MW00583545

Canaäd

Canaäd

D. A. Wood

RESOURCE *Publications* • Eugene, Oregon

CANAÄD

Resource Publications
An Imprint of Wipf and Stock Publishers
199 W. 8th Ave., Suite 3
Eugene, OR 97401

www.wipfandstock.com

PAPERBACK ISBN: 978-1-6667-6004-0
HARDCOVER ISBN: 978-1-6667-6005-7
EBOOK ISBN: 978-1-6667-6006-4

12/28/22

For my parents

Contents

Preface

The news of his death came as much less of a surprise than what it brought in tow. While still a young man, I received word of the passing of my great-grandfather early one afternoon driving down Calliope St. in New Orleans. It seems I knew the reclusive, wily-eyebrowed man about as well as his neighbors up the Thames. As a child, I summered with my parents to the outskirts of Oxford for six consecutive years to visit Great Grandpa Thompson. His limestone homestead, carpeted with a mossy roof, stuffed with thousands of friable tomes and foreign antiquities, where everything inside and out intimated ancient worlds of which I'd never heard—all this fascinated me. And although abstractly aware of being his only living descendant, I nearly scalded myself with chicory coffee when I learned that he had bequeathed his entire estate to me.

Taking a few weeks off work, I flew to London, then caught an early train to Oxford the following day for the funeral. Many years had passed since my last visit. I gave myself three weeks to decide what heirlooms to keep, which to donate, and whether to sell the house or to use it as a vacation home, for which I thought it might be perfectly suited. When I arrived at the house and saw its furnishings, my first thought was that nearly everything might be given to local colleges, museums, or curiosity shoppes. Most rooms looked like medieval libraries in the midst of repairs after a Norse raid, save the kitchen, whose larders (as he called them) remained stocked as if another siege might come at any moment. After settling in, I built a fire to dry my clothes and began to explore different portions of the house one by one, whiling away the evenings in nearby pubs. Two weeks passed, and the attic alone remained. In it I found an oak trunk with rusted dowels and latches. It contained a note and a hefty, hand-written manuscript, neither of which seemed unusual by this point, but still the documents intrigued me, not only as additional clues to aid me in unraveling the life of their elusive owner, but also because these were his only writings of note to be found in the entire cottage. The note astounded me then as it does now. I reproduce it here in full:

Preface

To Whomsoever's Found This Trunk,

The documents enclosed herein comprise my life's work, the which, were they ever again to see the light of day, should do so but posthumously. This manuscript requires some explanation, although I much doubt that what I say will inspire faith in my account.

In 1918 I accepted a joint position as Professor in the Department of Oriental Studies and the Department of Classics at Victoria College in Alexandria. Elaine and I moved to Egypt, and Rodney, our son, was born to us there. I taught until 1929, when Elaine left me for a halfwit wing commander, taking Rodney with her. Embarrassed and dejected, I went on sabbatical to clear my mind, leaving the coast to visit Charles Williams, a long-time friend in the Army who was then in charge of the small outpost at Umm al-Rashrāsh. That year I stopped reading and writing entirely. I lived simply, swimming in the Red Sea and hiking the nearby mountains to clear my mind.

One morning, while walking along a berm, my heel broke through a patch of earth into a hollow cavity. After regaining my footing, I kicked in more of the rock floor which broke evenly like plaster, as though it had been artificially constructed. I climbed inside the aperture and, removing a lantern from my rucksack, lit it. Working my way through the crawlway, descending down a steep shaft, I eventually reached a cool, dry chamber. There, all about me, lay countless dust-caked papyrus scrolls and soiled rolls of vellum, more or less untouched by substantial decay. Although an empiricist by disposition, I daresay that something like a divine ecstasy overcame me at the moment of that revelation. Overwhelmed, I carefully opened a scroll to find pages full of words I recognised as Koine Greek, yet which did not appear to treat of Hellenistic matters.

I exited the cave and made haste to the quarters I rented from Charles on the outpost's eastern edge. Climbing into my Crossley, I raced back to the cave and parked the lorry as closely to it as I could. I worked well into the night unpacking every scroll, gently placing them one atop the other inside the canvas-covered boot, then drove them back and unloaded them in my lodgings. All the while I contemplated whom to call about my turn up. As I did, images of my metropolitan colleagues being the first to read the scrolls, becoming legends in their own lifetimes what of my discovery, flashed before my mind. Which things, whether ancient or new, can petty academics not destroy a thousand times over in good faith? Thoughts of the ensuing argey-bargey over who proved worthiest to work on what I had found kept me awake the rest of the night. The next day, Charles came by, amazed at what I had found, but I convinced him to keep quiet about the scrolls, and he swore himself to secrecy.

That yearlong sabbatical became fifteen. My days were spent examining, ordering, and translating the scrolls. Their words possessed me, obsessed me, linking a mere scholiast like myself to ancient unknown worlds, and as I carried on with my solitary work, I became not unlike a hermit, living an ascetic life on small loans and smaller grants from the London School of Oriental Studies for articles I would never write. The epic poem (for that is what my haul comprised, once organised) took hold of me. What person or community had written it, and for what end? Had the cave been meant to preserve it or to hide it? Do other copies or fragments remain to be unearthed? Such questions flitted round my ears while the poem's content worked upon me day and night like an historiola. Its olden words cured me of my loneliness, at least in part. I only left them to visit Rodney when I could.

I completed the epic's verse translation in the summer of 1944. I could now go on about the idiosyncratic linguistic struggles that beset me then, winning your accolades, but as the world already has enough of these navel-gazing Translator's Notes, I shall spare you. Nonetheless, allow me to mention two particularly intriguing patterns which occurred in many of the scrolls. First, it became clear to me quite early on that the texts had been copied from tablets, as sequential numerals were used to indicate stoppages which rarely corresponded to proper sense-units, yet which separated segments of text that would have mirrored the length of an average-sized clay tablet. That the action of the epic takes place during the Bronze Age lends further weight to this hypothesis. Secondly and more interestingly, the scrolls contain quite a few unmistakable errors, the first sort of which can be explained by reference to mistranslations of various ancient Near Eastern homonyms, homophones, &c, while the second type comprises those sporadic copying errors which occur with expected regularity given the poem's size. But enough of this. I shall speculate no more about such matters as they have become pointless, as you will soon be given to understand.

While preparing my manuscript for publication, I decided to send the scrolls along with a copy of their translation to a close friend at the American Oriental Society in New York City so he could pore over them as a gift for his seventieth birthday. I instructed him to send my find to the British Museum when he had concluded his examination. The idea of his smiling stupefaction filled me with joy. With the unflagging support of dear Charles, we arranged the transport of the crates with assistance from the British Army, to whom I paid a most exorbitant sum for my contents' safe delivery. Weeks went by without word from New York. But soon I heard. The cargo plane had encountered a raging storm over the Atlantic, lost all external communication, and was never heard from again.

My heart followed that plane into the depths beneath the ocean's cold and endless barrows. The guilt of having destroyed those ancient relics devoured me. In years gone-by, I would pass a day of euphoric work without realising I had not eaten, and now I could not eat from stultifying shame. On top of that, I now had no proof whatsoever that all my labours amounted to any more than bumf, never mind the fact that I have not written an original line of verse my whole life, having never felt the need. Straight away, all of my efforts in that desert became a joke. So, I returned to Oxford after the War, where I took up work as a private tutor. Needless to say, I have never been able to forgive myself, much less publish my translation. I leave my manuscript in this attic—another cool, dark, and dusty cave—so that one wiser than myself might find it, to deal with however he sees fit. And herein lies my only solace, to wit, that perhaps in doing so I become still more like the anonymous scribes whose life work, too, lies only in this trunk for all we know, resting, bound up again in the strings of the Fates.

yours truly,

Alfred J. S. Thompson

As you might imagine, reading the above letter cast an entirely different light upon the uncanny and sometimes peevish great-grandfather of my youth. I immediately withdrew the manuscript from the chest, cut the strings that twined it, and began to read it, day in, day out, fueled by bottomless cups of Darjeeling tea. Having no background in matters concerning the ancient Near East aside from what I'd half-heard in Sunday School, I took in what I could, enjoying my escape to distant times and places. Upon my return home, however, work, relationships, and life's snowballing chores precluded me from giving much attention to the manuscript, so it receded from my mind, blurring with my other fond memories of England.

Many years later, after I was able to retire, I returned to my great-grandfather's translation and began to prepare a version for publication. During this time I attempted to uncover the truth of the note. Charles Williams, unfortunately, had long since passed away. And while I was able to verify my great-grandfather's tenure at Victoria College and his return to Oxford in 1945, I have not been able to secure any proof of his stationing at Umm al-Rashrāsh. Moreover, the relevant military documents to and from that station remain classified. Yet I doubt that even they would prove helpful given the liminal, unofficial nature of his sojourn.

I hesitate to share my own view of the translation's scholarly or artistic merits, as my affection for my great-grandfather would likely skew a more detached analysis—assuming, of course, that one should want to experience archaic poetry in a detached manner. I've made some standard adjustments throughout to make the text more reader-friendly and have included a map, glossary, and selected bibliography with the kind assistance of various scholars.

Dr. Thompson might have played a role in the tragic destruction of the work that you now hold. And, it would not be entirely wrong to say that the epic basically comprises stolen material. Yet I hope we might also remember that he gave much of his life to its preservation. If the story proves useful or enjoyable in some way, perhaps the spread of such pleasant feelings might allow him to rest more peacefully still.

Acknowledgments

I am deeply grateful to everyone who inspired and aided me in bringing this work to life.

To Claire, who has supported me in all of my wanderings, real and imagined.

To my parents, without whom I could not have pursued my passions.

To Dr. Zack Hugo, my philosophical comrade, for helping me make important preliminary stylistic decisions when this project first began.

To Dr. Pauline Viviano, for introducing me to the Canaanite pantheon.

To Drs. Eugene C. Kennedy and Jim Wetzel, who in their own ways opened my eyes to mythology's peculiar powers.

To Dr. Adam Kryszeń, for kindly sharing his expertise in ancient toponymy.

To Fred Kroner, for his beautifully-crafted map.

To all those scholars whose meticulous and painstaking labors afforded me so much grist for the mill.

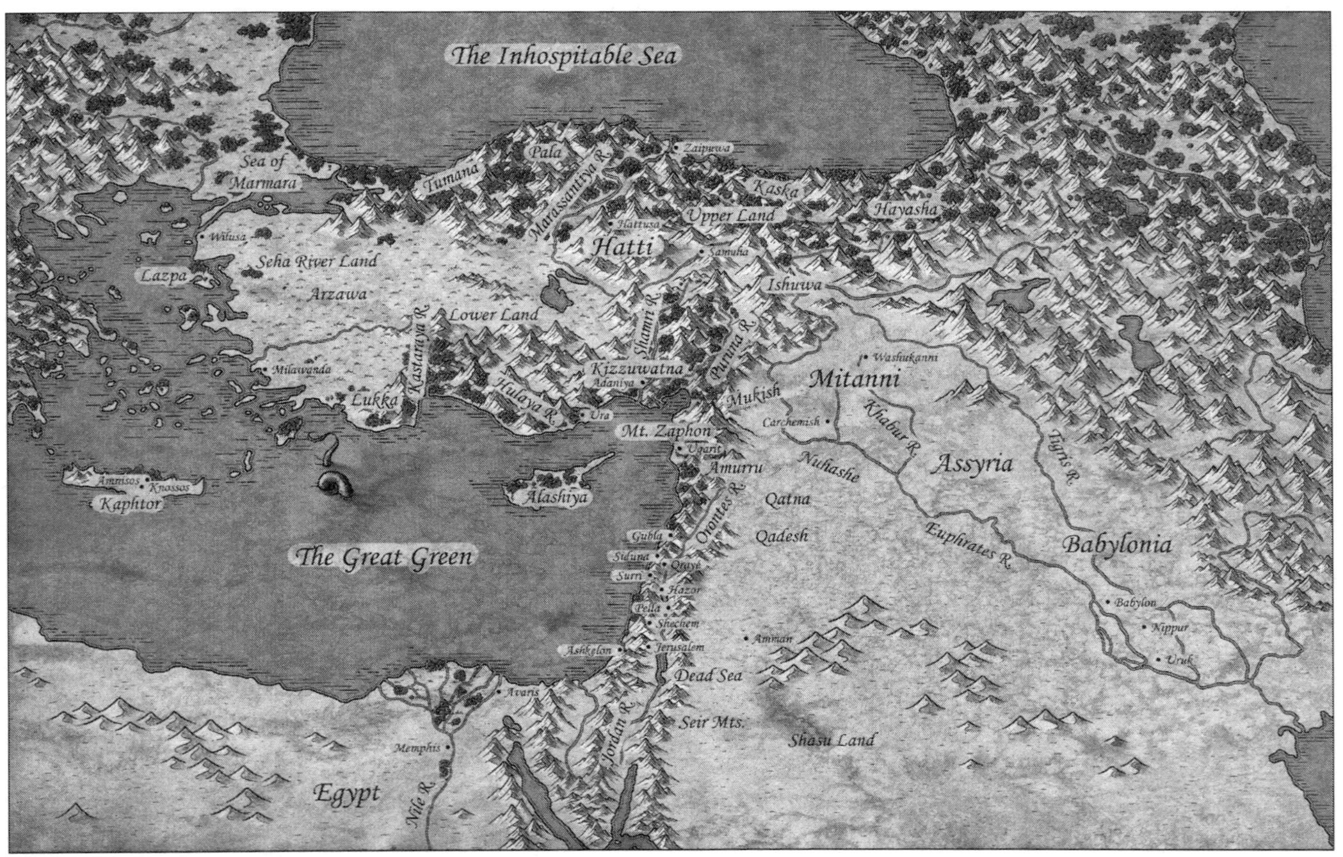
The Inhospitable Sea
Sea of Marmara
Tumana
Pala
Marassantiya R.
Zaipuwa
Kaska
Upper Land
Hayasha
Hattusa
Hatti
Samuha
Wilusa
Seha River Land
Lazpa
Arzawa
Kastaraya R.
Lower Land
Ishuwa
Shamri R.
Puruna R.
Washukanni
Mitanni
Milawanda
Kizzuwatna
Adaniya
Lukka
Hulaya R.
Ura
Mukish
Mt. Zaphon
Carchemish
Khabur R.
Tigris R.
Ugarit
Amurru
Nuhashe
Assyria
Amnisos
Knossos
Kaphtor
Alashiya
Orontes R.
Qatna
Gubla
Qadesh
Euphrates R.
Babylonia
The Great Green
Siduna
Qraye
Surri
Hazor
Babylon
Pella
Shechem
Nippur
Amman
Ashkelon
Jerusalem
Uruk
Dead Sea
Avaris
Jordan R.
Seir Mts.
Shasu Land
Memphis
Egypt
Nile R.

Book I

Swift Messenger Ilisha, you who seal
immortal dispatches within your breast,
withholding them until their chosen time
whereat you wing your way from heaven's halls,
drifting on downdrafts over mountaintops
and past our mortal realm which, though it be
prosaical, is god-enwroughtened still—
delay your journey; keep us company!
Sing! Sing of Aqhat Danel's Son, Slayer
of Deathless Ones, the Seir Mountain Man
whose fame has even reached the Netherworld
(where names have never been of much concern).
What drives a man to theomachic heights?
Whence came that hero's might unparalleled?
Unending might and main comprising, rest
with us now notwithstanding round this hearth
by which Kinnaru and Tiratu wait
for you with their greathearted offerings.
Hold nothing back and don't dumb down the tale.
Reveal and translate all you've seen transpire,
brimming our hollow hearts with lively verse,
commencing only where you see most fit.

Time it was when Amenhotep the Third,
both human and divine, the consequence
of Mutemwia's love for Amen-Ra,
ascended to his vested place within
the Mansion of the Dazzling Solar Orb.
The real embodiment of Lord Aten,

Amenhotep the Lion Hunter gained
distinction as a pharaoh who surpassed
his predecessors in regality.
The son of Hapu (healer and savant),
erected one hundred—no, one thousand
tremendous monuments to honor him.
Expending heaped-up treasure hoards, the king
had deep vivaria dug for his wives.
Transported over nome and Nile alike
within his shouldered baldachin befringed
with filigree, the pharaoh overlooked
his pyramids and gold-foiled obelisks
while contemplating his next enterprise.
Determined armies stood by at his beck,
impatient to extend their influence,
awaiting word from the uraeus-crowned.

But in those days Egyptian guards did guard
instead of conquering aggressively,
for diplomatic peace—infrequent gift
enjoyed by multitudes most fortunate,
and yet, no less an outrider of wars
to come—bound the Mitannians with Thebes.
Shuttarna, Second of his Name, the king
of Washukanni, clutched Assyria
within his grasp and kept their troops at bay.
His reign extended from the Taurus' spine
unto the fertile Tigris River's mouth.
Now old, Shuttarna had grown tired of war,
and so, in order to commemorate
the tenth regnal year of Amenhotep,
he forged agreements that forestalled chaos
between Mitanni and Deltaic Lands.
He proved the honesty of his intent

by gifting King Amenhotep whole troves
of copper and the purest lazurite
along with Giluhepa, daughter though
she was, all stowed in ships to cross the seas.

Northwest of King Shuttarna's stomping grounds,
Lord Tudhaliya sat on Hatti's throne.
He laid the groundwork for the Hittite realm
by riding out when hordes of outlanders
laid siege to cities on the north frontier.
He quashed their regular incursions, sealed
perimeters, rewarded loyal towns,
and trekked from shrine to cultic shrine in his
incipient imperial domain.
Neither Arzawan Lands to Hatti's west
nor Kizzuwatna to the south could hope
to stall this king's expansionary dreams.

But it was not among these storied climes,
all of these Somewheres ruled by Somebodies,
bespoken by the pomp and circumstance
of Theban sistra, prescient choruses,
prelusive chants, or Hurrian hoorays
that Aqhat Son of Danel's tale unfolds.
Beginnings of a homelier design
befell our hero, which befits the boy
besides, since from great people one expects
more greatness still, and from no one, nothing.
How more impressive, then, his rise to fame!
So sing, Ilisha, overwhelm our hearts;
of Nobody from Nowhere spin your yarn.

Four wooden boats coursed over the Great Green
as Shahar the Crepuscular awoke.

The mates of two ships baited metal hooks
attached to hempen lines and let them plumb
the cloudy depths—not satisfied with tugs
and noncommittal nips, waiting instead
for mouthy, brassbound jerks that chafe and burn
the palms with promise of a hefty haul.
The trusted methods of their forefathers
came through as silvered swimmers thumped the hull.
The other vessels strode the one beside
the other, partnered up, as men from one
tossed flaxen seines to trawlers opposite
them, both crews paying out the fishing net,
the northern boat now distancing itself
with confident control from her consort
before she turned with grace and circled west,
the first ship holding fast and pivoting.
The dragnet's weights of stones sank out of sight
to glide along the floor, the mesh stretched wide,
its lattice like an underwater sail.
Having turned toward their point of origin
in synchrony, both boats now made for land,
arm's length apart, then slowly joined as one
again and hoisted in the lively droves.

A soft alluvion aroused the coast.
The foreshore stretched and yawned up toward a town
which bustled with the din of daybreak toil.
Two centuries or so had come and gone
since folk had made this littoral their own,
the town comprising nine and twenty homes
of relatively equal size and build
whose floors were made of dirt, their wooden walls
upholding sturdy, wattled roofs of reeds
upon which rested flattened earth to be

rolled out again once winter rains returned.
Beyond the hamlet's long perimeter,
pastoral grasses mantled virid ground
where rams and ewes could sleep and safely graze.
Because in those days empires much preferred
the timber to be found in northern lands,
and since the War of Trees and Men would not
begin in earnest for some years to come,
a halesome wood still hedged the lea's east edge.
This sylvan neighborhood kept watch at night,
providing forest fowl, wild herbs, and game
for sacral, long-awaited festivals.

The families rooted here were modest ones
that pledged their very lives to Baal-Hadad,
whom sea and thunderstricken earth obeyed.
Among Hadad's most faithful followers
was Danel, Hallowed Man of Rapiu,
the God-Fearing One of the Harnemite.
A well-respected judge, he oversaw
the town's affairs with other eldermen.
Not three years' earlier his faithful wife
named 'Danataya' bore the judge a girl,
her advent catching everyone off guard,
for Danel's spouse outnumbered most in years.
As when with age and by necessity
a prickly pear begins to fortify
its walls with countless spearmen standing to
and storing water for impending wars—
as such a one betrays the tenderness
kept hidden in these years of toil and heat
now that his central, primrose promise blooms—
just so did Pugat crown her father's life.
She brought him solace heretofore unknown.

Yet Danel felt his life was incomplete.
Awakening one night, he walked along
the coast, and Danataya found him there,
"Why do you wander here alone at night?
Does something grieve you? You've not slept so well
of late, now tossing, turning, heading out
at night to look upon the astral kings.
Have you misjudged another's crucial case?
Perhaps you've sealed in stone the fate of one
whose innocence now weighs you down with guilt.
Did I offend you or neglect some task?
Confide in me. Or come to bed, at least."

Now Danel's seaward glance collapsed downward.
He inhaled, turned to her, and made reply,
"My dear, no guilt impinges on my heart,
nor have you done a thing to send me on
these nighttime blunderings (aside from snore).
Each day I venerate the many gods,
uplifting thanks before my labors start.
Between each dawn and dusk, however, I
take note of how our Pugat lives and plays,
each morning older than the day before,
her beauty never waning all the while.
I on the other hand grow old and gray.
But as with ingrates, my experience
of joy is tempered by a painful lack.
I have no son, no trueborn follower
to carry on our ways and family name.
How long until my spirit rises up
to disappear, my corpse becoming dust,
my shade no better than our brazier's smoke?
Our line will molder, dead to future times,
my girls left fending for themselves . . . alone.

Although the gods have given us the world,
who profits from such flighty usury
if in the end loans have to be repaid
in full, accompanied with that interest
which first binds debtors to their creditors,
that is, advance's only reason: hope?"

Now Danataya's words, compassionate
and warm, consoled her husband's careworn heart,
"The ways of the divine ones slip our grasp,
but when we persevere in faith they hear
and answer prayers that rise with incense wreathes.
Without fail, Baal Most High preserves our soil.
He wind-drives rains to sate our thirsty land.
With his help, barren plowlands drink their fill.
Impelled to joy the earth's glad choristers
cannot but praise Zaphonian Hadad.
Even the dumbest cow lifts up his prayers
from birth to death when he looks up and lows
his daily thanks amidst abundant gifts.
Could Baal not know your tears' effects and source?
When in his might he fashions the next storm,
be sure to offer sacrificial gifts
and let Ilisha's wives relay your hopes
if they, like me, would journey to the ends
of earth to give their husband peace of mind."
Agreeing to this last resort, the judge
turned in with Danataya for the night.

One month thereafter, Danataya rose
alongside Shahar as she had each day
since work and chores supplanted, one by one,
all of the serious frivolity
and rule-bound freedom found in childhood games.

She dressed and met Inumi, her close friend.
The pair meandered out beyond the town's
periphery, supporting large clay jars
upon their shoulders, lumbering like mules.
As they continued to approach the old
well, Danataya's perspicacious friend
endeavored to unearth the origins
of her apparent lornness—hidden by
intent, betrayed by mannerisms' prose,
for friendships weathered by a common past
are like those seasoned travelers who can shift
from tongue to tongue with glib proficiency
yet who with evening's comfort of strong ales
become indecorous toward custom's stout
injunctions barring loud and truthful speech.

Danataya came out with it at last,
"Why should I try to hide my thoughts from you?
My scrape is not some unknown mystery:
I've failed to bear my loving man a son.
What did I do, or whom did I upset
to end my husband's noble family line?
Perhaps I've irked the Kotharat—ideal
embodiments of purest womanhood,
illumined daughters of the crescent moon.
What could a person from a village like
our own do so that Fate might intercede
on our behalf, attracting Athirat's
attentiveness and capabilities?
As you know and as I have always feared,
my parents' sins pursue me even now."

Inumi hmphed, replying in this way,
"Since when have you been troubled by such things?

Without a doubt, we have indulged our share
of innocent impieties, each one
the more enjoyable than previous
amusements: In our youth we'd steal some fruit
from time to time, then let some scamps steal us
away for pleasures even juicier.
Remember how by day we'd torture them
with pranks, by night with well-aimed coquetry?
Postponing chores indefinitely, we'd
explore the forest depths and misinform
inquisitive adults about the day's
adventures filled with secret, reckless thrills.
We're cursed indeed—not since we're bested by
past sins, but since the best sins have long passed.

"Now heed this parable my mother told:
There rests a port in Gubla to the north
far vaster than our little set of docks.
Its piers extend the length of twenty ships.
Where the main pier abuts the solid ground
there stirs a marketplace in which one can
exchange all manner of impressive goods,
from provender and cloaks to swords and wine.
Amidst its swarm of truck-and-bartering,
a group of Gublan gossipmongers stood
beneath a stall's umbrageous tarpaulin.
They'd huddled to kibbitz about the month's
most pressing matters—lists of topics that
were commonly provocative and grim.
One morning's news, however, had surpassed
the norm: A mutual acquaintance had
announced that she was with child. Oh what luck!
Excitement uncontainable! How far
along was she? What if it were a boy?

What names were they considering for him?
(No less delectable: Exactly how'd
the newlyweds conceive the babe—was he
home-brewed or planted in an open field?)

"And then, as certain opposites attract
(as demonstrated by the newlyweds
of whom the girls had spoken, he a cad
and she as dewy-eyed as a lambkin),
the conversation flipped and settled on
another woman known to be barren.
Ill-omened, damned misfortune! How would she,
a desert, ever know the fruitfulness
and joy of womanhood's accomplishment?
Had she (poor girl) incensed the Kotharat?
To not experience the growth of life
itself, unfurling in one's womb, to smile
and be fulfilled with blessèd jolts and squirms
while asking him what he would like to eat—
what had she done to merit such demise?
With speculative pity, they discussed
this cruelest paradox: to be condemned
to have no issue as one's sole issue,
all youthful rutting left stuck in a rut.

"Now in those parts there was a madwoman
who like an unkempt bitch roamed round the port,
the locals leaving her alone so long
as she could keep her ravings minimal.
From sympathy some tossed her scraps of bread,
but that peculiar afternoon she roved
with no docility, dawdling on up
beside the aforementioned hearsayers.
A flopping fish—a sprightly, large sardine

netted not long before—caught the crone's eye,
and like a cormorant, the urchiness
took hold of it, devouring her prey
with one emphatic gulp and two small burps.
She felt the jolts and squirms of life itself
fulfilling her, unfurling in her gut.
Though needing nothing else to make her smile,
she bent in half and asked her former snack
what he might want to eat—turns out he liked
petite sardines, so she downed more of them
until the fishmonger drove her away.
With uppity and scandalized ado,
the women looked on as the crazy loon
wheeled round and gamboled on, much satisfied."

Here Danataya laughed. Inumi said,
"Believe me when I say: Gods care for us
with other, different eyes than you might think.
Infrequently do they concern themselves
with trifling mortal cares—and here you're right.
But even less do our inconstancies
or faults affect their self-sufficiency.
They set down laws and rules to gratify
their wants, yet it is not compliance on
our part that pleases them, but the reverse.
Gods' standards are impossibly high-set,
and herein lies the reason for this choice:
As Gublan girls make fun out of thin air
at other folk's expense, so too do gods
get off at finding butts for all their jokes
since it empowers and delights at once."

When evening fell, a tempest's downpour raged—
with gusting gales it shook the hunkered town.

And in that cataract the judge set out
to find the whitest lamb within his stalls
as sheets of water soaked his grizzled beard.
He chose the yearling best among his fold,
secured its fore and aft legs with a rope,
then took a salted knife in hand and prayed.
He swiftly drained the animal's warm life—
the instrument of bronze no sooner wet
with blood than cleansed with rain.
The underside cut, Danel then removed
the offal, tossing it to birds nearby
before he sliced through flesh, setting aside
the yeanling's bright red shanks and loins and racks.
The lamb now dressed, Danel washed and undressed
to be adorned with tawny sackcloth garb.
Weighed down by more and more amassing drops
and yet uplifted by his pious hopes,
the Man of Rapiu gathered himself,
returning to his family's fireside.

While Danataya stirred the lambent coals
beneath her household's fire, Pugat cried
and screamed at every bolt and thundercrack.
Now in came Danel, skins of wine in hand
with hunks of marbled mutton—crimson plains
divided by webworks of snowmelt rills
and tarns, of late barraged by saline hail.
Upon a wooden stool he set these things
before revealing graven gods whom he
positioned on a sacred postament.
He first placed El, kindly patriarch,
the Ancient Father of the pantheon
who breathes new life into the world yet who
no less engendered Mot the God of Death.

Enthroned, the statuette looked out across
the room with noble confidence.
The seven-headed figurine came next,
the god unequaled in ferocity—
Litan—the beast who stalks the ocean depths.
The Conqueror who gives and takes away,
Zaphonian Hadad, took center stage.
His weapon Driver in one hand, a rod
of lightning in the other, Baal loomed large
as did the giants of a former age,
his head that of a longhorned, untamed bull,
his muzzle's septum pierced with a gold ring.
With care the judge cleaned every deity
while litten incense sanctified the space.

The flames began to roast the salt-sprent meat
as logs hissed intermittently.
Just as a wine jar blackens, hardening
amidst a conflagration that's consumed
a storehouse whole, its contents heating up
and boiling till deprived of flintiness
(and so, alas, of inspiration too),
just so did Danel char the cuts of lamb,
surrounded by a crust of fired fat
within which life's red liquid roiled anew.
His horn of wine uplifted, Danel poured
Baal's first libation and began to pray,
"Hadad whose exhalations move the winds,
who lances lightning bolts from lofted heights,
respiring with the thunder's aftermath:
Do my laments not reach your gracious ears?
I'm confused—I feel unfulfilled.
Accept this offering of meat and wine.
To no one have you given more, and yet,

when one gives something to another, who,
expectant with a fool's undying faith,
awaits his heart's contentment, he it is
whom blessings curse and satiations drain.
In mortals (how it is with gods I do
not know), there often works supreme desire:
Like quicksand's underlying force, it grows
with steady might the more that which
atop its shifting surface yanks and pulls,
the two opponents vying back and forth,
the latter doomed without external aid.
But you who see below the surfaces
of things, attend to what's inside my heart:

"The pit within my breast requires an heir.
Who'll hold my hand when I am drunk with wine?
Were I to die tonight, who'd tend to me?
No son could free my spirit from the earth.
And who would watch my stela or protect
my tomb from thieves when I have fled this world?
Who'll guard me from untruthful badmouthing?
(I've not the slightest doubt that writhing snake
called Slander, whose enormous jaws ingest
the dead, his mouth and gut distending so
his vicious venom might rejuvenate,
stored up for still more victims yet to come—
no doubt this snake will live beyond my time,
although he has no feet on which to stand).
And who will serve as steward of our gods,
supplying offerings throughout the years?
Forebodings such as these disturb my soul.
So, Lord of Lords, the One Who Rides on Clouds,
entrust to me a male descendant . . . please."

His prayer now ended, Danel filled his cup
and with his deities imbibed strong drink.
His wife beheld the scene and shed a tear;
her husband's gestures and encomium
called forth her admiration, yet she wept
as much from love of him as from concern
for the futility of his requests,
which either never reached the ears of gods
or, worse still, pestered them without relent.

Nearby, the vultures that received their meal
from Danel (who in fact were messengers
of Baal returning to him from the Nile),
spread wing and soared, now fully satisfied
with fare far fresher than the norm as well
as with more information for their Lord.
Ascending just above the breaking clouds,
they caught the South Wind in their wingèd arms,
glissading effortlessly out of sight.
For three long days they cruised the oceanside
until Mount Zaphon crested into view,
arising on the Great Green's northeast shores.
Atop its peak sat Baal's magnific manse,
a citadel enclosed with battlements.
Kothar the Craftsman had designed and built
the palace in the days of yore, from its
large Eastern Gate and ashlar walls of stone
to the tall tower topped with blazing fire
that never waned, as if it were a torch,
while Baal had pleaded with Astarte to plant
the vineyard thriving on his northern slope.

Alighting on a parapet, the birds
transmogrified back into godlike form.

Their wrinkly legs expanded and filled out
liked desiccated stalks soak up the rain.
With shakes and squawks and much ado they rid
their pinions of black feathers as their bones
filled in with marrow, lending them support.
Their beaks retracted, softened, widening
as lips while talons lost their knifelike tips.
Gapn, Hirgab, and Ugar entered Baal's
palatial home as Hirgab plucked a sole
remaining feather out of Gapn's back,
at which he loudly yawped in pained surprise
then reassumed a dignified veneer.
Two sentinels, meantime, led them inside.
The five strode down high-ceilinged corridors
within which rested armed and foughten men,
that morn returned from months-long raids with Baal
along the coast, and though they'd found success,
the hirelings ate a mediocre meal
and boredly baubled with their paltry spoils
beneath the archways frowning down on them.

The messengers drew near twin-columned doors
of thick and sturdy cedar on which were
arrayed vignettes of warriors unseamed,
flung from their chariots, remorselessly
decapitated by a beast with two
extruding horns atop a bullish glare.
Each episode portrayed a different tale,
but all were knit together round one god.
Admittance being granted, six hall guards
and the escorts of the messengers strained
against the entrance, parting both its doors.
The godlings tip-toed through the hall where an
extensive wooden table showed itself

like a retired and battle-tested keel,
its stormy pilot resting at the helm.
There he sat, Baal, the taurine Conqueror,
his cloud-hued horns large and penetrant,
surpassing every crown of earthen kings,
his nose ring flaunting disregard for pain.
He emptied cups of wine while to his right
along the wall his sister, Dread Anat,
looked on, befouled with battle-gore, white skulls
engirding her as sundry human hands
collected from her kills aligned her sash.

The Thunderer addressed the ones who'd come,
"Choice day you've chosen to return to us.
We've just come back from raids along the coast.
A portion of our navy set upon
small towns for the first time, assisting me
in the extraction of outstanding debts
from those who beg and plead for rains but who've
forgotten their From Whom and For How Much.
Why wait for harvest festivals when my
reserves require drills to keep them sharp?
What better than remind our denizens
of piety's requirements, collect
my dues, and train my soldiers all at once?
These days such husbandry's gone out of style.
Enough, though: Tell me what you three have learned."

Now stepping forward, Hirgab made reply,
"My Lord, it pleases me to heap good news
concerning all the lands on which we spied
to your most recent naval victories.
Egyptian prowess, it is true, accedes
to ever new extremes, their sea-trade routes

extending farther to the West than ours,
but their aggrandizement—in our belief—
fixates on navel-gazing art alone.
It seems that after finishing your home
Kothar the Memphian's resigned himself
to building monuments for them,
shellacking boulders with his trowel by day,
by night erecting temples, hammering
on bronze and launching sparks into the sky—
the disappearing streaks shot from below
confounding nearsighted astrologers.
To be sure! Edifices such as these
still lag behind your dwelling's prominence.
As long as Kothar, that supernal god
who puts to shame all earthborn smiths, does not
construct machines and means for warfare, then
his artistry distracts and keeps the peace.

"But of the folk you rule, you will be pleased
to know that your own commoners confide
and hope in your unparalleled largesse.
The heartfelt faithfulness of one of your
allegiants, Danel, moved us with his love
for you as the most honored of his gods.
That judge sends offerings, the scraps of which
he shared with us unknowingly until
his reverent prayer uplifted us homeward.
He's known his wife but as yet knows no son.
Yet I relay this to you, Eminence,
not to prejudge the point, and even less
because this man is noble, strong, or great,
but only to report your folk's morale—"

Anat then interrupted them, saying,
"Enough of local trifles, Hirgab. Baal,
should we not act upon this scouting report?
Your men have had their practice now, and you
have waited countless seasons to assert
your place as emperor of emperors.
It seems the perfect moment to attack!
How could we not avenge those killed at our
Megiddo's armageddon by Thutmose,
Third of his Name, sworn Enemy of Wine?
Let's not delay. Amass your strength once more.
Let's lay the pharaoh low and disembowel
his bloodline, retinue, and populace,
our gore-drenched victories enheartening
and reinvigorating enlistees.
You know I goad our men to fight just like
a pack of starved and cornered lions by
my own example, flaying flesh to eat.
The Sphinx herself will soon avert her gaze.
Her puerile riddles shall reduce to groans
still more bemused, her song a fading dirge!"

Baal chided her with different plans in store,
"Be still. How can your battle-thirst foment
despite our having just returned from it?
I don't deny the pleasures to be found
in confrontations like the ones that you
imagine, but you mustn't only serve
relentless Strife, neglecting needful Rest.
Our father still goes unaware of our
affairs, and this, my dear, is for the best.

"Now, Hirgab, Gapn, Ugar: Many thanks
for your commitment to our broadened view.

Discovering that those within my land
increase their praise and their obedience
enlivens and propitiates my heart.
This Danel: Grant on my behalf his wish.
A pious man should reap his just reward.
While sleeping, tell him that I've heard his prayers,
but that in sixteen years from his son's birth
he must give up the property he now
most cherishes as testament to me.
Judges know how informal contracts work."

At this, Baal motioned that his envoys leave,
retiring with Anat to mount their bed.
Baal's messengers departed from the hall,
resuming avian identities
for their return back South to Danel's home.
The vultures flew along the seaside's edge,
delaying now and then to rest their wings
on top of boulders purified by tides.
Like huddled children, mussels slept beneath
these algaed rocks, competing and rustling
for best position only in the dawn
to be discovered sprawled haphazardly
under, across, and over each other.
Unlike such creatures, Baal's entrusted birds
refused to sleep until they had arrived
in Danel's humble town in three nights' time.

The Sun passed her flambeau on to Shalim,
the God of Dusk whose soft and flowing robes
of Surrian purple with saffron trim
inspirit some of Kaphtor's frescoed halls.
His brief diurnal trip below the earth
now at an end, Yarikh of ivory tusks

arose to come stand guard among the stars.
All soundly slept in Danel's town except
one elder who awoke, remembering
that he had left his scythe out in the field.
Having retrieved it, Kirta walked back home.
But at the clearing's edge he froze, his face
transfixed with terror at what he beheld.

He dove behind a hedge of tamarisks
before he gathered strength to lift a branch.
On Danel's house there landed three black shades—
like sickly vultures but more ominous,
their claws unnecessarily prolonged,
their wingspans over twice the normal size.
Appalled, the elderman assured himself
that, once again, his senile eyes mistook
something's appearance for reality.
And just before he had convinced himself
that shady silhouettes like these were naught
but average migratory birds, each beast
descended through the solid roof like souls
sucked downward through the earth for Mot's dark realm.
Now Kirta gripped his scythe as if he were
a first-time soldier waiting for commands.
In time the eldritch shadows soared back out,
at which point Kirta scurried for his home
and slept beside his implement, which is
to say, he clutched his newfound weaponry,
wide-eyed, awaiting any specters bold
enough to try to seize him unawares.

The morning came and Danel shook his wife,
arousing her with childlike eagerness.
He told her of his dream in which three birds—

the couriers of Baal, no less—relayed
the god's designs (to which the judge agreed).
The old man's boyish glee and faithfulness
alarmed his spouse who checked her joy so as
to not leave open windows for let-downs.
But as the months passed by, and as her womb
began to swell, proof's burden fell to her,
outmatching her defensive disbelief.
Anon the couple could no longer ward
off Rumor's minions, choosing to address
the obvious with faith: The Cloudrider
had promised them an heir to call their own.
The judge choked up each time he told the tale,
and while the vast majority in town
rejoiced with Danataya and Danel,
it must be added that Envy the gull
had litten on their shores around that time.

She'd flown to this specific stretch of coast
with other mews who let her tag along.
Each set about perfecting their own nests,
purloining threads of wool and fallen twigs
for their forthcoming young, and though Envy
possessed the inborn knowledge requisite
for such designs, she eyed the prettiest
among her colony to mimic them.
When time it came, and just as she had feared,
her peers begot their perfect specimens
of alabaster and mother of pearl.
While everyone produced at least three eggs,
Envy'd produced but two lopsided ones.
Her covey left to pirate scraps of food
with subtle tact from unsuspecting runts,
but Envy stayed behind to put to test

her worries, sitting on the others' eggs
to find, alas, that they were healthier,
more uniform, and warmer than her own.
Each day she settled on a different clutch,
and each day her presentiments increased,
though such affections were abated by
the emulousness of her escapades.

When her friends came back to the rookery,
Envy would roost just out of sight to see
if others saw to her as she saw them,
her core a sinkhole of resentfulness.
Was she not lovable enough to spite?
In time her neighbors' mottled nestlings hatched,
and just as soon as they had learned to fly,
they left to summer on more pristine shores.
Impatient and distempered, Envy tried
to nudge along her young's development,
pecking and beaking her cool eggs until
her nest dripped with vitelline, addled gore.
So even though her young had died, let no
one say that Envy neither breeds nor broods.

The winter rains subsided for the year,
the harvest's intimations springing forth.
Up from the dew-washed earth, with arching backs
pushed onward by the will to stand up straight
though bursting at the seams, green pregnant bulbs
arose with a slight wince and then a smile
while laughing at their awkward girth, and through
the strain of this delightful labor, they
expressed, although despite themselves, the key
to the earth's inner risibility.
The kinfolk in the town began to work

their garden plots, collecting vegetables
like legumes, lentils, and white onion bulbs.
Throughout the moons that followed soon thereon,
slumped women slashed and reaped the golden fields
of wheat with sharpened bronze while others saw
to gathering the season's amber stalks.
The bundled sheaves ascended up slight hills,
arriving at the slanted threshing floor
composed of slabs of stone where oxen tromped
the clustered crop, their cloven hooves tramping
and stomping, separating grain from husks
whereat the evening sea breeze lent a hand
by winnowing the cereals through sieves.
The chaff distilled, mules hauled Baal's gifts away
to granaries of fieldstone and brickwork
where in the coming days they would be burnt
and ground with querns employed by callused hands.

When Danataya readied to bear fruit,
insatiate Mot spread his prehensile jaws
to welcome his expected sustenance,
for childbirth often gives him two-for-one.
And this time—after hours of endless strife
where bloody pangs and screams admix with sweat,
a healthful body rent in two, as when
an earthquake threatens to destroy both soil
and seed—this time such cataclysmic signs
proved false, a whimper giving them the lie.
Mother and son had lived. The midwives cut
the baby's cord and cleaned the birthing stool.
Relief redoubled joy as, cradling her
son, Danataya welcomed Danel in
to meet the offshoot of his piety.
Though excess happiness now bleared his eyes,

yet he could still discern every unique
and precious feature of his newborn boy.
Taking him in his arms, Danel pronounced
Baal's miracle fulfilled so all the room
could hear, revealing his son's name: Aqhat.

That month an unknown wanderer appeared
with foreign goods for trade with those in town.
A gawky, lanky creature—like a horse
with knars for kneecaps—ambled at his side.
A puckered pout adorned its face and two
hillocks of straw protruded from its back.
Some children in the town were first to see
these new, wayworn arrivals, running up
to both of them without the slightest fear,
imagining them first as part of their
ongoing games of make-believe, but now
too overcome with curiosity
about these newcome visitors' intents.
A town well-practiced in the age-old art
of hospitality, the people took
them in and tended to their every need.
While tasting supper with his hosts, the man
regaled them with his journey's obstacles,
entwining and beknotting them with yarns.
But no escape from desert ruffians,
no melee fought with mountain fiends, and no
depiction wrought of foreign palaces
compared to the surprise he held in store.

He pulled a bow and quiver from his pack
and held them in his hands, saying to them,
"Never have I transported workmanship
of such divine make—this I swear to you.

A child was born this month, a gift bestowed
by He who Rides on Clouds—is it not so?
Kothar-wa-Hasis must have overheard
the news of Baal's late generosity
some time ago, touched by his kindliness
and longing to contribute like support.
Unable to lay hands of blessing on
the boy himself, the bowyer set to work
producing substitutes of expert make:
With timber harvested from northern ash
and annulated ibex horns he shaped
this dexterous, unbreakable bowstave.
He then removed long tendons from the hocks
of Apis' son and sinews from an ox.
Each night he stretched these cords and dried them
by day with Shapshu's aid, enfastening
the fibrous ends to their respective nocks.
During his afternoons the Skillful One
strolled down the reedbeds of the Nile, wherefrom
he plucked the straightest stalks for arrow shafts,
now fletched with feathers from young avocets.
Alloying tin shipped from Assyria
with copper from Mitanni's delven mines,
he smithed these deadly arrowheads of bronze
before securing them, the arrows set
within the quiver as the final touch.
I'd stopped in Memphis on my eastward trek,
and Kothar offered me protection charms
of untold worth should I convey his gifts—
an offer that no sane man would refuse."

Those thronged around the god's envoy shot looks
Danel and Danataya's way the while,
the godheads gifting them a second time,

the parents blushing from unworthiness.
Since Aqhat couldn't crawl, much less unloose
a godsent arrow, the recipients
decided that, when she had come of age,
Pugat would teach her brother how to wield
his present not unlike Anat had trained
her brother Baal to hunt eons ago.

In time the day for Aqhat's first rites came.
The village graybeards gathered in a tent,
awaiting Danel for the ritual.
Considering the moment opportune,
Kirta began to verbalize his fears,
"Good men: You know that I, like you, disdain
uncalled-for melodrama, which is why
I hesitate to even bring to your
attention matters seemingly opaque
and private, marked by their impertinence.
I also know that what I'll soon divulge
may very well call into question my
ability to judge and to perceive.
But since these practiced powers constitute
the means by which I'm proud to stand by you
and call you peers, accept the words I speak
as if I were an unknown witness who
would risk his standing for the common good.

"Around the end of last year's harvest, late
one night, I went into our fields because
I had forgotten to put up my scythe.
Atop a nearby homestead (Danel's own),
there landed three enshadowed shapeshifters
who moved with human-like demeanor, or,
worse, it seemed, with a demon-like humor.

Heading back home, I saw these skulking shapes
descend at once through Danel's very roof.
At first I disbelieved my eyes, which fool
us all from time to time, but soon enough,
those black-winged, thoughtful entities again
rose through the roof, departing for the sea.

"The days passed by and once more I began
to doubt my senses, so much so that I
resolved to drop the whole ordeal at once.
Then Danataya, as you may recall,
began to show, and now she's given birth.
Does no one find this strange? You know that I'm
an honest man with children of my own
who's nothing of which to be envious.
Who in our people's ancient history
has been with child at Danataya's age?
Judge Danel says that Baal accepted his
oblations, those he sent from his own hearth.
But Baal is Lord of All: Together do
we praise him, honoring his name as one.
The Cloudrider's no household deity
or some ancestral shade with biased bonds.
If this were not enough, we're to believe
that Kothar hopes to garner their esteem!
Even assuming Danel's pioneered
especial contact with our gods, should we
not benefit as a community?
If we as elders cannot sift the prayers
of suppliants, then our role's nullified.
No ill will do I bear toward Danel's son.
Yet if you heed but one of my concerns—
even if you should crack up at the rest—

as leaders you must not omit to grasp
and judge these issues for our people's sake."

No sooner than he'd finished voicing his
unease, another entered who appeared
to be the senior of all gathered there.
His distant and unfocused gaze searched round
between a hairless pate and toothless grin.
An overhanging paunch and flimsy neck
required that he be helped in—carried even.
Unbothered by all questions and demands,
surely admiring birds and dozing off
were his two primary activities.
These attributes endeared him to the men.
Could they perceive his friendships, struggles, loves?
Did they see his defining triumphs—not
those of the past, but ones still yet to come?
Just so did Aqhat come into the tent,
encradled in his father's sturdy arms.
As when a ship that makes for land amidst
the forenoon fog attracts the sight of those
on shore who welcome it and all the goods
it promises, not noticing how it
has broughten in its tow a crystalline
air, as if on its own, so too did their
approach transfix and then dissolve the air
of wariness brought on by Kirta's speech.

With smiles the patriarchs embraced them,
ensuring Danel that they were prepared
for the initiatory ritual.
He offered them his solemn gratitude
before performing his allotted task.

Removing Aqhat's swaddling garb, Danel
took wet, maroon clay in his hands and smeared
it over Aqhat, covering the boy
from heel to head, and when he'd finished this,
he gave him to a figure dressed in black
who like a cobra leered beneath his hood.
Including Danel, every elder left,
proceeding toward the anxious crowd outside.

A moment passed, then yet another one.
Uncanny in his stride, the hooded one
emerged and drifted toward the foreshore's marge.
Midway, he halted—setting Aqhat down.
The personage enshrouded like the night
retired to the tent whence he had come,
when with celerity seven men dressed
as nocent demons rushed upon the child.
Wild howls and snarls erupted from behind
their vizards—the observers shrieking too,
revolted by the minatory scene.
Surrounding Aqhat so that he could not
be seen, the spirits mock-aggressed the boy
then lifted him, rejoicing in his death.

But while the wicked celebrated their
infanticide, a holy heptad rushed
out of the tent, and in their gilded garb
replete with crescent moons, the Kotharat
assailed those seven baneful bloodshedders,
annihilating some while others ran
for shelter to the cheers of standers-by.
The Daughters of the Sickle Moon then stood
about the boy, lamenting his demise.
Upraising Aqhat in the salty breeze,

the eldest woman bore him to the shore
(the other six arranged in a cortege)
where Danataya waited in the shoals,
adorned with drab attire besmirched with blood.
Soon ululations from the Kotharat,
from Danataya, from the audience,
and from the newborn swirled into the vault
and bristled every upraised blade of sward.
Receiving him, Danataya immersed
her son into the sea, rubbing the clay
and dirt from him till he'd been washed anew,
then cleansed herself, the surf beclouded by
ablutionary whorls of blood and mud.
Arraying him in dry habiliments,
the Kotharat reclothed Baal's conduit,
bedecking her with unstained livery
to match the new regalia of her son.

Concentric rings of townsfolk rippled out
as from a unitary cause around
a ligneous colossus of Hadad,
their solemn visages turned toward the god.
Approaching them with Aqhat in her arms,
Danataya came to the circle's edge.
A low and wary voice called out to her,
"Who goes there? What would you request of us?"
to which the outsider made known her wish,
"A seed interred in your own earth has died,
but by the power of the Kotharat
he has been promised life and puts down roots.
Help cultivate him and he'll bear you fruit."
Another nameless voice now prodded her,
"Who goes there? What would you request of us?"
Once more the one beyond their bounds replied,

"A seed interred in your own earth has died,
but by the power of the Kotharat
he has been promised life and puts down roots.
Help cultivate him and he'll bear you fruit."
Two rows of sages opened up a path
for them to pass and Danataya walked
into the center of the fold to join
her husband and the priest Kilamuwa.

Tall carven Baal looked down on all below
as the cleared path resealed just like a door.
Now Danataya stood beside her spouse
and Kilamuwa asked for one last time,
"Who goes there? What would you request of us?"
In unison the couple made reply,
"A seed interred in your own earth has died,
but by the power of the Kotharat
he has been promised life and puts down roots.
Help cultivate him and he'll bear you fruit."
Once Kilamuwa washed his either hand,
a servitor stepped forthright, carrying
a tray supporting bowls of argent make,
and Kilamuwa took the ruddy clay
from one bowl, mixing it with fragrant oil.
He scooped the unctuous paste and plastered it
on Aqhat's forehead, followed by these words,
"My child, wherever you might wander to,
would that you keep your fatherland within
your heart as long as you have breath to draw.
Bethink to yourself the rich clay from which
you have been shaped, the soil that nourished you.
Give thanks to Baal who irrigates our fields,
thus strengthening the roots of ancient trees
who plunge beneath the ground with rugged force."

The priest then dapped his thumb in the third bowl
containing lucid water from the Green
and dabbed it on the boy's soft lips, praying,
"And may you ever praise Nahar, whose smell
and taste of salt give flavor to our lives.
We know that Baal already favors you,
but don't forget your seaside origins."

Now the officiant gestured for the bowls
to be removed at which his servitor
brought back a laver and a water jar.
He handed both to Kilamuwa who
anointed Aqhat's brow and lips before
intoning orisons to El the Wise,
"Oh El, great Father who looks after us,
Progenitor, no less, of Mot, Astarte,
and Yam, look kindly on this devotee
of yours and with this water which derives
from Lel, bless him; help him to emulate
your eminence and so become like you,
a wise man and a father too, and grant
his life be driven on by holiness."

Although remaining poised, the townsfolk beamed
at Aqhat's reverent irreverence,
for now, as had become a ritual
unto itself, the babe let out a cry—
the small initiate's antiphony,
a psalm of praise no less than of lament.
The old community's new denizen,
Aqhat was hoisted in the air to cheers
and cups of wine were furnished from the tent
by servers and distributed to all.
A grateful Danataya passed him round,

the people holding their longevity.
The ceremony ended, the village
caroused away the evening, tippling wine
and sharing roasted meats into the night.
With joy, in Aqhat all the town beheld
their future, and yet, unbeknown to them,
so too were they beholden to his past.

Book II

Years passed—so far as mortals number them—
the present harvest season beckoning
the gods to congregate atop Mount Lel
where El would feast them with the offerings
confected, poured, and raised by human hands.
El's mountain palace overtops thick clouds
which sever its incomprehensible
affairs from the presumptive nosiness
that so distinguishes the human race.
His citadel upholds the firmament
with seven turrets that can safely house
a thousand bowmen each (and comfortably).
Connected by long ashlar battlements
arising from the mount's perimeter,
these towers stretch seven and seventy
cubits from the interior outside.
The stronghold looks impregnable, though were
it necessary, one could surely cast
another from its walkways through the blue
abysms gaping on its every side.

Across the vales of wild and wind-warped grass
the gods trod, making for the halidom.
Anat and Baal were first to reach the trails
of marly duff that switchbacked through the wood
of pine comprising Lel's periphery.
Downrushes of a resinous perfume
swashed through boughs of evergreenery,
warm sunlight-shafts nielloing the floor.

Brother and sister huffed up limestone bends,
discharging tumbling scree from high aloft
and circumscribing still and lonesome lochs
as glinting snow clumps lost their grip and fell
through branches, splatting on the sposh below.
Beleaguerment eterne within her breast,
Anat scanned Lel's defenses for weak points,
observing that the mountain's vertical
northeastern face held small, unguarded caves.
Baal breathed in Mount Lel's ether, rarefied
and cleanly, sending scud clouds from his nose,
his wolfhide buskins craunching the sheets of grue
beneath which meltwater minnow shoals ran.

Tallay and Yatpan followed close at heel,
advancing to the forefront so they could
announce their masters' imminent advent.
Behind them came Tiratu, Kinnaru,
and Kothar-wa-Hasis with donatives.
Astarte and Yam-Nahar no less than Arsh
and Horon followed them, ascending side
by side, conversing on the way about
the meal and passing other godlings up.
The last to trek, because they lit the way
for all who came before, were welkin-gods:
Yarikh and Shapshu, Shahar and Shalim.
The moment they departed all the earth
descended into blackness, lost, much like
an empty hull that wavers side-to-side
alone upon a cave's pyritic pool—
all while the crown of Lel illumed as if
it were a bonfire fixed by giants' hands.

Awaiting the arrival of their kin,
El lay across from Athirat, who'd passed
her day in Lel's unrivaled library
comprised of row on row of organized
tablets—omniscience etched in fired clay.
For time unfathomable Athirat
served as El's faithful consort, guiding him
in troubled years and managing affairs
of state when caprice or exhaustion took
the reins, preferring detours of their own.
Upon the lofted balcony affixed
to their bedchamber, Athirat reposed
upon a byssus pillow stitched with gold
designs and plumped with plumules of wild geese.
Between them lay a favorite game of theirs:
a decorated faience rectangle
divided into thirty colored squares—
the steps or the eventualities
by which their pieces sought to liberate
themselves by skirring for the Underworld.

The potentates were midway through their race.
El's three remaining pieces held the lead.
He cast twin knucklebones and laughed aloud,
positioning his staff-shaped ivory piece
beside his hawk and taurine figurines
to form an unsurpassable blockade.
After imbibing a large draft of wine,
El looked to Athirat, and smiling said,
"Such a reproachful glare does not befit
your emerald eyes—besides, I always lose.
Even if I desired to let you win
I couldn't do so: Every roll falls out

just as it must when deities throw down,
our outcomes forecasted by our own hands.
For instance, you would not deny that we
were meant to meet those centuries ago?
Immobilized by beauty such as yours,
I couldn't speak. I'd never seen your like.
And now since you can neither speak nor move—
whether because of this game's rules or my
good looks—I'll play my part and go again."

The Lady of the Sea made no response
as El let fall the knucklebones once more,
advancing his hawk-piece beyond the board
but forced to separate the other two,
thereby disintegrating his defense.
Her turn now come, she cast the bones and said,
"Perhaps all is as it must be, in which
case I cannot but be someone who loves
to entertain all possibilities.
That may be why, unlike the others whom
you face, you still have yet to beat the one
who plays at wife as well as strategist."
She took her buck-shaped figurine and slid
it down four squares, replacing El's bull-piece
with a surprise attack. The goddess grinned.
Her black buck now maintained the foremost place,
becoming vulnerable to attack—
her figurine formed like a lioness
surrounded by El's ill-intentioned pawns.
She studied the array, examining
her options when a loud knock shook the door.
El gestured for his doorwardens to grant
admission to whomever'd just arrived
as Elsh and Qodesh came before their Lords.

Elsh bowed before Lel's paramounts and said,
"Apologies for interrupting you.
Our scouts report that those you've summoned here
to share your company will soon arrive.
Let me assure you that we've overseen
to everything: Whole flocks of lambs and herds
of cattle sacrificed by human hands
have roasted for a day with herbs galore
atop the firepits; ancient jars of wine
have been unsealed, inhaling mountain air
for the first time; the dinner hall is lit
with lamps of olive oil that can't run dry;
and sleeping quarters for your guests have been
arranged and cleaned by hands most sedulous.
We've drawn a heated bath for both of you,
the royal stolists waiting and prepared
to preen you in the finest linen robes."

Surprised their guests had summited so fast,
the gods postponed the outcome of their game
as El bade Elsh refill his cup of wine.
With valedictions they excused their aids,
for though the scattered pantheon would be
awhile yet getting settled from their trip,
Lel's rulers could no longer fritter time
away as if it were a normal day.
The Lady of the Sea called to her pride
of lionesses who came bounding out,
competing for the pleasure of her nails
before they followed her and El beyond
their sprawling rooftop garden in which mixed
bright crocus flowers, gentle white at heart
with violet tips like living amethyst;
trusses of sociable wild chamomile;

clusters of efflorescing sage; scarlet
tepals of be-so-bold anemones;
and others that they'd not had time to name.

Moved by this rainbow-dappled greenery,
El warmed at thinking of their lineage
united under his paternal roof.
He reached to pet a lioness who, scared
by his encroachment, snapped at him with her
resistant chaps from which he quickly reeled,
recoiling from the beast and bludgeoning
his wife below the eye with his winecup.
She cursed and cupped her face, reminding him—
with more insistence this time—that her pride
befriended few, protected her, and took
offense on her behalf (though meaning well).
Bypassing him, she felt her throbbing skin
begin to bruise, appareling herself
in silence as her lionesses climbed
atop her bed and made themselves at home,
recumbent yet remaining ill at ease.
El dressed and poured himself another cup.

The gods ascended up the mountainside
until the foremost chert and limestone walls
of El's erect massif came into view.
A sturdy base formed the unshakeable
foundation for his manse whose looming sides
could only be approached by one thin berm
which wound its way behind a waterfall
gushing above their heads amain, falling
down through the clouds below and out of sight.
Although they came to visit Athirat
and El each year, one year in joyful song,

the next in dour hostility, the day
had not yet come in which a single god
could duck behind Mount Lel's cascade without
renewed respect for El, the head of all
the land and its inhabitants of old.
Behind the waterfall there stretched a long
and torchlit passageway, the only route
to the interior, whereat the guards
that Elsh and Qodesh placed in charge stood watch
with ivory handled swords just like a wolf's
white fangs defend its pitch and dark-red throat.

The underlings of El's and Athirat's
attendants were instructed to obtain
and safekeep every implement of war
or magic power that the gods had brought
until the repast's end, and so they did.
Baal handed over Driver first, the club
he used to shatter his opponents' skulls.
Unto the sentries Kothar-wa-Hasis
gave swage and mallet, his fine instruments.
So too Anat, compliant but no less
chagrined by customs such as these, removed
her scourge of scorpion tails, holding it
for a moment just like a mother who
must leave her newborn infant for a while,
though never-ending punishment it seems.

Up through the rock-hewn tunnel each god rose,
their footfall on the wet stone echoing
throughout until they reached the gullet's end
which opened on a verdant peristyle
where green vines clambered over trellises.
Now Elsh and Qodesh greeted their esteemed

and worthy guests—Yadi-Yalhan, Samal,
Rabbim, Pidray, Athtar the Short Leggèd,
and all the rest, directing them to where
they'd sleep before escorting each to Lel's
incomparable and storied festal hall.
Ensconced oil lamps aligned the room along
the table's either side while inglenooks
well-tended-to housed fires of oaken logs,
their chatter joined by jokes cracked by the guests.
Some only met for such festivities,
like Shapshu and Yarikh, whose calendars
prevented them from routine rendezvous,
or like sworn enemies Nahar and Baal,
who with pretended cordiality
and feigned decorum struggled to disguise
their codependent animosity.

The clamor dwindled as the double doors
far toward the feasting hall's north side unlatched,
outspreading wide for Athirat and El.
Bedizened in a white and purple robe
embroidered with electrum-colored prints,
El strode into the hall beside his wife.
An elegant white gown clothed Athirat,
her wavy umber tresses falling on
her shoulder blades—a carcanet of gold,
to which a pearl, triangular pendant
suspended, necklacing her décolletage.
The convocation gestured deference
ere sitting at the cedarn table's sides,
their regal hosts positioned at the head.

El greeted the Foregathering like this,
"Children! Be welcomed to my home again,

which you are free to visit anytime,
though I must say, to have you all come here
at once, to eat and sing until the morn,
enjoying every well-earned sacrifice
that's due to us, as much for taste as from
the knowledge that our faithful partisans
prepared these gifts from duty to us all—
I say, much better that we dine as one!
I don't see Shegr, Ithm. Where are they?
In any case, I offer you my thanks
for having journeyed as you always do,
allowing your old Father to recline
and wait for you to visit him at home.
But now, enough: It's wrong to overstuff
the ears before the belly's had its fill,
so let us sup and sluff off every care!"

Thus spoke the Lord, and in came servant girls
supporting earthen tuns of ruddy wine
that genuflected when to cups came near,
relinquishing strong drink, commoving guests
more heartily than any earnest prayer.
Lithe girls brought fig cakes set in porringers
with bowls of raisins, nuts, and apricots,
arranging them near tallow tapers who
foretold with fragrance courses yet to come.
The hall doors opened once again and men
brought trays of bread and safflower oil inside,
accompanied by twelve legs of lamb
confit'd and fatling cuts prepared by cooks
with cumin, sumac, onions, thyme, and salt.
They banqueted as only gods can do.
All gobbled gobbets and clanked their goblets,
downing enough to glut their appetites

(although their drinking never waned) until
each one recounted tales that lifted up
their fettle higher still, descanting times
whose nobleness could not be overmatched.

During the feast, the Wise One summoned Baal
of all the other gods, the son for whom
he held choice grandiosities in store.
El hugged him, asking him of Zaphon's news,
refilling both their cups, and with a nod
insinuating that he'd found a way
to feel revitalized and young again
before inviting Baal to sit back down.

His ivory oliphant drained dry, the Lord's
demeanor changed as he addressed his guests,
"My kin, it pleases me to see you here
enjoying food and drink and fellowship,
but as the night grows late, I think we'd be
remiss to squander convocations such
as these (since rarely do they come) without
discussing tidings that concern us all.
Perhaps as some of you already know,
the many peaceful years that graced our land
have reached their destined twilight, so it seems.
Our people find themselves in need of aid,
engulfed within a conflagration not
of their own making or due to their fault.
Shuttarna recently took ill and lay
upon his royal deathbed, muttering
his hard-won wisdom to his eldest son,
Artashumara, pleading with the man
to look to his own safety just in case
his imminent accession to the throne

be challenged by internal enemies.
But Artashumara ignored his words
of exhortation, looking out beyond
Mitanni's boundaries with ambitious eyes,
for maugre his impressive skills and all
his father's knowledge, Artashumara
proved so unwise to think that enemies
beyond his boundaries posed the greatest threat.
The halfwit! Those he should've feared the most
hadn't a need to manufacture plans
to escalade his city's walls, for they'd
been machinating from the inside out,
awaiting their subversion's proper time.
Upon Shuttarna's death, his eldest son
prepared to take his rightful place as king
only to be decapitated by
someone from Uthi's secret rebel force.

"Accounts of Uthi's coup and its intent
soon spread to governorates far and wide.
Concerned, and not without apparent cause,
that Abdi-Ashirta, Amurru's king,
would seek Mitanni's aid and sack his port
at Gubla, King Rib-Haddi sent his men
to Egypt to relay the recent breach
of peaceful ties established and upheld
between these empires up to this point.
And word did reach Amenhotep, but found
its way as well to Giluhepa's ears,
who'd late begun to love her time abroad,
accepting strange Egyptian ways of life
with solace that her sacrifice as wife
to King Amenhotep stopped boyish feuds
before becoming cause for butchery.

Yet now, just as the gash inflicted by
the separation from the kith and kin
she'd left in Washukanni had begun
to heal, this same scar sundered once again
as she imagined, overwrought by self-reproof,
her brother's head end-over-ending down
the palace steps, and so she grasped a dirk
to give material form to her heart's
deep wound, her soul sent westward with the sun."

El quaffed strong drink as Athirat spoke up,
"The more experienced of pharaohs, let's
presume, anticipate receiving news
of strife and disarray, for no one stays
in power long if he assumes that men
are good and sound of mind, but none expects
a word to skim across the seas to slay
his wife before you, Shapshu, redescend
into the Netherworld until the morn.
Assuredly, what hopes there might have been
for measured actions from Amenhotep
no longer have an air of likelihood.
Without a doubt he will commission troops
up through the southern desert to entrench
that influence and power which extends
with self-importance past Orontes' mouth.

"With this in mind I would advise our towns
to circummure themselves with bricks of mud
and fieldstones, readying themselves for war.
Your parents counsel digging secret shafts
to springs and joining these with tunnelways
in preparation for whatever comes.
We must be swift erecting forts and walls;

there's little time for perfect symmetry.
What matters is our people's unity.
Moreover, we must not lay waste to towns
that neighbor us and on whom we rely
for trade, as this would be like one who fears
the pain of being stung, and from this fret
decides to kick a beehive, striking first.
If with adjacent empires we must side,
we should refrain from hasty guessing games
and wait in patience for alliances
to prove themselves instead of erring now."

Anat—whose ichor boiled from violent thoughts—
became irate at Athirat's advice.
The Goddess of War first extolled the mauve
eyeshadow decking Athirat's left eye,
inciting snickers and continuing,
"In realms like ours, a period of peace
is like a beachhead burnished by the sea's
caress and lulled into a thoughtless daze
only in order to be pounded by
gigantic breakers whose retreat had been
a trick to gather jagged rocks and whelks.
We all remember Thutmose's assault
on walled Megiddo and the terror he
inflicted on our people, none of whom
he buried with the proper rituals.
To smithereens he smashed our ancient walls,
destroying vineyards like a man possessed.
Untold Egyptian men survived that fight,
establishing themselves as go-betweens
for future Delta interests in our land,
remaining here with wounded leftovers.
That bitterest defeat has since refueled

my efforts to amass and train strong troops
in subtle arts of war, for I, just like
our enemies, have made the most of years
that have been ones of amity for you.
Moreover, in addition to all this,
Resheph (who as you see cared not to join
us here), has recently unleashed cruel plagues
upon our cities. Don't you care for them?

"But no! You'd counsel all our villages,
the people who depend upon our might,
to hastily withdraw within their walls
and wait just like a tortoise who retreats
into its shell, afraid of eagles far
away who will, indeed, descend from heights
and thrash the reptile fore and aft, as feared.
With such a plan the slowpoke cedes the first
and most important battle to his foe,
the bird of prey who like a general
awaits his chosen moment to attack.
With heat and hunger banging at the gates
until they crack—his talons go to work
and breach the scutes, sped on by whiffs of blood.
At best erecting higher walls will shield
those foreigners already here; at worst,
if Egypt or Mitanni sieges us
while plagues pollute the beggar and the king
alike, our towns will be reduced to cesspools.

"But those who lack strong enemies need not
cry out in angst, much less prepare for Mot.
For too long Egypt has affixed her eyes
upon our land, conducting infantries

to capture southern city-states and quays.
You surely don't pretend to overlook
the creep of her bureaucracy toward us?
When ants crawl here and there about their work,
collecting the most miniscule of motes,
their sparseness seems to pose no threat, but soon
enough those files of convoys reach their mark,
assembling into colonies—whole seas
of black that teem with sinister intent.
So too reviled Egyptian garrisons!
Thus let us be the first to strike full-force.
We'll start with target practice using men
that I've equipped to root out every fiend
who sacrifices to the birdbrained Ra,
commanding men of weapon-bearing strength
to seize our seaside ports, ensuring that
all trades and raids begin and end with us."

Now Horon's heart uplifted with the thought
of his commander's grin at hearing news
of their expanding empire down below,
for whether mortal warfare leads to loss
or victory or stalemate, Mot succeeds,
receiving shades whose food is clay and dirt
while he devours human flesh and bone.
Yarikh too listened to Anat, his round
blank face turned colorless by words of war,
and in disgust he stormed out of the hall,
returning home at once to rest alone.
Though unsurprised by her rapacious plans,
El found them insolent per usual,
the ichor in his veins now tannic drink.
Before the great Creatrix of the Gods

could voice her thoughts, El from his dais rose
to intervene but stumbled headlong toward
the floor, propped up by nearby servant girls.

Recouping his composure, El declared,
"Please, please—we cannot fight amongst ourselves.
Remember that we all abet our land.
For now, let's leave off talk of war, for I
have seen enough to last a thousand lives.
One thing, it seems, we can agree on now,
to wit, that our folk can't defend themselves
or take up arms if they have been becharmed.
You think the magic of Resheph escapes
my sight, that I don't hear my people's cries
as he bedevils them from dawn to dusk?
Yet who among you has upbraided him
or tried to heal the ones that he afflicts?
Which one among you drives the plagues away
or has created spells to stay their spread?
Your silence tells me all I need to hear.
In that case, and because I'd like our feast
to end as cheerfully as it began,
allow me to present the remedy
that I've alone devised to put an end
to all the pestilence Resheph transmits."

The Lord then waved his hand embossed with rings
to one among his retinue who turned
to open wide the antechamber's door.
In strode a goddess whom none of the guests
had ever seen, nor could they—though possessed
of knowledge and foresight driven on
by imaginations that are next to none—
nor could they comprehend the beauteous

new wight who'd joined them in the festal hall.
The nubile goddess made her way toward El
as unmet gazes fixed on Athirat
and warmed her dimples to an ember-red.
Her stomach plummeted from Mount Lel's heights
down to its base, and she desired to leap
from some high overlook to follow it.

Imbibing still more garnet wine, the Lord
began to foreannounce his handicraft,
"Only when like commits to fighting like
can any hope for victory upsurge.
Resheph's contagion—insofar as it
diminishes the status of our land
as one where moderation and respect
take precedence over self-centeredness—
imperils our home as a neutral zone
for empires otherwise inclined to fight.
Therefore, so as to neither laden you
with dirty work nor grant more potencies
to the high priests of temple shrines (who seem
oft wont to swell with pride and who'd employ
their newfound force with their own gain in mind),
I took good clay and fashioned Shataqat,
a cure-all for emasculated men,
a goddess given breath to aid us all.
I have enjoined her to revive and heal
all those who've fallen or who've taken ill
from our land's plague, and without prejudice
regarding fealty, family, or estate.
Moreover, I've demanded that she work
in utter secrecy, transfiguring
herself as needed to evade the eyes
of gods and men alike (who're quick to be

corrupted by ambitions), and because
it's tawdry to indulge one's skills in full
display, ordained by gods though they might be.
She'll see to her vocation come the dawn,
but now it's late, and I must go and rest."

El's sons Shunama and Thukamuna
assisted him, holding their father up
as he lurched down the hall with Shataqat
whose buxom figure moved with graceful step.
Insisting that his boys return to join
the feast, El thanked them for supporting him.
The Lady of the Sea'd retired as well,
walking along a corridor to find
the Lord and Shataqat outside their door.
Now hoping the Creatress of the Gods
appreciated his creativeness,
the Lord invited Athirat to join
him while he entertained their newest guest,
to revel in each other as one god—
distinct by name, united by their love.
The queen beheld the two of them and then
declined the Lord's proposal with calm tact
(although her rage could hardly be tamped down).
She turned and made her way to the far end
of El's great citadel, now standing near
the balustrade along a balcony,
admiring the freethinking of Yarikh
who'd acted of his own accord and left
the banquet to resume his brilliant seat.
There she began to contemplate all things
as she attended to her golden pride.

Although the gods who lacked the stamina
for the Assembly's afterparty slept,
the hall still roared with toasts and merry song
until Habayu interrupted them,
"Now that the Oldster sleeps or toys the night
away with his new amatory friend,
we can at last speak truthfully, I hope.
The Lord—for once, despite himself—gave good
advice when he suggested that we not
let slip away our time together here.
I fail to understand why idly by
we lounge and watch the so-called King of kings
fall prey to daily drinking bouts,
each stoup more stupefying than the last.
Anat, it's true you spoke to El tonight
with critical determinedness, but in
so doing you presume his masterdom.
Would we not call a fool the one who, long
immured within a room against her will,
inured into habitual dismay,
inserts wrong keys time and again in hopes
that subsequent attempts will set her free
yet thereby never notes the once-stout door's
dilapidated state which needs but one
swift push in order to be knocked aground?
Before we cast a thought toward war, defense,
debating this or that potential plan,
we must decide what course of action we
will take with the incontinent old fart
since his aberrancies will ruin us."

Though some divine ones found Habayu's words
veracious, nonetheless, his tongue's supposed

impunity surprised the ones convoked.
His insolence offended Shunama
the most, who countered his daredevil speech,
"Why don't you bite you tongue off, saboteur,
and tuck that fiendish tail between your legs
so that you may lay claim, at least for now,
to the appearance of that manliness
which you do otherwise pretend so well.
You have forgotten Father's origins,
his feats, the reasons for his eminence.
Listen, then. Unclog your worm-infested ears
while I remind you of our Father's past:

"I sing the noblest warrior to come
from eastern lands, Ellil's own son, the one
whom Mami loved the most of all, more swift
than plunging highland gusts, ferocious as
a host of firefiends, he who'd requite
the gods in time of need—a god himself
no less, benevolently showering
dry fields with rain and boring oases
from desert dunes: Ninurta was his name.
Tonight I shall not hymn this warrior's
defeat of the unparalleled half-man,
half-bull far out at sea; I won't recite
his battles with the seven-headed snake
who terrorized large villages before
Ninurta stabbed its chest, lopped off its heads;
nor yet will you be told the tale when he
held contest with the ram whose horns were curved
stalagmites, each one fifteen fathoms long.
No—I shall sing of Anzu's fateful schemes
which brought the Eastern pantheon near doom.

"In those days Earth was new. Not everything
had yet been formed. The young gods of the sky,
the Igigi, had nowhere to recline,
ranging and roving about as they pleased.
One morning they passed over Hehe's peak,
its side distending like a craggy boil
until the mass burst open, giving way
to avalanches snapping girthy pines
as children break up kindling twigs with ease.
Out of the mountain's wound Anzu emerged,
an eagle fitted with a lion's head.
The myriad Igigi darted off
to tell Ellil, the King of All the Lands
who dwelt within Duranki's ancient walls.
Ellil sat back and pondered what to do.
Far-sighted Ea, Lord of Wisdom, Lord
of Incantations, saw within Ellil
the reasons for the god's confusedness,
addressing him with reassuring words,
advising they distract the neonate
as a probationary initiate,
entasking him with sacred busywork
so that the lion-headed bird might not
wreak havoc up and down the riverbanks—
encharging him to guard Duranki's door.

"Ellil agreed to Ea's plan and sent
Igigi to the feline bird of prey
to summon him unto Duranki's gate.
They soon returned, the orogenic god
agreeing to the honor they'd bestowed.
With eyes both keen and fierce the doorkeeper
secured the threshold, nid-nodding not once,
permitting only the most sacrosanct

of priests into the temple's central court.
From time to time, however, Anzu glanced
inside and saw Ellil remove his crown
and jewelry, taking off his finespun garb
before submersing in a bath to read
and fathom the Tablet of Destinies
upon which were inscribed the fates of all.

"The days droned on and seagulls winged their way
up from the gulf along the riverside,
alighting on Duranki's highmost walls.
One evening, Anzu turned the priests away,
assuring them Ellil would not require
their services that night, and though they did
insist, eventually each took their leave.
When Lord Ellil reclined within his bath,
the Tablet in his hands, his ward crept in
and with his talons he submerged the god
who gazed up through the turbulent surface
with panicked eyes until his gurgling waned.
Now Anzu seized the Tablet, taking wing
for Hehe's heights with surging anxiousness.
But in his reckless haste, swift Anzu crashed
full tilt into a sturdy coign of stone.
A fragment from the Tablet broke and fell.

"The temple's foremost priest, a man with dark
black hair extending past his shoulder blades,
his face adorned with reddle streaks, rushed toward
the blast which rocked Duranki's very base.
He found the broken Tablet piece and held
it, studying its pictographs with awe.
This quondam systematizer of things
to be foreknown, unmatched interpreter

of strange anomalies, who understood
why sometimes severed heads will fleer and laugh,
what should be done when babes refuse to leave
the womb and clench their mother's wrist to pull
her in—nativity turned inside out—
or what the mating of the cow and horse
shall signify for ne'er-do-wells and kings
at home—this deep officiant now beheld
the meaning of his life with clarity.
That day, Ellil's chief priest collected all
the tablets and the magic instruments
in sight, compiled them in a caravan,
and with a lashing whip he drove his team
of mules down dirt roads unto the West
where, it is said, he found a cave inside
a palisade where he could dedicate
himself to black arts, purling with the dead.

"Nightfall bitumened Lord Ellil's abode.
Its radiance had disappeared, its frieze
of copper which recounted epic deeds
of old immediately putrefied
with verdigris, the doors and cedar stools
began to rot, and all the rites surceased.
Anu, the father of Ellil, had gone
to see his son and—horrified—he found
him floating in the water, motionless.
A long and anguished cry flew from his lips
as Anu scrambled for his satchel filled
with air from an empyrean locale,
embreathing some before exhaling it
with incantations into his son's nose.
Though weakened by the act of treachery,
the King of Populated Lands awoke.

"Now raging Anu summoned every god.
He called his sons, Ellil's own kin, and said,
'Adad and Gerra, hunt down Anzu—slay
that wretched and perfidious outlaw.
Adad, take up your shining lightning rod,
and Gerra, shatter Anzu's hollow bones.
Whoever strikes him with the final blow,
in Ekur temples shall be built for him;
he shall be called 'the Lord,' be favored most
among the gods who will remain in debt
to him, their destinies safeguarded by
Ellil's just hands once more, where they belong.'

"Renowned in arts of warfare, Gerra made
reply, 'Decisive One, you know we'll root
out dreadful Anzu if you so decree.
The odds are stacked against us nonetheless,
since Anzu clutches destiny itself,
foreknowing when and where we will attack,
the number we shall bring, and how he must
prepare to guarantee his victory.'
Dejected, all the gods concurred with him.

"Ninurta watched Adad, beheld Gerra,
his loving uncles who had taught him how
to fight and use the bow, to hurl the spear
and wield a heavy shield of layered bronze.
He'd followed them in battles heretofore,
commanding smaller units of his own
and celebrating their accomplishments.
So too he saw his father, Lord Ellil—
unable to sustain another loss.

"Commoved to voice his heart, Ninurta faced
Mami and Anu, uttering these words,
'Our situation's bleak, but we must act.
I've heard it said that Anzu's callow when
it comes to thinking, and provided that
the Tablet's dense to the illiterate,
I say our best hope's to engage at once.
Up Hehe's southern ridge Shara and I
will lead our own Igigi hosts—Adad
and Gerra striking Anzu from the north
assisted by their own Igigi troops.
Brave Uncles: Which campaigns have you not won?
Our record's perfect—so it shall remain!
If we succeed, may Anzu's feathers flit
across the firmament and be a sign
of hope for those of you assembled here.'
Those present roared assent, enheartened to
possess some strategy instead of none.
Mami and Anu backed their only hope.

"The legionnaires enarmed themselves in haste
just as they'd done so many times before.
Both regiments set out that night and marched
as one through forested expanses till
they reached Mount Hehe's foot and parted ways.
Adad and Gerra headed north as planned
when Anzu, false in word but true in aim,
beset the unsuspecting regiment.
Ninurta, Shara, and their throngs engaged,
dispatching troops to scale and infiltrate
the beast's lair while the rest distracted him.

"Returning for another divebombing,
Anzu caught wind of the intruders who'd

invaded his domain with hopes that they'd
secure the Tablet, altering their fates.
He winged for them and from the mountainside
detached a ziggurat-sized boulder, soared
aloft, and set in stone those brigands' course.
He then searched Hehe's northern pediment
for the commanders of the ambuscade,
forthwith espying Gerra and Adad.
The latter nocked ten arrows all at once
as Gerra gripped his sword, frore from the air,
lusting to warm itself in Anzu's guts.
Adad loosed arrows at their enemy
but they were met midflight by Anzu's curse—
stopping and decomposing, each long shaft
returning to the reedbeds whence they came.
Descending like torrential rain, Anzu's
teeth sank into Adad's helm, and with one
ferocious jerk the monster rent his skull
in half, Adad's corpse falling down jaw-first.
Then Gerra charged the beast who held him off
with imprecations too, the fighter's sword
now melting as the singe of his hands' flesh
became inaudible amidst his screams.
With molten stumps he tried to fight the god,
protesting till the monster ended him.

"Ninurta, sickened with a rancorous
dismay, had witnessed every carnage-filled
affront upon his kin, the ones whom he
convinced to join the fight not long before.
Without an eyeblink's hesitation, he
and Shara raced toward Anzu who appeared
to them as if surrounded by a void.
The brute encircled them aloft before

he dove straight for Ninurta's jugular.
With his brand Shara punctured Anzu's leg,
the bird vociferating roars of pain,
abruptly taking hold of Shara's chest.
Awaiting the most opportune of times,
Ninurta drew an arrow in his bow,
and though it weighed more than a spear, his gaze
remained unwavering and ready—his
arched bow as still as twilight's crescent moon.
He fired the whooshing pointed shaft which cut
the air like lightning, though Ninurta glimpsed
each moment of its gradual advance
until it pritcheled Anzu's lungs, at which,
amidst strewn feathers, blinded by prolonged
chaotic pain, Anzu dashed Shara down
against a rocky outcrop, killing him.
The monster groaned and turned to meet the wretch
who had transpierced his lungs—but much too late.
Another arrow slaked it thirst for blood
as Anzu foundered downward to the earth.
Ninurta stood above him, mace in hand,
and dealt him seven blows for every god
he'd murdered, suggilating him until
he liquefied the traitor's bludgeoned mass.

"Three days thereon, all the divinities
inside Duranki roused and wrung their hands.
Like dandelion puffs propitious tufts
of down rode gentle winds, some plumes stained red,
no omen list required to know the signs
which vivified Ellil and washed away
the holy ones' anxieties and dread.
They raised up toasts for their deliverers
and drank away the early morning hours

like only those with diadems know how.
Each danced and sang so loud the temple walls
joined in, percussing with their rhythmic quakes.
By sundown, warrior Ninurta reached
the temple with Igigi veterans
bespattered with the evidence of war
as gods rushed out to meet them, hoisting up
the Tablet of Destinies, hugging them,
saluting their achievement with applause.

"But Anzu's slayer looked like one who'd known
defeat, and Ea grasped his vacant stare.
Ninurta placed the Tablet in Ellil's
still-convalescent grip and detailed what
befell them, how Adad and Gerra died.
Their father, Anu, couldn't bear the news
and wept, besmearing dirt upon his face
until it turned to brackish mud just like
one finds in estuaries near the coast.
Victorious Ninurta saw it all.

"Entrusting Anu's care to love's godhead,
Ellil addressed Ninurta with these words,
'My Son, you have succeeded in what none
aside from you would have set out to do.
The gods can write and read the world again,
and had your dauntless battle fallen out
some other way, would we yet be ourselves?
As promised, temples will be built for you
in Ekur and the world will know your deeds.
From henceforth you will take the name of 'El,'
the Lord, and though you owe your life to me,
I equally now owe my life to you.'

"To which Ninurta, now called El, replied,
'Good Father, I don't merit any praise.
Much nobler ones defended destiny,
cut down by Anzu's gruesome wiliness.
I won't protest if you and others call
me El, but please don't build me temples here
or in Ekur, where every sound and smell, all those
haunts where my uncles loved to pass the time
with me will just remind me of their loss.
I cannot bear to look in Anu's eyes,
nor would I dare accept his pardoning
for my role in the death of his two sons.
So, King of Populated Lands, reward
me rather with a mountain to the west,
a far-off place where newfound memories
will thrive so guilt can dissipate like smoke.'

"And so it came to pass," Shunama said,
concluding his opponent's chastisement.
Most there had heard the song before, a fact
which did not lessen its impressiveness.

Meanwhile, concerned for Athirat, Qodesh
searched Lel's unnumbered corridors for her.
He found her and inquired as to her needs.
With dizzied enmity she said to him,
"For all his errors that I've fixed, and sins
forgiven in the silence of my heart;
for every foolish curse he's spit at me,
not able to recall them the next day;
for each and every hardship I've endured,
though rarely with a word of thanks repaid—
for those she loves a consort bears such things,
upholding thoughtless jilts—a greater good

both calling and eluding her the while.
I've tried to bear this load with dignity.
For shame! One night of insuperable
disgrace outweighs his other faults combined.
I utterly refuse to smile and vie
with some repugnant courtesan to whom
tasks are allotted so that she can live
in ignorance, distracted from her Lord's
explicit and lascivious designs.
From queen to cuckquean he'd disparage me,
and right before our children's very eyes!

"To make things worse, he thinks his odalisque
will aid him better than I have, all while
Anat hatches her hawkish subterfuge,
intractable as she has ever been.
For one last time I'll intervene on his
behalf, diverting our land's course from war.
Qodesh: Conceal this vial of somnolent
bane, pouring just a drop into the cups
of Baal and the War Goddess, putting them
into a harmless sleep for half a month.
When Sleep enshrouds them, find Mot's vizier
Horon, instructing him to furtively
consign Anat to Mot beneath the earth
where he's to jail her, obviating her
attempts to stir and reignite the coals of war.
Her sinister aggressions must be barred.

"As for myself, when everyone turns in,
we shall effect the plan we once discussed:
I'll leave El to his biomantic games
and steal away as no god's ever done.
In limitations unbeknown to them

and which for all their strength they'd not endure,
I'll veil myself, assuming human form.
There's little time to spare. Take this and go."

She handed him the vial as he replied,
"My Lady, have things truly come to this?
What will we do without the unseen hands
that cater to our folk behind the scenes?
Soon Shataqat shall leave your home and tend
to El's commands, not needing to return
while busying about, invisible.
Excuse El's foolishness once more and stay.
I pray you. I need not remind you that
assuming the appearance of mankind
seems harmless at the start, but what if you
begin to live and to perceive like them,
since practiced likeness bears upon essence?
Of all the places you might hide, of all
the things you might become, why must you choose
that petty, squabbling herd of clayborn men?"

His words had touched her but she did not budge,
"You're right that feigning likeness bears on one's
whole being, which is why I won't pretend
to love this life or put on festive airs
or go on simpering atop this mount.
Make ready my Sidunan hideaway
with utter secrecy, for soon I'll sail
from Ugarit, returning nevermore.
See to Anat's imprisonment below,
disclosing not a word to anyone
and bidding Horon do the same . . . or else.
But most importantly, look after my
four-leggèd loves. See that they thrive on Lel.

Slaving no more, in solitude I'll rest.
Now go, before I opt against good sense!"

With heavy eyes, he took the vial from her,
departing and bypassing El's bedroom
from which salacious, tickled squeals snuck out.
Arriving at the raucous feasting hall,
Qodesh relieved a servant girl of her
night's duties, sending her away to sleep.
Pouring the bane into a jug of wine,
he served Anat and Baal, who had assumed
their parents' seats, presiding in their stead.
Hadad the Cloudrider now took the floor,
"The night is late. We must decide upon
a plan, a mean between the ones proposed.
I speak with the coregency of El
and in the spirit of the warrior
Adad in whose great honor I am named.
Remember that Shuttarna sired two sons.
The second one, Tushratta, may have scaped
the bloody coup that Uthi organized.
If Prince Tushratta kept his wits and head,
then it behooves us all to find and make
an ally of Mitanni's rightful heir.
A malleable, vengeful heart in straits
so dire could be developed for our ends.
I'll send search parties to discover him,
avowing to his restitution if
he pledges Washukanni's warriors
and chariots whenever we're in need.
Should he be found, Anat and I will train,
compose, and fashion him in our interests."

Thus Baal. His argument persuaded them.
The gods, now weary from their revelries,
took leave to seek out their respective rooms.
Before Mot's vizier retired, Qodesh
conveyed his Lady's messages to him.
Horon accepted her commands and knew
her plans would hearten Horon's overlord.

As sleep enshrouded the immortal ones
(save Horon, who lay wide awake from fear
and eagerness faced with the task that fell
to him that night), the Lady of the Sea
descended toward the foot of Lel and past
its guards with drooping eyes and lazy ears.
She quickly reached the woodland at Lel's base,
emboldened by the ease of her escape.
Amidst the sappy pines, she held within
her bosom an existent to exist,
the likeness of a being yet to be,
the gorgeous mortal she would soon become,
composing it with calm until the form
inside her inmost omphalos was fired
and struck upon an anvil with full force,
removed and brazed within a water tub
of similarity and variance,
examined, then put back into her core's
kiln where her passions fought for pride of place.

Her royal raiment frizzled into shreds
and ripped asunder in frustrated tears
before it turned into a tunic brooched
together by a copper toggle pin.
Her liver changed the ichor in her veins

to human blood which pumped and flowed with verve
to her extremities, and from behind
her softened face sharp cheekbones overtopped
the faultless fault lines of her even jaw.
Her eyes of malachite remained but filled
with charged, reanimated youthfulness.
She took the gold chains and the bangles El
had gifted her and threw them in a stream.
This beauty, now becloaked in human form,
then sought her stabled purebred destrier
who whinnied at her presence right until
her touch gave her identity away.
Mounting her horse, she gripped the reins and rode
with liberated pace for Ugarit.

Book III

The next day Shahar Lord of Dawn awoke
before the other gods and journeyed down
Mount Lel, arousing birdsong on the way.
Shapshu pushed down her coverlet and climbed
the palace steps to peak over the tip
of Lel's walkway, and from that vantage point
she warmed the sleeping pines and followed Dawn,
her stableboy, before she took the reins.
The mountain's cataract, the fountainhead
of all freshwater on the earth, gushed out
its endless substance, roaring from on high
until it smothered smoothened rocks below,
its water calming for a stretch before
rough rapids riled it up once more just as
outbursts of rage rhythmically subside
over time only to fume once again
when confrontations one has grown to loathe
resurge, provoking anger's sharp return.

In days gone by, Mount Lel's chief chine carved
its path through limestone while within the wood
a channel broke from it—not the result
of any fault—but due to tendencies
and inclinations of divergent kinds.
A cloudy sediment moiled in the first,
its offshoot boasting pristine clarity,
maturing in its independent flow.
With time their separation grew till on
a promontory's opposite divide,

far from their origin, both rivers heard
each other, rushing for their childhood friend.
Both met and wimpled side by side within
a confluence, reunified afresh,
forgetting why they'd ever gone their ways.

As eyots increased in number and in mass,
portentous fears of their forthcoming bourns—
of predetermined downstream destinies—
redoubled violent rapids that arose
from love and from the sorrow at love's end.
A dry and unmoved mountain edge then cleaved
the flume into two separate waterways
which aboresced into more creeks and rills,
embittered all the more by every rift.
Observant of these multiplying pains,
El charged Nahar to form the seas to spur
all runnels, ghylls, and brooks to muster hope,
progressing with the confidence that they'd
unite again as they once had on Lel.

A new beck forked from those who'd fathered him,
a river now subsistent in himself
yet made of the same stuff from start to end.
In emulation of his mother's ways,
he ventured southward through a dell beside
which rose a vibrant vineyard on a brae.
Adjacent to the vineyard's canting edge
there stood an ancient, gnarly olive tree
which looked as though a maundering giant
had taken massive forest vines in hand
and with excessive force fused the bouquet,
replanting it atop the hummock's head.
That tree, almost as wide as tall, adorned

the loamy hillock centuries before
a soul had thought to till the nearby rows.
It was the earth's first instance of its kind.
And yet its own age it could not recall
since winter's dormancy erased and rinsed
every last word its greenery'd enclosed.
In the same way, the vines were ignorant
of just how many years they had, and so
each spring renewed their common youthfulness.

With cautious hesitation, turtle heads
began to stretch their necks out of their brown
protective logs six pallid moons ago
as from a half-year's hibernation both
the vineyard and the olive tree awoke.
Growing reluctantly at first, their buds
soon burst with confidence, the tree's white blooms
faced with the other's flowering as if
for the first time, as when a child finds out
that there exists another just his height,
each sizing up the other warily.
Neither the vineyard nor the olive tree
concerned themselves with what distinguished them,
the skinny, wiry one content to share
the bees and breeze with his quixotic friend
who, perched upon the hill, could see far off
and liked to dream of traveling one day.
Their toes embogged deep down in sandy soil,
the twain endured the scorching afternoons,
at night perspiring till the coming dawn
when the belovèd Sun would pat them dry.
When green eggs sprouted whence white blossoms had
once bloomed, they laughed at one another since
the grape cluster's great girth better beseemed

the tree, from whom the smallest drupelets drooped.
The olive tree began to fret when his
friend's green fruit bruised, but since he showed no signs
of pain, he sighed relief and rested his
five hundred eyes and six thousand sage ears.

One morning they awoke to find a group
of twenty women walking down the bank
toward their terrain, accompanied by mules
and miniature versions of themselves.
Not even one branch recognized the lot,
the vast majority of whom had come
to train and prune them not so long ago.
The children tromping with their caretakers
wore faces of fatigue, and when the mass had reached
the vintner's mudbrick home, he helped them prop
their tents as the exhausted took their rest,
way-weary from their long autumnal trek.

After they'd taken bread and drink, the group
split up, the older children brandishing
their delegated billhooks with conceit.
They slumped down rows and sliced the peduncles,
tossing the ripened bunches to the girls
who guided jennies flanked with basketry.
And once a mule could bear no more, she hauled
her loads to youngsters who destemmed the grapes,
delivering them to the lucky ones:
The eldest of the women stood upon
the winepress—squishing, squelching, squashing grapes
with their old crows' feet, screeching with delight
they'd misremembered as impossible,
their heels empurpling in the messy marc.
Juice from the dancing sluiced along a carved

depression where more women filled up skins
and unfired jars of clay to be stopped up
and left to swell for one last ripening.

The first few days of harvesting gone by,
the vineyard learned to bend to the new hands
attending to his needs with constant care.
Distracted by the chitter, toil, and mirth
surrounding him, he didn't hear his friend
the olive tree when he called out to him,
enjoying his taut necks' disburdening,
his incidental creativity
concelebrated with the laborers.
The days progressed and the tall olive tree
stood motionless, a bystander to all
the fuss these strangers made for fruit contused
first by the gods, then by old women's toes.
The taciturn olea only watched,
his fruit's flesh indurating at the scene.

Come eventide, the workers lounged around
a candent campfire as the vintner's wife
brought sycamore figs, fresh-baked barley loaves,
and jasper-like, emmarbled mutton shanks
to feed the migrants, joining them at wine.
As the bright blaze with every crack gave birth
to wingèd sparks, a pious woman filled
the young ones' ears with old didactic song:

"Once back in primeval times,
Yam and Mot were feasting,
conjuring their newest crimes,
sinisterly scheming.
As a common foe they had,

they would work together:
Both would chain up Baal Hadad,
conquering the weather.

"Emissaries flew to Baal,
auguring subjection.
He then held them to the wall,
yet they found protection
(rescued by Ilisha's hand,
fleeing through the casement),
while Baal forged his counterplan,
wroth from his abasement.

"To the Craftsman he made haste,
pleading for a weapon.
Kothar forged a magic mace—
strongest in the heavens.
Eager for a violent scrum,
Baal dove through the deepness,
dicing Yam up like fish chum,
bloodying the bleakness.

"Zaphon's king then marched for Mot,
confidently storming,
but he chanced upon Anat,
who gave him this warning:
'Mot will drub you in the field,
so you must be clever.
As a shade remain concealed,
then him you'll dissever.'

"Outside Targuziza's cave,
Baal bestrode a heifer.
Him a replica she gave,

like him in all measure.
To the Netherworld they roamed,
where Mot heard the ground shake.
He defended his fell home,
raging like an earthquake.

"Mot transported his fresh kill
where he could behold it.
Seeing that Baal's blood he'd spilled,
his black eyes turned molten.
Those on Lel then mourned Baal's fate,
as Death himself laughed on.
Mot then flew through his black gate,
subjugating Zaphon.

"Throned upon Hadad's dais,
Mot received a servant.
Humbly cloaked he stayed his gaze,
prostrate and observant.
Mot bade him now kiss his ring,
thus he came unto him,
reaching the usurper king,
planning his undoing.

"Taurine teeth then mashed Mot's claw—
two bull's horns impaled him.
Mot spread wide his vasty jaws,
wrawling and inhaling.
Both gods fought the whole night long
till Cloudrider conquered,
felling him who did him wrong,
winning back his honor."

As vineyard harvests come but once a year
at best, there never being dearth of drink,
the mothers and their children danced and sang
past evenfall, the youngsters clapping hands
to songs saved for occasions just like these.
The women sang with gaiety, their mouths
and eyes upraised as if to guarantee
their words would fly above their children's heads:

"From rooted stocks there grows a leader,
a grafted scion with promises.
He sights a lark and vows to feed her
when she alights and blows soft kisses,
turning an eye to gauge his worth
just as two greenish buds sprout forth.

Oh noble vine, stay grounded
and don't you step out of line.
The lark can call the vintner's wife
to stomp your grapes once rounded.
To stomp your grapes once rounded!

Upon his branch she settles,
his woody stem attending.
His arms are firm, his clusters gentle,
their sired his shoulders bending,
until a finch comes from afar
whose coos distract this cultivar.

Oh noble vine, stay grounded
and don't you step out of line.
The lark can call the vintner's wife
to stomp your grapes and pound them.
To stomp your grapes and pound them!

With flails the lark now cools her young,
bringing them to ripeness,
while the drooping leaf-bearded one
lies round as if lifeless.
She squawks in plight while he keeps napping,
yet soon takes flight, her wings aflapping.

Oh noble vine, stay grounded
and don't you step out of line.
The lark can call the vintner's wife
to stomp your grapes once rounded.
To stomp your grapes once rounded!"

The olive tree could find no rest, and he
came to abhor those termagants' shrill cries.
Beneath the moonrise he beheld the lot
of them swigging his friend's fermented swill,
appalled by how the drink deluded them.
A part of him desired to join their ranks
though questions kept him rooted where he stood:
Could no one see his monumental height?
Or did his stature fill their hearts with fear?
It's true, he had produced less fruit than his
friend, but did no one want a single drupe?
To keep the night's festivities alight,
the vintner's wife brought out illuminants
whose mild aroma harkened to good times—
whether to a forgotten memory
or as the image of a better life
to come flits across the heart's cave entrance,
no sooner sighted than it's gone for good.
Thus while the lit perfume agreed with him,
its wafts eluded his decipherment,
frustrating his interior till he

turned sour and astringent, looking down
upon those witches dancing round their pyre.

At sunup, two mischievous girls left
their boring work and climbed the nearby knob.
Aroused, the tree lit up and stood erect
with the anticipation of a groom
the day he's set to wed his lovely bride.
When they approached, the girls inspected him,
running their soft, inquisitive hands down
the currents of his bark, a waterspout
made still beneath its cloud cover of green.
The smaller of the two girls climbed atop
her playmate's less-than-stable shoulder blades
to shake some olives from his outstretched arms.
The tree was glad to give them some, the girls
each taking one in hand, counting to three
and plopping their first pick into their mouths.
For but a moment each one chewed their bite
before they screwed their eyes up, faces squinched.
They shrieked and spit verjuicy mush upon
the ground, attempting to scrape off the taste
while laughing and logrolling down the hill.

Dew bleared the treetop's eyes. As days wore on,
he caved, capitulating to the vine
as drupes began to take the form of grapes.
They purpled and relaxed and even tried
to weazen pits to pips—without success.
Still no one came. Nor would a soul arrive
for one moon when the vintner came to beat
the tree's stout bole, collecting all that it
would let go of, and with his patient art
and time's slow-brine he softened up and cured

the bitterest and thickest-skinned of ones.
And though their ingrown stony pits remained—
a hard reminder of the past—they learned
to live with salty, dry exteriors,
matured and humbled, ready for a laugh.

Among the vintner's migrant laborers
were Danataya, Pugat, and Aqhat.
The first pressed grapes, Inumi at her side
for balance (though the latter pulled her down,
creating something of a royal mess)
while Pugat steered her mule down trellised rows,
her brother cutting bunches of ripe fruit
and underhanding each of them her way.
He would have loved the labor even if
he had to work alone, so partnering
with his friend Gabbar and the sister he
admired compounded his exuberance.
Each twelvemonth harvest puppied back to him
all smiles and bounding playfulness until
he left, its time for sleeping come again.

Together Aqhat, Gabbar, and Pugat
would suck the grapes' sweet juice, propelling wads
of seed and skin in competitions which,
however affable, sometimes required
resorting to the ancient, tried-and-true
imperatives of juvenile justice:
Pugat or Aqhat or Gabbar would stoop
down unawares and take a fallen grape
in hand—no shriveled raisin but a lump
internally putrescing in the heat,
its sleek and leathery exterior
ensuring good projectability.

In secrecy they stockpiled armaments
to whip fruit one another's way like rocks
from slings, kersplattering their target sites
with grape-gore till some killjoy intervened,
not from pacific inclinations but
to put an end to tunic-slubbering.

Upon the last day, Aqhat and Gabbar—
alleging grave exhaustion earlier
though now miraculously energized—
pled with Danataya and Inumi,
their mothers, for permission to go play.
Under condition that they make for camp
before the sun went down, they gave them leave.
The two scamps praised them, making for the hills.
Far from the vineyard, Aqhat grabbed a branch
both long and sharp-tipped, brandishing his sword
ere challenging his friend-cum-enemy,
"Which foolish field marshal commanded you
to take me on, or did you, coveting
renown, elect to head the van yourself?
You must be unfamiliar with my name
to forfeit life with such haphazardness:
I'm Aqhat, Baal's Predestined Warrior
and Gift to Danel, Man of Rapiu,
the God-Fearing One of the Harnemite,
Descendant of the Highborn Hyksos kings.
The Conqueror has chosen me to lead
his foremost northern outfit which—"

A clod struck Aqhat in the chest mid-vaunt,
eliciting a shriek incongruous
with his pretended, manly airs, his claimed
succession having granted no success.

He dodged the second round that Gabbar flung,
the latter taking up a sword, saying,
"Unless you hope to bore me to the grave
to meet your ancestors before my time,
it's you who's foolish to rely on words
for weaponry upon the battlefield.
Who fears some made-up tale of origins?"

Now Gabbar swung for Aqhat's side but missed,
his target having nimbly dodged the blow.
Aqhat then lunged for Gabbar's chest and swooped
down from on high, but each assault was blocked
and parried with a flurry of ripostes.
Their swords clanged with inserted sound-effects,
their battle-cries sufficiently high-pitched
to rouse decumbent dogs ten leagues away.
When one diminutive belligerent
fell back, the other'd give him chase until
they squared off once again to fight, yet when
their swings struck true too often, trespassing
the bounds of make-believe, the warriors
joined forces, slaying fang-toothed serpopards,
grim firefiends, and wyverns till they'd cleansed
the hilltops of facinorous archfoes,
their hands still stained with grapes' blood as the proof.

Forspent from war (not least because they'd had
to conjure up the very brutes laid low),
Aqhat and Gabbar climbed a sunburnt hill
to overlook the widespread wilderness.
Against a tree they sat and took their rest,
disburdening their shoulders of their packs.
Plucking a blade of grass and holding it
reed-like between his thumbs, Gabbar began

to play it, making expert locust chirrs.
While taking in the vista Gabbar asked,
"Do you think one day you'll depart from home
to fight among the legions of Hadad?
Our town's not known for generating troops,
and I have heard that Baal's made enemies
of Litan, Yam-Nahar, and Mot, the three
of whom I'd just as soon as not confront.
Still, sowing barley, seining, tending sheep—
we're not cut out for drudgery like that.
I'd only stay if Pugat looked at me
as I do her—even a knowing nod."

To his best friend the other made reply,
"You know that Pugat's wed to Yarimmu,
so why harass yourself with thoughts of her?
And yes, in time I hope to fight for Baal—
unless the Conqueror decides that I
should serve another purpose, sending me
clear signs of how to glorify his name.
Imagine riding at his sides, a spear
in your right hand and Kothar's bow in mine.
What better way to know the gods receive
our sacrifices than make them with them?
We'd stick together, holding Zaphon's gates,
disbanding waves of reckless infidels,
replenishing our spirits afterward."

Smiling and opening his pack, Aqhat
removed a hefty wineskin that he'd snatched
from camp, arousing laughter from his friend
in part from simple, knavish joy, in part
because he'd brought a gift to pair with it.

Into his sheepskin rucksack Gabbar reached
and hoisted up a sloshing pilgrim's flask,
its potbelly a cautionary tale.
They drank into the evening, sharing lore
to clarify the bestiaries they'd
committed to their memories' deep vaults,
for the heart's images need dusting too.
The more they drank, the thirstier they felt,
relaxing in their unrestrainèdness,
authenticating the old adage that
'Libations for Tiratu sell themselves.'

Amidst their sotted mirth, Gabbar called up
a song which, although unaccompanied
by customary instruments, they sang
with full awareness of its proper lilt,
"Long labor has left our feet well-worn,
these hands strained and stained as if torn.
There's naught come next but seek out rest
alike the Sun on ruddied mornes—
who in the morn our faces tanned
and warmed the naked ochre sand,
afore high-hung but now far-flung
she sighs and plumbs the hinterland.
Her presence she as yet betrays
with softened alpenglow displays
that disappear as we hide here—
horizon's flame fading away.
Our life she's still engendering
as we sprawl out remembering
day's good and ill now that all's still,
this solitude our rendering.
The twilight's secret's yours and mine,

reminding us there comes a time
when gone are cares for life's affairs—
and all that's left's to drown in wine!"

With splitten skulls and swollen eyes they woke
to yells reverberating through the hills
when morning came—their names upon the wind.
Abandoning the paraphernalia
of last night's revelry, the two made off
in dizzied haste as new recruits prepare
to square off with battalions, knowing that
they only rush to their betimely doom.
The garish light derided them, but both
ran back full speed, evading briar shrubs
and kicking up the stones beneath their feet,
their heartbeats racing neither from the heat
nor from their winding course's length, but dread.
Rounding a bend, now drenched with sweat, they came
upon tall women with disheveled hair
whose eyes transpierced them, turning them to stone,
their mothers' worries turning into rage.
Aqhat and Gabbar stood immobilized
by nauseating fear till Gabbar slewed
and spewed his stomach's contents on the ground—
Tiratu's penalty for avarice.
Both mothers marched their scoundrels earlobe-first
to camp, too furious to chastise them.

When they'd regained the vineyard, everyone
shot glances at the hangdogs who delayed
their opportune homeward departure time
(except for Pugat who could not but help
to laugh, relieved that they'd been found and glad
to not be party to their punishment).

Now that the clusters had been harvested
and processed (save the gleanings for the poor),
the migrant laborers set off for home,
whereupon Aqhat's mother said to him,
"Oh Aqhat, why this turn to theft and lies?
I trusted that you'd keep your word and come
to camp at sunset, so I laid my head.
Have you tried fathoming a mother's care
and worry when her son's lost—gods know where—
amidst those things that only lurk at night?
Before you came into this world I felt
a shame for being sonless—now my son
himself humiliates our family name.
Your father won't be pleased to hear of this.
For now, our footslog's punishment enough.

"Do you recall the stories that I told
you when you refused to lay your head to sleep?
Then you'll remember there once lived a fox
who relished vintage time, for he would slink
along the clustered trellises at night
to reave sweet grapes until his gums turned black.
He loved them more than any animal,
and yet he savored more than fruit alone:
Upon the woody vines he honed his teeth,
digging his burrowed bed beneath the rows
and chewing through the roots so he could curl
into a ball and groom his matted beard
before he snoozed away the livelong day.

"One night, an owl perched in a tree called out,
'Hoo hoo! You there! What do you do for us,
the vineyard crew, who only take our due
when we these vines are able to renew?

Hoo! Ask around how you might be of use,
or very soon, young man, you'll meet your doom!'
The owl took wing and, frightened, the red fox
tore off a cluster, quickly dragging it
into his burrow for the night where he
would not be bettered or bested by fowl.
When morning came, the burglar left his hole
and loped around the vineyard's rows until
he chanced upon two sheep and seven geese.
At seeing him they panicked, scattering,
but he convinced them that he meant no harm
and asked them how they helped improve the land.
The larger of the sheep replied, 'We chomp
the weeds the whole day long so they can't choke
the vines, and then give ordure to the earth
to fertilize the rows with nutrients.'
Affirming their vocation's magnitude,
long bobbing geese necks honked in unison.
He snickered at the weeders, turning round
to look for animals of nobler stock.

"The fox next found a flustered partridge whose
sheer terror at his sight took soothing words
to calm her down so he could ask what she
exchanged for living off the vineyard's gifts.
She said, 'I, well, I eat cutworms and bugs
from leaves before they eat the leaves themselves,
and, well, Oh! I too fertilize the ground.'
Without intending to, the frantic bird
then proved the point ere flapping out of sight.
Repulsed, the fox sought birds of loftier
descent who might have dealings with the owl.
In time he found a hawk who like a king
sat perched untouchably within a nest

from which to scan the borders of his realm.
The fox sought answer from the hook-nibbed king,
the latter deigning to respond to him,
'I scare off covetous and ravening
small birds with just one glance, and with the skill
of an assassin, plunging from on high,
I hunt until my aerie's filled with bones . . .'
The fox retreated two uneasy steps
just as a raptorette popped her bald head
out of the nest to fortify his claims,
'And father gives great ordure to the earth!'
His brimstone sightline censured her, the fox
guffawing, heading for his hidden den.

"Inside his tunnel underneath the vines,
the red-furred thief reflected on the day,
'My neighbors prove no better than myself:
They eat their fill and do their business just
like me but pat themselves upon the back.
Why let a wiseass daunt me with his taunts?
The vineyard isn't his or theirs, a point
which I'll drive home before the sun ascends.'

"That night the fox took cover in the leaves
and waited for the one who'd menaced him.
Glissading down the rows with gilded eyes
inlaid beneath recurved and feathered horns,
the owl scanned left when from the right the fox
sprang forth, his fangs clamped down upon his wing.
The owl unloosed deep-bellied hoots of rage
and turned to claw the fox who dodged his strike
while jerking, tearing, shaking him around
until the owl beaked him and freed himself,
boo-hooing to the safety of a tree.

"Elated to have thwarted doom's mouthpiece,
the picaroon adorned in red returned
to pilfering sweet grapes, which had acquired
a pleasant, aromatic burn of late.
The more he noshed, the wider stretched his grin.
He savored their new funkiness and found
himself becoming dizzy with delight.
Relaxed and warmed, a wisp that smelled of blood
and charred meat titillated his keen nose.
Although with far less grace than usual,
he traced the scent back to its origin:
the vintner's home, his front door left ajar.
Determined to discover roasted meats
that pair with tannic fruits, he crept inside.
At dawn the sheep and all the fowl arose
to eat and labor, looking to the west
to note the vintner exiting his stead
and hammering a red pelt to a stake
to desiccate beneath the sun's dry heat."

Allowing for her son to contemplate
the fable's message, Danataya said,
"We may descend from simple folk; perhaps
we haven't much to trade at market stalls;
and maybe future generations will
malign our name: But reciprocity,
hard work, and justice spur us ever on.
When we ignore life's prophecies or fail
to give back what we owe or, even worse,
refuse to honor promises we've made
and do what's just, then we are not ourselves.
To do the right thing's hard enough as is,
becoming harder still with too much drink,
so pay attention to those times when you

have foxlike thoughts—for craftiness may look
like wisdom though they're distant relatives."

As their long plod's commencement fell from sight—
the warm familiarity of home
alluring the array of laborers
southward, their steps up-tempo—thoughts of their
delay and of its cause were left behind.
In two days' time, with skins of wine in tow,
the workers reached their longed-for intimates.
Danel embraced his weary wife and son
while Pugat joined her husband Yarimmu
inside the home that he had built for her.
The day was late, and soon the seaside town
resounded with its former lively din.
The sky inhaled blue wreathes of smoke and then
exhaled deep sleep on the community,
a timely gift, for most would need to rest
their arms and legs before they plowed the land
for wheat and barley in the coming days.

Though normally sent out to work the fields
when Shapshu shone, the next day Danel's son
accompanied his father through the town,
bypassing racing children, women who'd
fetched water, ostlers, and the tanner's place
until they came upon the potter's kiln.
Bidding his friend good morning, Danel said,
"Look here, Son. Watch Yattanu's daughters work
their clayey masses, careful to remove
even the smallest rocks and sediment
so as to ornament their finished wares.
Just when you think they've all been found, see here,
another pebble shows itself, unseen

by untrained eyes, but not from practiced hands.
Once they have purified those lumps, look how
they add in pestled cattails and manure.
Now come this way. These cruses, tuns, and pots
will be among the last that Shapshu dries
and these girls bake to guarantee their sheen.
If they're subjected to excessive heat
too hastily, they either turn out dull
or shatter into sherds which have no use,
divested of their possibilities.

"If you look properly, you'll come to see
just how the potter's calling teaches us.
It's no coincidence the Wise One, El,
elected clay as the material
wherewith to form us and our holy land.
Each child begins as unformed clay within
which certain chunks of gritty dross reside.
Such rubble might go by the name of 'sloth,'
'impatience,' 'disobedience,' or 'rage.'
Though difficult, one can and must remove
such vices and their like before the heat
and time of habit ossifies the mass
of mud into the person one becomes.
But in their stead one must instill those dry,
well-grounded, sometimes loathsome practices
that virtue needs—for good though simple deeds
give sturdiness and structure later on.
You're still young, Aqhat, strong and pliable
within the hands that mold you and want you
to shine before you come into your own.
There was a time—"

Just like Yattanu's finished earthenware,
the boy's eyes had begun to glaze over
when on light feet his sister ran toward them
with Kothar's bow held firmly in one hand,
his quiver round her back, and she broke in,
"Father, Aqhat: So good to see you two!
I'm glad you both remembered that today
I take my brother for a practice hunt.
Aqhat, it's time you mastered bowmanship.
Before you know it, your bare chin and face
will stubble and you'll have to hunt for does
alone without your sister's being-there."

Attempting to conceal the joy he felt
at her salvific, intercessory
appearance, Aqhat voiced the lesson learned,
"Father, a hunt demands maturity,
stick-to-itiveness, patience, and trained eyes,
the lot of which I need to work upon.
My clay needs shaping yet, just as you've said.
Still something more impels me to the wood.
I fear I might upset the Craftsman if
I don't take ownership of his kind gift,
unable to command it as he'd want.
Please let me go. Pugat won't steer me wrong."

The patriarch gave his assent, at least
in part because he couldn't call to mind
having permitted or prohibited
this outing that they both remembered well.
They kissed him, vowing firstfruits from their hunt
as Pugat tossed a goatskin waterpouch
to Aqhat ere they crossed the village bounds.

Before they reached the threshold of the trees,
she handed him the bow, instructing him,
"Let's practice for a moment here before
we track down deer in earnest: Aim for that
tall sycamore ten fathoms to your left.
Remember what I've told you many times:
Relax your straightened bow arm, pointing toward
the ground in front of you. Don't squeeze it tight.
Support it with an easy hand and nock
the feathered end between your fingertips.
With one smooth motion, push and pull the bow
and string with little tension in your arms,
your elbows pointing sideways, yes, like that.
Now. Trust your aim as we trust Father's word."

Attending to her counsel, Aqhat then
let loose a bronze-tipped arrow at the tree.
He struck it squarely, trying to conceal
his boyish satisfaction while Pugat
looked on agape, congratulating him.
They started eastward, Pugat scouring
the wood for spoor-signs such as cloven prints
and bark abraded by possessive bucks.
For half the day they ventured through the wood,
her brother trailing her just like a cub
who learns through imitation rife with play,
observant of his mother's ways from time
to time yet easily distracted as
he shambles to and fro, far less alert
than is his caretaker who hunts perforce
and from innate responsibility.

Coming upon a river, Pugat found
a group of trotter tracks, distinct in size,
imprinted on the muddy bank's downgrade.
She gestured that her brother stay and wait
while she crept forward, following the trail
to an eroded tip-up mound from which
there dangled mangey strands of clotted roots.
She slowly parted them and soon beheld
a wild boar drinking from the riverside
some fifteen fathoms northward (give or take).
A farrow squealed down to the water's edge
beside the sated tusker, taking drink as well.
At once the huntress sensed that they must leave
the game alone, intuiting the rage
that such a mother could unleash and since
these sucklings wouldn't last without her care.

No sooner had she set her mind to this
than Aqhat supplicated Dread Anat,
the goddess of the hunt and warfare's arts.
His bowstring snapped, an arrow whooshing through
the air, the she-boar's muscly withers grazed.
She hurled a stertorous uproar his way,
the bristling beast preparing to attack.
As Pugat strove to intervene he twanged
another shaft which struck a boarlet's hock,
at which the seething grunting mother charged
with fulminant furor, her hackles up,
and as she ducked and drove to skewer him
his sister tackled him into the stream,
delivering them to the other side.
The rager snorted with such truculence

the treetops swayed, affrighted at the sight.
She then sought out her babe and nuzzled it,
abandoning the piglet unavenged
and fleeing through twisted thickets of thorns,
her family, minus one, pursuing her.

Expelling water, Aqhat cried aloud,
"You saved us both just in the nick of time!
I barely missed that grisly sow—she won't
have Fortune on her side next time around.
But why'd Anat not guide my arrow shafts?
Did I implore her with too little strength?
Or should I have prayed to her earlier?
Let's journey down the bank until we find
a shallow place to ford and give them chase.
If we can't find them, other game will come
to take their drink upstream, don't you agree?"

While wringing water from her umber hair
she castigated Aqhat Danel's Son,
"You nimrod! We were nearly gored and maimed.
I had instructed you to sit and wait,
and what if I'd not been here by your side?
That boar was no imaginary beast,
as now you know, and even had you hit
your mark and killed her, what of her young ones?
My future children and your own will traipse
these woods and spoor for fauna too, so we
must leave them gleanings though they're yet to be.
Today's hunt's ended. Even if we tried
to carry on, the snarling of that boar
resounded far and wide, so any game
nearby has scampered off, taking cover."

Contrition scrawled across his face as she
recouped her former equanimity,
"But buck up—we don't have the slightest scratch!
You have more nerve than I had ever thought,
correct in shooting for the biggest game,
but one must do so at the proper time.
The hunter's virtue lies not in his bow
or knife, since anyone can kill, but in
just whether, how, for what, and when and where
to fell another creature by his hand.
Your bow and arrows are divine in make,
and prayers are good and well, but gods won't heed
or even hear your every cry for help.
Divine things in a mortal's hands have no
perfection we'd not find a way to botch.
You must become reliant on yourself,
acquiring vision for what isn't there:
The best of huntresses and marksmen see
potential consequences would that their
arrow fly wide—observant of all things
that might arise so they might be adjudged.
Now for the hardest part. Let's cross the stream."

They jumped back in the stream and swam across.
Arriving at the other side, Pugat
unsheathed a bronzen blade that she kept stowed
behind her waistline horizontally
and handed it helve-forward to her kin.
His head held low, he plodded down the bank
as Pugat gathered kindling for their fire.
He reached the runt and overcame his rue
(or tried to, as befits a pious man)
before he called on El to please receive
the firstfruits of his hunt, at which he drained

the suckling's viscid life, shedding a tear
he hid from oaks who'd bowed their heads in prayer.
He took the carcass to his sister who
bade him to sit down, gralloching his kill.
She set the pig to roast upon the flames,
consoling and distracting him at once,
advising that they eat their fill before
they made for home, and though he hoped that El
was honored by his offering, still shame
imbued his repast such that holy thoughts
and words in no way eased his heart, which burned
as the indelible aroma spread.
They both retraced their steps, and no one learned
about the details of that hunt's events.

Book IV

Baal's consort woke, or so she thought, for thick,
impenetrable darkness compassed her
as though she were enchained to the seafloor.
Infuriated and befogged, Anat
began to grope about the lightlessness
for tactile signs regarding her locale
until her digits smarted, having touched
the giant stolid bars encaging her.
The Huntress screamed and wailed within her jail,
her hair on end, the human skulls around
her cincture clattering, her spitefulness
resounding down dark tunnels hewn from stone.
Unstrung, she bit her fist and tasted blood,
the which intensified her wrathful mien.
With untold strength the Bellicist beset
the confines of her adamantine gaol,
but maugre her unparalleled puissance
it wouldn't budge. She only harmed herself.
And though vociferating violently
and without end deep in the House of Death,
Anat's amassing madness didn't reach
the earth, and so, for a short while, peace reigned.

In course of time two rivulets of fire
ran parallel along a tunnel's sides,
a litten byway leading to her cage.
The brightness singed her unexpectant eyes,
eliciting a string of malisons.
With steady clops upon the limestone ground

her gaoler's footfall—measured, ponderous,
and slow—echoed down the blazing path,
their fey effector drawing nearer still.
A tall cowled presence closed upon her cell,
its talons clutched around a mighty haft
composed of neither bronze nor silver but
of iron—metal's coveted ideal.
Atop the mammoth scepter handled like
a stave there sat a double-bitted cleaver's head
with edges sharp and inwardly recurved.
Upon one blade was written 'Impotence,'
the other one incised with 'Widowhood.'
He then approached her prison—Mot, that is—
for Death himself strode toward his prisoner,
observing her like some exotic bird
here trammeled for his entertainment's sake.
She recognized Lord Mot and shrilled at him,
demanding that her seizure be explained,
to which the Master of the Pit replied,
"The Lady of the Sea would have it so."

Thus Mot, at whom the goddess spat rebukes,
"You idiot! You rule the Netherdom,
whose vastness rivals that of earth above,
whose power always has the final say,
and yet you take your orders from your foes?
You dumb, anemic beast! Even the worst
of mortal rulers knows (despite himself,
often enough) not simply to obey
commands from neighboring and weaker sorts.
But you, the Emperor of All Decay,
have let your mind disintegrate and rot.
Oh, had I known that everyone I've killed

should have to suffer such a servile king,
I might have spared them all for my own use!"

Her swelling passion angered and aroused
Lord Mot who tightly grasped the ferric shaft
of his ax, rusting from his lethal grip.
But now he'd finished visiting his pet
and turned to leave, at which she changed her tune,
"Wait, Lord! Forgive me. I have spoken ill.
While down here, trapped inside this cell,
I cannot help men kill their kith and kin
en masse—my purpose being wrenched from me
just like a husband who has lost his wife.
But think now: Maybe I've been brought to you
not to accomplish Athirat's designs,
but to fulfill yours. Do you eat enough?
I don't intend to slight your chiseled face,
but I would guess that since I've been restrained
you drink and sup far less than you deserve.
No emperor should have to wait to feast.
Allow me to engift you with the flesh
and blood on which you dine like bread and wine,
preparing feasts of which you've only dreamed.
Permit me to recruit and fortify
your numberless Rephaim, to build for you
an army answerable to your word,
unmatchable in scope and potency.
Imagine all the ways that you might glut
yourself, besotted with red viscous drink
until you're fat and happy as a tick.
And when and only when this army meets
your satisfaction, I shall go my way,
attend to my affairs, and send you my
own slaughtered offerings from up above."

Mot harkened to the Goddess of War's plan.
When she'd completed her persuasive speech,
he moved toward her and gently clasped a hand
that hung from her stained sash to study it.
King Mot examined her and kissed the hand
to signal his acceptance of her terms.
He closed his eyes and concentrated till
the lock fell from her door, and as he turned
to go, he motioned that she follow him,
and she accompanied him whence he'd come.

Atop Mount Lel, the Wise One couldn't brook
Baal's sloth a moment longer, entering
his room to rouse him from excessive drowse,
"Wake up, wake up, Son! Surely you have dozed
enough to be revived from too much drink.
I'd gladly have you rest still more, but there
are pressing matters to which we must see.
It's Athirat. Your mother's gone and no
one's seen her since our former revelry.
I don't recall her ever turning in
that night, nor have my stewards witnessed her.
Of course, she has her own affairs, but still,
I'm usually kept abreast of them,
if not by my informants then by her.
Perhaps she's set to work constructing walls
and towers in our towns, restrengthening
our land's defenses as we'd spoken of
(unless another god—Habayu or
Astarte, mostly likely—disesteemed her
again with their large personalities).
If so, however long it takes, I'll see
to it myself that whosoever drove

her off shall be demoted from their place.
Come, rise! We must send men to search for her."

Far groggier than he had ever been,
Baal tried to cast off sleep and heed El's words
like one whose ill begins to convalesce.
He stretched by reaching up to grab his horns,
then yawned, responding to the Ageless One,
"Apologies. For how long was I out?
A banquet for the ages I would say!
Do you remember how you left that night?
No? Well, allow me to remind you, then.
You introduced us all to Shataqat,
then left with her when you'd grown wearisome.
Thereafter, Mother took her leave as well.
If you say she did not join both of you
in bed that night, the reason for her flight
is plain enough: She envies Shataqat
and grudges you for the attention that
you've given to a beauty such as her.
But these things pass with time. Her jealousy
will soon subside and she'll return to Lel
to find that Shataqat has set to work."

The Lord took worried thought and stroked his beard
before he left his son to his affairs,
the latter summoning his viziers.
Gapn, Hirgab, and Ugar came at once,
ears readied for the longhorned god's commands,
"There—fetch my tunic; bring my buskins here.
It's time we got to work. But where's Anat?
Perhaps she's headed for Inbubu or
Mount Zaphon's halls, impatient as she is.

No matter. Listen up: The rightful heir
to Washukanni's throne, Tushratta, fled
Mitanni's capital in recent days
and could be anywhere by now—in towns
unheard-of, hunkered down in some dark delve,
or on the run beneath night's coverture.
Manhunt this fugitive. Explain to him
that Baal Hadad the Conqueror requests
his audience on Zaphon straightaway,
his restitution forefront on my mind.
If he should be so bold as to refuse,
not knowing what is good for him, then take
the boy by force and bring him nonetheless."

Baal's messengers bowed low and exited.
With swift step each bestrode Lel's corridors,
bypassing Elsh, attended by his guards,
until they reached a turret's lower door
which Gapn opened for his kin who scaled
the limestone waterspout's upwinding stairs.
Egressing from the stairwell's upper door
and having metamorphosed into birds
again, they leapt into the clouded sky,
sped onward by a chilly Easterly.

Below, in a wide chamber, Elsh addressed
his guardsmen standing to in ordered rows,
"Good men, our land's belovèd queen is gone.
El bids us track her down and bring her back
to Lel where she belongs so that she can
look after those things that befit her role.
To Hazor you along the wall shall go
while to Aleppo march the tenderfeet.
Those trained in seamanship will wet their oars

in the Orontes, sailing day and night.
Megiddo, Shechem, and Jerusalem
require our more experienced of troops
while my contingent heads for Ugarit.
Report to Lel with tidings good or ill.
No one must know of our reconnaissance
and rescue mission—such are El's commands.
Well, don't just stand around and stare. Let's move!"

Attired in human guise, having made it
to Ugarit's surrounding farms at night
and coming to its city gates by dawn,
the goddess Athirat ventured down
the southern residential quarter's streets
to take the inn room Qodesh had arranged.
She lay abed and fell asleep with ease.
The Sun peered through her window and began
to warm the inn's east wall, refiring
its elements before the evening breeze
would cool them—work its builders thought complete.
But buildings are the earthen wares of gods
as cities are the kilns of goddesses,
preserved and cared for in the secrecy
of broad daylight, invisibly remade
often without due recognition by
industrious, distracted workhorses,
for while the gods are generous to grant
insightful visions, taxing labor blinds.

Despite her humble quarters, Athirat
woke rested, reinvigorated by
the freedom she'd seized of her own accord.
She had arrived in Ugarit two days
ere her Sidunan vessel would depart,

and so, without responsibilities,
without palatial or political
polemics to clean up, Athirat chose
to stroll the busy streets, accustoming
herself to daily human life firsthand.
She first walked west along the central road
that bustled with the comings and goings
of costermongers, nondescripts, and scribes
returning to the eastern library
which sat north of her husband's house of prayer
and southwest of that skyward orthotope
where citrus fumes of frankincense and hymns
ascended into heaven for Hadad.

Two palaces hemmed in by temenos
partitions rose along her either side.
The large Necropolis lay to her left.
Without prejudgment and without a care,
a newcome foreigner in her own land,
she breathed the city in and made her way
toward the postern on Ugarit's west side.
Upon her right a tower and redoubt
stood at the ready—upright, shoulders back.
In time she reached Makhadu, Ugarit's
main port between the foothills and the sea
where foam-tipped rollers mark time's steady pulse.
Cranes chevronned overhead in unison
while merchants eyed the dockworkers who stowed
Egyptian ships with ingots, cedar logs,
large jugs of wine, and battened treasure chests.
Dockhands unloaded Alashiyan ships
whose wooden gangplanks groaned beneath the weight
of copper troves, escorted from the pier
by swordsmen from Niqmaddu's entourage.

The one who hid in plain sight wondered why,
despite her epithet, she'd not returned
to walk the Vast Green's shoreline for so long.
She passed the afternoon in peace then left,
exploring Ugarit's interior.
Not wanting to come off like royalty,
the visitor reined in and curbed parlance
of highfalutin provenance and pitch
while gathering provisions for her stay.
The city's heartbeat, breath, and energy
enlivened her and stirred her to perceive
it with increased awareness, opening
her senses to the excess otherness
attracting her while holding her apart,
a vital tension sanctioning her flight.
But stormclouds brooded in the West, and so
the city's underground flaneuse turned in.

Perched by the window of her upper room
she watched as cloudbursts volleyed slashing rain
upon the neighborhood, the arrow shafts
becoming hailstones buffeting the roofs.
In normal circumstances, Athirat
could ask her son, Baal, to abate the storm,
or to suspend it for a while at least.
But ordinary times had ceased for her.
Her ordered capture of Anat and flight
from Lel had broken long-established laws
and rendered contact with kin direful,
for while transgressing edicts of the earth
imperils one, to breach the regulae
of gods endangers everything that is.
The storm afforded pleasure nonetheless:
Because the hail and bolts could harm her flesh,

and since her lodging's warm security
contrasted with such pain—the latter but
a thought—ease flowed from the discrepancy,
an aperture unknown to her till then.

Suddenly soughs erupted from the room
next-door, echoed by cries of succorance
as Athirat unlocked her door in haste
to help, auxiliaries promised by
the footsteps running thumping up the stairs.
A sweat-drenched woman in travail, gripped by
unfathomable throes two moons before
her proper time, implored her neighbor's aid
with wincing words and terrified regard.
The wife of the inn owner, Athirat,
and three more women tried to calm her down,
rushing to gather towels and water bowls,
the one in labor begging for the group
to fetch a midwife of the Kotharat.
The innkeep's wife said that Baal's fury out
of doors prohibited such luxuries
while Athirat began to dab her brow
and reassured her, coaching her to breathe.

A blazing streak of bronze transpierced the sky,
shaking the earth's foundations as the one
with child cried out and cursed from searing pain.
From curious concern, a man unknown
to them peered in no sooner than he was
dispelled by blistering remonstrances.
The war began—some raising rally cries
to spur the woman on to victory,
another making bold to organize
recruits under her spearheading command,

still others stanching blood as best they could
amidst bloodcurdling and horrific screams
while Athirat enheartened the assailed
that peace was nigh and squeezed her squidgy hand.
And just as many battles—though they be
more bravely fought than others that were won—
prove fruitless in the end, an afterthought
of reckless men who will not sing of them
in festal halls or taverns by the sea
and who know not the names of those who've died,
just as such fights forerun new waves of tears
that end in silence, so too this conflict.
The women mourned both strangers that they lost,
unable to reopen the gateway
dividing those alive from the deceased.

Upon lamenting one they hadn't known—
yet whom in scant time they had come to love
as one attaches to their neighbors in
a shield wall, interlocked in common cause—
the women left the room to search about
for cleanly shrouds and oil infused with myrrh.
The neighbor of the fallen stayed behind,
digesting the outright fragility
of human life, a truth that she had known
but never fully felt until just then.
She sat alone with hollow heart until
the stillness of the room distempered her.
Then outrage checked her sadness, twisting it.
Looking behind her as to verify
that she remained alone, Athirat raised
her hands and held them over those who'd passed,
speaking apotropaic benisons.
Resounding thunder rocked the inn, for Mot

despised her violation of his right.
Deadlocked in tug-of-war for two Rephaim
of little note, Lord Mot and Athirat
exchanged blows in a spiritual fray,
offended by the other's greediness.
Anon they both relinquished their intent
as Athirat collapsed, doubly saddened.
Since fleeing Lel, her ownmost plenitude
had partially deteriorated.

The women clambered upstairs, entering
the room where Athirat lay in defeat.
Another scowled at her for lazing by
while they worked, as if they weren't also sad.
Anointing the departed, cering them
in cloth, those present stripped the blood-soaked bed,
one woman with the stillborn in her arms,
embracing her for the first and last time.
She then unswathed the lump with frantic hands
to find the girl could move her fingertips.
The babe's face soured as she puled in fear,
her sharp discomfort brightening the room
and flooding them with joy unthinkable,
as if the world were not so hideous
as they once thought, but rather mystical.
While cradling the revived babe, the patronne
vowed to adopt the chickpea as her own,
the indoor tempest dwindling, passing on
in lockstep with the one that raged outside.

On Lel, upon a stately bed beside
his paramour, El sprung from a nightmare.
She tried becalming him with gentle strokes
but he threw off his covers, leaving her.

El robed himself and searched his giant home
for any of Ilisha's wives, whom he
could trust to carry confidential words
to Elsh and his array of recon men.
He chanced upon one in his library,
dismissing everyone else in the hall.
Recounting dream scenes to Ilisha's wife,
El spoke to her with imprecise alarm,
still she could ascertain the Lord's intent,
taking her leave at once to Mount Lel's heights
where she assumed an eagle's form and soared
aloft beneath the moon to seek out Elsh.

Before dawn came, an eagle circled round
the eastern farms that nourish Ugarit.
Espying Elsh's camp, Ilisha's wife
descended spirally until she neared
his tent and heaved the air with wings splayed out
to cast aside her aquilinity.
She summoned Elsh and roused him with these words,
"Awake, good servant of the Lord. Our king
imparts to you the content of a dream
so that your errand might have swift success.
El dreamt that Athirat and his beloved
Lord of the Hereafter had an affair
and chose, of all locales, a dirty inn
of Ugarit's southernmost neighborhood.
I shall not tell you of the potency
and meaning of his dream, as time is scarce.
Go now. Assemble those in your command.
Investigate his consort's whereabouts,
detaining her by force for her own good
if she resists or proves intractable."

Elsh thanked her for her tidings, entering
his tent to don his armor wrought of bronze,
then blew a ram's horn, waking his encharged.
Once they had mustered, standing in a file,
their officer debriefed them as to their
good fortune, readying them to decamp
and ride for Ugarit without delay.
After he'd specified their stratagem—
the likelihood of their accomplishments
becoming clear—they raced the westing sun.

Arising after midday on account
of the preceding night's calamity,
from which at least some minor good emerged,
the Lady of the Sea considered how
to spend the day before her ship pushed off.
She stretched and dressed, departing for the day
then stopping—two guards at the stairwell's foot
conversing with her host who pointed toward
her floor, a simple gesture threatening
the floodgates that immured her fearfulness.
Without a doubt the guards belonged to El:
The workmanship of Kothar-wa-Hasis,
their round shields bore the Lord's insignia.
She bolted for her room and closed the door,
confused by how she'd already been found
and quickly weighing how she might escape.
A fist now rapped a wooden door nearby,
knocks sending rills of panic down her nape.
Her fretful gaze surveyed the room until
it lit upon a pewter amphora
on which there shone the unknown personage
she had become—a stranger to Lel's guards.

She smiled at her unfounded anxiousness,
remembering the strength of her device.

Knuckles now slammed her door and Athirat
bade entry with a feigned humility,
beseeching reasons for their stopping-by.
The taller of the troops replied to her,
"Apologies, my Lady. Last night we
received complaints of shouting being heard
from this floor of the inn, and we have come
to make sure all is well—and ascertain
the origin of these disturbances.
Tell us what happened if you wouldn't mind,
then we'll be on our way and leave you be."

She daubed herself with womanly distress
and wrung her hands before responding thus,
"Yes, good men, surely. Last night tried us all.
A woman in the nearby room began
to give birth well before her time had come.
A number of us tried assisting her.
She screamed, of course, and we did too perhaps.
We did the best we could—of that I'm sure.
The blood was everywhere, you'll understand,
as men who've no doubt fought on the front lines.
I've never seen such gore before last night.
Shall I go into even more detail?
No? Well, alright. The mother passed from us,
although the girl, the strongest runt I've seen,
somehow survived—praised be the Kotharat."

The guards beheld each other, satisfied,
and thanked her, readying to take their leave.

Relief washed over her and she exhaled
just as the other guardsman paused and turned
to her to settle one more point, as if
in passing, asking her if it were true
that, as they'd heard, the woman who gave birth
compared in comeliness to Shataqat.
Her countenance flushed red, her eyes agog,
her body having fallen for their trap.
A mutual awareness of the game
at hand united hunter and hunted,
the former set on roughly taking her—
beginning to—yet like a lioness
who's cornered by a pharaoh's retinue
so that their king can safely make his kill
knows what shall come should she withhold her rage,
she grabbed one of the guard's arms, yanking it
with unexpected force, delivering
a blow before defenestrating him
three stories down to his neck-breaking end.
Climbing onto the sill, she pulled herself
out of the window onto the clay roof
before the other could manhandle her.
He saw her flee and from her lodging blew
his horn to signal clanking men-at-arms
to hound her from below, some giving chase
on foot as others rode on chariots,
the drivers steering their accomplices
in range to hit their target with arrows
whose barbs were dipped in paralytic sap.

With pounding heart and nimble feet, as if
the lioness became a mountain goat,
the beast of chase cleared rooftop parapets
as arrows darted by like furied wasps.

Great havoc circumfused the runaway
as in the busy streets below new waves
of undammed guards debouched to follow her
and overtoppled mendicants who sought
their daily bread, first struck by poverty
or plague but now by bronze-rimmed wheels,
onlookers seeking shelter in their homes,
afraid their city had come under siege.
Guards shouted, keeping each other abreast
of Athirat's location best they could.
Ahead of her their yawned a thoroughfare
within which some of Elsh's henchmen lay
in wait, their swords withdrawn, their arrows nocked.
Anticipating their proximity,
she hefted a large krater with designs
of white and brown and sprinted for the gap
whereat she launched the vase to her right side;
it smashed against a wall beside the troops,
alarming and distracting them as she
leapt overhead for the opposing roof—
landing then rolling headfirst—safe for now.

Swift of foot, Athirat eluded them
until she ducked into an upper room
where women sewed, her entrance ruffling them.
One tossed a shawl at her (presumably
in self-defense) so Athirat enveiled
herself with the apparent gift and ran
downstairs, departing from the house with poise.
She headed westward down a narrow street
(the world now weaponry or hiding spots),
discovering a woman carrying
a cumbrous load, a weight which Athirat
invited her to share, and so she did,

her work and less-than-fully honest talk
providing her with welcome camouflage.

Between two looming palace walls they passed,
the innocent abettor having reached
her destination, thanking Athirat,
and taking back her customary freight.
Now hasting for the postern to the west,
the Lady of the Sea walked round the fort
but saw that it was barred by footmen who
interrogated all who came and went.
She pivoted, yet once again found guards
who hurried her direction, so she walked
with self-composure northward up a road
adjacent to a shrine and ducked inside.
While mimicking the pious folk nearby,
she kept her trackers' whereabouts in view.
A suppliant beside her rose and neared
the shrine, libating wine into a pipe
that trickled underground into a crypt.
She then set forth three candles, lighting them.
Before her votive offering she prayed,
"Oh Athirat, Creatress Most Divine
and Lady of All Populated Lands,
the Mother of Our Happy Gods, I come
to you in gratitude: My mother's healed!
Before she tottered on the precipice
of death, but you refused to let her fall,
attentive to the prayers and promises
of humble fieldhands who put faith in you.
As vowed, we'll slaughter all our livestock—life
for life—so you may feast as you deserve.
Although this trade-off will emburden us,
why seek to thrive if one's kin are no more?"

The prayer perplexed and panged the one who hid,
but Elsh now poked around the shrine himself,
and so it proved the least of her concerns.
She bowed her head. Another man then prayed,
"Anat, Light-Footed Goddess of the Hunt,
Highhearted Warrior, where have you fled?
We cannot find wild game, the birds and deer
upon which we rely have disappeared.
Black magic's driven them away it seems,
but we must supplement our stores of grain.
As if this weren't enough, Niqmaddu's troops
whom I command have lost all discipline
while sloth depletes their waning battle-lust.
My guards and lookouts cower at the sight
of those who loot our sovereign's treasuries.
Oh Huntress, intervene on our behalf:
Restore this citadel of yours to strength."

Soon Elsh and his accompanying guards
had left the shrine, discussing their next move.
Completely at a loss, El's consort sought
evacuation routes within her heart
until the image of a sewer drain
northwest of her which she had seen before
came back to her just like a scout returns
with reassuring news, though his report
forebodes a heap of dirty work to come.
With cagey eyes she stepped into the street
and started northward where professional
engravers, vendors, carters, artisans,
and merchants went about their daily tasks.
Her subterranean expedient
came into view and she slipped in unseen,
attempting with decided lack of luck

to keep from gagging, wading through the muck
whose stench reached from below, garroting her.
She tripped and plashed the waste before she rose,
her probing fingernails begrimed with filth.
A light like Athtar twinkling in the morn,
barely perceptible, peeped through the bog.
She slogged toward it, her stamina waning,
her bloated lungs like rotten carcasses.

Emerging from the ooze into the light,
she wiped the blood that trickled from her arm
and inhaled deeply, making for the port
where yesterday she'd reveried unseen.
A gleesome spirit then, today she trudged
along the pier, attracting notice yet
avoided altogether or ignored,
in such wise grasping the unfortunate
invisibility of wharf gamines.

Ensuring that she hadn't been pursued
and noticing the sigil Qodesh carved
upon a wooden hull to mark it out
as her own, Athirat approached the keel.
Hauling provisions and tackle aboard,
the deckhands stopped her at the gangway's end,
prohibiting her boarding of the ship.
She looked around and then replied to them,
"I am the export Qodesh would convey."
Annoyed and unimpressed, they shooed her off,
storing and stevedoring more supplies.
At hearing her the captain showed his face,
berating them for so ill-treating their
important guest whose passage had been paid,
although arriving earlier than planned.

He ordered one to show her through the hatch
into the hold, her private domicile
with water, nutriment, and new attire,
withholding nothing that the girl should want.
Nonplussed, the burly seafarer complied,
escorting her below deck where a space
of relative comfort had been prepared,
and here she changed out of her putrid garb,
inuncting her figure with scented oils.

As longshoremanly thuds battered above,
the Lady of the Sea hunkered aboard,
reflecting on her close-call's origins,
"Who tried to foil the plan I set in place,
and how'd El's hunting parties locate me?
Did Qodesh give me up? He wanted me
to stay, it's true. But no, he wouldn't have.
He's been more faithful than my husband has.
Nor would he have prepared this ship if he
did not intend to carry out our plan.
Moreover, he'd know untold punishment
were El to learn of his hand in my flight.
Did Elsh and his retainer follow me
from Lel, awaiting the right time to strike?
Impossible—for they'd have seized me ere
I came to Ugarit and would have had
less trouble doing so than came to pass.
How did they come upon the very place
in which I inned unless . . . unless my use
of magic for that unknown babe gave up
my whereabouts somehow. But yes, of course!
No prayers, no magic do the Lord's eyes miss.
How reckless of me to make use of that
which binds me to the life I'd sooner leave!

No more. Henceforward I'll do no such thing
as would betray me to those spooring me.
I swear this by no god except myself."

At vowing thus, she felt the boat undock,
her sense of liberation heightening
as from Makhadu her ship took wide berth.
A cautiousness curbed Athirat's delight,
however, urging her to stay below,
and with good cause, for some of Elsh's guards
now scanned the docks, investigating ships,
yet all they found were dunnage, jars of oil,
resin of terebinth, large elephant
tusks, hippo teeth, and other articles
arriving from or heading for the Nile,
Assyria, or Kaphtor's seagirt shores.
In synchrony the swash of oarage swept
the vessel's either side and echoed through
its pulsing womb, creating liquid whorls
to match the wooden eddies of the planks.
Behind the stern a white-winged skein spread out
to follow its forerunner's southward flight,
cooperative winds billowing the sails
until the rowers shipped their implements.

Sufficient time had passed to go topside,
so Athirat heaved open the trapdoor
above her quarters, climbing from the hull.
The crew beheld her, mouths agape, as if
she were a stowaway they'd never seen.
By just so much had water, sweet perfume,
and new attire wholly transfigured her.
Their captain's orders not to pester her—
which had before seemed obvious good sense—

now hung imperiously over them
like a condemnatory scimitar.
The young helmsman (who'd rather be engulfed
by Yam's abyss than keep his hatchway shut)
beseeched forgiveness on the crew's behalf
then asked if she would kindly share her name.
She hadn't thought of what to call herself
until just then, but told the company
to call her 'Laeya;' thus did Athirat's
new nominal identity take root.
Sitting along the caprail in the sun,
the salt spray seasoning the Southerly,
Laeya at last enjoyed the leeway she
had sought until, struck by Shalim, Yam bruised,
his endless body changing from light green
to date-wine purple, finally blackening.
Retiring, Laeya let the ship's hold rock
her sleepward where those seemingly absurd
illusions of a life beyond Lel's grasp—
for the first time—seemed less fantastical.

Enthroned on Zaphon, scratching his muzzle,
Hadad took thought as to how he might best
protect the interests of the land he loved,
which now fell further into disrepair
with every day that El's hagridden cares
distracted him from ruling properly.
The chamber doors flung wide, and through them marched
Gapn, Hirgab, and Ugar, followed by
a man with down feathers upon his chin.
Addressing Baal with pride, Gapn began,
"It pleases me, your Worship, to present
the ousted king of Washukanni whom
we tracked down with great efforts as you'd asked.

Absconding down the Khabur on a raft
by night, he boated till he joined the swift
Euphrates' watersmeet and southward fled
where no conspirator would follow him.
He chose a covert, taking a new name
while living almost like a feral man,
collecting plants and berries to survive.
He comes to Zaphon uncompelled and hopes
the rumors of your graciousness prove true."

Baal eyed Tushratta, scanning him from head
to toe with penetrative reckoning.
The lawful heir to Washukanni's seat
of power bent beneath his gaze's weight,
his head and shoulders sloping toward the floor.
Although no posture for a king, still Baal
interpreted the man's demeanor as
an outward sign of kneadability,
and since he hoped to shape the charge as he
deemed fit, a bit of give proved promising.
The Cloudrider addressed Tushratta thus,
"Stand tall, good man, if you are truly king
of Washukanni: I have summoned you
not to inflict your story with more pain,
but to propound a plan for forging strong
allegiances between your folk and mine.
The gods know of the traitor Uthi's coup
and discommend illicit takeovers
that sever rightful lines of royal men,
for mutinies—even those far from here—
may ripple over calm and steady seas,
amassing size and force to capsize those
who never thought that such a storm might come.

"In truth, a kingdom's like a cauldron set
atop hot coals—the king being the cook,
his people little more than boiling bones,
leftover scraps of meat, and vegetables.
The cook has little say regarding which
ingredients to use, but can dispose
with all those viands that have soured or spoiled.
He has no choice but to concoct a soup
from such a motley, earthy multitude,
exerting the pressure of heat on them,
like taxes, debts, customs, till they move
(of their own accord—they think), working round
and with each other, adding to the whole,
the herbs ascending to their place on top,
the bones accepting their lowly descent
as each contributes what it can and must.
A city's laws are like the cauldron's sides
of scorching metal, keeping everything
in place and setting limits over which
nothing can flow . . . unless the cook decides
some element needs putting to the test.

"But foolish are those cooks who, seeing how
the whole broth swirls in unison, infer
that it no longer needs attending-to.
For most inevitably, some will seek
to rise above their origins—and let
me tell you that they always come from deep
beneath the rest, the greasy lot stirred up
because they're riled up by incessant heat,
not yet inured to it like the old bones
from which they surge, their base progenitors.
These lowborn effervesce and slip with ease
between the rest, imagining they're but

the cream that rises to the top of some
dessert of their own making. What a ruse!
In truth, only the scum tries to ascend
above the highest echelons, the herbs
whose redolence and verdure mediate
between the cook and ordinary stews.

"When such sludge rises higher than it should,
the other elements forget the one
who tends to them beyond the mix, and by
this dreggy froth they're blinded out-and-out.
They cannot see that what they'd let float by
has cankered their collective work. You see,
insurgents and defiers are but scum:
They cannot but appear amidst the roil
yet are inimical to the cook's toil.
Thus, given what is best for him and those
pursuing the same end, an expert king
waits patiently just like a cook, and once
the filth has shown itself, he lends a hand
to it—assisting it in its intent
of finally transcending all restraints—
skimming and separating and lifting
it up above the rest below to be
bestrewn upon the dirt where it belongs.

"Now, listen to the offer I shall make
and weigh it carefully: I will assist
you personally, helping you reclaim
the throne that once belonged to your sire
since it belongs to you by right, and you'll
lord over Washukanni as is fit
with my protection, if, in turn, you come
with every sword-bearing man, chariot,

and warhorse when I call upon your aid.
Yet should you fail to heed my call, you'll be
disfurnished of Mitanni's governance."

Tushratta marveled at Baal's overture
and liberality, considering
the plan the Conqueror had just proposed.
He only had his newfound poverty
and famelessness to lose, their opposites
laid at his feet by Baal Hadad, no less,
and so Tushratta swore fidelity.
Expressing his delight, Baal bade his guards
escort their long-term guest to his new room
where he could bathe and rest before Baal would
begin instructing him on everything
pertaining to good rulership at dawn,
for he had much to learn, and even more
to practice if Mitanni would be his.

Tushratta and the god's attendants bowed
and exited, Hadad petitioning
what news they had uncovered of Anat,
to which the Father of Vultures replied,
"My Lord, we never came across your love—
and we traversed expansive tracts of land,
deep combes, and jagged tors—but I suspect
that she has traveled to those Eastern hills
where it is said that men are currently
at war, for Mount Lel's policy of peace
has often irked her, so much so that she
must vent her ire on populations far
from us, disporting bloodshed's warmth.
In all times past she has returned—refreshed.
Try not to fret, your Lordship. Let her come

to Zaphon once she's been revived by death."
Reluctantly, Baal heeded his advice,
turning his heart to Washukanni's crown,
arriding in the strength that it would bring.

Book V

One sunshot morning, Danataya woke
to find her gift from Baal had come of age,
nearing his sixteenth year. How could that be?
She'd only just conveyed him to the world
the other day, delighted to appease
his hunger, watching as his feeble neck
grew strong, chest down upon a bed of grass,
his chunky limbs each jolting with a mind
of their own till they worked of one accord—
crawling, standing, falling, dashing, climbing.
With wistful pride she eyed him from afar.
Although he proved more than a handful now
and then, she vowed she'd do it all again:
every melodramatic hissy fit,
every bullheaded overreach of will,
even the shit-filled loincloths he produced.

Old age had weathered Danataya's face,
her story sedimenting in her bones.
With stiffened gait she hauled her many years,
encumbered by their weight but not deterred
from relishing the evening of her life,
though ofttimes wishing she could recollect
what she'd forgotten, saying to herself,
"Oh Memory, you once were like a sack
I carried down an ever-changing brook;
in it I'd place all sorts of stones and shells,
removing them at any time so that
I could examine them with careful eyes.

But now the bottom of my pack is torn,
and though I try to carry it aright,
still much that I have gathered tumbles out.
And so, because you can't be sewn back up,
no longer do I walk the mudbank now
to recollect and gather what was mine
but skip the rocks I find across the stream,
enjoying every toss and hoping that
one day, upon that other bank, I might
discover them again with freshened eyes."

Less headlong, far more nonchalant was Time
when she'd been younger, a nonentity
who dallied here and there, as loathe to bug
her as she was to plead with him for gifts,
the unseen god's routine predictable
till punctuated by irregular
experiences woven into tales
where every doing proved significant.
A forthcoming event of such a sort
hung over the horizon, cheering her.
The labor of the last amorphous years—
although it often felt like clumsily
assembled patchwork—now assumed a shape
and form all of its own, a work of art
which, like all others, hides within itself
invisible exertions one has wrought
so that it might shine in autonomy.

Aqhat assisted Danel with the day's
innumerable tasks, for that night they
would celebrate the young man's birth with song
and dance and orisons to those on high.
From the first moment Danataya swelled

with the Cloudrider's boon, her husband had
begun to plan how he'd repay the god.
Eleven calves awaited slaughtering
come eventide; communal firepits
were stocked with kindling and thick oaken logs,
large jars of claret wine surrounding them;
with curds the meat of yearling kids slow-braised
within their mothers' aromatic milk;
large lanterns brimmed with oil to light the night;
and tuns of beer brewed from fermented bread
began to effervesce expectantly.
Such were some of the pious judge's gifts.
Because the celebration of his son's
nativity aligned with springtime's feast,
the men who often furnished rituals
throughout the year augmented his largesse
to wine and feast the gods as they deserved.

While children chased each other in the fields
the townspeople got ready for the fête,
dividing up their work as usual.
And since the evening's sumptuous festival
aroused unanimous excitedness,
all gladly bore the morning's lightweight yoke.
Come eventide, all preparations made,
the people joined around a central fire
as elders led the sacrificial calves
behind young maidens hoisting crescent moons,
green boughs, and votive statuettes of clay.
Fresh water consecrated by the priest
then circulated through the gathered throng
which downed the lustral drink in unison.
As was their duty, cupbearers poured wine,
the town libating to great goddesses

like Athirat, the Lady of the Sea.
Anat was sated next, and Athtar too
as knifestrokes drained the umber calves of life.
Now Kilamuwa's servitors prepared
the quartered cuts of veal, arranging them
above hot coals, the winecups filled once more.

The rite began in earnest as two groups
of women dressed in flowing, dark-blue robes—
encircled stars embellishing their brows—
stood opposite each other round the fire.
One woman and four men then came before
the flames to mime the scenes the vernal chants
of old would recreate and bring to life.
In antiphons the choristers sang out:

"Hail, Fertile Goddess, Lovely One,
Bright Lady of the Evenstar!
We shower you with gracious praise.
Creative Guarantor of Life,
come sing through us, your acolytes,
who gaze upon your liveliness.

"She burned to be with her beloved,
repining over Tammuz' touch—
the one whom Death gripped in his clutch.
No less did he want her, that girl
with lips like dates from Mararat,
whose eyes were beautified with kohl.

"Astarte braved Tharumagi's mouth
where Horon, God of Lesser Deaths,
vowed entry if that Conqueress
of Hearts both mortal and divine,

anomalous in that dark place,
obeyed the ancient rituals.

"His vision clouding from the smoke
of sacrificial offerings
within the realm possessing him,
Tammuz explored the unknown land
before him with regardful care,
aflutter with desire to see.

"Without her constant vibrancy
collapse beset the living realm.
The earth dried up and cattle died.
All life refused to multiply
as sable scarabs rolled their orbs,
their sunbaked young entombed inside.

"For days and nights she traveled down
until she reached the Netherworld,
yet he was first to find her, glad
to pluck the laurel from her hair
as she her lapis trinket shed—
a lovely goddess, to be sure!

"After their fingers intertwined,
however, a great asp aggressed
at Mot's behest until, enclosed
within a cave, it drew her blood,
but not before she'd bested it
and drained its pulse up to the hilt.

"Emerging from that raucous fray,
they ferried over Mot's black stream,
ascending skybent from below.

Earth fructified where all things green
and golden tryst, and from within
the scarab's sphere there burst new life.

"Oh, let us come together now,
enlocked in raptured unison!
With all creation we you praise,
adoring your fecundity.
Now dance with us into the night,
Bright Goddess, Guarantor of Life."

The multitude raised their assent as slabs
and chops of smoky meat were offered up.
Now Kilamuwa nodded Danel's way.
He kissed his children's foreheads, grabbing hold
of an enshrouded, longish article.
He took his stand along the fireside,
his presence silencing the onlookers.
The pious man unwrapped a noble staff
of barkshorn cedar, carven with designs
bespeaking long-forgotten mysteries
that spiraled from the rod's base to the top.
A fearsome wolf's head crowned its pinnacle.
Addressing those assembled, Danel said,
"My friends, I have no mind to keep you long.
As many of you know, some sixteen years
ago I prayed that Baal grant me a son.
He did, requesting that I give to him
that property I held most dear to me.
And so, behold the rod whose name is 'Fate,'
passed down from my forefathers to their sons.
Upon it's etched our kindred's origins—
which I won't here recount—because tonight

this backward-looking man's eyes gaze ahead.
Good friends, bear witness to my sacrifice!"

The judge now staked his forebears' wooden staff
into the center of the firepit
as tongues began to lick and feed on it,
whereat the Harnemite invoked Hadad,
"Oh Baal, you kept your promise to this judge
who worships you, now let me do the same.
You are the Holy Rider on the Clouds,
the Valiant One whom wind and storm obey.
Who'd dare compete with your prerogative?
Who'd better balance force with lenity?
Which god or man evades your lightning bolts?
Receive my grandsires' stave along with all
the immolations of our gathering.
Although I haven't much, I offer you
the very best of what I can procure.
Let no man say my debt goes unrepaid.
If I've reneged the oath I swore, then like
my precious heirloom now engulfed by flame
reduce your benefactions to mere dust.
I thank you for the gift of my young son,
Aqhat, the one who'll carry on my name.
Would that he live up to his status as
the consequence of simple holiness
and serve our town until he's bent with age.
Now, lift your cups and drink with this old man
who's waited long for these festivities!"

Thus Danel. Those foregathered found that he
had spoken well, approving of his prayers
no less than his behest that they carouse,

wassailing on account of Aqhat's birth
and in the name of gods and goddesses.
The women danced to flutes as children played
around the fires, the slightly older ones
describing semicircles near old men
who with no scarcity of garniture
fed famished little ears with fictive lore.
Nobody wanted for a thing that night.
In steady waves of individuals
or households, people greeted Danel's son,
felicitating him and thanking his
most generous of parents for their gifts.
When all had wished him well, his sister came
before him, noting that the time had come
to take possession of the instrument
that Kothar formed for him and that she'd bring
the bow and quiver to him in the morn.
Of all the day's exuberant rewards,
what could compare to Aqhat's joy just then?
The boy-turned-man embraced her, whereupon
she beamed with pride, refilled his cup with wine,
and then saluted him with her own drink.
In time the young man helped his father, drunk
with sweet date wine, back to his bed of straw.

By midnight all had lummoxed into bed,
the village growing deathly still beneath
the ebon cowl of night as winds skimmed cross
the dwindling coals, among which lay a charred
wolf's head, its molten countenance provoked
to anger, smoldering at each caress,
its spirit liberated by the gusts
that lapped then howled up at the distant moon.
The once-calm sea began to stir with swells

and spindrifts through whose blackened blustering,
far off atop the offing's razor edge,
there cut foul figureheads of beastly form
as shadows dug their sculls into the waves.
Just like the sightless heart knows when to pound
deep in the dark recesses of one's chest
when new external threats present themselves,
so too did that armada set about
tattooing drums of war amidst the gloom.
Loud plashing oarage timed itself against
the magnifying thumps as on they sped.

Incensed with him, his father mourned the staff
he'd burnt, the scepter's sacrifice his son
had not deserved, discovering the truth
about the outcome of Aqhat's first hunt.
Upbraiding him, his father raged as boars
with bloodied withers raved throughout the town,
unleashing raucous grunts that harrowed everyone.
Behind a distant house there issued shrieks
of playfulness and Aqhat made for them,
the outcries of delight inviting him
till they crescendoed algedonically,
a metamorphosis that daunted him.
Rounding a bend, a longhorned bull appeared,
pursuing Aqhat down an endless cave,
the stench of soot upon its age-old walls.

As if a demon wailing misery
or like the benu bird's creative cry,
a piercing scream woke Aqhat from his dream,
his hair horripilating at the sound
which multiplied in number and in pitch
and tore him out of bed to peer between

his home's door slats, aghast to recognize
the waterside abodes of town ablaze,
a host of raiding ships along the shore.
He woke his parents from their peaceful drowse,
the three beholding their beleaguerment.
Frenetic livestock bolted up the streets
while tail-tucked mongrels ki-yi'd anxious wrath.
Unsheathing his knife, Danel whisked his wife
and son outside, impelling them eastward
while he struck out for Pugat's residence
to safeguard and deliver her along
with others to the woods where they would meet.

Amidst the chaos, Danel ran from house
to house clandestinely and slank along
their eastern walls as screams and cracks of bone
gave way to morbid silences within.
Yet Danel hastened onward nonetheless.
While crouched behind a wooden wain, he heard
a rustling underneath its covering.
He lifted up the outer flap to find
Bitea, elder Ahiram's daughter,
alongside Hayya, her only brother.
The children winced and cried at being found,
but Danel calmed the siblings, telling them
they need not fear for anything—that they
should run with one another for the woods
as fast as possible, not looking back.
Obeying him, they sped off hand in hand.

Attaining Yarimmu and Pugat's home,
the judge espied a mammoth pillager
whose feathered headdress danced afore the fire;
the Harnemite's affections pregnated

the barren silence, growing, dilating
until they could no longer be contained—
his bronze blade boreholing an aquifer
of lifeblood from the raider's clavicle.
He grabbed the brute's curved sword and rounded shield
and rushed inside where he found Yarimmu
upon the ground—a sword-gash through his neck,
the judge's daughter nowhere to be found.
Eastward he raced with rescue in his heart,
dead set on extricating those in need.

Before, when Danel'd made for Pugat's home,
assailants neared his own house, pressuring
his wife and Aqhat to retreat and keep
inside—a mattock as their sole defense.
Aqhat urged Danataya underneath
her bed of straw, instructing her to stay
well out of sight until he called for her,
affliction for him writ across her face.
He knelt beside the doorway, giving thought
to their escape, each instant billowing
with dread as nearby screams replied to shouts
in foreign tongues whose meaning neither he
nor anyone in town would come to learn.

A moment passed, then yet another one.
Between two pinewood sideboards Aqhat saw
a kilted brute with ursine arms and legs
approach their dwelling, reaching for the door.
The giant with a dented turban on
his head, a bow slung round his back, a sword
in hand, flung wide their door and edged inside.
And like a farmer who has only sere,
effete land that he tries to till each year

frustratedly removes deep clumps of stone
day in, day out, reaches his breaking point
and hacks the rocky earth in futile rage
until he hits on wet and ox-blood clay,
just so did Aqhat slam his plowshare's blade
through the intruder's spine, dispatching him.
As Aqhat, shaking, recomposed himself,
another bearded raider knocked him out
with the butt end of his enormous lance.
Darkness descended over Aqhat's eyes.

His dirty visage caked with dried black blood,
Aqhat came to and found the ground beneath
him westing toward infernal disarray.
As Danel hurried Aqhat out of town,
a foreign sword within the former's grasp,
the boy invoked his mother's name but met
with silence as his father's sole reply.
A fulminant resurgence of alarm
tore Aqhat from his struggling savior's grasp
and sent him sprinting for their family hearth
across their doorway's threshold where he found
his mother—she for whom he would have died,
whose preciousness did all else render vain—
left lifeless on the floor, bestrewn with blood,
her vibrant life cut short.
Despair possessed his feeble body like
demonic nothingness, a power that
now trilled a litany of anguished No's,
coercing him to grate his nails into
his cheeks and through the dirt to scoop it up
and pour upon his head and smear across
his face as if he might inhume himself.

These keens tipped off some of the razzia
precisely as to Aqhat's whereabouts,
and two assailants came to do him in.
Now weapon-strapped and hopeless, Aqhat stood
between the wooden jambs of his home's door.
He welcomed death. And while those sea people
preferred a worthy challenge when it came
to blood sport, they were happy to oblige.
With his crescentic sword a large berserk
lunged toward the boy and raised his glinting blade
when from behind a bronze-tipped arrow shaft
transpierced his cheek just as another barb
impaled the throat of his accomplice, both
marauders crumbling to their knees in pain.
These square hits exorcized from Danel's son
whatever fiend had taken hold of him.
Forth came his sister; like an archeress
she stepped on each foe's head and jerked
the barbed flanes backwards through the marks they'd hit
to expedite their underworldly trips.
Embracing Aqhat briefly, Pugat grabbed
a sword and to her brother handed it.
She read his face, and through the burnt-orange light
emitted from her childhood home she saw
enough to sicken her and nothing that
would lighten her responsibilities.

By now a charnel reek suffused the air,
a fetid fug that overhung the town.
Inspecting the perimeters of homes
adjacent to them, Pugat turned around
and waved her hand whereat a frightened group
of mainly women and their children ran
behind a dagger-wielding elder who

ensured their safe conveyance: Ahiram.
Together they endured their smokey course,
retreating like gazelles in exodus
from savage lions who can taste their fear,
arriving at a flat expanse of grass
that opened toward the cover of the woods.
Their refuge lay but fifty fathoms east.
All ran as they had never run before.
Looking back, Aqhat witnessed Ahiram
collapse next to a tussock, doubling back
to help the elder, only reaching him
to realize that what he had thought to be
tall blades of sedge were scores of arrows sunk
into two children's arms and legs and backs.
Despite the darkness Aqhat could make out
Bitea and Hayya, struck down as if
for target practice in a pool of blood.
The graybeard kissed his children's visages,
beside himself with grief, his heart transfixed
by every arrow he beheld, and more.

Now warriors in feathered headdresses
bulked on the edge of town to hunt their prey.
To no avail the Son of Danel spurred
the elder's flight, endeavoring to lift
him as a lusting sortie charged their way.
Their straits made known to her, Pugat returned
to help her brother, Gabbar seconding
her efforts, dragging Ahiram away.
Now at the black mead's cusp Pugat roused
their pace, emboldening their needful flight
as she sought shelter by a sycamore's
broad trunk and prayed to Kothar-wa-Hasis.
Her first shot missed the mark, but not the next.

An arrow pierced through one assailant's knee,
immobilizing him in agony
just as two more whipped by to kill his mates.
Another wave of seven pillagers
appeared between two burning homes, a sight
persuading Pugat to away and join
her remnant kin stampeding through the wood.

They fumbled through the forest at full tilt,
the muscular and greaved footfall of their
pursuers pounding on the shaken earth
like mallets on the alligator skins
men wrack across a tambour's wooden mouth.
Rotating fenestrated axes clanged
off rocks, sparks flying from hard ricochets.
Without their sandals, mothers and their kids
ran over stones and thorns as arrows snapped
at their heels, striking trees beside their heads—
the silences disparting strikes and screams
like inhalations of a mourner's dirge.
Yet as when packmates hunt for sport instead
of hunger tire of their charmless game,
returning to their well-stocked dens, so too
these giant sea wolves let their quarry go.

Continuing to run still further on,
the last survivors called into the night
till those uprooted had reunified:
some sixteen women and eleven men
along with fourteen girls and thirteen boys,
not counting three of the town's eldermen—
Aqhat's father, Kirta, and Ahiram,
the last assisting a disabled boy.
The Man of Rapiu addressed them all,

"Those murderers and looters from the sea
have stopped their hunt for now, but come the dawn,
recovered from their savage crimes, they will
set out again to look for us so that
we won't return to seek our just revenge.
We have to stick together and walk on
despite fatigue in case they've hunting hounds.
Our home's been taken and we've not the strength
or wherewithal to take back what is ours.
Thus I propose we drink our fill from that
dark stream then march until bright Shapshu makes
her way below tomorrow, stopping when
we must and hunting in the afternoon.
We must ensure our safety first of all
before we brace for challenges ahead.
No one could sleep tonight in any case.
You men of largest build, support the small
ones in your arms or on your shoulders till
they're capable of walking on their own.
And those of you like me who took a sword
or shield or any other armament
amidst the chaos, split in two—one half
to guard our front, the other at the rear."

The fearful lot adhered to his commands,
for even if some might have disagreed,
no soul possessed the strength for quarreling.
Aweary, rank with sweat, their feet contused,
the exiles plodded through the loury night,
depictions of the ruthless massacre
before their eyes with every labored tromp.
And with each trudge away from home, their legs
grew heavier, not only from waning
endurance but also from the remorse

of leaving loved ones' bodies in the sun
for heat and birds to do with as they pleased.
The march was tedious and sorrowful.
Resourceful women shod the escapees
with tunic strips torn from their garment's sleeves,
a recourse that alleviated most,
stanching their lesioned soles, yet which would seem
a curse when later they would be unwrapped.
When overexerted they'd rest their bones,
but anguish always caught back up with them,
their dropped guards sites for parasitic woes
that creep and crepitate throughout the night.

The morrow came too fast. The band trod on
as through the bowers Shapshu gazed on them.
Initially the godhead only saw
their file's well-armored head, and so she rose
above the trees in case their march meant war.
But seeing them in full she pitied them
and even tempered her intrusive glare.
Extemporaneously bivouacked,
the exiles searched for life's necessities
while Danel sent his children on a hunt.

They left at once as Pugat took the bow
and quiver from her shoulder, handing it
to Aqhat, fishing for a passing smile.
Accepting them, the Son of Danel said,
"You're always loyal to your word, aren't you?
The purpose of this bow's made manifest
to me at last: With it I will protect
and feed us—refugees who've lost our land—
until the day comes when we shall return,
reclaiming what belongs to us by right.

I swear it by the long-lived gods: One day
I'll hunt those savages and make them pay.
The sackers shall be sacked, the killers killed,
heaved back into the ocean whence they spawned.
Within my grip they'll beg for slavery
or deathblows, never having known such pain
as I'll bring down upon their heads that day."

Pugat embraced him, making her reply,
"I know, my brother. Trust me when I say:
Not only shall our mother's slaughterers
be brought to justice—so shall Yarimmu's.
I won't exhale my last till they're avenged.
I swear it, just like you, by all the gods.
Yet we must wait, prepare, and only act
when we can be assured of victory.
Anyone can react, but few can plan.
Success prefers the latter (as a rule).
For instance, we could storm our town right now,
take out some men, exact our reckoning,
but we would surely fall before we knew
if they'd besieged us from a common will
or if some foreign lord dispatched their raid—
establishing a beachhead for more troops."

The kin tracked game away from camp, the bow
in Aqhat's hands. His sister carried on,
"A singular concern of paramount
importance lies before us, binding us
although demanding we walk life's thin edge.
We can't entomb the one who with her heart
and body nourished us, nor can we give
her food and drink, because of which she'll turn
to using dust as flour to bake clay bread.

No one will prop her stela with due rites,
and so her shade will find no resting place—
a ghost unworshipped, wandering the world,
untethered from our land, and once she's gone
so is our hope since justice appertains
to those with breath and to the dead, but not
to those who vagabond between these states.
Do you see? If her spirit's lost, then our
revenge would not reorder things afresh
but only gratify our fleeting wrath.
There's only one on whom we might rely:
It's said a Necromancer dens northeast
of us deep down within a mountain cave.
Of all men he alone could help us now.
We must set off to visit him at once."

Though harkening to her advice, Aqhat
directed his attention to the woods
as well, and, hearing rustling up ahead
he held his hand up, peering round a tree
to see a hart that browsed in quiet peace.
Ingathering the scattered, raging thoughts
within his breast, the hunter nocked and drew
an arrow, letting the projectile fly;
it struck the noble beast who belled and wried—
her stout neck punctured by the bronzen tip.
They followed her until she breathed no more,
upon which Aqhat bound her fore and hind
legs and proceeded to give answer thus,
"Our duty lies with those who live, our town's
survivors who depend upon us now.
Our mother cared for all the least ones more
than anyone I know, and she would want
us to protect and to provide for those

who've nothing now—no family, home, or hope.
You're right to say our situation's bleak
and that our vengeance won't be swift, but things
are not so dark that dark magic's required.
Let's plan the justice that is ours without
involving those whom it does not concern."

They hauled the game as Pugat pleaded him
to reconsider, giving up her case
when he repeated his unbudging stance.
Yet his composure and assuredness
disguised their opposites, which prodded him,
"Of all those taken, why are you alive?
Because they celebrated you, the town
caroused and slumbered, wholly unprepared
to stand up for their loved ones and themselves.
You only had your mother to defend.
One person. How did that work out for you?
You saw an osprey harry nesting chicks
three days ago, the easiest of signs
to read, yet you ignored the auguries,
forewarning no one, lifting not a hand
except in preparation for your feast.
Far better had you never walked the earth."

A great though brief relief descended on
the exiles at the sight of Aqhat's kill.
By litten fires children gathered round
for warmth, awaiting their apportionments.
When all had tasted supper, women lay
about the fire like so many divans
for little ones assaulted on all sides:
by past duress, by coming vagaries,
and by the Rippers that beheld them, eyes

aglow, from deep within that beastly bosk.
One woman held an infant not her own,
a girl that circumstance bequeathed to her,
singing to her adopted child much like
her mother had when she could find no rest:

"Once a young hatchling,
white with black patching,
couldn't lay down to rest.
Three rocks of her color
made sleeping a bother,
so she flounced away from her nest.

"Bouncing along now,
Peep found some soft ground,
hoping to shut her eyes.
But babblers and whoopers
left Peep in a stupor
as did the brown warbler's shrill cries.

"Finding some quiet
far from that riot,
Peep tucked her stilts and dozed.
Then bramblings got ruffled
and ruffs brawled and scruffled
while darters and coots came to blows.

"Fleeing that mire,
flustered and tired,
Peep thought she chanced her spot.
She hid in a sallow,
yet here found fowls callow,
who heckled her as they'd ought not:

"'Look at this game bird.'
'That's not the right word.'
'Fine, what's her stock, you nag?'
'A bustard for father
and booby for mother,
result of some negligent shag!'

"Starting to whimper
(legs a bit limper),
Peep cheeped for Mama's aid.
That spear-beaked descended,
their insults she ended,
and cradled Peep back whence she strayed.

"Gliding a mistral
clear as bright crystal,
she who was down soared high,
her eyelids now swooning
to Mama's soft crooning—
the sandpiper's soft lullaby.

"High in the distance,
both rode a cirrus
back toward their place of rest.
While gracefully swooping,
Peep's neck started drooping,
and soon they arrived at their nest.

"Gone were Peep's rivals,
stones colored piebald,
fuzz balls now in their stead.
Among them she nuzzled,
relaxing her muscles,
and finally rested her head."

Ere long Sleep blanketed the exiled lot—
all save the graybeards who ignited brands
together, congregating in a grove
some ways from camp to contemplate and weigh
the meager options that confronted them.
Unable or unwilling to restrain
his curiousness, Aqhat followed them
in secret, careful not to give himself
away by stepping on dead leaves or twigs.
Forth through the dimness Aqhat stepped and crept.
He hid behind a tumulus-shaped mound
in earshot of the elders, watching them.
Among the patriarchs his father said,
"What will we do? My wife—they butchered her
in our own home and spilled her blood upon
the floor before defiling her in turns!
I couldn't save her—couldn't do a thing.
Those images will haunt my heart until
they lay my body in a pit of dirt,
my final day that can't come soon enough.
But why? Why have the gods unleashed their wrath?
Did we not celebrate and placate them
just as our forefathers instructed us,
even surpassing their requirements?
We must have erred in some egregious way,
our unatoned-for sins avenged on us.

"I'm old enough, my friends, to know that most
of heaven's mysteries elude our grasp.
Perhaps the truth regarding our mistakes
will only be revealed when we're made clean.
And so, instead of letting Whys haunt us,
let's look to Wheres and Whens and In-What-Ways.
We must get everyone as far afield

from those barbaric men as possible.
We know a sprawling desert lies southeast,
across which brutes enladen with their spoils
would not give chase; we might find haven there.
Thus I suggest we march that way each day,
surviving on what we collect and hunt.
Our journey will be arduous, but if
we are indeed impure, then our due pain
shall act as our redress to those on high.
And if we've done no wrong and were attacked
by foreign heathens, may our gods set things
aright and pay them back a thousandfold."

Thus Danel. Kirta then addressed them both,
"I've not yet failed to gratify our gods
for safeguarding my daughters, sons, and wife,
though I will never know why we were spared.
But still I mourn our dead as though they were
my own, and as we've plodded through the woods
I've struggled to make meaning of our pain,
to strike upon our ruination's cause,
for we're a pious people, as you've said.
Why were we punished after having sung
the vernal hymns, not even half a day
since we had venerated Bright Astarte?
The only difference from past feasts was that
we sacrificed more animals and poured
out more libations to the deities,
to which were added Danel's heartfelt prayers.
And who'd take umbrage at loud praise and gifts?
I'm with you: We provoked the gods somehow.
But we won't find our refuge in the wastes
but rather in a thriving northern town,

specifically, within a temple's walls
where priests are trained to handle such affairs."

Smarting at their words Ahiram replied,
"I've ruminated on our schlepp as well.
One story in particular won't give
me any rest—I've now unraveled why.
Do you recall the grandsire Zakir's tales
of olden kings and queens and all they did?
The tale that will not let me rest concerns
Khamudi, one of Zakir's most preferred
exempla (as you'll both remember well).
Khamudi ruled Avaris long ago.
From his own subjects he filched everything,
enslaving those with nothing left to eat.
Yet King Khamudi coveted still more.
Dissatisfied with his large palace, he
designed another, grander one himself,
commanding able hands to mine its stones
and then construct the edifice despite
his architects' insistence on the thing's
demonstrable impossibility.
But in the gods he had unrivaled faith.
And when the palace, top-heavy and grand,
collapsed full-force atop the workers' heads,
he sprayed the blame upon his architects.
To make a show of them he clubbed their skulls
in front of everyone and tossed them in the Nile
before he tortured their extended kin—
those whom he late suspected of dissent.

"One day, a regicidal enemy
arose: great Ahmose, bane of Hyksos kings.

Up from the south he came with armies at
his back, astride a hairless, leathern beast
whose nose was like a thick and braying snake.
He took Tjaru with facility,
but Lord Khamudi showed no sign of fear.
Avaris' mudbrick palisades attained,
the conqueror attacked with all his men.
They sieged the city once but were repulsed.
Khamudi stood his ground. A second, third,
and fourth day Ahmose and his partisans
aggressed, held off yet one more time, but not
before they'd killed two thousand Hyksos troops,
demolishing the city's garrisons.
Examining the war's realities,
Khamudi's counselors advised a truce,
the tyrant gruffing his unmoved response.
Yet growing fearful for his lineage
Khamudi ordered that his daughters, sons,
and wives be convoyed down the Nile at night
until they reached the safety of the Great
Green Sea, awaiting word for their return.
Avaris fell the next day, and with ease—
the king and his suspected allies slain.

"I've asked myself just why this story haunts
my heart, and now, tonight, its meaning's clear.
Khamudi ruled with unmatched power till
the end, and though both mad and evil like
all tyrants ere and since his tenureship,
still some small speckle of unalloyed gold
hid underneath that tarnished copper clump.
Would we not say he acted for the best
and with a modicum of wisdom when
he shipped his family off, for in them lay

the future of his line, unblameworthy
in their relation to their father's crimes?

"Now if a king as stupid, vincible,
and wretched as Khamudi could decide
what's best when necessary, then of course
the gods you claim are wise, benevolent,
and powerful—No!—wisest, kindliest,
and strongest—surely they would likewise save
their guiltless children from unmeted pain,
from torture and gratuitous travails.
Yet they do no such thing! And if you're both
to be believed, those Just and Clement Ones
may even mastermind such suffering.
And so your gods prove weaker, more insane,
and more malevolent than potentates
who lord it over crumbling monarchies.
Still, mortals can depose or kill a king
(unlike a god), and thus, despite the dark
depths humans reach, justice might have its say.

"I see you've brusque rejoinders on your tongues,
but still them or I'll cut them from your throats.
You're hard of hearing not because you're old.
Strong prejudice beclouds your stubborn hearts,
you who'd extenuate the ancient ones
where nothing less than execration's due.
Even so, what's the use if I am right?
Will truthful stories wash my eyes and ears?
My heart beholds four children's visages:
the two wan, empty stares of Bitea
and Hayya as their punctured corpses slouch
beneath the moonlight in my helpless arms,
having respired their last, their flesh still warm,

and alternately, their appearances
tomorrow and the next day and the next,
emaciated by the ruthless sun,
with flies alighting on their unclosed eyes.
The selfsame gilded portals through which life
once freely passed have closed forevermore,
and though I bang and hammer on those doors
my every effort echoes hollowly
until I, too, am emptied of all life."

Unable to eke out another word,
the elder keeled over and dropped his torch
with heaving sobs as Kirta and Danel
embowered their heart-riven intimate.
Through tears and hard-intaken gulps of air
their bodies—proving wiser than their words—
expelled their grief in broken unison,
the ecstasy of mutual concern
immixed with loss arresting Time himself.
At length the necessary purge let up,
their eyes like ones back from the Hereafter.

When Silence the most eloquent of gods
and goddesses had said her peace and left,
judge Danel stood, addressing his compeers,
"Brothers, we have no food, no tents, no plan.
Our people—they must see us of accord,
especially in days to come, for we'll
be tested as we've never been before.
Good Kirta, I too thought that we might march
northward to seek out shelter in some town,
whether abandoned or inhabited.
But then I realized that convoys like
the ones that stormed our shore wouldn't have come

for one small town, but probably have set
their sights on others up the littoral.
Asylum in the north would be short-lived
whereas the wall-less waste provides defense."

Exhausted, Ahiram agreed, and though
demurring thoughts plagued Kirta, he concurred
as well, if only to debate no more.
The elders started backtracking and sent
the son of Danel scurrying to camp
where he feigned sleep beneath his flaxen cloak.
But though he lay aground, he never slept,
his eyes interrogating starry kings
who voyaged high above the canopy.
What were the gods in actuality?
Had they forsaken elder Ahiram
or had the forlorn man abandoned them?
Where'd Baal been when his mother was attacked?
Could he have had some hand in slaying her?
Upon him suchlike questions climbed and crawled
like spiders whom one splats—incognizant
of spawnlings clustered on their backs—each hit
diffusing numberless derivatives
who, even when they've been dispelled, one feels
abounding, skittering across the skin
and watching one with six-too-many eyes.

Come first light Danel and the elders told
the people of their plan, and though all feared
Mot's shore, their leaders' reassurance helped
to solace them, allaying fevered fears.
Decamping, women scattered the remains
of last night's fire so as to leave no trail.
The remnant trod southeast, dehydrating

fresh venison and berrying for fruit.
The coastal woodlands gradually lost
their former thickness, trees becoming sparse,
till in a few days' time the travelers came
upon a streambed such as some would not
behold again as long as they drew breath.
And so, expectant of the worst, they each
partook of it, englutting stomachfuls.

A few sword-wielding men led everyone
beyond the lowlands past the desert's marge.
They walked and cast the only shadows as
far as a hawk could see. The sun was hot.
Most worried whether they'd survive until
fatigue expunged these very thoughts as well.
The days droned by. The days were dun and dry.
At night the refugees would spread their cloaks
upon the ground and in the morning wring
what little dew the textile had absorbed
onto the divot of a limestone slab
from which they'd slup whatever they could get.
Aqhat had fitful luck in tracking game,
procuring shrews and thewy tortoises.
Days humdrummed on. Each day was hot and long.
On one stale morning Pugat came across
a massive tree, a lone pistachio
surveilling its environment just like
the last grunt standing on a battlefield,
undaunted by the Sun's panoptic gaze.
With eager children's aid, she shook the tree
till every drupe had fallen to the earth.
The women hulled and dried and roasted them.
They bowered underneath the giant's limbs,

distributing the nuts between themselves,
their restless stomachs settled for a time.

Some days thereon, while walking, Aqhat said,
"Gabbar, I've something to confess: Some nights
ago I followed father and the eldermen
to learn our plan and so be put at ease.
Indeed, I heard we'd venture south and east—
a bit of a surprise—but nothing like
the other things I heard the men discuss.
The three could not decide upon the cause
of our attack, but the alternatives
boil down to two grave possibilities:
Either some foreign king dispatched the raid,
in which case either Baal refused to come
to our defense, was powerless against
their arms, or never knew we'd be assailed—
or, Baal foreknew we'd be laid low and could
have intervened, but didn't, since he was
the one to orchestrate our ransacking.
In both scenarios, the Conqueror's
unfair, a weakling, or improvident.
And yet such names are blasphemous and false.
Can you unravel these perplexities?
I've not slept well since overhearing them."

Considering his friend's words, Gabbar said,
"Such things exceed the limits of my thought,
and while I think I grasp the paradox,
perhaps it's nothing more than that, and thus
should go untouched, for what good could result
from speculating on such quandaries?
A servant might not know just how or why

his master's tail-tied his old mule, and if
he tries undoing it without due care
he might get kicked or accidentally
release it, asking for the master's lash.
Maybe some knots are best left to themselves.
Our home's been razed. The deed's already done.
We know this and upon it we must act
by getting everyone to safer lands.
To do so, you will need your sleep, my friend."
The questioner agreed with reticence.

The heat with each day grew as did the walls
of rock that flanked red wadis' either sides,
the exiles trooping through a constant war:
Just as in ages immemorial,
humongous scarps continued to stand fast
against erosion, that clandestine foe
who gains ground on rivals by losing it;
large insects fought deathstalker scorpions,
envenomated by the latter's strike
only to be devoured while alive;
yet even they would soon experience
the black bat's fangs that dive and crunch and kill
all while the leopard stalks the ibices
whose recurved horns stand primed for self-defense.
But Shahar's presence augurs Shapshu's climb,
and when that goddess takes her seat and scours
the world below—all-overseeing yet
unseeable on high—the predators
who prowl by night agree to a détente,
knowing the dangers of the Potter's kiln.

The remnant footslogged over trackless dunes,
through yawning gullies, snaking in between

the corrugated steeps of knuckled spines.
They hiked a half-moon's time. Two scorching days
had passed since their morale's last drops ran dry.
The desert—heartless trickster—forecast pools
of water just beyond broad waves of heat
that sinuated just like floodwaters.
One evening, when the lot could drag themselves
no further, seeking refuge in a pass,
the armed men pulling up the rear began
to quarrel with the vanguard—neighbors, friends
not long before now at each other's throats.
With stern rebukes judge Danel intervened
to quell the mutineers, in part because
irascible dissension weakened them,
but first and foremost since a retinue
of five and twenty archers with long shocks
of kerchiefed sable hair and black deer eyes
surrounded them atop the ridges' sides
as strains of tautened bowstaves filled the vale.
A spear in hand, their titan leader boomed,
"Desist and lay your weapons on the ground.
What right have you to trespass on our lands?
What pharaoh furnishes so mean a troop
to infiltrate our territory's bounds?
Get on with it. Speak truthfully or else."

Establishing himself as spokesperson,
Kirta stood forth, replying with respect,
"My Lord, we come with no ill will towards you
or any of your kin. We're refugees.
Some time ago barbaric warriors
laid siege upon our waterside abode.
They raped our women, slaughtering for sport,
with torch-fire burning down our homes and boats.

We're all that's left. These armaments aren't ours.
Their strength and style and shape are proof enough,
for none of us has ever seen their like.
Nor could our fallen smith have crafted them.
We took them from the few that we had killed
in self-defense, escaping with our lives."

The leader of the bowmen turned around,
conferring with adjacent men-at-arms.
A hushed debate ensued before the man
in charge about-faced, gesturing for those
obedient to him to ease their bows,
addressing those corralled beneath his stead.
"We are the Shasu—desert-born and proud.
We call these noble Seir Mountains home,
their height bestowing a farsightedness
upon us, elevating our desires.
Yet Fortune's been unkind to us as well.
Of late Resheph has worked his magic on
some of our women, stealing breath from them.
So too we lost good men two moons ago
when we waylaid an eastbound caravan.
Our independent plights might bind us yet.
Pledge fealty to me, promising your men
of sword-bearing capacity to us
that we might guard against invading tribes,
your women joining ours in their travails.
Do this and we won't call you guests but kin.
But be forewarned: A vow is absolute.
Should anyone who swears his loyalty
abandon us, that one shall meet their death."

Judge Danel, Ahiram, and Kirta joined
together to discuss the leader's terms.

The Man of Rapiu made known his view,
"Hear me, we are and have been peaceable,
just as our fathers and their forefathers.
Were we despoiled to become despoilers?
Deprived of everything, can we forego
what made us venerable, pious men,
that which till death we might still call our own,
that is, the morals that unite our folk?
And what about our clan's self-governance?
If we forsake our customary rule,
what might these strangers order us to do?
Perhaps the Shasu leader will allow
us to remain nearby and work with him
on our terms and—"

"Danel, we do not have the upper hand,"
said Kirta, fed up with his lecturing.
"The forces pressing us are stronger than
traditions we have held as good or bad.
For too long have we lacked the means to fight
with skill for those we've promised to protect,
and now such opportunity appears.
We've stumbled into territory not
our own—and on your own advice, mind you.
Do you think self-reliant highlanders
will share their resources with mendicants
who hope to settle on their holy land?
No leader abdicates his place of strength
unless he must, and in this wilderness
we are the ones who must abjure our roles.
Or like Khamudi shall we stubbornly
defend our ways from pride and foolishness,
endangering our people needlessly?"

The graybeard Ahiram concurred with him
as silence bound and separated them.
Here Danel took a moment to behold
the famished faces of the escapees,
the people who relied on his good sense
and followed him into this arid waste.
He then knelt down before the Shasu chief,
avowing fealty to the man till come
the day he have no further need of him.
Without a word the others mimicked him,
at which the leader smiled and beckoned them
to rise and to ascend the steeps as kin,
conducting them toward darkling ridgeline caves,
the lofty sockets they would call their home.

Book VI

Having recuperated from their march,
the newest members of the Shasu tribe
began to learn and ply their stations' trades.
Attending to those sick and bowed with age,
the women wrung out dew from woolen rags,
preparing meals and sewing near the caves
while beardless boys set to their goatherd's work,
some wary kids instructing them with rams
below the cincture—lesson number one.
With armaments of motley origin
the Son of Danel and the other boys
of weapon-wielding strength began to train
for their surprise raids on Egyptian troops.
The Shasu taught them how to grip their swords,
a process taking far more energy,
correction, and forbearance than they'd hoped.
Next Gabbar, Aqhat, and the rest received
directives on their weapons' proper care—
for one blunt edge could equal early death.
But when (and only when) they'd grasped these skills
did the recruits begin their exercise.

Fit out with leathern corselets, oxhide shields,
headgear, and bronzen swords—the lot of which
had suffered combat six and sixty more
occasions than they had—the tenderfeet
descended the glacis beside their caves.
Deep in the gorge, berated by the heat,
their drilling now commenced. The men paired off.

A raspy-bearded man took Aqhat as
his new trainee, and while they sparred he said,
"Keep that shield up and hold it steadily.
Pull back your right foot, keeping off your heels.
Now, lunge and aim to strike me in the chest.
Good. Keep an eye on how I block attacks
as we'll work on defensive stances soon.
Again. No! Bend your knees a little bit.
If your legs move like trunks, your enemies
will hack them, felling you just like a tree.
Again. Not bad, but loosen up your grip.
Attack me once again with this in mind.
Don't let your forearm do the work that's meant
for your whole body or you'll tire out.
Now hit me with a horizontal stroke.
Alright. Resume your stance and go again.
Why are you sucking wind? Are you worn out?"

The Shasu worked the novices until
the afternoon when all let up and stopped
to rest, consuming water and dry loaves.
After they'd drunk and eaten, each took up
their swords again, including Gabbar who
sparred with a heavily-accented man
who wore a scar across his face. He said,
"Let's start off simply. When I come for you,
lift up your sword to parry my assault.
No! Hold it firmly, boy, or what's the point?
That helmet takes a blow far better than
your skull, but not by much. Now use your shield
to counteract my blade, then have a go.
Once more. Again. No! Don't block passively.
If you unbalance me, then you control
your next move. Win the little battles first.

Defend your head, then grapple and respond.
Ha! Hard when your opponent's massive, no?
Just stick with me and I will show you how
to use a giant's girth against himself,
though I'm afraid you've months of work in store."

When roseate Dusk took pity on the boys,
the Shasu drillmasters conducted them
up paths that ended at an overlook.
Like flightless fledglings the initiates
drew close to one another for support
as the tribe's leader came and passed around
charred meats and wineskins, captivating them,
"So you've survived your first of untold days
of training in the cutthroat school of war.
For those of you who feel you're not cut out
for fighting, you may leave without disgrace
or mockery to learn another trade.
Reflect on it, for we don't tolerate
deserting dastards once the fight is on . . .
No one? Last chance. Well, good. We need more men.
I pray your swordsmanship improves in time,
because while we don't know when caravans
will pass, our livelihood depends on them.

"Men—combat is a language. In the months
to come, my Shasu brothers shall repeat
and translate it until you're literate.
An armed man, though he only grunt and shout,
becomes a vast array of signs when he
attacks—his muscles, movements, pauses, eyes
speak prose or poetry, however well.
With unremittent practice you will learn
to read and speak with lettered expertise.

Most you'll encounter know violence's
tongue better than you ever will, thus strive
for fluency not only in the sword's
smooth sound or the curved ax's consonance,
but also in your foeman's dialect,
his accents and his oddities of phrase,
not to converse, but because only when
you can interpret and anticipate
a flashing body's idioms will you
be able to cajole and kill a man.
In turn, know that he reads you too and waits
for you to gaffe so he can gaff you through."

Continuing to sate their appetites
with goat and garnet wine, the fuglemen
conversed with the recruits, harassing them
at times as does an older brother who
from deep love wants to harden younger kin
for life's invariable cruelties.
Soon all returned to their respective caves
in order to regather fighting strength
but found a group of onetime refugees
engaged in necromantic rites to call
on the unburied they had left behind.
The starlit vault embreathed their frankincense.
Participants set beer and strips of meat
out for their loved ones, crying out their names,
imploring them to come but for awhile.
No specter stirred. Once more they summoned them,
repeating conjurations time and time
again, their strophes circling back around
to where they had begun yet magnified,
each revolution surging frantically.
With dwimmercraft of varied cadences

one woman tried communing with the dead.
Alas, no word, no voice, no visages
appeared to them, so they gave up the rites.

Along the entrance to the westmost cave
slept Danel, guardian of those inside.
One night, arising to relieve himself,
he ventured down a moonlit bluff's corniche.
A sharp crisp whirlwind lashed his neck and sent
ants scuttering along his vertebrae.
The path snaked down the mountain's northern face.
His right hand's fingers crept along the wall
of jagged chert to feel their way as do
a blind whip-spider's probing legs and palps
just as a dreadful skirl pealed through the night,
obliterating Silence's vigil.
A full-throated roar challenged the high shriek
before another screech tore through the black.

The elder rushed toward the continual
exchange of high and low-pitched sounds which rose
into the night like devils' antiphons.
Although the noises colonized the land,
judge Danel knew he neared the battle's heart
because their tone and pace transmogrified,
transcending anything he'd heard before.
Grabbing a sharp branch, Danel hurried on,
but now the netherworldly chorus ceased.
Quiescence had resumed her suzerainty.
With scattered rapidness the Harnemite
sought out the pandemoniac chorale,
concluding when two irises met his:
Its eyes were set within a bloodied face
from which there dangled coral viscera.

The graybeard raised his club, a beast himself,
but the bespeckled cat flashed blackened fangs
and growled, protective of its recent kill.
Beside himself with furor, Danel charged
the leopard, ready for his life's last fight
as with one last indignant jerk the beast
tore off a limb and fled into the mirk.

At once he knelt beside the ravaged corse,
unable to identify the girl
whose frame and face had been so mauled, defiled.
The Man of Rapiu began to sob.
His hands and knees shook. Gathering himself,
he took her, carrying her up the berm.
The graybeard stumbled up the mountain path
in icy sweat, a murder of black crows
alarming one another of his course
but much-intrigued by hints of carrion.
By now those dwelling in the Seir cliffs
had risen at the awful sounds, the chief
enarming men beside the entryways
of their abodes with blazing brands in hand,
preparing to descend when Danel came
into their sights, his face befouled with dirt.

The Shasu chieftain dropped his spear and ran
to him, disburdening his weary arms
and cradling her, lamenting, crying out,
"Sharelli! No, no! Oh, my gods. My girl.
My precious girl! What have you done to her?
You're home, Sharelli, speak a word to me.
I've got you now—we'll stitch your wounds and you'll
feel better soon enough. Be strong for me.
Was that a sigh? Fetch me some water. Now!

Oh, El! Why do you scourge and cudgel me?
What have I done to merit spitting on?
You, old man! Tell us what you did down there."

All watched the shaken elder as he spoke,
and he recounted what had taken place
down in the vale, explaining that he knew
not why she'd ventured out so late at night.
Despair stopped up the Shasu leader's ears
to all his speech's content, but the tale's
grave tone and Danel's visage testified
to his sincerity and empathy.
Responsibility held back the flood
of sorrow as the Shasu women took
Sharelli, readying the girl's remains
for burial, performed at dawn's first light.
After the exequies, the leader trudged
to where his daughter had been slain and wept.
For three whole days he mourned her on his knees.
Upon the fourth day, women came to bring
him home where they consoled and fed the man.

Despite that bleak night's sudden tragedy;
despite the fact that it had not rained once
for sixteen months; despite the growing growls
of hunger circulating through the camp:
the people worked together to survive,
and combat training carried on each day.
One evening Danel walked a wimpling path,
a rocky trail that led him to a tor
from which he scanned the men-at-arms below.
Although they were rigged out in battle-gear,
he had no trouble picking out his son,
for Aqhat had grown tall and swift and strong

as if he were predestined for such work.
His son attacked and feinted, blocked and struck
with poise and grace, a match for Shasu men
who set strong troops against him, challenging
him overmuch until he had to yield.
So too did Gabbar's spearsmanship improve.
The elder watched him proudly, doing so
as if vicariously, for the man's
mother, Inumi, couldn't see him now,
not having ridden out their town's demise.

Set off from others by the evening fire,
roasting a bird, Pugat spoke to Gabbar,
"I'm sure the grape harvest is underway.
Oh, what I wouldn't give to be back there,
to drink my fill beside the fire and sing
or peg you and my brother with old fruit,
our mothers dancing, letting down their hair.
When will we know such happiness again?
Only in daydreams can I venture back:
I hear the luscious goat's milk simmering
and wait for tender lamb just like the gulls
who, uninvited, make themselves at home
until some cranky widow shoos them off.
I smell the salty sea breeze from in my bed.
At times the strength of such sensations makes
me wonder whether we really belong
out here—this wasteland where no swath of cloud,
no rain, no fish, and nothing green's at home."

All smiles, he watched the coals and made reply,
"You've said it well. I'm twice as hungry now,
as much to swap this bird for roasted fish
as to jam up your hair with mushy grapes.

One day we will return—I'm sure of it—
reclaiming what is ours through counterraids.
Our training's going well. They work us hard,
and Aqhat has a shtick for swordsmanship.
Within a few years' time, we might improve
enough to spirit other fighting men,
sons of our own perhaps, to head back west,
and I have seen you wield a bow, so I
would gladly fight beside you, come what may . . .
There's one more thing that I—"

A breathless man cut Gabbar off and said,
"They're coming—trains of eastbound caravans
a hundred fathoms to the west of us.
Suit up, recruits! Your swordplay ends tonight.
Prepare yourselves and say what prayers you must."

The Son of Danel found his friend and took
his arm, the latter briefly glancing back
while hasting for the mountain armory.
The two men tied their leathern corselets on
and crowned their heads with helmets wrought of bronze.
Aqhat slung Kothar's bow and quiver round
his back (the envy of his desert hosts),
and grabbed a whettened and well-balanced sword,
his comrade taking up a pike and shield.
With expletives the Shasu boldened them,
bestirring one another's battle-lust.
The thirty warriors crept noiselessly
into the gorge and reached the blackened sand
all while a lookout climbed a southern peak
from which to mark the progress of the train.
A multiform barrage of imminent
disasters ambushed Aqhat and Gabbar's

imaginations, broadening their eyes.
They hunched and waited on the cusp of life.
The scout returned, informing all as to
the whereabouts of those who'd set up camp
and detailing their guards' positionings
before the Shasu leader thanked him, wheeled
around, and briefed his soldiers of their plan.

Aqhat wished Gabbar strength and turned to go,
proceeding in the wake of marksmen who
assumed their high positions round the north
side of the bivouac of thirteen tents.
Enlivened by the torchlight, hieroglyphs
incised upon the covered carts began
to dance while beasts of burden lay about
beside their masters, weary from their march.
Sharelli's father led his company
through a defile, the sandy floor of which
absorbed the normal clunking of their steps.

One guard, made cautious by experience,
surveilled the lightless channel made of stone.
He looked about and traveled deeper, brand
in hand, suspicion overtaking him.
Around a corner he caught sight of men
intending war and made to shout for help
when from above the Shasu leader fell
upon the lookout, covering his mouth
until the man's wet life ran down his neck.
Gabbar interred his torch to snuff it out
and lugged the guardsman's body out of sight
whereat the Shasu leader reproduced
a throaty, swift, and full facsimile
of the horned eagle owl's vernacular,

an arrow volley—economical
because well-aimed—dispatching sundry men
who stood around their tentage unawares.

The raiders set upon the nescient camp
in pairs, waylaying those inside the tents.
Descending from their nests, the archers joined
the fray as frightened horses neighed and men
beset on every side cried out for help
or hacked their way to freedom, running off.
Full-blooded Memphians-at-arms hove spears
and harsh obscenities each in their way,
impetuous and whelming as the Nile.
Now for the first time squaring off to fight,
Gabbar swung for a man but missed, his foe's
riposte delivering a painful gash
that shocked his martial drills back into place.
He blocked a series of intrepid strokes
then feinted, driving home his spear into
the man's uncovered heart from which the crack
of broken ribs resounded, followed by
the copper smell of blood, impressions which
throughout his time on earth he'd not forget.

Unsheathing his curved blade—the same some brute
had used to spill his people's blood—the Son
of Danel added to the clangoring.
He killed two men and then a third, his thigh
nicked by a whizzing lancehead's course, a close
call crystalizing his resolve until
he found a boy not one year his younger
alone within a tent, afraid to fight,
still more afraid to feed the swordsman's blade.
Condolence cumbered Aqhat's surety,

and when a Shasu brother found him there,
declaiming victory, he asked him what
he waited for, advising him to not
torment a boy so young but do him in
at once and out of generosity.
The warrior retreated from the tent
while Aqhat looked into the boy's brown eyes.
Decided, blood stains on his crescent blade,
Baal's gift stepped forward to lay low the boy
who in his sweat-soaked panic shouted out,
"Please! Don't kill me! I cannot die out here,
for if I do Anubis won't appraise
my heart upon his scales, nor will I come
to know an afterlife, beholding Ra
descending into Duat, blazing fire!"

Astounded that he spoke their tongue (still more
bemused by what his words meant), Aqhat sheathed
his sword, assuring him no harm could come
to him should he do nothing foolhardy.
He seized his arm and led him from the tent.
The Shasu leader saw the two come forth,
detaining Aqhat and his prisoner,
interrogating his unbidden act,
to which the Son of Danel made reply,
"I do not pity this Egyptian boy
but think he might prove useful for our work.
He speaks our tongue. Could he not tell us when
more caravans plan to traverse this land
or what their counter-stratagems entail?
Might he not know what officials now
propose to do about our hillpeople?
We can't prejudge the value of a man

familiar with our constant enemy.
What risk could such a coward really pose?
Once you have gotten what you want from him,
you might dispose of him as you see fit."

The Shasu lord rebuffed his brazen speech,
"In case your binding oath has slipped your mind,
you call no shots round here, nor do you choose
who lives and dies or how the deed is done.
I'd have you kill him now to prove the point.
To show you—all of you—that I'm a chief
who'll lend an ear to those who've bent the knee,
ignoring none no matter what their rank,
I'll condescend and let the prisoner
provide what information he has stored
away, if advantageous to our folk.
But when the boy's utility runs dry,
I'll sell him to a slaver—better yet—
I'll reunite him with his caravan."

By now the raiding party had begun
to rummage through the covered carts, the first
of which contained wheat beer and savories.
The men rejoiced, libating to Lord El,
enflamed with eagerness to tear into
the other wagons stuffed with heaps of loot.
The next cart likewise harbored nourishments,
a revelation that excited them,
though far less than would hoards of golden jewels.
With increased haste the Shasu tore apart
the other vehicles to find some gads,
pickaxes, and cheap adzes strewn about,
the five remaining carts all but vacant.

Observing his men's disappointed looks,
the Shasu chieftain queried Aqhat's boy,
"Is this some sort of joke? Does powerful
and haughty Egypt export onions now?
Who traffics in these worthless implements?
Speak now, boy, for it's just for this that you've
been spared, and I am not a patient man."

Plying what words he knew, the boy replied,
"We are not merchants, Lord, but men employed
to mine the minerals within these hills.
The lords of Alashiya's coast inflate
the cost of metals far beyond their worth,
and so the pharaoh has seen fit to send
out trains of prospectors on Horus' Way,
dispatching us to bring home copper ore.
We hauled provisions in our chariots
along with tools for our allotted task,
intending other carts to carry back
the precious metals which we might unearth."

The chieftain tried to stay his disbelief.
He ordered some to take the equipage,
supplies, and vittlings to their tenements,
instructing others to inter the dead.
To show their worth, Aqhat and Gabbar hauled
more than their share of tools up to the caves
but found they'd also borne the hapless job
of passing on ill tidings from the raid.
When some inquired about the captive boy,
he answered them himself with deference
and introduced himself as 'Ameni,'
ensuring them he'd serve them best he could.

When morning came, the leader called his folk
in order to address their mounting fears,
"My friends, by now you know that last night's raid
secured provisions for some time to come,
but little else withal, if truth be told.
This year our crops and livestock haven't fared
as well as usual, and there is talk
of moving out to settle better land.
However, I must counsel otherwise.
Though meager, winter's rains will soon return.
So here's what I propose: Let's send a group
to trade our loot for life's necessities
while others shall keep adzes for themselves,
endeavoring to dig an aquifer.
It's time our settlement establish routes
of trade and have a wellspring for our own.
El sees our struggles and he hears our plight
as do his scions Shegr and Ithm.
They won't abandon us in time of need."

Excitement at the thought of a refined
existence rippled through the hillpeople
as swiftly as debates concerning which
of the assignments best befitted whom.
To settle them the local patriarchs
accorded those the roles that they deserved.
Ameni set about the abjectest
of tasks, dissolving the suspicious looks
that kept him on his guard, transforming them
from cold acceptance to a certain kind
of gratitude, however transient.
Even the chief—although not saying so
himself—accepted his utility
instead of seeking to dispense with him.

Pricked by accountability for him,
Aqhat stood up for the Egyptian boy,
encouraging his friends to do the same—
in part to justify the sympathies
that motivated him to spare his life.

Around a cliffside fire one eventide,
they asked Ameni how he'd learned their tongue,
being a foreigner, and to apprise
them of his former life and provenance.
Ameni hesitated ere he said,
"My mother welcomed me into the world
in the Black Land along the Nile's right bank.
She passed away when I was young, so my
first memories involve my father's care.
He was a fisherman. And I can see
him now, a sharpened bident in his grip,
stock-still until a catfish erred—spitted and bagged
with fidgety tilapia, nor would
he let me live down, even to this day,
my first encounter with a crocodile,
or how in my fourth flood season I approached
a bloat of hippos, thinking they'd be kind.

"But none of these compares to one image:
the River's blue lotus. Father and I
would rise before daybreak and walk the banks
where I would play as he began to fish.
As Ra ascended in his chariot,
the lotus too rose from its watery
abode, its dripping petals spreading wide.
When I would cry from hunger, heat, or thirst,
my father'd pluck the flower, giving me
a taste to still me, eating some himself.

He'd fish the whole day long, and when Lord Ra
descended in the West, the lotus bloom
would furl itself and dip down for the night.
Becalming me and sleeping when I slept,
its perfume on the air—that water herb
was like the mother I had never known.

"In time pharaonic fisheries and vast
vivaria reduced the price of fish
so much my father had to seek new work.
With friends' help he secured a job along
the Way of Horus, working in the Walls
of the Ruler, a mudbrick fortress through
which many Asiatics make their way
for commerce or as royal messengers.
It's in that caravansary where I
picked up your tongue and many more besides,
and from which I set out to mine these hills—
an unwise expedition, you'd agree."

The ones now clinging to his every word
had not expected such a treasure trove
of strange remembrances within his breast,
inspecting his exotic articles
while he defined what 'hippo,' 'crocodile,'
and 'Asiatic' meant in great detail.
Attempting to convince them of the Nile's
perennial deluge, Ameni drank
and supped with them as if an honored guest.

As moon succeeded moon, adversities
compounded for the Seir highlanders.
Those having left to truck and traffic in
the winnings of the raid had not returned

while those who plumbed the unforgiving earth
hit bedrock, watercourses snubbing them.
From dawn to dusk the Goddess of the Sun
slow-roasted stringy herds of sheep and goats,
her glutinous desires insatiable.
Though far more patient than the average folk,
acquainted with the desert's challenges
and unified by common poverty,
the Shasu now had cause for discontent,
a shared affection growing in the caves.
Nor were they ignoramuses, aware
that every outcome has its origins
in mortal or divine purposiveness,
a fact provoking them to speculate
and root about for causes of their curse.

No king who hides away within the walls
of his majestic home, the Shasu chief
could sense his people's struggles, sharing them.
A native woman and her child had died
the night before in labor, an event
now bearing down upon his need to act.
At twilight while alone inside his delve,
the leader welcomed Kirta who brought food
and drink to him. The chieftain questioned him,
"Thank you, my friend. Can I confide in you?
You were an elder once, is this not so?
You strike me as a knowledgeable man.
Of course, you don't know what our life was like
before you and your people came to us,
but we have never suffered times like these.
Our livestock plumped themselves and slept at ease,
the forenoon dew relieved our thirst, our raids
were prosperous, and I possessed a child

whose radiance competed with Astarte.
I pledged to take your people in if you
transferred all loyalty to me, and so
you have, yet I cannot but help perceive
your coming as a curse upon this land.
Marauded in the dark of night, you scaped
with little more than fear and your own names.
But think now: Could your people have been stained
in any way, transmitting sinfulness
of some sort to our mountains unawares?"

His interlocutor looked round to check
that they were still alone and sidled up
to him, divulging worries of like mind,
"Just rulers like yourself can't overlook
grave matters like the ones of which you speak.
It's good that you've sought my experience
since I have weighed this matter many years.
My once-desultory hunt has become
a searching guided by real evidence,
suspicions having led to truths hard-won.
Allow me to recall to you events
pertaining to the case: Some years ago,
the elder Danel made a pact with Baal
through the Cloudrider's private couriers.
Apart from Danel I alone saw them,
and at the time I found it hard to think
that sky-borne beasts of such a monstrous form
could serve Hadad. Since then I've wisened up.
Baal's emissaries promised, on our god's
behalf, that Danel's wife (advanced in years)
would bear the man the son for which he prayed
if after sixteen years he offered up
that which he then loved more than anything.

She—Danataya—soon conceived a child
named Aqhat who now raids beside your men.

"When sixteen years had passed, we held a feast
in honor of the springtime deities
as we have always done, identical
in every way except one—Danel gave
the best he had: young bullocks, leavened bread,
fresh milk, wine, goats, and sundry other goods.
Our folk had never seen such lavishness,
nor do I think we ever will again.
Upon the rites' conclusion Danel prayed
to Baal, uplifting thanks for his great gift.
He then unwrapped a cedarn shepherd's crook
legated by his father's forefathers,
ornately etched with lore from his long line
and crowned with the head of a gnarling wolf.
Invoking Aqhat's tutelary god,
he sacrificed the heirloom to the flames.

"That very night our town was brutalized,
our people mauled and gutted in their sleep.
Apart from Shasu hospitality
no blessings have befallen us since then;
instead, divine connivances assault
us, spelling ruin for this settlement.
And each night I reask myself how we
have come to rankle gods so long appeased
when last night truth revealed itself to me:
The judge's immolation went awry,
not in intent but content, don't you see?
The gods are just, demanding like for like,
but his oblation lacked equality.
The dumbest peddler knows a shepherd's staff

amounts to nothing like a living heir.
The Cloudrider asked Danel not for his
most precious What, but for a certain Who."

The grimness of the graybeard's reckoning
weighed down upon Sharelli's father's face.
Continued drought meant famine, penury,
and thievery—Death's faithful forerunners.
Dispatching Kirta to assemble men
of prominence, including Ahiram,
the chieftain sat amongst them, seeking their
advice, disposing of irrelevant
additions and considering their words
till a consensus had united them.
The leader sent for Danel who appeared
before the group, just having watched his son
outwork his overbearing drillmaster.
With pity harnessed by a firm resolve,
the holder of the judge's loyalty
adjudicated Danel's penalty
in full view of the gathered elderman.
As Aqhat's father fell upon his knees
and impetrated him between hard sobs,
two elders justified their reasoning
to Danel though he couldn't hear a thing,
oppressed by how they thought to reconcile
themselves to Baal and by guilt's callous noose.

The rumor of a ritual to call
down rains sped through the ridgetop settlement,
exciting everyone and prompting them
to wash and garb themselves appositely.
Night fell. When time it came a man approached
the caves and blew his solemn horn to lead

the people to a sacrosanct plateau,
the desert's Altar of the Highmost Ones.
Ameni trailed the shambling denizens
with Aqhat and Gabbar, the three of whom
assisted elderwomen up the slope,
arriving at the peak where warriors
encircled men in robes of waxen-gray—
the Shasu elders standing in a file.
Despite his liminal positioning,
the Son of Danel saw his father's pride
of place by Ahiram and Kirta, glad
to see their once-suspicious hosts had found
it in their hearts to welcome eldermen
of foreign origins and lifeways as
coequal servants of the living gods.
He smiled upon his father who perspired
from the steep climb and whose face shone pale
beneath the light of the moon and the stars.

Examining the faithful, Aqhat asked
Gabbar if Pugat planned to join them there,
to which his friend confessed his ignorance.
Into two halves the line of elders clove,
the Shasu leader gliding through the seam.
He wore a priestly cope and painted face,
proclaiming to the eager multitude,
"Good friends, we gather here to please the gods.
Of late we have refused to recognize
that which, in common, we well understand,
afraid to wake a beast by naming him.
But let us not deny what we all know:
We're cursed! But I, consulting with the wise
who read heraldic signs, shall purify
us all from our unwanted, baneful blotch.

Long ago, Baal demanded an exchange,
the binding terms of which have been infringed.
This sin, whose consequences shall not cease
until the Bull receives his recompense,
must be atoned for on this very night.
Thus shall we be restored and sanctified."

The mass of people cheered. The leader turned
and motioned to a costumed acolyte.
Forth from the warriors' periphery
the servant led a girl caparisoned
in garmenture befitting of a queen,
her tunic Surrian in undertone,
its foreside decorated with gilt bolts
of lightning over emerald meadowlands.
She gazed up, showing that her mouth was sealed,
her hands tied round her back with hempen rope.
All watched as Pugat maundered into view.
Enraged, Aqhat and Gabbar pushed their way
between the compact cultists, halted by
the warriors with whom they'd trained and fought.
Outpouring water onto Pugat's head
the Shasu leader purified the girl
and summoned Baal as witness to their faith.
Now Danel doddered toward his blossoming
and dew-stained flower, pruning knife in hand,
convulsed by horrors heretofore unguessed.
His eyes met hers, and then he said to her,
"My light, I love you far more than myself.
Forgive my grave impieties and rest
with Mother in the Place where we shall meet."

So saying, Danel slit her throat, her blood
caught in a bowl held by the ministrant

as she beheld the melancholy stares
of Aqhat and Gabbar before her life
receded steadily—as when night-tides
retreat to the abysm whence they rose.
Two servitors propped Danel as he fell.
The Shasu chieftain gazed upon the stars
and prayed, pouring the blood on Danel's head.
Retreating to a nearby chamber hewn
within the plateau's crust, the celebrant
entombed the girl upon her side, her arms
around her knees, surrounding her with loaves
of bread, a spear, and earthen jugs of wine
to ease her netherworldly pilgrimage.
Those gathered watched and chanted hymns
save Aqhat and his friends who pulled their hair
in utter agony and disbelief.

Young men began to cover Pugat's corpse
with dark earth, heap by heap, and when they tamped
the last bit down, the desert took a breath,
inhaling wind as if returned to life.
Before long, hosts of cloudbanks filled the sky,
arising from the West like billowing
haboobs kicked up by horse-drawn chariots
who thunder toward their enemy en masse.
The Shasu folk stood overawed, transfixed
by hope and fear as the black clouds approached.
Soon some began to shout and lift up prayers
as the stormclouds closed in, the people's cries
intensifying till their tears admixed
with downpours as no desert's ever drunk.
Beside if not beyond themselves, the men
and women stumbled forthright home for jars
in which to capture Baal's beneficence.

Gabbar collapsed, his head between his hands,
while Aqhat stood immutable and dumb,
an unformed metal on an anvil's face.
Bright flauchts of garish lightning veined across
the welkin, heating Aqhat's rugged jaw
while gusts as from a mammoth bellows fanned
the flame that glowered deep within his bones.
Defiance raised his rain-soaked head, his sharp
eyes hissing at the maelstrom while his core
redounded with transforming hammer-strokes.

The raging storm continued through the night
as waterways carved channels where they willed,
the smaller runnels joining greater ones.
When Shahar's wakening dispersed the rack,
five Shasu men pursued the draining rills
into a valley where, to their surprise,
they lighted on a sinkhole newly formed.
When one let fall a stone to plumb its depths
a splash responded, signaling a well.
Now rushing back to tell their kin, they saw
their traders had returned with livestock, food,
and drink by cartloads, beaming at their haul.
Spontaneous festivities commenced,
the hillpeople assured their snakebit days
had ended, raising shouts of gratitude
while dancing, singing, and imbibing wine.
But Danel hid himself. Like trampled chaff
he lay upon a cave-floor, riven, sere.

Aqhat and Gabbar mourned their murdered love.
Unable to communicate their pangs,
the two sat silently by Pugat's grave
till words refilled their breasts, the revelry

below becoming utmost loathe to them.
Addressing Gabbar, Pugat's sibling said,
"My malice knows no bounds, my love respects
no bonds—save those which bind me to yourself
and to the women whom my gods and kin
have wrenched from me in their insanity.
What's happened to this world? Has it gone mad?
Or does our grief exhaust and madden us?
In either case, we cannot dwell among
our opposite with any hope of peace.
Though scenes of slaughter play before my heart,
I hear my sister's counsel to avoid
those impulses that quickly foil themselves.
It's time I heeded her—perhaps too late.
But to what end? Where has she gone, and has
her shade found rest of any kind, or does
she roam about the desert, lost, morose?
We have but one alternative, a path
she recommended when our mothers died:
There lives a Necromancer deep within
a northern mountain's innards, so they say,
a peerless conduit of lost Rephaim.
Tonight I leave to seek his tutelage.
The journey will be dangerous, and while
I wish to have you by my side, I won't
persuade you to break oath or risk your life."

Thus Aqhat. Gabbar made reply at once,
"You've never left my side, nor have I yours.
Why should the future differ just because
we've yet to see how it will menace us?
Should I remain with happy idiots
who gloat over their evil victories,
imagining how I might take revenge

against the dogs who've killed the ones I love,
I would become a monster through and through.
Tonight we venture north. If Pugat wished
you seek this Necromancer in the hills,
let's not delay but make good her request.
I'll be your sword and shield, and you'll be mine."

When all had fallen fast asleep that night,
the two companions stole back to the caves
to pack provisions: skins of water, bread,
dried meats, and vegetables, enfastening
new sandals to their feet and grabbing spears—
one falling to the ground with a loud clank,
awakening a girl whom Gabbar tucked
back in and reassured that all was well.
Aqhat slung Kothar's gifts around his back
and sheathed a knife within his cincture's side.
Propelled by wrath, allured by desperate hopes,
they fled the Seir bluffs along a berm
of sinuous configuration down
into the hollows where no light survived
whereat they lit their torches, marching north
until they reached the Highway of the King,
notorious for arrant banditry.

The God-Fearing One of the Harnemite,
the Hallowed Man of Rapiu awoke
the next day, having won the mountaineers'
respect for bringing off what they could not.
But Rumor whispered into Danel's ear,
apprising him of Gabbar and his son's
nocturnal larceny and running-off.
He knew himself to be their cause of flight.
Now that they'd broken from the Shasu tribe

without endorsement, they'd be hunted down
by native warriors or beasts of prey
at best, or finished by the wild at worst.
Deserting thieves could not be reconciled
with those who cherished honest constancy.
And so, without his wife, without his girl,
without the son he'd prayed for all his life,
adjudging himself cursed forevermore,
the elder wandered through the wasteland's heat
until he lighted on his chosen place,
ascending an acclivity of stone
that towered six and sixty fathoms high
from which to scan the widespread barrenness,
and from its outcrop Danel cast himself.

Book VII

Ilisha! Surely you have more to tell,
Supernal Herald, you who entertain
the gods on Lel and Zaphon but who
have condescended from those holy heights
to fill our hearts with wisdom and with song.
Accept these cordials we libate for you
to coat your wearied throat and ease your mind.
Recall to us those things transpiring next.

Beneath a sky whose gloaming never wanes,
Anat perched on a looming palisade
that overlooked a hundred thousand leagues
of swarthy mountains, moors, and watersheds.
The vastness teemed with living death betrayed
by quarriers who clobbered baetyli
that had descended from the Underworld's
dark vault before the First Wars had begun.
With whips the dead flogged coffled hircine beasts
to haul extracted wagonloads of ore
to smelters and unworldly blacksmithies
who midst the giant foundries' molten ghylls
and with the stricken anvil's clangoring
cold-forged the iron into sturdy greaves,
curved swords, and felloes for swift chariots
while casting javelins fourteen-forearms long.
Near cantonments of carven rock, forgefires
afforded light for pale Rephaim who fought
each other, practicing the arts of war,
impassioned with new purpose in a place

where meaningfulness oft absconds itself
and where cooperation's not the norm.

Anat gave order to the Underworld,
providing its Rephaim new means of death
by playing to their strengths, provoking them
to join her for a chance to have their share
in blood spoils—fluid lacking in this realm.
How many men have died since Time was born?
Who, having had their breath expire, would not
forego their tenebrous and tenuous
existence for one little taste of life,
the faintest scent of which can flood a soul
with memories alive and well?
This number joined Anat—no questions asked.
Chthonic creatures rallied to her cause.
Her host comprised great armies that were slain
on earth and disremembered champions
as well—Mot having equalized the two.
Before black strongholds generations trained
their shieldbearers, brigaded once again—
a second shot for winners and losers.
But ordinary shades enlisted too,
for who could be afraid to lose their death?
Anat refused no one's support and put
to work eons of dormant skills just like
a queen's high expectations shape her hive.

Beside her, towering above her head,
stood Og, last of the giants' ancient race,
Anat's head general and substitute
should she be granted leave of Mot's domain.
They both beheld the churning industry

below and swelled with procreative pride
as Mot the King of Wraiths approached them both
and grinned with pleasure at their efforts' fruits.
In time Anat addressed the Lord of Rot,
"Your Eminence, the horde has now matured,
attaining to a self-sustaining form.
Cascading hierarchies know their place
and whom without ado they must obey.
The world of preparation and travail
that lies beneath your feet can only grow
in strength and number, wholly nourished by
their bread of clay and muddy runoff drink.
Meet Og. I've groomed him in the government
and oversight of all activity,
of every officer and motherlode
of iron ore your miners excavate.
Not much escapes his sight—or would dare try.
Now go ahead. Assay what's yours by right."

Like a baboon Mot bared his teeth—perturbed,
excited, and protective of his realm.
He looked to Og and loosed a clicking growl
informing him to goad the swarming mass.
Og blew a giant caprine horn and hurled
an order in an unknown tongue to all
below, at which the muss of clattering
and clobbering ground to a frozen halt.
In unison the dead stood to in rows,
black chariots behind the legioned throng,
as if Og had becalmed a storm that raged
against a port, reorchestrating ships
that companies had given up for lost.
Together every throated animal

upsent a shout that shook the palisade
and echoed to the Netherworld's far end,
disturbing crows on distant mountaintops.

Mot placed his taloned hand upon Anat
then turned to leave as Horon took his stead,
the ruler's mouthpiece uttering these words,
"Your work has pleased the emperor, Anat.
He bids you stay in order to improve
your handicraft, accomplishing still more
than you've already done—achieving fame
commensurate with your proficiencies.
Yet he is just, and though he fails to grasp
why you love lesser gods like Baal Hadad,
Mot won't transgress your prearranged accord.
From the Below I'll transport you, but know
that long as Mot shall reign you're welcome here."

The goddess thanked him, telling Horon she'd
neglected necessary deeds above
which summoned her, yet promised offerings
to Mot and all his henchman in due course.
Anat and Og locked arms while taking leave
in recognition of the bond they'd formed.
Descending from the precipice, the two
immortals mounted mammoth destriers
whose nostrils snorted smoke, ascending grots
lit only by their torchlight, bypassing
gateways and fording snake-infested streams
that rippled underneath the dusky air.
They wended for a long, uncertain time
until they came to Targuziza's mouth,
diverging with a mutual respect.

The Goddess of War longed to hold Hadad,
yet vengeance got the better of her needs.
With murder of her mother on her mind
she raced for Lel, arriving at its base
and hiking its northeastern forestland
ere escalading up a sheer couloir,
exploring entryways the lot of which
turned out to be dead-ended dens of stone.
At last she found a smallish opening
that burrowed deep inside the high massif,
pursuing its contorted tunnels till
she reached a hypogeum carved in rock.
She pried into a secret passageway
that granted access to El's residence
where her inconstant coconspirator
Sleep had already overtaken all.
The Goddess of the Hunt sought Athirat.
Closed doors presented her with morbid hopes,
but vacant thither-sides gave them the lie.

Frustration boiled the ichor in her spleen
as she drew near the library, inside
of which she found a tablet yet unbaked.
Inscribed on it were local toponyms.
She pondered it, then grasped that it contained
the names of places where they'd searched for her,
a revelation filling her with pride.
Footfall disrupted her unriddling.
The goddess hid beneath a table as
a pair of Elsh's scouts, just back from work,
approached and made their marks upon the clay.
The goddess reeled at scaring them to death,
deciding otherwise as one scout said,
"I doubt we'll ever find her. We have searched

Damascus and Irqata, Ashkelon
and Yursa, leaving not a stone unturned.
Suppose she's gone for good. What then? Who will
devise our stratagems and guide the Lord?
No beauty—not excluding Shataqat—
could fill her seat in looks or intellect.
No goddess supersedes the Lioness."

Two fire-demons fought within her breast,
the first one fueled by hatred for these men,
the second spurred by chafe for Athirat.
In time, the latter proved victorious,
and so she didn't disembowel the guards,
preferring that her presence go unknown.
Once they had gone, Anat climbed from the floor
and took the vial of drench she'd brought with her,
deliberating on its usefulness
since Athirat was nowhere to be found.
She searched her memory then lit upon
a truly satisfying supplement
to a fulfilling vengeance which must wait.
With leashes and raw meat she scoured Lel.

Upon their stallions, Baal the Conqueror
and a matured Tushratta marched across
the silvery Euphrates' eastern plains
with Zaphon's well-accoutered legions lined
in perfect symmetry not far behind.
The infantry's bronze sheaths and baldrics clanked;
warhorses' hooves beat down upon the earth;
and spears held vertically swayed like a vast,
deracinated reedbed on the move.
Behind Tushratta rode a woman who
looked after Taduhepa, nine years old,

the daughter whom Astarte had given him
for his cooperation with the gods.
Deciding that his epigone had been
sufficiently prepared for governing
his warranted demesne, Baal rode with him
in order to fulfill his covenant.
By now that empire's scouts detected them,
relaying word to the seditious king—
Uthi—who readied chariots and troops
for the inevitable war to come.
But he did not rush recklessly to meet
his foes in unfought field, preferring walls
with keen-eyed archers, waiting patiently.

Along the Khabur's riverbanks Baal camped,
well out of Washukanni's arrowshot.
Tushratta and his tutelary god
rode for the capital, arriving at
a riverplain before the Western Gate
where two of Uthi's generals approached,
the brawnier of whom Tushratta knew
to be one of his father's former guards,
Mush-teya—one time trusted for his sword.
Baal formally indicted Uthi thus,
"The Storm God and Shuttarna's Living Son
hereby declare war on the Scepter Thief,
Uthi the Treacherous, who by his deeds
unleashes chaos in and well-beyond
Mitanni's proper sphere of influence.
By means of villainous conspiracies,
the traitor and his lickspittles arranged
and carried out a most unlawful coup,
decapitating Artashumara
as he was poised to take his father's seat.

Such bloodletters and serpents suffocate
an empire yearning for enfranchisement.
If Uthi and his men refuse to cede
what they have stolen, facing punishment
for unjust crimes, then we shall war with them.
Surrender by the dawn or meet your fate.
We call upon Mitanni's gods to leave
the city and abandon those at fault,
as we've no qualms with righteous deities.
Listen! Hudena, Eya, Nubadig,
Timegi, Keldi, Hebat—all you gods—
Attabi, Pidadaphi, and Talan—
desert Mitanni's wrongful throne-warmers!
Thus speak Tushratta and the Cloudrider."

Shuttarna's heir spit at the traitor's sight,
returning to the camp beside Hadad,
dismounting to commence the rites of war.
Baal sat upon a makeshift throne for trips
abroad, his protégé at his right hand.
The war-priest then appeared before them, troops
amassing round them as ten servitors
led tethered pigs into the open space.
He raised his arms. The din came to a halt.
With intonations that empowered all
he praised Tushratta and the tauromorph.
The war-priest next outheld a cruse of clay.
Inscribed upon it was the traitor's name.
He then removed a offertory blade
and drained the porkers' lives into the jug.
Unleashing imprecations in the air,
accursing Uthi for his sinfulness
and promising reprisals come daybreak,
he smashed the amphora upon a stone,

the blood disploding from within before
it soaked the ground amidst the army's cheers.
The drudges holding lowest rank then cleaned
and cooked the meat, the choicest cuts of which
were offered to the leaders of the host,
the generals allowed the next-best hunks
while soldiers rationed the unwanted scraps.

Came the dawn, Uthi failing to renounce
his arrogation of Mitanni's crown
and thereby daring Baal to keep his word.
Earthshaking lines of Zaphon's infantry
took to the riverplain succeeded by
a fleet of chariots ready to roll,
the skin of every soldier purified
with lustral waters from the Khabur's flow.
And yet they met no enemy upon
the battlefield, for Uthi knew of their
approach and mustered resources to last
two years, ingathering the populace
beyond the capital's perimeter.
The king's array stood ready for a siege:
His massive gates had been refortified;
proficient bowmen hawkeyed every swath
of sward from high atop their parapets;
too young to fight, small boys ran news and food
to soldiers who patrolled the city streets;
and high-stacked boulders lined the battlements
in order to deter brash escalades.

Astride his courser at Hadad's right hand,
Tushratta begged to signal the attack.
They hadn't marched so far to falter now.
Baal stayed him, frustrating his battle-thirst.

The Conqueror then closed his eyes and peered
within his breast, inhaling through his nose
and elevating his almighty arms.
Over the city thunderheads amassed,
and when with his spear Baal impaled the earth
white bolts erupted from the firmament,
emblazing wooden rooftops ere the clouds
unleashed their unexpected fusillades
of hailstones—ice and fire joining sides.
Chaos ensued as residents were forced
to choose between the battery without
and sheltering in ovens filled with smoke.
Tushratta and Baal's coastlanders-in-arms
exulted in the easy victory
as Uthi scrambled to revise his plan.
His panicked army now aligned itself
beyond the wall—half-ready to make war.
Despite the hailstorm's onslaught, Uthi's men
still rivaled Baal's in number and in strength.
Soon the Usurper took his place in front
whereat Baal plucked his spear, the storm becalmed,
and reappropriated all the force
which he'd expended in his first assault.

Ballistic, Uthi charged his multitudes
to guard their birthdom from brute Westerners
who shunned the long-established codes of war,
commanding them to take no prisoners
and leading them against their enemies.
Baal likewise gave the signal, followed by
Tushratta and the first wave's soldiery.
Discordant squalls of war were first to clash
as through the glaucous clouds protrusive beams
relayed the battle-scenes to Shapshu's eyes.

Appealing to Ashtabi or Anat,
great marksmen shot their arrows from the rear.
Just as a boy who walks a riverbed
attempts to trident huddled shoals of fish,
far likelier to strike than miss, so too
those shooters loosed their arrows into crowds.
Anon the hoven pikes of foremost lines
hit home, the vanguards clashing head-to-head
and hand-to-hand with swords and oxhide shields.

One Talmiyanu, a recruit of Baal,
had plowed his bract-shaped lancehead through a foe's
ribcage, unable to dislodge the point.
A man from Ugarit, the warrior
incurred a catena of damning debts
the day an accident reduced his home
to ash, and so he turned his farmer's knack
away from thankless haymaking and cursed
the prospect of his family's indigence.
Thus Talmiyanu joined the Longhorned's troops,
collecting pillage for his children's sake.
Charging, his spear poised on his clavicle,
a man of equal strength named Zita ran
toward Talmiyanu, eager to relieve
the foreign farmer of his current job.
A homeless boy reared by the alleyways
of Washukanni, Zita made a life
by filching fruit and bread from market stalls.
One day a vendor caught and drubbed the boy,
yet Zita stood his ground and boxed the man
with god-given dexterity and speed
as passersby took in the spectacle.
When King Shuttarna's guards broke through the crowd
they saw they'd come too late, for Zita'd knocked

the wits out of his peddling counterpart.
They captured Zita, planning to immure
the guttersnipe, but, seeing how he'd fought,
enrolled him in the army's lower ranks.

The one-time pauper heaved his heavy spear
for Talmiyanu's chest, but the old man
employed his shield, deflecting Zita's shaft
and redirecting its trajectory
to hamstring an offensive Hurrian.
Abandoning his spear, the coastlander
unsheathed his sword, and Zita mimicked him,
the latter striking first but blocked aside,
a swift riposte outjutting from behind
the plowman's shield and grazing Zita's helm.
It stunned him yet the soldier went unharmed.
Now Talmiyanu feinted to the left
and Zita took the bait, his corselet torn
by Talmiyanu's onset—falling to the ground.
Baal's servant lunged in for the final strike
as Zita flung a heap of detritus
into his eyes, a recourse giving him
a hairbreadth moment to decapitate
and leave the man, forgetting him just like
a harvest worker scythes and bundles sheaves,
no sooner done with one than to the next.

Nearby, Pizziya and his firstborn son
Tubbenu plied the instrument of their
descendants' handicraft—the forester's
large fenestrated ax—but for new ends.
Empires encroached upon their boreal
domain of late, expropriating land
and wood with no compensatory plan.

New colonists uprooted sacred trees
unmeant for lumber, firewood, and troughs,
disparaging the holy timberland,
devaluing the fruit of laborers.
A man can only tolerate so much.
Pizziya nudged Tubennu's reticence
to join Baal's efforts till his scion caved,
both son and father warring for the Bull
now, hoping to reclaim their way of life.
Upon them Puhi-Shenni rushed beside
his firstborn Tehip-tilla, out for blood,
the younger pining after war-renown,
inspired by Kumarbi's wide repute.
The smithy Puhi-Shenni tried to talk
some sense into the boy, explaining that
their place was by the anvil, with the forge.
When word of troops approaching from the West
hit home, however, Puhi-Shenni gave
into his son's ideas, making sure
to craft a mace for each of them so that
should war come, they would be the best bedight.

Undaunted by the gore-drenched earth and screams
of those whose organs saw the light of day,
a brazen Tehip-tilla ranged midfield,
now sizing up Tubbenu whose
ax paid men's passage to the afterlife.
Sped on by thoughts of grandiosity,
Tehip-tilla applied his massive mace
against Tubbenu who with outspread grip
diverted it and swung for the man's legs
as Tehip-tilla cleared the singing miss.
Tubbenu then let fall a log-splitter,
his foeman's shield of collocated hides

and bronze dirempt, the ax's bit dug deep
into his arm, enjoying marrow, blood.
Right when the woodsman tried to tug his ax
away his enemy pulled just as hard
and helmbutted him, knocking him aground.

Although like many men who fight with rage
requicken just as much from fearfulness
as by new triumphs—when Pizziya saw
the savagery of Tehip-tilla's blow
he rushed on him with animosity,
berserkly hacking hapless busybodies.
By this point Tehip-tilla had acquired
a new shield from a lifeless lump nearby
and used it to impede the lumberman.
The high-pitched stridency of mace-on-ax
rang through the air as like a raving fiend
Pizziya swung with forceful downward strokes,
repeating his attack in synchrony,
creating rhythmic order out of rage.
Upon what would have been his tenth assault,
he disrupted the pattern:
When Tehip-tilla braced for the assault,
his shield raised overhead, he blocked his eyes
but not the ax right as Pizziya halved
the man and strode between his roots and trunk
as Hittites do a sacrificial horse.
Late-coming Puhi-Shenni struck his son's
annihilator, killing him in turn.
The blear-eyed bronzesmith gaped upon his son.
Much like the midday shadow of a tree
rejoins its bulk, Tubbenu's shade returned
to him enough to throw his hook-beaked ax

and thereby aid the father to his knees
ere hooves dispatched Tubbenu's clinging ghost.

Those hooves belonged to Baal's black destrier
who roamed the battlefront for challengers.
With Driver firm in hand Baal smote those bold
enough to cast a fleeting look his way,
not least of whom were Halu-shenni's men,
Ar-tidi's outfit, and the sizeable
platoon encharged to Akip-tashenni.
Invigorated by his killing sprees,
he only wished Anat fought at his side
to witness just how much he'd learned from her.
Tushratta's training also served him well,
for while he bore contusions and deep wounds,
he rallied roughshod over those who chose
to fight against their destined emperor.
While countless dead from both sides overstrew
the proving ground, the scales of war seemed tipped
in favor of the allies of Hadad.

Atop a distant battlement a file
of ovine horns let loose their deep-set brools,
at which a sortie of swift chariots
emerged, preparing to outflank Baal's troops.
Astride his mount, King Uthi grinned at his
maneuver—having saved the best for last.
The Conqueror obliged his infantry
to disengage and fall back. All obeyed.
War-cars and shieldbearers alike turned tail,
retreating headlong toward the Khabur's banks.
At length they stopped and turned to face their fate,
blockaded by the river's breadth and depth.

But that which seemed a grave impediment
to mortal vision showed itself to Baal
as one more rearguard now abandoned by
its riverine protectress—gone for good.
As Uthi's men-at-arms gained ground full-speed,
the taste of victory upon their tongues,
Hadad dismounted, wading to his waist.
With measured movement he turned round and took
a knee, his eyes closed, murmuring those spells
determined and possessed by gods alone.
Above his head, and not without much strain,
he hoisted up the stream, a sapphire tinge
imbuing the erect hairs of his arms.
Hadad now hurled the water through the air
with gale-force, every droplet cold-snapping
into sharp barbs of hoarfrost, puncturing
and exiting Mitanni's foremost men.
The high-speed chariots rigidified
and hearts of foot soldiers congealed with rime—
whole rows of swordsmen crystallized in place.

As hikers in the Kizzuwatnan peaks
hole up beneath a cornice to protect
themselves from icy winds, so Uthi ducked
and cowered underneath a cambered row
of battle-hardened Hurrians-in-arms.
When Uthi made to flee and save his life,
Tushratta ran him down as Baal's recruits
uplifted cheers, their armaments held high.
Tushratta captived Uthi in full stride,
enfastening a rope around his neck,
his wrists securely bound behind his waist.
Victorious at last—so too remiss
to squander long-lost time upon his throne—

Tushratta dragged his chattel through the gates
of Washukanni to a central square
while summoning the city's citizens
into the twilight, promising no harm
would come to those at his investiture.
The bravest (or the ones with least to lose)
approached the rebel's place of reckoning,
inquisitive pariahs following
the devotees of curiosity.
Atop a platform centered in the square
Tushratta stood above his prisoner,
condemning him for murdering the prince
Artashumara, King Shuttarna's son
and brother of the prince before him now.
Baal's right hand offered Uthi parting words.

While kneeling, Uthi raised his eyes and said,
"You think you're ready to be king, to lead?
It's true, I killed your brother. He'd have made
an awful king, a despot like your dad—
a truth which no one gainsays in their heart.
But while unfit, he wasn't dumb like you.
You think I acted of my own accord
with some cabal, I'd guess. What foolishness!
Who stood to gain the most from his demise?
Not me. Not some imagined coterie.
Your brother's offing was an outside job.
Who needed to emplace a guarantor
of ceased incursions into northern lands,
the only goal that drove your family line?
King Tudhaliya, Second of His Name
and Hatti's king paid for my services.
With him I fostered new concurrences
to benefit Mitanni in the end.

And now, insensibly, you've broken these
accords, destabilizing three empires'
relations, whining over legacy
just after slaying your own countrymen.
Oh, what inaugural stupidity!"

Mitanni's traitor having overpassed
the time allotted him, Tushratta smote
him, splattering his brains onto the street,
thus ending his pretended sovereignty
and forecasting a telltale warning sign.
Baal's mercenaries roared. Tushratta smiled.
Approaching his trainee, Baal said to him,
"Congratulations to Mitanni's king.
You fought well. And I must commend the nerve
and fortitude with which you led your men.
There will be time for celebrations soon.
But we must first attend to Uthi's words,
for though he was an enemy of ours
and morally corrupted from without,
intending his confession as a curse,
his revelations have utility.
Lend me your ear: Amenhotep will not
be pleased to find that one of his longtime
alliances should prove so volatile.
Send Taduhepa to the pharaoh as
a gift and symbol of your good intent,
for he is predisposed to foreign brides.
Next, bury every fallen legionnaire
regardless of the side for which they fought.
Since you are Washukanni's king, those men
we killed have families now in need of you.
Hence treat their kinsmen well, or you'll incite

a riot long before the morrow dawns.
Now, cleanse yourself and rule as you've been trained."

Baal's counsel that he ship his daughter off
dejected him, for though he knew that such
a time might come, that it should manifest
upon his first day's rule afflicted him.
Tushratta and Hadad then cleansed themselves
and shared drink to commemorate their bond,
their soldiers clearing out the dais-room,
ensuring that Tushratta's home was safe.
In course of time, well-rested from the war,
Baal rounded up his men to journey home.
Despite persistent wounds, the knowledge that
one's cheated death and won a heap of spoils
goes a long way to spiriting the troops.
They plodded over endless pediplains
and bister steppes, footsloshing through cool streams.
The days were drab. The nights were dull and black.
Excited for their billet-beds as well
as for the feasts that sealed their victory,
they shouted when Mount Zaphon rose to view.

Fatigued, Baal entered through his palace gates.
Attendants rushed to tend his needs, but he
dismissed their meddling, heading for his room
and opening its door to find Anat
before lashed lionesses, whip in hand,
rewarding them for bowing to her will.
Baal called to her. She turned and they embraced,
the Rider on the Clouds addressing her,
"Anat, my love! Where have you been these years?
I dispatched heralds round the earth and seas

to bring you home, forever seeking you.
No matter—you are here and that's enough!
Are those the remnants of our mother's pride?
So much has come to pass since you took off.
We've just returned from Washukanni where
Tushratta sits enthroned, prepared by me
and pledged to Zaphon should we need his aid.
Mitanni's ours at last—but much remains
to set aright, for Uthi didn't work
alone but for the Hittite overlord
whose northerly domain will pose a threat
so long as it exceeds our influence.
But let's leave empirecraft for other days
and celebrate your timely homecoming
in any way you like. Just say the word."

Knowing the ancient rivalship between
her love and Mot, Anat well understood
that she could not reveal where she had been.
She made the lionesses sit and said,
"I've been away—adream with thoughts of war,
unable to enjoy its festiveness
in living breathing actuality.
So Uthi's power grab was not his own
but rather orchestrated by the North?
How generous of them! We needn't find
a pretext for waylaying Hittite lands
if Hatti gives us one preemptively.
My dutiful Sutean Warrior
has eyes on Tudhaliya's every move
and has confirmed what other scouts report:
The king's son Suppiluliuma fights
in northern backwaters, subduing clans
of Kaskan braemen with his father's troops.

With such diminished numbers, we might take
the capital and overthrow its lord.
This—this is how I want to celebrate.
We sack Hattusa with Tushratta's aid.
Abihumbaba shall be notified,
allowing us to pass at your behest.
Tomorrow we inform our rank and file,
conveying word to Washukanni's crown."
Taken aback by her desires—although
he should have guessed them—Baal obeyed her wish,
for what things won't one do from ardent love?

Residing in an unassuming yet
commodious abode along the coast
which Qodesh had prepared her, Laeya lived
a happy, uneventful human life,
looked after by a live-in maidservant
named Eliawa paid in monthly gold.
Qodesh had carpeted the coast with spells
whereby incised upon the hearts of each
Sidunian that Laeya came across
were fabricated memories in which
her upright father—having passed away—
bequested Laeya her inheritance,
such as her dwelling on the waterfront.
Although he'd never lived, inhabitants
would readily describe remembrances
of him—a soul averse to usury
whose ships were nothing but reliable.

In such wise Laeya hid among mere men,
relaxing, sleeping, strolling—passing time
however and whenever she saw fit.
The eons of administering Lel's

affairs beside incompetent and rude
divinities had left her leisurelorn,
a fact she scarcely recognized until
a goalless decompression bowered her,
imbuing her with time to pause and breathe—
without which Beauty often goes unseen.
Imagine melodies that soothe the soul
when fine musicians bless us with their works.
Who'd care to live without their resonance?
But should even the loveliest of songs
lack rests of varied lengths throughout their course,
the senses which had sought abandonment
therein would find themselves dissatisfied.
Just so did Laeya beautify her life
with balanced restfulness until repose
clandestinely transformed into malaise—
a metamorphosis whose origins
deserve repeating and remembering.

In days before the giants went to war,
the goddess Silence bore identical
twins, Rest and Boredom—handsome as could be
and similar in every outward way.
As they grew up, however, Rest became
his mother's favorite of the pair since he
proved far less fidgety and much less prone
to melancholy than his other half.
Boredom tried mimicking his brother (who
maintained a lightsome poise without effort)
but failed, and each setback embittered him
until he came to loathe his ownmost aims.
Mortals and gods alike came to adore
Rest as his mother had, inviting him
to dally or recline with them at home.

The god obliged them not from vanity
but from his carefree outlook on the world.
Even when messengers flew from around
the earth in order to solicit Rest,
not once did their commotion flummox him.

Demand for Rest's companionship accrued
a thousandfold each day, such that both work
and conflict dwindled far below the norm.
The gods called Strife and Labor noticed this,
incensed that he should nonchalantly spread
infectious sloth throughout their stomping grounds.
Aware of Rest's renown and knowing that
he spent less time with those he visited
(his schedule being booked), Labor and Strife
contrived a plan to put things back in place.
They sought out Boredom, purposing that he
slip unawares into the company
of those whom Rest left, imitating him
in all things till the proper time had come,
at which he'd tincture the communal jug.
To their proposal Boredom gave assent.

Within a vial the gods immixed their bane:
Strife poured in fickleness, his counterpart
immitting dosages of tedium.
They handed Boredom the insipid drink,
whereat he flew to carry out their task.
None noticed his arrival. With one drop
to unsuspecting partisans of Rest
the god effected his kin's opposite—
an itchy restiveness impelling one
to long for Strife and Labor's harnesses.
The three gods benefited equally

and so continue in their partnership
even today, at work behind the scenes.

In this way Laeya downed the threesome's draft,
and while its substance hadn't changed, she sipped
it now with mortal lips, her youthful frame
affected by the cordial in new ways.
A long-forgotten sort of restlessness
upsurged through her, possessing her desires.
An energy excited every limb
to dance or fight, but at the very least
to move, exerting its inherent strength.
One night she dreamt the next day would bring storms,
and though no cirrus could be seen, Laeya
persuaded Eliawa to begin
her errands earlier than usual
come Dawn's arousal, taking her along.
Agreeing, Eliawa brought her friend
down to Siduna's market where they laughed
and chaffered for fresh meats and vegetables.

Possessing that for which they'd erranded,
the women started home and passed a stall
with goods in high demand by women, men,
and children struck by life-destroying plague.
A huckster filled the alley with his voice,
"Come and be healed! Salvation's near at hand!
Of those here, who's forgotten Ilkuya,
this boy beside me cast beyond the walls
and left to fester as you all will be,
but who now stands before you, whole and clean?
Yes, go ahead, examine him and look
in vain for lesions, wens, and weeping wounds!
The blessèd shall not tolerate those cursed

for very long, so come and give of what
you have that you might know the hailing salve
of Shataqat, the Virgin Deity
who rectifies our grimy sinfulness.
This boy's but one of many cured by her.
Some say she's even healed the plagued who've died.
I formed and baked these votive statuettes
before you, spirited by the reborn
to leave my much-more-profitable job
to serve our new Protectress and yourselves.
But my creations shall not sit here long!"

Laeya then knit her brows and scoffed at such
a sordid scam, but as they walked back toward
their dwelling, Eliawa said to her,
"Perhaps that vendor trades in false conceits,
or maybe not, but which of us could say?
I only know that everywhere good comes
from bad and bad from good, reversals that
the deathless ones decide to bring to pass
for reasons that exceed our grasp, as when
within illusion one finds clarity,
or as one sees in honorable souls
who sometimes must dissemble truth in lies.
The sick are healed, the vigorous take ill.
All those one thought to be one's enemies
become friends, allies showing their true face.
So let us not be quick to judge, but leave
the task of justice to our distant gods."
Laeya accepted Eliawa's words
respectfully just as a mannered child
chokes nauseating nostra down in bed.
Returning home, the two prepared a meal,
delighting in the other's fellowship

as over the horizon stormclouds strode
before cold rains stampeded overhead.

One month thereafter, Laeya ambled down
Siduna's docks and found a place to sit.
A Hittite trading vessel ran downwind
this-side of the horizon, setting course
to glide into its destined mooring-point.
While distant yet, the ship seemed not to move,
a smoldering ember enkindled by
the late-day sun, now kept aglow with wind.
Observant of the gentleness with which
Shalim dipped saffron Shapshu in the sea,
from whom there shimmered flickered flecks of gold,
Laeya watched as the ship increased in size,
cooling and blackening just like a log
from which a fire can extract no more.
The crewmen took in sail and took to oars,
rowing in unison until they reached
the boat's allotted berth, at which one heaved
a coil of painter to a man who stood
upon the dock and tied it to a beam
as starboard deckhands oared their vessel's side
against the wharfage, the worn joinery
conversing with its kindred cedar hull.
In earshot of this common ritual,
Laeya looked on with half-advertent care.
The ship's strong beak secured, a gangplank thwacked
the sturdy pier as sailors took their leave
to ransack alehouses until kicked out.

The Hittite vessel's pilot disembarked
with far less gusto, two men greeting him—
the harbormaster of Egyptian birth,

the other one a weathered Hurrian.
Upon exchanging pleasantries, the man
who oversaw the quayage introduced
them ere the Hurrian made known his wish,
"I shall be brief, good man, since wine and bed
belong to you by reason and by right.
I am a go-between around these parts,
a man once calling Washukanni home.
When with my wife and daughters I had hoped
to head back for our fatherland today,
word came to us of its beleaguerment
by Baal and Prince Tushratta—now the king.
Word is he's rounded up men like myself
for questioning if not imprisonment.
Thus we cannot return but must make due
with broad-hearted Sidunian support.
If it's no imposition, I would like
to trade with you tomorrow afternoon."

The Hittite captain sighed and made reply,
"It seems not only trade unites us, friend.
I sailed down Shamri for my final time,
most fortunate to find myself abroad
when the archenemies you named attacked.
Hadad, the Dread One, and Tushratta marched
their troops through Anti-Taurus valleyways—
Humbaba's son not standing in their way.
They murdered multitudes, destructing walls,
King Tudhaliya gutted like a fish.
But count Mitanni blest if Dread Anat
did not lay siege to it as she did us,
commanding lionesses ravenous
for human flesh strapped to her chariot.
She feels no sympathy, nor does she shirk

a chance to wet the earth with excess gore.
Such carnage carried on until the king's
eponymous firstborn gave up the fight,
the spoilnapped capital pledged to the Bull.

"Meanwhile Prince Suppiluliuma fought
insurgent Kaskan renegades up north.
Although victorious in his campaigns,
ill tidings of Hattusa's massacre
and of his brother's quick surrendering
discovered him and undermined his joys.
Prince Suppiluliuma bivouacked,
deploying surreptitious outriders
into the capital to neutralize
whatever loyalists to Baal remained.
And so they did, in cloak-and-dagger style.
When Suppiluliuma came back home
he found his brother in a whorehouse, drunk,
a plushy, plump excuse for leadership.
Disgusted, Suppiluliuma slew
him, adding fratricide to urbicide,
and made a Tawananna of his wife,
Queen Henti, mother of his many sons.

"Like you I find myself a refugee.
Who knows what contacts I have left at home.
I'll trade these shipboard goods with you along
with my aquatic chariot itself.
With what I gain I shall retire here,
but let us speak tomorrow afternoon."

The men agreed. While leaving to break bread,
the thoughtful harbormaster said to them,
"As one who works within Hadad's domain,

I fear what all these wars presage for me.
Will populaces of your motherlands
so soon forget which gods and goddesses
waylaid their livestock and their legacies?
And what am I to local deities?
Will they look after me as someone born
upon this soil should vengeance sweep the land?
I shudder at the image. Knowing war's
inconstancies, however, let us treat
each other as if we were common blood,
for who knows when we'll need each other's aid."

Lel's fugitive attended to each word
of popular Akkadian they spoke,
each syllable enraging her the more.
Hadad had spurned her parting strategy,
and either he or El had made a deal
to free Anat from her imprisonment,
Mot going back upon his worthless word.
Deprived of any prescience, her own kin
incited needless pain and jeopardized
advances centuries of work had wrought
while running roughshod over her advice.
Be all that as it may, no single breach,
no swift betrayal or self-centered sin
compared to what her daughter stooped to do:
purloining her belovèd, golden pride,
enchaining and reshaping them for war,
accustoming their tongues to human flesh.
Only imbruted foes could act this way.
Her passive restiveness hereby became
procinct, detaining and examining
the images and words that flurried round
her heart with rising speed and petulance.

Book VIII

Beneath the unrelenting sun, Aqhat
and Gabbar hiked the Highway of the King,
supposing that the Shasu search parties
sent after them had given up the chase.
And so the runaways glanced backward less,
turning their thoughts toward obstacles ahead,
escaping ever further to the north
and living off the rations they had packed.
While plodding over sand and khaki loess
that crunched beneath their sandaled feet, the friends
began to speculate on where to find
the Necromancer's hidden dwelling place,
their thoughts delimited by ignorance.
From an escarpment's roof the two beheld
the great expanse before them, stretching like
a sea of stationary russet waves
immobilized amidst creation's storm,
Order and Chaos reaching a détente.

The days droned on. The days were hot and long.
The two companions rarely spoke to save
what little energy they still possessed.
On every side the heat hummed round their heads
and slowly leeched what grip their senses had
on Shapshu's wide domain before the words
within their hearts evaporated too.
Their spitless tongues were burrowed lizard trunks.
One day, when evening came, they camped beneath
a fanning wattle, relishing its shade.

Ascending a plateau's slope, Aqhat scanned
the road ahead then sat upon the ledge,
his heart depleted of excessive noise
when far below the goddess Silence showed
herself to him in pure simplicity.
Like most, he thought he'd met her many times
before, but perched upon that bluff he knew
he'd never known the deity at all.
Only a chosen few encounter her
because the babbling world misapprehends
and fears her singular propensities.
If one brings prayers to her she disappears,
and she deplores the groans of thudding bulls
whose blood bespatters altars, all in vain.
To imitation only she responds,
sometimes in kind, sometimes with wisdom's gifts.

Aqhat and Gabbar carried on at dawn,
continuing along their northern trek,
the gradual abatement of their food
and water piquing their anxiety.
The men schlepped over earth devoid of life
as nighttime overtook the reddled world.
Beneath Yarikh's dim pallor, the two men
slogged down a path which seemed to be a road
that migrants of the past had utilized,
choosing this lesser-trodden route so that
they might ward off the main road's highwaymen.
The path bisected facing outcrops like a trough
between disastrous swells in breaking seas.
Around a bend some way ahead, the men
thought they could see a fire's flickering,
progressing thitherward with cautious step.
Distinctive voices gruffer than the norm

arose in tandem with façades of orange
enshadowed by twin disembodied shapes.
The trekkers trained their eyes and pricked their ears,
a compromise in perceptivity
amounting to incaution with their path,
the which gave way beneath their heedless step
as sounds of cracking branches compassed them.
Both men cried out, descending through a mouth
with dust and marl until they hit their heads
upon the rocky floor deep down below.

Half-reattuning to the formless night,
Gabbar tried locating his fallen friend,
bright light attacking him in throbbing throes.
He felt his blood-caked hair and looked around
to find that Aqhat, like himself, now hung
within a net that dangled from a tree's
opposing arm, as if they were but fish
uphoisted as a vessel's happy haul.
Adjusting to the blazing light, they peered
between their latticed prisons to behold
two naked creatures, strong and sinewy
with limbs almost as long as they were tall,
reclining on a cookfire's other side
with sharpened sapling roasters held in hand.
Behind them on a cliff was pitched a tent
of horsehide while beside them were bestrewn
stone daggers and self-fashioned wooden bowls,
wild herbs and wineskins bursting at the seams,
among which lay the travelers' armaments.

Observing that their abductees regained
some of their senses, one of the brutes said,
"We weren't expecting visitors tonight,

but we're sure glad to have you for supper.
I'm Shegr, this is Ithm—we're the sons
of El, erstwhile protectors of all sheep
and cattle, born to guard the herding class.
Did you once think that you'd be privy to
a repast hosted by the deathless gods?
Tonight's main course is a familiar one:
aged and slow-roasted saddle cuts of kid."

They loosed wry laughs and raised their horns of wine
to one another, chugging down their lot—
or most of it—not counting the red rills
that dribbled from their chins onto their chests.
Refilling their potations, Ithm said,
"At feasts immortals typically regale
each other and their guests with ancient song
or entertaining legends spiced with myth,
and since we can't have you two looking down,
let's lighten things and put your wits to test.
Three riddles I will set before you now.
Solve them and we will cut you down at once.
Alright, let's start off with an easy one:

"I give the world its harmony,
on me all trade depends,
and though one add or take from me,
my substance knows no end.
If my reality were shunned,
you never could account
on anything or anyone
since you'd have neither sense of some
nor know your love to be the one.
My parts compete for higher spots:
Considering their lesser naught,

each other they surmount.
Search your mind, find what you espy,
and answer me this—who am I?"

Aqhat and Gabbar looked bewilderedly
at one another, at a loss for words.
But fearing for their lives, they tried to think
of a solution to the problem posed.
They listed names of gods they could recall
and tried to think of those said to be large.
How trade compared to wives they couldn't guess,
entangled and entwisted and beguiled.
In no rush, Shegr and Ithm bestowed
them ample time, attending to the fire
and making merry, munching dates and nuts.
Indignant and ashamed to die because
of some gods' stupid game, and, even worse,
to be the cause of one's best friend's demise,
Aqhat bemoaned that Ithm's riddle must
number among the sickest jokes on earth.

Amidst their festive banter Shegr paused
and stilled his brother, eyes agog behind
loose strands of long and grungy hair, now asking them,
"Did you say 'Number'? Ah, but how'd you know?
You must have cheated! Have you heard that one?
Well then, here's one that I made up myself.
Let's see, how does it go? Oh yes, that's right:

"This one's opposed to every norm
and always gets a laugh,
yet since he's not in proper form,
I'll speak on his behalf.
A constant threat to minds most keen,

perforce misunderstood,
he's friend to infants and to priests,
who know him as the much esteemed
Flummerious Flumadiddlry.
If one with luck should clear the haze,
or his skullduggery appraise,
then he takes flight for good.
Blithering jabber and blathering jibber—
gather your wits, should you be a winner!"

Those netted hung in utter disbelief.
As if a run-in with two puzzling scrags
weren't weird enough, and as if lighting on
the right solution in their first attempt
by accident weren't stranger still, now these
purveyors of conundrums doubled down.
The captives broached the whirl of words at hand.
As their discussion circled round and round,
digressing into dead-end alleyways
that bored the gods, Shegr and Ithm turned
to their cavorting, easily amused
by overflowing horns and ribaldry.
The men's thoughts raced to no avail, their hearts
once beating hope now palpitating fear.
Gabbar then wondered if there even were
an answer, or whether the trick itself
weren't just a trick, and this thought grew inside
his gut until his lips gave form to it,
dismissing the ordeal as plain nonsense.

Mid-gulp, just catching wind of Gabbar's plaint,
a flabbergasted Ithm spat his drink
onto the ground and questioned Gabbar thus,
"Did you say 'Nonsense'? Shegr, you assured

us that they wouldn't disentangle it,
yet here they are, just one more lucky guess
shy of attaining freedom undeserved!
Perhaps these men are sorcerers, or worse,
young hierarchs, so let's try something new,
a quandary unlike those posed before.
I have the paradox to do them in.
Listen, you two, and try this last one out:

"I'm one upon whom lives depend,
you need me to exist.
Though I the eyes of youths offend,
they cannot long resist,
for I'm a much-sought-after bout
who sucks out every breath.
Their hands unhandy sort me out—
my novices—who bleed and shout,
still even they to me will lout
the more adroitly they attack,
for what one gives one gets right back,
till comes a little death.
Now don't sit there and look so shy.
Let's get on with it—who am I?"

Without a second's pause, the prisoners
began to contemplate some workable
solutions to the last of their resorts.
Remembering the raid of which they'd been
a part in Shasu territory, both
recalled their skirmishes and noted that
their lives depended on successful fights,
admitting the exhilarating rush
of setting on Egyptian caravans.
However, neither Gabbar nor Aqhat

were killed on those excursions, and although
men died, they didn't fall concurrently.
His patience ebbing, Ithm prodded them
to proffer their response, to which Aqhat
confessed that they had nothing to propose.
The gods then howled delightedly and mocked
their captives' ignorant virginity
as they began preparing for their meal
by whetting knives and sharpening their spits.

Unsure of what to do yet unresigned,
Aqhat began to temporize like this,
"Before you said you were the guardians
of livestock and their herders—sanctioned by
the Father, El, to see to their good health;
but here tonight you've only raised a cup
to one another's health and livelihood.
We're goatherds having lost our droves, in fact,
returning north now that the rains have ceased,
the desert grass and shrubs all drying up.
A gang of thieves attacked us, stealing our
possessions—hence our present meager state.
And now we come to see that you were near.
Could you not hear our pleas? Or don't you care
for us like we were members of your flock?

"In youth we learned to call upon you when
in need, and so we did with much success.
Our fathers told us of your shepherd-like
protection, modeling parental love.
They said that not unlike pastoralists
you're patient yet most vigilant, all ears
for wolves and plunderers who'd dare appear
to face your walnut crooks with sharpened points.

It's said a shepherd boy in town, when he
first plied the trade out in the fields alone,
was once assailed by six gray wolves, but you
protected him, disbanding white-fanged foes.
And now it seems that you've become the wolves
yourselves, your purpose turned upon its head.
But how did this fall out? What of your flocks?"

The cut and rangy deities eyeballed
each other, knowing they need not respond,
desiring nonetheless to disabuse
the boys of tiresome inanities
ensnaring backwoodsmen and gods alike.
Before addressing Aqhat's inquiries,
Shegr first reasoned with his drunken kin,
"Ithm, the night's still young, and while I know
that you're as famished for red meat as I,
we needn't expedite our feast which, as
you've said, improves the more with well-sung lore.
So fetch the olives, bread, and fruit (which go
so well with wine in any case) so we
can do our part to teach these virgin boys
some minor truths about the world before
it passes from their sight forevermore.

"It's true, boys: One time we looked after sheep,
long-horns, and drovers but, detesting it,
we quit such work eons before your births.
Had you been born to bygone centuries
perhaps your prayers would not have fallen flat.
You see, one evening after dinnertime
we afterpartied with a visitant
who hailed from Babylon or thereabouts.
And that god told a tale we'd not forget,

a story whose interpretation soon
unbound us from illusion's throttlehold.
The tale went something like the following:

"One day the goddess Mami overlooked
creation, finding it still incomplete.
A thought then filled her breast, inviolate
and true, a word she breathed into a pinch
of clay and set upon a mountain rim.
The clump dislodged itself and tumbled down
precipitately, gathering wild grass,
small rocks, and topsoil, snowballing in size
until an angered avalanche outran
the mass, now talus-covered at the base.
Nine moons thereon, a creature clawed its way
from underneath the rubble-heap, a man
adorned with coarse black hair, his arms and legs
resembling stone, his neck that of an ox.
Although unnamed for his first eighteen years,
that wild man's called 'Enkidu' to this day.

"Enkidu the Untamed roamed over steppes
with undomesticated animals.
An aurochs and gazelle adopted him.
He relished milk from onagers and lapped
his fill of water from the clearest brooks,
delighting in wild berries from the branch
alongside animals he knew as kin.
When any fell into a hunter's trap
Enkidu would release them from the snare
or help them from the pit, refilling it.
With feral creatures he would range beyond
the hills and imitate their sundry gaits,
allowing them to lick his honied hands.

"The hunter from the city Uruk who
had set the traps and dug the pits to catch
his equine prey had now become unnerved
at his interminable mischances.
Instead of setting snares as usual,
he waited overnight and hid behind
a boulder on a nearby mountainside
to see if he might not descry the cause
of his ill fate, his failures' origins.
As dawn awoke, the huntsman roused to find
wild beeves and harts beside the waterhole,
imbibing and conserving energy.
He rubbed his eyes, amazed to catch a glimpse
of a wild man on the oasis' bank
who leaned on four limbs, slurping with his mouth,
his presence unvexatious to the rest.
Inferring what had happened to his traps,
the hunter waited till the wild man left
and crossed the treeline back into the woods,
accompanied by those who'd drunk their fill.
The trapper ran to Uruk to apprise
his friends and family as to what he'd found.

"Attaining Uruk the Euphrates' Pen,
the huntsman told the leader of the flocks—
the unmatched Gilgamesh—of what he'd seen.
The Son of Lugalbanda dropped his games,
attending closely to the huntsman's speech,
enthralled by the uniqueness of his find.
The hunter asked what they should do, to which
the herder said that he should go and find
the harlot Shamhat, bringing her unto
that distant pond from which Enkidu drank,
and, when the wild man saw her, she should doff

her garb, revealing her bare nakedness,
for only then could he be tricked to leave
his kind and come to know the ways of man.
The shepherd's interlocutor agreed.

"The hunter scoured Uruk's alehouses
until he found the slattern, telling her
of Gilgamesh's plan, a scheme which she
could not ignore, assenting to the task.
Together they departed, journeying
beyond the Sheepfold's outskirts to the haunt
in which the hunter'd seen the primal man.
They didn't wait particularly long.
Enkidu crossed the threshold of the woods
upon all fours to satisfy his thirst.
With caution Shamhat neared the creature, her
companion gaping from his hiding place.
The wild man caught her scent, his nose upraised,
his tensive vision schooled by predators
who stared at the nonresident's approach,
and when she'd come within ten steps of him,
she doffed her lacey tunic to the ground.
Enkidu studied her, inhaling her
perfume and stroking her oiled arms and legs.
She tantalized him, frustrating his touch
before rewarding it, his progress stalled,
reversed, advancing yet again as she
allured him to a mead, instructing him
in self-deferment's most exquisite pains
for seven goatish nights beneath the moon.

"When Shamhat and Enkidu reappeared,
the stallions, kine, white storks, and other beasts
misrecognized the man deprived of verve.

A new arcanum's aura circled him,
its foreignness dispersing those he'd loved
since he was now a stranger in their eyes.
Before Enkidu could decrypt their flight,
however, the impatient trapper showed
himself, inviting them to come with him.
With sounds and gestures Shamhat tried to show
her lover what the hunter had proposed,
and though he didn't understand a thing
he left with them, abandoning his home.

"They reached the Sheepfold in a couple days
and all the shepherds gathered round the brute
whose girth and bosky beard enchanted them.
Outpouring cups of copper-colored beer
fermented with brown barley loaves, the men
imbibed together, sharing spongy bread
which they declared the hallmark of their life,
the yeasty meal dissolving former fears.
Intoxication cleared their minds of chores.
That night a pair of lions and three wolves
who'd followed Shamhat and Enkidu home
beset the ewes nearby, their bleats—much like
Enkidu—anthropoid yet bestial.
Both partial to his hosts and tortured by
the screams of his four-leggèd relatives,
Enkidu bolted to deliver them,
successfully forfending all but one.
Those present were amazed, applauding him,
requesting of the man to keep their watch
so that they could recover and sleep in.
It pleased him to please them—an inkling new
to him—and so he readily complied.
At his assimilation all were pleased.

"By daybreak rumor of Enkidu's feats
had spread like yellow cattail pollen through
the air and down the inlets of a fen.
When the increasing adulations vexed
great Gilgamesh more than he could withstand
(now worrying that he would be replaced
as Uruk's bravest shepherd), he oppugned
Enkidu, challenging him to a fight,
yet since the latter understood no word
directed at him, he stood silently,
the Son of Lugalbanda taking this
as an affront, demanding that they brawl
before the city gates where all could watch,
reverifying his preponderance.
And on that destined day when Mami's craft
transgressed the Sheepfold, Gilgamesh upstirred
the people's fears and vowed their safeguarding.

"Now Gilgamesh attacked Enkidu—their
affray amounting to the latter's first
experience of daily urban life.
A vicious, cornered dog with hackles up,
Enkidu blocked the first blow dealt to him
and grabbed the brawny shoulders of the great
aggressor who in turn clung onto him.
The two opponents wrestled for their lives,
crashing through doors of pine and smashing chunks
of dried brickwork with such brutality
the earth groaned, people havening indoors
and vacating the city's public square.
For three days they unleashed their rage, and no
one intervened or knew a moment's sleep
till sapped of power both of them collapsed.

The stalemate saddened Gilgamesh who called
out for his mom and dad, but neither came.

"Having expended every bit of hate
that coursed throughout his limbs, Enkidu now
felt pity for the man bewailing so,
for Gilgamesh's pleas reminded him
of how a chick ensnared will screak for help.
As was his habit in the countryside,
Enkidu sought to aid the forlorn man,
consoling him and nuzzling cheek-to-cheek.
To Uruk's stupefaction, both men left
the city limits, having formed a bond.
The punctured pride of Gilgamesh now scabbed,
eventually returning to its past
degree of pulsating vitality.
Together at his homestead, Gilgamesh
instructed him in wordcraft, cutting off
his excess hair and trimming up his beard
as if to make a likeness of himself.
He then began to teach Enkidu how
to care for flocks as one now civilized,
employing him and tending to his needs.

"One burning afternoon, their flocks at ease,
the men disrobed and ran down to the brink
of the Euphrates, diving in to rinse
the sweat and griminess encaking them.
Far off, three goat-skinned rafts cast out their lines
and pulled aboard the river goddess' gifts.
Contented with his purified physique,
the Son of Lugalbanda lay ashore,
sunbathing in his copper clotheslessness.

The goddess Ishtar sighted him and longed
to have him, making known her inner wish.

"Addressing her entreaty, he reproved,
'Astucious Ishtar, why should we be wed?
Are you reputed for your faithfulness?
You shower us with rains so grass and grains
can grow, and then, without a second thought,
your shaduf halts and everything dries up.
You give us water and gold wheat for beer,
entasking alewives for our benefit
while cursing us with drinking's aftermath.
You taught the fisher and the fowler how
they might preserve their kills no sooner than
you smite their storehouses with lightning bolts,
reducing them to windswept trails of ash.
As if this weren't enough, you teach the young
how to beget new life, impelling them
at the same time, with more vivacity,
toward war's internecine and rotten fruits.
So no, contrasted to yourself, I'd say
the ficklest and cheatingest of wives
would strike me as devotion's paragon.
A man like me would be remiss to brook
your famed, consistent inconsistencies.'

"Infuriated, Ishtar sped her way
up through the firmament, demanding that
her father, Anu, give to her the Bull
of Heaven that she might avenge herself
on Gilgamesh for his unjust critique.
Lord Anu, god of Uruk—whose great fane
Eanna renders null those that belong

to other deathless ones—now glowered at
his daughter, chiding her discourtesy.
Quite overwhelmed by his rebuke,
Ishtar cried, tantruming tempestuous
torrents in front of the assembled gods.
He pitied her and could not bear to see
her suffer any more, so Anu changed
his last decision, granting her the Bull
to do with howsoever she saw fit.

"Without delay she sicked the Longhorn on
the city and it smashed the Stockade's walls
in search of that shepherd who dared blaspheme
and disrespect a goddess like herself.
It snorted steam that melted womenfolk
and children near the gates, interring them
within a widemouthed chasm opened by
the hoofing and earthshaking animal.
By hundreds Uruk's people tumbled down.
Enkidu heard the chaos first and rushed
to help while Gilgamesh caught up with him,
and when the first arrived on scene, the Bull
began to paw the ground with his right hoof
(which weighed that of a temple's cornerstone).
It charged, and just before it gored the man,
Enkidu leapt into the new-formed rift,
the public tomb that Heaven's Bull had made.

"The wild returning to Enkidu's veins,
diffusing through his blood, he scaled the pit
and seized the longhorn's tail, avoiding bucks,
gyrations, and attempts to skewer him.
It threw him, finally, across the street
against a plaster wall and stormed again.

Once more Enkidu sprung out of the way,
an animal contesting with his kind,
but not before its horn transpierced his thigh,
the gash exsanguinating on the earth.
Enraged beyond restraint he blitzed the Bull,
at which point Gilgamesh held to its horns
and dealt it blow upon ferocious blow.
He drew his sword of thirty minas' weight
and helve-first tossed it to his counterpart
who while his life continued pouring forth
impaled and pithed it in an ichor-spray.
A mix of triumph, wroth, and justified
relief at having made it out alive
impelled them to defame their sacrifice,
ecstatically eviscerating it.

"Amidst the paeans pealing through the streets,
Enkidu contemplated what he'd done
as vestiges of former days appeared—
of days where men and gods were not estranged,
of days without indenture or travail,
without the lies that symbols multiply.
And who had taught him how to best survive?
Who fought off beasts of prey when he was young?
None but his taurine father, kind and true.
Enkidu's legs lost strength. His head grew light.
He fainted, parting for the world of dreams:
The gods discussed what sort of punishment
befit the crime of Lugalbanda's Son
and his accomplice for their massacre.
Lord Anu said that one of them must die,
Ellil suggesting that the talus-born,
Mami's experiment, deserved such fate,
but that bold Gilgamesh be spared, for he

might still prove useful in the coming years.
Ishtar concurred and bright Shamash demurred,
but those in favor of the plan won out.
The gods unleashed a teratonic beast
like Anzu to reclaim Enkidu's life,
now exiled to Kurnugi's endless waste.

"Enkidu wakened in his friend's abode
in terror, coulees dried upon his cheeks,
recounting what his dream revealed to him,
to which his lone companion made reply,
'My friend, it's normal that one has bad dreams
succeeding mortal skirmishes akin
to that in which we proved victorious.
But all has ended, all is well, and you
need rest to ease your soul and heal your leg.
Dispel Kurnugi from your heavy breast.
I've mustered every unguent and herb
which with my prayers will put you on the mend.
Sleep soundly knowing that you are the first
to make a hecatomb with one axstroke.
The city has commissioned your reward:
a statue built with half a sar of bronze,
its pedestal cast from palladium.
Thus even when you've passed on decades hence,
the city will remember you and lay
out flowers, offerings of meat and beer
to satisfy you and Ereshkigal.
When you have gone, the cypresses will weep
for you; the myrtle copses will cry out;
the leopard and the stag will strike a truce
to mourn your loss beyond the open tracts.
But none will keep you in their heart like me.'

"His friend's condolements failed. Enkidu said,
'No cures or supplications could suffice
to safeguard me from higher powers that
would see me dead—of this I am convinced.
And what a curse such knowledge proves to be!
I used to roam the woods carefree and range
wherever I would please, at no one's beck.
I couldn't read the signs of gods or men,
oblivious to premonitions' pangs.
My gut and bevy pointed out my path.
The hunter who beguiled me for a laugh—
may he be always lacking in regard
to wealth and may his storehouse know decay!
Let all the gods unmake his livelihood.
And Shamhat, Uruk's public chariot
whom everybody rides—may she array
herself with mud, indebted to cruel men.
Would that no silver pile up in her home,
her only shade beneath the outer walls.'

"His imprecations cast, Enkidu slept,
his friend awaiting on him hand and foot.
Come dawnlight Gilgamesh sought to arouse
Enkidu, but the man would not be stirred.
A second time he gently prodded him.
He looked to heaven, asking when his friend
would rise, and shook Enkidu with more force.
Now realizing what had fallen out,
the Shepherd wailed and beat upon his chest.
In chorus with him, wild hyenas shrieked
and asses brayed, the moors and desert hills
intoning their peculiar threnodies.
The cypresses bent over. From the sun
they hid as myrtles perished by the score."

Here Shegr ceased as both gods noticed that,
although their detainees were much intrigued,
their faces wore incomprehensive looks.
Ithm imbibed another draft of wine
and wiped his beard before he said to them,
"Incredulous at such a fantasy,
we left for Uruk with our visitor,
and what do you think we discovered there?
Nothing but Gilgamesh installed as king,
the statue promised to Enkidu gone—
or, likelier still, never having been.
That day we recognized the lie we'd lived,
becoming privy to our origins.
Do you not grasp Enkidu's travesty,
that everything determining his fall
unites the two of you to gods like us?

"That wild man knew the only freedom worth
the name—a lightsome lawlessness—before
with pride and shamefulness they broke him in.
No sooner did they bring him to that cote
called Uruk, giving him too much to drink,
increasing his dependency on them,
than they enslaved him to a life of work
to rest and benefit at his expense,
applauding him that he might do their chores.
Becoming emulous of the result
of his own plotting, Gilgamesh struck out
to repossess the man outdoing him,
Enkidu changing hands from pen to pen."

The throat of Ithm knotted up, and as
he binged more wine his brother took the reins,
"Thus while a hunter has his bait and snares

and prostitutes defraud with lurid lures,
it's only fitting that the greatest ruse
that this confounding world has ever known
sprang from a shepherd's lips, returning back
to him with every unearned benefit.
For shepherds' ways prove most duplicitous
of all: Enshrouded by an aureole
of deep concern, the shepherd's thought to give
his life for kids and yearlings, looking to
their safety come what may in terms of risk
or harm accepted for their flourishing,
the quintessence of true self-sacrifice,
an image that the man himself absorbs.
But what a sham that lofty vision proves
to be, for everything a shepherd does
brings good to him and damages his flock!
Only a sheep accustomed to the knife
(the shepherd having fleeced it into trust)
relinquishes the inborn fearfulness
of dying at his hands. And so it will.
Pastoral power's bourn's to have one shorn
until the day of slaughter rears its head.
The shepherd beats the wolf at his own game:
His dogs corral the fold, but just for him.

"So what, I ask, could be so great about
a shepherd god—like either one of us?
Why should we be our father's bellwethers
or feign we want to be your caretakers?
Neither shepherds nor fawning sheep we'll be,
renouncing every domesticity
in imitation of the primal one.
We seek his spirit in the mountain pass
and underneath the cypresses, inside

abysmal depths and on the westerlies.
We neither look behind us nor ahead,
eschewing arbitrary artifice
to do whatever comes to mind without
observance of restrictions we've not made.
I'd recommend you do the same, but at
this juncture that's become impossible.
Our screed's gone long enough. It's time to feast!"

The gods took pride in having spoken well.
Although they had consumed their whole supply
of figs and nuts, yet they had much to eat,
imbibe, and ready for their crowning course.
Taking a pestle, Shegr ground up salt,
dried sumac, rosemary, and safflower,
dividing stolen aubergines by knife.
Beside him Ithm threw logs on the flames—
always the first tongues to enjoy their meal.

The runaways depended from their nets,
unsure to whom they could or should now pray.
Smoke curlicues ascended, disappeared.
The fragrance of the herbs and vegetables
beknotted their unsated appetites
as Aqhat eyed their captors with contempt,
imagining the embers flitting off
to nestle in their horsehide tarpaulin,
now fearing for his grip upon the world
because that far-off tent appeared ablaze.
He doubted what he saw till Gabbar's face
confirmed his senses hadn't come unmoored.
The firebrands set to their cookery
till Ithm—worried that Shalim had come
already though the night had just commenced—

wheeled round to find their tent engulfed in flame.
As when a mountain she-bear overhears
her cubs in dire need and heaves her bulk
their way, unleashing roars that blench the pines,
just so did Ithm race to save his home.
Reacting likewise Shegr gained his feet,
the rebels stumbling-crawling up the steep
corniche, a sotted Shegr catching hold
of Ithm who had almost plummeted.
They reached the peak and stomped and smacked the tent
like giants waging war upon the sun
to no avail, the fire's furor fanned,
the valley filled with its miasmic fumes.

The hoisted runaways gaped at the mad
affair—although by now, it must be said,
they'd reckoned on continued lunacy.
At length the tricksters managed to reduce
the flames by hurling gravel onto it,
the firelight waning down below as well,
all visibility submerged in pitch.
A moment passed, then yet another one.
Forth from the earth beside which Aqhat hung
a hefty thud broke tandem with a grunt.
He too fell down and struggled on the ground
before a dagger-wielding imminence
who with the help of Gabbar lifted him—
Ameni charging them to flee at once.
Yet Gabbar gestured toward the deities'
foodstuffs and tools, and each of them took hold
of what he could, including weaponry
of which they'd been deprived, escaping now
in fear and from a newfound love of life.

The trio sprinted northward and away
from doubled roars reverberating through
the mountain pass and closing in on them.
Each one could feel the thudding panting brutes
who gangled after them with malintent.
Like jackals Ithm and his brother sensed
the course of their delayed meal, tracking them
with the resolve of apex predators
who need good hunts to keep themselves shipshape.
The gods split up to corner the pursued,
the volume of their growling waking crags
of limestone from their deep, eonic drowse.

With ears about to bleed, her realm disturbed
by insolent cacophony, Silence
began to fume at El's sons' clamoring.
Discerning their position, motioning
her hands mysteriously, she unloosed
a spell that pierced the desert air and struck
the turbulent gods just as Shegr neared
his prey, the three of whom dove underneath
the cover of a rock's protuberance.
Approaching them, now craving uncooked meat,
Shegr called out to ascertain his kin's
location but his gullet made no sound.
He stomped his bony feet to no effect
and cried without emitting any noise.
Ithm ran round a bend amidst the black,
awaiting Shegr's customary call.
Anxiety then surged up in his heart.
Had mortals somehow done his brother in?
He shouted for his sibling voicelessly,
the gods divided by a soundless void
and groping with the senses left to them.

Dark digits searched the cavity beneath
which Aqhat, Gabbar, and Ameni hid.
Scooching away from them, they held their breath
as dirty streams of sweat ran down their brows.
Not only had the nighttime's upheaval
aroused peaks and primeval goddesses
but it had also angered shapes that creep
beneath archaic stone, like scorpions.
One skeltered toward the sheltered men to guard
its threatened lair, four pairs of armored legs
ascending the Egyptian's gooseflesh arm.
Imploring his companion not to move,
by nothing but faint starlight, Aqhat then
reached out and grasped the scorpion's arched tail
and tossed it onto Shegr's thumb whereat
it lanced the god who raised a silent squall.
He burned and bumbled, turned and tumbled till
he crashed into his brother who could sense
that something was amiss, but neither could
communicate his thoughts, so Ithm took
his kinsman's arm, retreating to their camp.

Now unimperiled, so it seemed, the men
abandoned their redoubt and gathered up
their spoils, escaping northward through the night
until they clambered up a precipice
from which to spot aggressors and to rest.
Here Aqhat asked their liberator how
he found and rescued them. Ameni said,
"I never did belong in Shasu land,
nor had I ever planned to stay with them.
For months I worked to earn their leader's trust,
for what could better serve a servant's needs
than leeway from the man who masters him?

When you two ran away, they first refused
my help in finding you, but I assured
them that I knew you better than the rest.
I thereby joined the Shasu search party.
When three long days passed by without success,
just as Fatigue and Night gave birth to Sleep,
I mimicked you and stole away from camp.
And though I am no hunter, I picked up
your trail and followed it until I saw
those monsters' fire and you two strung aloft.
Not knowing what to do, I circled round
the mountainside and set their tent ablaze,
distracting them so I could cut you down.
Where I'm from, good turns must be paid in kind.
You saved my life. I owe you nothing less,
so let us be as equals till we part."

A moistureless Levanter then announced
Lord Shahar's first intaken breath, the which
erased the footprints of the wayfellows.
Aqhat embraced Ameni, thanking him
as Shapshu's Stableboy prepared her reins.
Intoxicated by their former fugue,
impatient to keep moving, and convinced
that, somehow, somewhere, he'd experienced
this moment long ago, Gabbar upheld
a winejug he'd freebooted from the gods,
taking a pull and passing it around
ere greeting the new day with mirthful song,
"Long labor has left our feet well-worn,
these hands strained and stained as if torn.
There's naught come next but seek what's best
alike the Sun on ruddied mornes—
who on this morn our faces tans

and warms the naked ochre sand,
afore far-flung but soon high-hung,
she flies and climbs the hinterland.
Her presence she as yet betrays
with softened alpenglow displays
that reappear as we hide here—
horizon's flame to light the way.
My life she's still engendering
as we set out remembering
past good and ill now that all's still,
dawn's solitude our rendering.
The twilight's secret's yours and mine,
reminding us there comes a time
when gone are cares for life's affairs—
and all that's left's to drown in wine!"

Book IX

Rejuvenated by their god-given
comestibles in Silence's domain,
Ameni, Aqhat, and Gabbar made north
when Aqhat spoke to the Egyptian thus,
"My friend, you have a right to know our plans.
We haven't taken to our heels from fear
but venture for a Necromancer's aid,
a conjurer of spirits from the dead.
Whether the women whom we love are now
at peace or roam some phantom waste between
the worlds of El and Mot keeps us awake.
You're free to come with us or go your way,
nor shall we judge you for the choice you make."

Moved by their common plight, Ameni vowed
to join them, promising that he would help
them any way he could until the souls
they sought were found and shepherded below.
A doubtful pity lingered in his breast,
however, knowing what becomes of one
who's unembalmed, left to the elements.
Yet he elected not to broach such things,
deciding that their present unity
outweighed the parsing out of morbid truths.
All revelations have their proper time.

Together yet alone, the three friends trekked
for days on end until, atop a bluff,
they spotted an encampment in their path.

In need of water and direction, they
set out to greet those of the tented town.
When they approached four guards impeded them,
demanding reasons for their trespassing.
Aqhat spoke first to put their minds at ease,
"Good men, we come intending you no harm.
My name is Aqhat Son of . . .
Son of the Seir Mountains to the south.
In truth we're parched and hungry refugees.
Should you be kind enough to let us use
your well, we'll quickly carry on our way."
Because Ameni much resembled grunts
from the Two Riverbanks with whom the guards
had frequent run-ins, they examined him
with wary looks until the precedence
of hospitality outclassed their fears.
The guardsmen bade them welcome for the night,
explaining that they would return their arms
when they departed. Aqhat thanked the men
and once again abandoned Kothar's gifts.
In passing, Gabbar asked the four if they'd
heard tell of necromancers in those parts.
The men eyed one another ere a guard
assured them that they needn't dread the man
so long as they stayed close, appending that
they hadn't suffered him for many years.
With pride he grasped the hilt of his sheathed sword
and told them that there'd never been a breach.
Taken aback by his response, the guests
hung close and wished they'd been allowed their blades.

In camp the hosts provided them a tent
to take shade from their voyage's white heat
and gave them water to assuage their thirst,

receiving heartfelt gratitude in turn.
Once rested, the three guests broke trail to find
whatever word they could as to the place
wherein the Necromancer denned and worked.
The tanners, weavers, and engravers chored,
acknowledging the men with chary nods
before returning to the task at hand
as caprine blattings of a humanesque
alikeness circumvolved the twilit camp.
Gabbar, Aqhat, and Ameni approached
a mother standing, watching her child play,
exchanging pleasantries before their names,
at which point Aqhat asked the woman if
she knew a necromancer's whereabouts.
Abashed, she looked up as her daughter klutzed
face first upon the unforgiving ground.
And just as lightning strikes a distant peak,
admitting of a drawn-out, quiet lapse
before its violent afterclap explodes,
so too the poor girl struck the rocky earth
and stood back up as if unharmed—yet when
she noticed how she bled, she loosed a scream
of shocking and horripilating pitch.
The mother darted to her daughter's aid,
and when the threesome tried to lend a hand
she turned on them with ire undeserved.

Distrustful glares transfixed the foreigners,
the weight of which compelled them to move on.
In time they came across a farrier
whose seeming jollity attracted them
and tokened freer-hearted dialogue.
Continuing to mend a mule's rear hoof,
the seated man addressed his visitors

with hope of hearing good news of the world
beyond his rather uneventful home.
Gabbar spoke first, explaining that their town
had been beleaguered, forcing them to flee.
The kind soul asked them for particulars
if they were comfortable in sharing them
and they obliged (although they left much out).
For quite some time the men discussed their lives.
As Evening showed his sunbrent face, the guests
made known their sojourn's true intent, to wit,
their searching for a storied psychopomp
whom Rumor'd said to domicile nearby.
The farrier's regard examined theirs.
He shifted on his stool. His focus lost,
he pricked his mule's left ankle, causing it
to haw and buck in place, dissevering
and shattering the bones within his hand.
With curses and retaliatory
lambasting he provoked the mule to flight,
and when his new acquaintances stepped in
to help he shunned their interferences,
contending that they'd helped more than enough.
His wife cast scowls their way as they withdrew.

They hurried to their tent uneasily.
Ere reaching it a figure called to them,
inviting them to come and sup with him.
Though nervous, each complied. To guarantee
that no one overheard them, he resealed
the tent flap, bidding them to eat, and said,
"My name is Abdiyarah. Welcome, friends.
Whispers are swifter than Ilisha's wives,
I hate to say. You seek the one who knows
those words, techniques, and rites that rouse the dead.

Because you were not raised around these parts,
you don't know what you seek—how much you risk.
Since none should act from ignorance, and since
good hosts should keep their visitors informed
of local dangers, I shall counsel you.
Before my father Kum-U breathed his last
he wanted to impart our history
to me, a tale whose details I'd not guessed
but whose malefic outgrowths I'd observed.
Listen—and I shall tell you what I know.

"Our people once inhabited a town
of sturdy mudbrick homes a three-days' march
due north of here, encircled by red hills.
Like every hearth deserving of the name,
the village tended to its elderly
and youths, permitting them their oddities.
One widow of some ninety years (whose spouse
had long-escaped collective memory)
delighted in recounting myths about
a man who dwelt within a cave's black bowels
for centuries. Shatanu was her name.
The village brooked her silly old wives' tales,
but children basked in them, for she could sing
with such a lilt and summon imagery
with such seduction that her words took life.
One day, four boys sought out the fabled cave
by means of her descriptive words alone,
arriving at its entrance right at dusk
to sight the Necromancer in his lair.
Encouraged by his peers, the eldest boy
challenged the youngest one to enter just
a little way into the cavern's mouth.
Not wanting to surrender their hard-won

esteem, he raised his chin and doubled down
ere infiltrating farther than they'd dared.
He never made it out. When Dawn arose,
the frantic parents of the disappeared
extracted what had happened from his peers
before the young boy's father and a group
went off to find him, none of whom came home.

"Around that very time, a twittering
ascended from beyond the mountain ridge,
outspreading, bruming like a heavy fog.
The eldermen convened then warned the town
that locusts were resurging and that all
should gather even their unripened crops
so that the pests might not descend on them.
The people heeded them accordingly.
Each night the swarm's thrum grew, but as it neared,
the vast insectile hum transmogrified
into a susurrus resembling speech.
At night, unable to get any rest,
the people huddled in their homes and ate
acerbic produce, praying for relief.
One dusk a fusillade of rain beat down.
Kum-U recalled how old Shatanu burnt
with rage throughout the storm, supposing that,
like other superannuated souls,
she suffered from the tempest's oncoming.
The storm ceased, whereupon the residents
rejoiced when they discovered that the rains
washed out the danger, such that nobody
once came across a single locust shell—
those crunchy, ghastly sepulchers from which
there burble pteric plagues, reminding one
how firmly blank-eyed specters cling to life.

"But restful sleep did not result in peace
because a famine gnawed upon the town.
More than a few resented the advice
to harvest crops before the proper time;
a few denied that any coming harm
had ever lain in store; and others set
to taking matters into their own hands,
obeying counsels from Shatanu's lips.
One night it happened that an anxious man
assailed an elder while the latter walked
alone and threw his corpse across a mule
to do away with it and leave no trace.
Into the murky cave he dumped the corse,
but not before a claw took him as well.
That night the sibilating sounds returned,
though louder than before and with a tinge
of agony admixed with hollowness.
The echoes tormented both young and old
till Kum-U took his undesired lead.
He mustered those he could, advising that
they leave at once to go someplace where night
did not resound with imprecating noise,
and when the counterarguments fell flat,
the people followed him without delay
to seek a new home in the wilderness.

"Observing that Shatanu hadn't come,
some noted that the journey would have been
too difficult for her in any case
while some conjectured that she'd stayed behind
for reasons far more ominous than that.
Now one and eighty years have passed since then.
They say the first years were quite arduous
to say the least, and while our lives are much

improved, and while those born here aren't aware
of our past in its fullness, still a sense
of fear predominates among our clan.
However, since such fear helps us survive,
its origins remain unspoken-of.
No townspeople adventure whence we came,
and rovers who've passed by the place report
that it's abandoned to this very day.
But even though it's now untenanted,
avert that place and its surrounding hills.
Foul presences have claimed it as their own."

Thus Abdiyarah, who poured wine and fetched
dehydrated fruits and a loaf of bread,
refections that in turn brought forth repose.
Now that the monitory tale was told,
the host reclined beside his footsore guests
who soon repaid his story with their own,
regaling him with details from their bout
with Shegr and Ithm, the which would sound
fantastic to most people, but their host
had heard and felt things much more horrible
than he would dare acknowledge or make plain.
They drank and laughed until the venturers
regretted that they needed to turn in.
But Abdiyarah bade them wait and stepped
away before returning with some food
and water for their trip; they thanked the man
effusively as new drunk friends are wont.

At daylight Abdiyarah rose to see
them off but found their tent unoccupied.
He wandered to the camp's edge where he saw
a trail of footprints heading the wrong way

and hoped those birds of passage would well-mind
his words so that they might break bread again.
Alas, their first encounter proved their last.
Now reaccoutered with their weaponry,
their sojourn in the dust, the trio traced
a rusty backbone, rationing their meals
and drinking only when the need arose.
Came the third day when they hiked up a draw
then climbed a mountain's rim so as to spy
the village of which Abdiyarah spoke,
desiring to discover travelers who
perchance could point them to the sought-for delve.

Ameni, Aqhat, and Gabbar beheld
the town and made for it, the golden disc
sundowning, changing places with Yarikh
whose wan, cislunar light cereclothed the earth.
Malnourished skeletons of scrubs reached out
their arms in welcome to the visitors.
Yet undisturbed, the hollow lay dormant—
that state between a temporary rest
and the more permanent, impending sleep
that comes to all regardless of station.
The men approached the town of twenty homes,
inspecting their dilapidated state
by torchlight, splitting up and scouring
the ruins, checking for a shred of life.
They ducked inside the foundering abodes
but nothing stirred—no breath, no bat, no breeze.
Not even spiders called the place their own.
Decrepit mudbrick tenements comprised
the sole unscavenged signs of Kum-U's time.

Discouraged, Aqhat found Ameni who
had likewise come up empty in his search.
They watched as Gabbar exited a home,
confirming their presentiments that it
remained devoid of any curiosities.
With stillborn hopes he slowly walked their way
when from the hovel's orifice from which
he'd come a horrid harridan crept forth.
Gabbar at once perceived their dumbstruck looks
and wheeled around to find two ashen eyes
set in a wroth and hoary woman's face
enshrouded by white wisps of matted hair.
He stumbled backward, dropped his torch beside
the doorframe, sand-crabbing away from her.
The brand cast just enough orange light to see
a portion of her rugose face as she
kept hidden in the drear, beshrewing them,
"Foul trespassers! Who sent you here to steal
into my home, to end my slumbering?
Which one of them commands you? Which of you
suppose that you could do me any ill,
as if my time had come, as if I've failed
in any way to keep the covenant?
Who dares to obviate my recompense?"

Although distrained, Aqhat replied to her,
"We mean no harm and no one sent us here.
A stranger told us of this place, but we
have come into this valley of our own
accord, as we are searching for a man
they call the Necromancer, truth be told.
We have no mind to stay, much less disturb
your peace or take a thing that's yours by right.
We'll leave. Ameni, Gabbar—let us go."

Her brow retracted and she chortled like
a gambler whose long streak of mischances
has ceased, her smile revealing rotten teeth,
a few of which were missing, all of which
were olive-brown along their broken sides,
and none of which touched. She addressed them thus,
"I see, I see, then you are good boys, yes.
And lucky you! You've found the only one
who knows the one you seek as well as his
location in the hills. But come, come in!
You must be hungry. Hurry, right this way."

She screwed and scuttled back into her home.
Gabbar gesticulated that they leave,
Ameni in agreement, but Aqhat
refused to turn tail quite so easily.
They'd traveled much too far to stand down now.
Chagrined, they followed him, yet not because
they thought it wise but to protect their friend.
Across the threshold of her home they strained
and entered an adjacent room in which
a fire boiled a fetid pot of stew
whose steam rose through the roof, a part of which
had crumbled, leaving crossbeams jutting out
like fractured ribs that penetrate the skin.
With blandishments she seated them and stirred
the mush, appraising its development
by fingering and savoring the gruel.
While doing so she eyed Ameni who
eschewed all eye contact, his supplicant
mistaking it for teasing coquetry.

The glop-top blistered like a rheumy slough
and reeked of burning hair and sour feet.

She pertly splurped some into bowls for them.
They watched the contents of their retch-buckets
take on a blobular consistency.
Wringing her venous hands she said to them,
"My good boys, eat, eat! Don't delay on my
account, as there is plenty left for me.
In truth, I'm most delighted that you've come
to see my friend, as few believe in him
these days, these worst of days before the end
when all shall reap what they have earned in life.
I will direct you to his den if you'll
be good and transport wares I have for him.
You will? Oh good, my boys, so very good!
Surmount the northern hillcrest just beyond
this vale and hike its backbone, following
its wends until you reach a brake of thorns.
There you'll rappel along the eastern slope
with pendent roots projecting from the rock
until you reach the ledge and sidle down
its thinness, parting brambles on the way.
Behind those final shrubs you'll find a rift
that hews a path directly to the cave.
To make that climb you'll need to get some rest.
Choose any home to stay the night, my guests,
but not before you finish up your meal;
you're growing yet and nothing more than bones!"

Surpassing everything Politeness in
the flesh would dare to stomach, each of them
choked down the festering and mucoid schlop.
Retreating for a house some ways away,
Gabbar looked back and saw Shatanu's eye
poke out behind her splintered jamb, and when
their gazes interlocked she drew inside.

The three sojourners of the ghost town found
a hovel on the east side, satisfied
with a pariah's distance from their host.
Inumi's son addressed them, reasoning,
"We can't stay. Abdiyarah spoke the truth.
Shatanu shouldn't even be alive.
She's found a way to cheat the god of death,
and at what cost or for what ends—who knows.
I checked her home before we went inside:
Neither an unbathed woman nor her stew
was there—I'd never miss such awful things.
Witches alone make something from nothing.
We've got directions; let's be on our way."

Unswayed by Gabbar's words, Aqhat replied,
"You'll get no counterargument from me:
Shatanu's strange. But she's no one to fear.
Tonight's full blood moon, this deserted town,
and our wayweariness barrage our hearts
like so many mirages of the night.
Once rested, we'll laugh off this whole ordeal.
But if that elderwoman frightens you,
then we can sleep in alternating shifts."

Ameni then expostulated thus,
"No. We should leave as Gabbar has proposed,
not where Shatanu has directed us
but fathoms from her evil influence,
nor when she's wide awake but when she sleeps.
Do you not feel her presence even now?
She's worse than Abdiyarah would confess."

The three companions took to quarreling,
the beldam's baleful sludge unsettling

their guts, their livers, and their racing hearts
until they opted each for his own home,
Fatigue and Time foreclosing more debate.
Inside her home, a candle burning low,
the bunioned ronyon crooned a plangent song
through which a hitching laughter came and went,

"Oh tall dark man who waits for me,
my first and last obsession,
remember what you said to me—
that I'm your prized possession.

"We'd just escaped into the hills,
our Where and Why kept hidden;
That memory still gives me chills.
Who says our love's forbidden?

"Stay here with me; come back to me.
Let's have a little fun.
Stay here with me; come back to me.
Our nights have just begun.

"Some say you found a better match,
while others think you vanished.
Their jealous tricks won't leave a scratch,
my faith they will not damage.

"For I recall your wise advice
our final days together,
that 'love requires sacrifice
if we're to last forever.'

"Stay here with me; come back to me.
I know that you're the one.

Stay here with me; come back to me.
Without you I'm undone.

"Who knows the promises we made,
the oaths of blood that bind us?
From me I know you've never strayed—
I hear you in the silence.

"And when I close my eyes come night,
your gaze alights upon me.
You torture me with playful bites
until the new day's dawning.

"Stay here with me; come back to me.
Let's have a little fun.
Stay here with me; come back to me.
Our nights have just begun.

"I whisper words to wingèd friends
who tell you of my dealings;
then back to me they soon descend,
descanting your true feelings.

"Our time apart's annealed us—
Yes! It's never been clearer.
Your absence gives me purpose,
our distance brings us nearer.

"Stay here with me; come back to me.
I know that you're the one.
Stay here with me; come back to me.
Without you I'm unstrung!"

In their respective ruins each man dozed.
Across Ameni's cheek a tepid breeze
now eddied, jarring him awake, at which
he sat up, scouring the emptiness
before he laid back down and closed his eyes.
Phantasmic images left him adream.
The night was calm. A lukewarm fetor grazed
his lip, awakening him underneath
Shatanu, spraddled on him like a belt.
His legs already trussed, she grabbed his wrists,
Ameni crying out as she stammered,
"He'll do just fine. No meaning to the thing.
Why should the Master get to have them all?
No longer shall I sit around and wait!
He squirms and writhes; be silent now, be still!"

Without the faintest sign of effort, she
manhandled him and dragged him where she dwelt
just as a mantis hauls off a cocoon.
He screamed for help and tried to wriggle free,
his nailbeds raking furrows in the dirt
as Aqhat and Gabbar sped to his aid,
Shatanu gnarling round to slam her door
with nothing but a look of raddled ire,
her entrance backed by a debarring beam.
The outsiders beset their obstacle
then looked about for other entry points.
Distraught and riled as he had never been,
Gabbar made for the northern hills as if
a craven soldier cowing from a fight.
His unannounced retreat disturbed Aqhat.
Of all the setbacks he surmised would come,
of all that they'd experienced thus far,

of all the trials to leave them worse for wear,
he never thought that anything could come
between the ultimacy of their bond.

The while Ameni shouted in distress,
each subsequent attempt at breaking in
left Aqhat reeling, bolstering his sense
that nothing matched against such witchery.
A locust crepitated in the night.
Its single burr arose and then surceased.
The clangor in Shatanu's house then stopped
as well, and Aqhat pressed his ear against
the door just as another locust's call—
much louder this time—sounded from afar.
The door burst open, bashing Aqhat's head
as sprite Shatanu sprung out of her lair,
and as she bolted for the hills she waved
as if in afterthought and slammed her door,
resealing her Egyptian knockabout.
The blow reshuffled Aqhat's memories.
He circled to the backside of her home
and, gripping crevices in broken brick,
he scaled the edifice and reached the roof,
now stomping joists besmoked and rotten-through,
descending through the hole and cutting loose
Ameni's limbs before he helped him up.

Meantime Gabbar (who'd plucked a blade of grass
to blow on, holding it between his thumbs
to emulate a locust's cry in hopes
that Abdiyarah's story held some truth)
beheld the nimble figure of the wight
depart in frenzied angst into the mirk.

Behind a shrub he blew the reed once more.
Although she couldn't hit on whence it came,
Shatanu trusted to her anile ears,
and when she reached the northmost pediment
she clambered up the incline on all fours.
Still deeper in the rolling wilderness
Inumi's son retreated, terrified
by his diversion's workability,
incapable of locating the lured
save by her fitful and phlegmatic heaves.
Against his better judgment Gabbar raised
another locust's call into the night.
An umbra flashed across a moonlit patch
of red ere reconverging with the black.
He loosed the plaguey ostent one last time
to give his friends' survival better odds
when from behind his brushwood hideaway
he saw four scabrous limbs encroach and halt.

Having unbound Ameni, Aqhat ran
with his relieved companion to collect
the few belongings that they'd left inside
their quarters, stumbling on their haversacks
and weaponry ere making their escape.
The echo of insectoid clittering
froze Aqhat in his tracks, bethinking him
of Gabbar's forte for such replicas—
the harmless pastime that would bring him harm.
The revelation sickened him because
his friend had sacrificed himself so they
might live and since he'd doubted Gabbar's faith.
He drew his sword, as did Ameni, but
the chirring chorused far away—so far

that realistic hopes of reaching him
in time were thwarted long before the fact.
And yet they hastened toward him nonetheless.

Just as a wounded mouse lies motionless
beneath a briar, hoping that the fox
that searches for it won't persist if it
hears nothing rustle on the desert floor,
so too did Gabbar regulate his breath
behind a bush, predated by the shrew.
She sniffed the air then lurked with manic step
toward Gabbar's ineffectual refuge,
and when she stretched her vesseled claw to part
the branches, one more locust sound rang out
nearby, Shatanu wheeling thitherward.
The high insectile pitch excited her
and she continued hunting for its source
just as an eager child plays hide-and-seek.
Yet when sufficient time has come and gone,
the seeker sensing that the game's become
unfair, her gaiety now tinged with spite,
so too Shatanu's pleasure blent with rage.

In course of time the chirrup multiplied:
First two, then four, then sixteen wingèd cries
resounded through the nighttime's nippy air:
"*Weeruh, weerruhh, wherhuh, we're here, we're here.*"
A rapid rushing overwhelmed the draws
like water through a gulch, and in a trice
the bombination circumfused the witch.
The vast, discordant susurrus consumed
pretended individualities
into a murmurous and single swarm.
Her pupils of obsidian enlarged,

up to the vaulted skies Shatanu raised
her palms and gaze, now whirling, crying out
exuberantly like a plowman's wife
who after years of drought reveres the rain.
The hunted risked his life and ran for it.

Shatanu nestled down and wrapped her arms
around her knees, now indurating like
a grizzled boulder—whereon underneath
her membrane there began to vex and vie
prodigious jostlings wrestling back and forth.
The various parturient effects
extruded from her exoskeleton
like vesicles intent to pop themselves.
Shatanu's neck tore as a fingernail
reached from the aperture to widen it.
Another griding group of talons rent
the cleft still further as the final stage
of molting ran its course, the envelope
now rupturing with moistened crunching sounds,
and from the shell emerged a youth unclothed,
surveilling her environs, grimacing.

Gabbar, throughout that metamorphosis,
remet his friends like brothers home from war.
The latter handed him the spear he'd left
behind before they huffed up northern slopes
while swatting skyborne pests that plagued their ears.
They scrambled to the top of a plateau,
refusing backward glances, racing on.
Beneath Yarikh's bright orpimental glow
they found (so they supposed) the fabled spine
of which the witch had told, ascending it
till coming to the thorn-brake, easing down

the steep façade by means of dirt-clung roots,
alighting on a narrow stretch of ledge.
One following the next they braved short steps.
Losing his footing, Gabbar slipped and fell,
discharging rubble to the valley's depths
before Ameni grabbed his arm and pulled
him back onto his feet with might and main.
Arriving at the bramble clusters like
Shatanu'd detailed, Aqhat held the arms
aside as each crept through, relighting brands
within the limestone, cave-bound alleyway
ere squeezing through its claustral bends.

They reached the cavern's entrance. Aqhat said,
"I was mistaken not to heed your thoughts,
my friends, and underestimated our
predicament—the danger that you sensed
and which I fear has hardly shown itself.
Forgive me, if you find it in your hearts,
aware that you need not descend with me
into this cave if you wish otherwise.
Of one sole thing I'm confident, to wit,
that if we're to survive then we must work
in harmony whenever feasible
before we act. What do you say to this?"

Ameni and Gabbar concurred with him,
averring that they'd act of one accord.
The new pact formed, resilient breaths indrawn,
they staggered through the cavern's lightless mouth.
Although devoid of manmade steps, the grot
permitted only one way of descent
so far as meager torchlight could discern.
They crouched and crawled and scrabbled through the delve

where everything seemed contradictory:
The men felt shielded from their enemies
without, as none would dare to follow them,
yet also sensed a peril more intense,
more imminent than any hitherto.
The fug of death and redolence of life
collided one against the other as
when victors send up incense to the gods
while just downwind the slain begin to rot,
awaiting Horon's immolation heaps.
Although the air grew colder as they walked
below, the men perspired more and more.
Attempting to emit no sound inside
a tunnel, faint disturbances of stone
would skitter down toom passages just like
unstifled giggles in a solemn space.
They plashed through shallow pools of groundwater
on which their shone a duplicate of what
lay up above, distorting their path's size.
Through such a sepulchral domain between
the vault of heaven and the Netherworld
the trio delved, endurance failing them.

An orange glim lurked behind a doorway down
below, both beckoning and threatening
the new intruders who like hawkmoths neared
the light unthinkingly and stepped across
the threshold where a torch-encircled room
permitted them and towered overhead.
Strange instruments lay strewn about; the walls
held thousands of clay tablets side by side,
the highest ones of which could be removed
by means of giant ladders made from wood.
Assorted human skulls were watchfully

aligned from miniscule to large upon
a ledge of chalk, beneath which rested sacks
just like the one Shatanu had at home.
Observant of these things, they grasped their hilts
when from a door a black-coped figure came,
his eyes bestreaked with ruddle patterning.

He moved as would a twisted olive tree
if such a being's roots unearthed themselves,
becoming tentacles wherewith to crawl.
His branch-like fingers clutched an ivory staff
atop which sat four graven ibex heads.
His words emerged from depths unknown, unseen,
"Approach. Or came you not to seek me out?
And if you have, then surely you're aware
that I can change swords into blades of grass.
Oh! How this blood moon has eluded me!
Yet Aqhat's brought a retinue, it seems.
Which one of you lays claim to such a name?"

Confounded, Aqhat answered him this way,
"They call me Aqhat. We have come to plead
your help, traversing mountain wastes where gods
have tried deterring us. These are my friends.
Who told you of my coming? How, alone,
so far below the surface of the earth,
do you know that a full moon shines tonight?"

The Necromancer grinned while gliding toward
a ladder, climbing to its midmost rung,
inspecting various compendia
before discovering the one he sought.
Descending, he returned to them and held
a clay-red tablet for their scrutiny.

Columnar starlore writ in astroglyphs
abutted pinpoint ephemerides.
He ran his fingers down the signs and said,
"As to your latter query, gods transcribe
their secret wisdom in the sky, ordering
the world in ways that literati grasp.
I know the odysseys the sun and moon
and stars took long before my birth, and know
henceforward how and when they shall appear.
Because the messages sidereal
anomalies present can be descried
in libraries, I have no need to leave
my home, no need to use my eyes and ears
to recognize what deities intend.
Alone—you really think that I'm alone?
Amidst the arguments embroiling gods,
the Underworld's incessant mutterings,
petitions from the desperate undead,
innumerable commentaries etched
by scribal hands—do you think that amidst
such endless chatter I find time to rest?
Oh, wearisome, domesticated souls!
But now you're here, and destiny awaits.
Who told me of your coming! Centuries
on end I've waited for this very night.
Along the narrow haft you've walked till now,
whereat you've come unto the bident's fork."

The Necromancer turned his arching frame
and floated toward a wall beside which sat
a cypress chest embossed with sinister
old runes that seemed to slither underneath
the courtship dance of nearby candlesticks.
Out of his cowl he took a silver key

and slid its teeth into the keyhole, clicked
the coffer open, pulling wide its jaws.
He reticently reached inside and took
its content in both hands with either fear,
respect, or some admixture of the two.
The Necromancer disenshrouded it,
returning with the sacred artifact.

So quoth the Necromancer to his guests:
"Behold a shard from Destiny's Tablet.
While still a young man, down to me it fell
when lion-headed Anzu, Hehe's beast,
Ellil's appointed bodyguard-turned-rogue,
attacked his Lord within Duranki's walls.
Yet as he fled in reckless haste he smashed
into a coign, at which, before my feet,
there crashed this corner piece of holy writ.
At that time I was Nippur's priest of priests.
Aware of what had come into my hands,
I clenched it, vowing to return it once
Duranki's chaos had been set aright.
But think—for one who dedicates his days
to analyzing portents from the gods
between upholding rituals which oft
result as foreannounced, but sometimes don't,
reviewing old recondite lists of words
and laboring well into the nighttime
to aid the rich and poor illiterate
while culling from a lifetime's worth of skill
and keeping tabs on temple offerings,
comparting them as deemed appropriate—
just think how such a man as that reacts
when holy words reveal themselves not through
a cryptic haze, but clearly carved in stone.

Would he not risk his soul to study them?
And so I did. The gods' own text I read,
expecting to outwrangle destiny,
yet I discovered that I carried out
the gods' decrees despite myself, the shard's
discretionary care encharged to me.
The fragment's broken but still legible.
Unplug your mind's ears; harken to its words,

"'Without delay, Duranki's Priest shall head
for the deserted Western Mountain Range,
and when the Hawk ensnares the Mouse, let him
pursue that Bird along the Mountain Spur
till he discovers an uncharted Cave.
Down in its Recesses he'll spend his Days,
and for his Needs Procurings shall be made
while there in Secret he shall come to be
a Master of, in, and with the Darkness.'

"And so I packed a mule-drawn caravan,
and like the sun I journeyed westward
until the promised signs unveiled themselves.
Unlike the sun, however, underground
I ventured, never to return above,
investigating what remains unseen.
The Tablet shard continues in this way:

"'To him shall come a Querent, One who seeks
Communion with the Shades of his Mother
and Sister when the Saffron Moon ascends,
and ere a Candle of a Shekel's Weight
expires, this Visitant, whose Given Name
is 'Aqhat,' shall decide between Two Roads.
Either he shall forsake his Arms and burn

his Bow and Arrows, offering their Smoke
in order to empower and appease
the Gods of Old, and with Apposite Rites
he shall, this Night alone, communicate
with the Deceased Ghosts whom he cherishes,
bestowing on them Sustenance and Rest.

"'Or he shall seek a Power yet unknown
to Mortals, infinitely greater than
any the Earth has seen before this Age:
the Mettle that belongs to Gods Themselves.
If he indeed desires such Potencies,
then let Duranki's Priest incant the Spell
befitting this Decision—Magic Words
that shall empower him to slaughter Three
and only Three Gods ere a Year's elapsed.
If down this Path he sets, then when the Third
One breathes no more, his Hands shall run with Blood,
and with the Squall of Warfare he shall roar
as Light surrounds and captures Sin Itself.
He'll never come to Death, and with his First
Words he shall name himself and thus become
Immortal, living to the End of Days,
his Reign inaugurated by Old Song.
If Aqhat should slay fewer than Three Gods
within this Time, henceforth he'll never know
a Mortal's Life, a God's Life, or the Life
of a Rephaim, but shall dissolve into
Oblivion for all Eternity,
that No-place without Form or Hope—the Void.'"

On iterating 'Void' the lector grabbed
a candlestick and rubbed two fingers till
a flame appeared wherewith he lit the wick.

Aqhat stood still, completely at a loss.
His vacant eyes and heart transpierced the flame.
In order to support his hesitant,
exhausted friend, Ameni spoke to him,
"Why don't you speak, Aqhat? Your path is clear.
To choose between two good alternatives
can devastate the strongest man alive,
but forking paths between that which is good
and what is bad present no challenges.
We've traveled all this way to mind your kin;
let's finish what you set about to do.
If piety does not persuade you, heed
the changeless bounds of possibility:
There are immortals and the rest of us.
Mere men cannot kill deities, much less
assume the quality of deathlessness."

At this the Necromancer laughed aloud
as does the council of an emperor
who, while discussing serious affairs,
perceives a naked prince not three years old
burst through their chamber loosing squawks,
his frantic caretaker in swift pursuit.
The men beheld each other. Aqhat searched
the Necromancer's wizened face for clues,
the Cavern Dweller making known his thoughts,
"You come from common stock, so it appears.
There's not much time, but listen to my words.
Two types of deicide exist, all told.
The first, which we initiates call the 'pure,'
occurs when one god kills another one.
Such deaths are like that of a seed which dies
for living's sake, to blossom and to grow
into a plant that sends forth further seeds.

Pure deicides result in perishing
but temporarily. They're to the point,
mere metamorphoses of godliness.
The second sort go by the name of 'mixed'—
a kind you seem to think impossible.
Mixed deicides are rare. Whole ages come
and go without a single one of them,
without a god's death by a mortal's hands.
Unlike its counterpart, mixed deicides
disrupt divine cyclicity itself.
You know it not—and many of the gods
themselves think it impossible—because
the recently apotheosized have
a vested interest in forgetting it
while getting others to forget it too.
To outright recompose a pantheon
requires breaches where the old must be
suppressed so that the new may sediment."

Ameni and Gabbar had hoped to be
enlightened, but they struggled following
the Necromancer's mist-clad reasoning.
To clarify what he'd said, Aqhat asked,
"So, in mixed deicide the gods who fall
by mortal hands depart for Mot's domain,
the Netherworld, as it is said that Baal's
begotten did through Targuziza's mouth?
Then surely they could exit once again
as Tammuz and his love Astarte escaped?
Why would a slain god not seek their revenge?"

The Master of the Darkness made reply,
"Have you not understood a thing? Too much
coarse stubble lines your chin and jaws for you

to think by means of childhood parables.
You think because you use one word, like 'life,'
or 'death,' that each picks out a single thing,
delimiting but one reality?
With pictures I'll describe life's deeper truths
so that you have some chance of catching on.
From animates a mortal shade departs
like smoke arising from a smoldering
wick—as will happen with this taper soon.
As long as other light remains, although
the flame's activity and vibrancy
have been snuffed out, still one can catch
a glimpse of its peculiar afterlife,
in which it seems to move by its own dint,
ethereal and far more venturesome.
The Netherworld's own deities, the ones
that you call Mot and Horon, for instance,
exude the light by which such wisps are seen.
But when a god lays low another, this
is like a torch's light extinguishing
a candle's flame with its irradiance.
In this case light occludes light by degree.
At length, the greater light can be outshone:
Intensities are interchangeable.

"An overarching balance keeps in check
illuminance that brims and then dislimns
in all that I have heretofore described.
Neither pure darkness nor its opposite
affect the steady equilibrium.
But when the days of theomachy come,
when mortals look to slay divinities—
a shadow swallows up its very source.
The Void itself allows for such a breach,

rewarded by a tasty sacrifice
which neither gives nor costs it anything.
On this night you alone may intervene,
Oblivion and Fate allowing you
to break the reigning bonds of gods and men."

In some way the instructed understood
the stakes that fell to Aqhat yet desired
more evidence to prove that what he'd said
was mantic (not just manic), asking if
some rite might simplify the choice at hand.
The Cavern Dweller turned around and skulked
back through the door through which he'd come and closed
it just before Gabbar could catch a glimpse
of what the antechamber hid inside.
Anon the Thaumaturge appeared to them,
a goat—caliginous and leashed—in tow.
The Necromancer fetched some eggplant ash,
a jar of castor oil, and muddled dates;
with incantations he decocted them
then gave the bulging goat a tiny sip.
Its blatting echoed as it yeaned a kid
with twin heads, each of which supported horns.
He helped the mother to the anteroom,
returning with a fired haruspex.
A whetted golden dagger let its life
into a bowl before the hooded one
unseamed its craw, the extant exta saved
for later use, its liver brought to light.

Interpreting the organ, he began,
"The kid emerged with two abutting heads,
an evil bodement, clearly; but its heads
have only right ears with none on the left.

Such signs are positive, significant.
But see these two and twenty liver marks?
An even number augurs benisons
to come, but only if they're uniform.
Eleven are misshapen, as you see;
the rest are formed just as we would expect.
And yet the good ones fall upon the left
hand side, the bad upon the other half.
Such cancellations never show themselves!
Univocal negations mean one thing:
All good and evil, right and wrong, have been
suspended for time indeterminate.
The Void excepts you from morality."

Now beetling to his shelves, the Sorcerer
examined old genethlialogies,
poured over turbid teratologies,
checked seven lengthy hemerologies,
investigated pharmacopaeia,
fumbled around with historiolae
and envoutements recorded in strange tongues,
and surveyed columns of wordlore before
exclaiming that the valuative terms
had disappeared from every one of them.
He eyed the men with anxious sympathy
as mothers do their battle-bound firstborns.
Then pointing to the shrunken candle he
withdrew from them, egressing through the door.

His heart beclouded by the aforesaid,
Aqhat addressed his anxious counterparts,
"The first alternative set at my feet
proves better, being safe and virtuous.
Ameni's right: We traveled all this way

to grant rest to the women whom we love.
What kind of son, what kind of brother would
deny them their entitled food and peace?
What man who shirked such simple pieties
could sleep at night, content with how he's lived?"

His comrades gave assent, and seeing how
the option's yoke bore down on him, avowed
support for him regardless of his choice.
A moment passed, then yet another one.
The litten candle meting Aqhat's window dripped.
An object he'd not seen, a large buck's skull,
distracted his attention now and gazed
at him with empty sockets from afar.
Its look conducted more significance
than every logogram engraved on clay
and stored along the room's surrounding walls.

Here Aqhat stood and voiced these inmost words,
"But would those women dear to me, now that
they're gone, desire that I chase after them,
or would they not advise me to take care
of those in need who still have breath, to see,
in truth, that bigger game awaits me yet?
Was mother not defiled before a god's
own eyes, the same one who demanded blood
from her own blood with trickery and greed?
Baal! What has he assured but misery?
Yet he did not create himself. From whom
would he take orders but his father, El?
Could such a Lord, the Emperor on Lel
who lets his son wreak havoc here below,
have any claim as leader of the gods?
Never! And who do they say El loves most?

El loves Insatiate Mot, the one who brings
decay and rot to all of life on earth.
But he who loves death must in turn loathe life
as well as every living thing, like you
and me and everyone we love and all
who'll populate the earth in future times.
No one admits these grave realities
or challenges them in the open field.
Let us, instead, behold these gruesome truths,
look deeply into them, unsheathe our swords,
and thereby truly venerate our dead,
imparting order on absurdity."

His furor had transfused his harkeners
whose needs and longings now converged with his.
Hope intermingled with astonishment,
uniting them not unlike newlyweds.
The candle's flame had almost run its course,
the Necromancer entering the hall,
inquiring as to Aqhat's chosen path,
to which that man, now resolute, replied,
"I seek to slay three gods in one year's time."

The Cavern Dweller hasted for the shard
that he'd preserved from Nippur's accident
to speak the spell upon its obverse side.
He looked to Aqhat—not derisively
this time, but like a brother who bequeaths
his younger sibling silent, heartfelt praise—
before reciting what had long been writ,
"Bold Hero, Aqhat: Go and seize what's yours.
I sanction your revolt against the gods,
whose deposition shall see you enthroned."

The Tablet fragment's final syllable
evoked a whirring draft extinguishing
the candlelight no sooner than the earth
began to lurch and groan on every side.
Abraded rock dust misted overhead.
The men grew terrified and rushed to flee,
but Aqhat turned around to aid the man
who, though unknown, had lived his life for him.
Resigned, the Necromancer urged him on,
"Be off! I've served my purpose at long last
and hope that you will yours. Your road is hard.
Oh yes, much harder than all heretofore.
But persevere and you shall have your wish.
Don't look at me with sympathy, for I
above all others am prepared to go,
equipped with know-how for katabases.
Head for Siduna—there you'll find support.
Take this. Forth now! Your second candle burns."

He handed him his written destiny
as Aqhat grabbed his torch and made to leave,
a last look thrown the Necromancer's way
before he exited and hurried on
and climbed with Gabbar and Ameni's help
up through the tunnels as the walls caved in.
Like Anzu in defense of Hehe long
ago, the ceilings cast down giant slabs
as dripstone daggers drove into the ground.
Whole limestone arches slammed the rocky floor,
releasing storms of chalky particles,
and faster than Khamudi's palace fell

atop his subjects, burying the lot
beneath that king's unmatched hardheadedness,
the cavern buckled under its vast weight,
imploding as the entryway ensealed—
the ones whom Chance loved having just escaped.

Book X

In bygone times, a lush oasis sprawled
across the desertscape, recipient
of cool fresh water from its northern stream
whose font, like every other one, is Lel.
Above and underground, on wing or craw,
whether sunbather or waterbreather—
to this oasis every creature drew.
Its southern coast was home to grasses wild
and shade-bestowing toadstools, underneath
which one could marvel at the lily pads
and blooms along the nearshore's boundary.
Their necks and windswept tresses stretched above
the surface of the water, bowering
sun-spangled shoals and lapis kingfishers,
large trees with boles unfathomable plumbed
past blooms of sluggard jellyfish below.
This sea—a desert miracle—lived well.

Ensuant on the Giants' Civil War,
successful tribes began their homeward march,
and though each step a hundred fathoms strode,
and while they were the strongest brutes alive,
yet they could not put off lamenting those
they'd lost in battle, shedding bursts of tears.
Still onward they progressed, perspiring
beneath the Sun's desertic, ruthless glare.
At length, through undulating heat, they glimpsed
the thriving sea (to them a washing pool).
Descending on it with uplifted hearts

they drank deep drafts to quench their emptiness
and ate what mushrooms they could find before
they leapt into the sea to cleanse the scurf
and blood that grimed their battle-weary brawn.
They spit spates, dunked their kin, and splashed about,
indulging in the water's playfulness,
forgetting for a time all Whence and Thence
until each giant felt revivified,
continuing the slog that beckoned them.

Once they had left, the sea began to change,
for unbeknownst to them, their salty sweat
and tears infused the water's every drop
six hundred times more than the Great Green Sea.
Ensconced in saline armor, lily pads
took on the form of hirsute mold and sank
into the depths, though some remained afloat.
The toadstools as yet unconsumed congealed
as though from ice, and horrent sedges rimed
near corrugated snowdrifts clambering
toward bone-white headlands. Trying to escape,
the jellyfish began to ossify,
some reaching the alongshore sands
while others scaled low scarps and fused as one,
their alabaster tentacles festooned.
The treetops died, broke off, and soon submerged,
their trunks like island chains of ivory spires.
When El discovered what had come to pass,
he sighed frustratedly but rectified
the giants' accident: So visitors
of the oasis might reflect on how
our simplest acts affect the world, and so
the creatures' bitter deaths might yet enrich
the living, El proclaimed this Dead Sea's salt

be used when sacrificing quadrupeds.
Thus he redeemed a purpose for the sea.

Midday, upon a chert and limestone crest,
Aqhat, Ameni, and Gabbar looked on
the Dead Sea not unlike the giants had,
for though their war was yet to come, still they
knew great fatigue and hoped to bathe themselves.
Descending down the sandstone gradient,
Ameni and Aqhat disrobed to swim
while Gabbar stood along the shore and knelt
to wash his fingers. Aqhat called to him,
"Gabbar, it seems the stories told about
the Dead Sea have some truth! Look how I float
here with Ameni, neither one of us
needing to tread to keep from going down.
The water's magic will support you, so
not knowing how to swim is no excuse.
Come join us! Since you are the smelliest
among our crew, we can't let you sit out."

Such badinage outdid his hesitance
as Gabbar laughed and jumped into the sea.
A strange and rare emotion worked its way
through Aqhat's heart: a perfect—better yet—
a future-pluperfect sensation that
one day he'd feel nostalgia for this time.
The Dead Sea rinsed their dirty hands and feet
and lavered—for a time—their agita
with turquoise brack akin to that from home.
While floating, Gabbar asked Ameni if
he might not teach them how to speak some word
or saying in a foreign tongue, since he
knew multiple, to which his friend replied,

"Of course, but let me think. Akkadian's
the idiom that's used officially
amongst great kings, allowing them to speak
in common though they be of different realms.
I learned much of this tongue while working at
the Walls of the Ruler, where we would say:
'*a-na ia shi shul-mu a-na ka-a-sha lu-u shul-mu*,'
which translates, 'It is well with me; may it
be well with you.' The phrase can oft be heard."

Aqhat and Gabbar drifted in the sea,
repeating what he'd taught them till the three
men made their way toward shore beneath the sun,
encaked in salt like fish to be preserved.
Shalim passed by, and in so doing took
the daylight's blitheness as an offering.
The men prepared a fire, aware of what
discussions need be broached. Ameni said,
"Demanding days await us, my good friends.
Aqhat, you've named the gods whom you would slay
in one year's time, and now there falls to us
the matter of deciding where to start.
The final say is yours, of course, for you
alone confront the Void, however much
our friendship binds us fast to your travail.
This notwithstanding, I would counsel us,
first off, to undermine the god of death:
Just think how many more we might recruit
for future wars upon the death of Death.
Although it's true that everyone shuns pain,
to fight without the slightest fear of death
would much embolden even nidderings.
I know a man familiar with the path
to Rosetau, the Underworld's dark mouth.

Should we round up like-minded men-at-arms
along the way, we might descend in league
and have a better chance of victory
before recruiting our own ancestors."

Amidst the fire's cracks, Gabbar demurred,
"We can't kill Mot too soon. We'll need to truck
and trade with him if warfare is our game.
We should assemble fighters, laying siege
to Lel before we march on other gods,
for Baal and even Mot, to the extent
to which they take their very life from El,
depend on him just as a tree does soil.
If one lops off the forearm of a foe,
the head remains in charge and may yet save
his neck, but when the head's abscised,
what use are sturdy legs and muscled arms?
If we assail Mount Lel and find success,
the gods enfeoffed to El shall lose their strength,
their discipline disbanding as when troops
look on to watch their officer cut down
just as protracted battles have begun.
Moreover, El the Elderly might prove
less difficult to rout than Baal or Mot.
To fire our men through victories and make
Mount Lel our bastion should be paramount.
I too, however, cede the final say
to you, Aqhat, since our fates don't compare."

Aqhat took his companions' words to heart,
the weight of his decision bearing down
on him once more, its gravity increased.
Self-willed and short-lived embers flitted off.
Some time elapsed before he spoke to them,

"You raise important matters which cannot
be taken casually, much less ignored.
I will consider them as we head north.
For now, I withhold judgment as to whom
we shall strike first, as I need time to think.
You're right that we will need devouts to fight
beside us, but I hesitate to seek such men
before we enter through Sinduna's gates.
Although he didn't say that we would find
support along the way, nevertheless,
the Necromancer's words entreated us
to seek out allies in that seaside town.
To safeguard our endeavor, I suggest
we take the sole advice allotted us.
Since we have but one year, and since each year
transpires more quickly than the last, let's race
onward, befriending the hospitable
but keeping our true purpose to ourselves."

His two companions gave assent, and soon
the three men took their rest beneath the stars.
The coming days were arduous and long
and would have been much more so were they not
surrounded by creation's comeliness.
Along the Dead Sea's western shore they trudged,
desiring that their view were potable.
Upon attaining the Dead Sea's north source,
they crunched the Jordan's saltbitten left bank,
which seemed obdured by thermophilic frost.
The tributary hadn't much of which
to boast at first, and yet its confidence
increased the more the men marched upriver,
displaying tamarisks and reeds before
producing willows and white poplar trees.

The current ribboned with flirtatious folds
and twists, its flow precipitating south
as stalwart crestings gaped at her on high,
desirous of her lithe fertility,
to them a silt-enshrouded mystery.
In time, the river deigned to let Aqhat,
Ameni, and Gabbar imbibe from her.
While following the bank's desultory
shoreline, the men encountered womenfolk
who'd journeyed from Sapuma to enjoy
the Jordan River's cleansing liveliness.
The bathing women waved to those who walked
the banks, and yet to Gabbar's great chagrin
Ameni and Aqhat insisted that
they concentrate, not straying from their course.
The river valley's folk availed the men,
attending to their needs and harboring
the travelers as tradition bade them do.

One night the men camped on the riverbank,
Ameni keeping watch while his compeers
slept stilly, tucked beneath their horsehair pelts,
the indestructible illuminants
on their unending racecourse overhead.
He prized the current's peaceful monologue.
Its course from north to south, however, much
unnerved him, seeming most unnatural—
turning on its head the world's right order.
He pondered whether Shay and Renenut
had brought him to these badlands for some good
beyond his measuring or whether gods
less kindhearted had exiled him abroad.
The sound of violent clops broke through his daze
whereat he roused his friends but not in time,

the trio now surrounded by three guards
accoutered with bronze helms and scimitars
that glittered underneath Yarikh's pale light,
each watchdog saddled on a destrier.
The cornered men stepped backward, gesturing
compliance and aversion to bloodshed.
Intuiting the men's Deltaic blood,
Ameni interceded with respect,
"Good men, Egyptian brethren, we traverse
this valley peacefully and don't intend
to stay, nor do we threaten your domain.
We're simple migrants heading for the north
where we have heard there's need for laborers.
If you'll allow, we'll carry on our way."

Atop a large and gray-black dappled horse,
the leader of the other two replied,
"As no doubt all of you are well-aware,
you're trespassing upon the East-West Ford
belonging to Beth-Shean's governor.
What do you, one of our own race, expect
to gain by plundering the caravans
transported to the land that gave you life?
What's brought you to this point of shamelessness,
this life of Asiatic banditry?
Silence! It matters little now that you'll
be sold as slaves to join the very train
for which you lay in wait. Upon your knees!"

Though neither Aqhat nor Gabbar knew what
Ameni and the guard had said, they grasped
enough to sense the direness of their lot.
Aqhat submitted to the guardians
and knelt between his friends, his hands at rest

upon their shoulders as a last farewell.
The watchmen of Beth-Shean's trading routes
dismounted, walking toward them, swords held tight.
When they drew close to bind their prisoners,
the ground met Aqhat's stare, his hands ahold
of each with valedictory malaise.
In one swift motion he then hove his weight
behind himself and rocked onto his heels
while springing from the riverain plateau,
his friends hauled in the Jordan, moonlit streaks
bescattering upon their sudden splash.
Beth-Shean's sentinels then strode their steeds
and flew along the river, leering through
the ramage brush like centaurs on the hunt.
The current dragged Ameni out in front
and Aqhat tried to tread the rapid's course
while keeping Gabbar's head above water.
Ameni paddled toward a fallen tree
beneath whose overgrowth they might hide out.
Attaining it, Ameni turned around
and saw his two companions drawing close.

Though wanting to continue downriver,
Aqhat could not bear Gabbar's weight much more;
he fought the current toward Ameni's hand
and grasped it, taking shelter with his friends.
A moment passed ere hoofbeats hammered by
accompanied by snorts and bellowing
as at a full stretch their pursuers rode
along the bank and southward through the night.
When a sufficient period had lapsed
the three discussed their move when from behind
the undergrowth shot weathered hands that yanked
them through the scrub and pinned them to the ground,

their heads forced to the dirt by sandaled feet,
their wrists constrained with unforgiving rope.
Relieved to catch their prey, the guards remained
perturbed, vituperating each of them.

Their coffled bondsmen tethered, the three guards
bestrode their horses just as arrows sung
from the surrounding wood and hit dead on.
With thuds Beth-Shean's lookouts hit the earth
as seven raffish cutthroats showed themselves,
emerging from the dark with blades in hand.
Three swaggered toward the captives, taking hold
of them, then cut the cords that fettered them
as others lugged the corpses to the stream.
Bedraggled and aweary, Gabbar thanked
them, asking who they were. One said,
"That all depends on who you ask: To some
we're nobodies, Hapiru, hijackers
and thieves, immoralists that run amok.
To others we're Mutbalu's right-hand men,
surveillants of the River Jordan's dale,
the guards who guarantee that Pella thrives.
But we have little interest in such names.
Beth-Shean's governor has set his sights
upon the East-West Ford, unsatisfied
with his hillfort and wanting every tract
between his city and the Amman Plains
so that he can control the caravans
from Washukanni and Assyria.
We see to it that he's not gratified.

"I know a pack of thieves when I see one—
and either you're the worst prepared of them,
no sooner setting out than being caught,

or you are only passing through these parts.
The latter seems the likelier to me.
Since there can be no trace of what's occurred
lest tensions rise still more between our towns,
take up those horses, ride the whole night long,
and speak of nothing that you've witnessed here.
This valley's not a place for errant men."

He tossed them bread and motioned for his men
to follow him into the eerie night.
Aqhat expressed his deepest thankfulness
as Pella's riders left to keep their watch.
Ameni and Inumi's orphan strode
the chestnut horses nearest them, their mounts
dispelling doubts as to the worthiness
of their ambitions, filling them with strength.
Aqhat approached the headshy dappled horse
which neighed and reared as though unbroken yet.
He took the hot-blooded's long leathern reins
in hand, assuring him with soothing words
and with a goodly portion of his dates.
With four attempts and not a little luck
he gained the outlaw's back, so recently
relieved of his subduer's ruthless rod.
The courser pivoted and moved about
of its own will, but as his team progressed
upriver, he pursued them, Aqhat's thighs
clenched firmly to the steerless runaway.
He'd never ridden, much less come across
a creature so imbued with might, and so
bestowed the name 'Aliyan' to his mount.
They rode back to their camp, collecting what
they'd left behind (including Aqhat's bow)

before continuing their northern trek
at a hand gallop by the riverside.

Spring moused about the wetlands to the north,
arising on its feet advertently
to sniff the air ere hasting underground,
preferring sleep to hunger's toilsomeness.
A few days' ride from Yanuammu where
they'd gained provisions for the days ahead,
another sea stretched out before their view,
inviting them to camp and cast their lines
along its waterfront, and so they did
until they reached the Jordan once again
where green and umber mountains flanked its course.
Endeavoring to win Aliyan's trust
and coax from him a jot of discipline,
his rider fed him apricots—but still
the temperamental ass remained unbent.
The company northwestered, following
a road dividing marshes, meadowlands,
and swards toward Hazor's backcountry where they
encamped a ways from the main thoroughfare.

Onward they rode when Shapshu wakened them,
arriving at Litani's riverfront
by sundown, looking for a place to ford.
They found what seemed to be the shoalest spot
to cross, dismounting from their backsore team.
With hempen ropes Ameni and Gabbar
conducted their surbated equine friends
across the water which, although it bore
no rapids on its surface, pulled amain.
Their victuals supported on their heads,

the twain crossed safely, Aqhat managing
Aliyan's fluvial deliverance
when midway undercurrents overtook
Aliyan's usual surefootedness
as on an algaed rock his hooves gave way,
his hip and barrel crashing in the flow
that captured him and wrenched the horse downstream.

Abandoning his gear and contrary
to better judgment, Aqhat coiled the rope
around his palms and leapt into the stream,
Aliyan gyrating now underneath,
now just above the surface, panicking
as silted mouthfuls rushed into his lungs,
short neighs obstructed by the force-fed drafts.
Aqhat clung tightly to the drowning horse
as Gabbar and Ameni raced to help,
the latter signaling a rooted stump
along the shore, and Aqhat swam for it,
embracing it, refusing to let go
despite his chafing palms and shoulder strain
just like a stiff-necked fisherman forbears
to let prodigious catches off the hook
although each promises to be his last.

The onshore backup hurried to his side
and pulled with all their strength as Aqhat swam
to his mount's other side and pushed his flank
with what remaining dint was left to him.
They dragged the soaken thoroughbred ashore
where he and Aqhat coughed and gulped down air.
Gabbar tried to remove Aliyan's tack
but only met with fretful bites and snorts.
When their immediate necessities

were sated, Gabbar found a place to camp,
collecting kindling to prepare their fire.
Alike the dead they slept beneath the stars,
and come the break of day Aliyan proved
far less indirigible than before,
outstarting toward Qrayé as if his brush
with death rejuvenized and hardened him,
his rested teammates hard-pressed to keep step.
The horse's lope surprised them, shortening
the last leg to Siduna's storied shores.

Along the way it happened that the men
discovered an abandoned garrison
or hidden outpost in complete disuse.
Its walls and edifices were well-built
although betraying signs of disrepair.
Who had forsaken it? Did no one claim
it for their own because it lay so far
from the main path amidst the wilderness?
No one inhabited it for some time.
As night approached, so too did memories
of vile Shatanu—though they kept all words
about her battened deep within their chests.

Worn-out and saddlesore, the travelers reached
Siduna's walls, unable to suppress their smiles
when riding through its gateway's turret-jambs.
Although Ameni'd seen such metropoles
before, Aqhat and Gabbar were amazed
by its enormity and bustling pace.
The city's market thrived, its streets were fringed
with khaki homes which rose three stories high,
and seaside noises circumfused the air.
Ameni then proposed they cast around

for lodgings, Gabbar countering his plan,
"I smell the Great Green Sea, beside which we
were raised and which we've not beheld for years.
Let's look on it before the sun descends
and then reward ourselves down near the docks
since we've not had a proper drink in months.
Come, celebrate our first of victories:
We've reached this northern city at long last!"

They raised no plaints and rode ahorseback through
the packed dirt streets and toward the lively port.
Arriving at the water's wide expanse,
the threesome marveled at its roseate rim,
a sight reminding Gabbar and Aqhat
of home, bestirring pictures of a life
long-gone—bright images of simpler times.
In this way the Vast Verd inspired them
and cleansed their hearts just as it always had.
They soon remembered that their memories
were only that, however, so they turned
from this selfsame occasioner of joy
and sorrow, trusting to the alehouse's
inveterate allure as a retreat
from everything that overwhelms the soul.

A burnt-orange glow alit the tavern's walls
with warmth and mirth, inviting them to come
inside to eat and drink and rest awhile.
And so they did. They ordered monkfish stews
and jugs of liquid bread from barmaids who
refilled their cups until they overflowed,
the strong drink running down their gullets as
libations flow down pipes to vaulted caves

where ancestors residing underneath
a city home await their rhyton's-worth.
The other patrons likewise downed their lot
(and more besides) for reasons that, although
quite heterogenous, anon dissolved
into a merry unanimity.
As slews of fishermen on shore-leave beat
clay cups of ale in synchrony, a man
stood up to captain them with raucous song,

"There once was a sober young sailor,
who left home to sail the high seas,
but day one he flew from our whaler
when our boat was grazed by a breeze.
He took to the air like a seagull
and in the blue water he flailed,
but soon he'd discover his new hull,
engulfed by a dopey-eyed whale.

"Chug, chug, gulp 'em down glug,
drink like a fish out at sea!
Chug, chug, gulp 'em down glug,
throw one more back, you sardine!
Storms own the offing and waves the wharves swash;
pull up your oars and get sloshed.
Oh, storms own the offing and waves the wharves swash;
so pull up your oars and get sloshed!

"We vowed not abandon our crewman,
unleashing harpoons at the beast,
and when a sharp barb nearly doomed him,
he succored the gods for release.
'If I'm freed I'll be yours completely,'

he raised up his prayer through the spout—
but then he revoked his entreaty
when that bloated fish shat him out!

"Chug, chug, gulp 'em down glug,
drink like a fish out at sea!
Chug, chug, gulp 'em down glug,
throw one more back, you sardine!
Storms own the offing and waves the wharves swash;
pull up your oars and get sloshed.
Oh, storms own the offing and waves the wharves swash;
so pull up your oars and get sloshed!

"We yanked him up over the port side,
and scrubbed him down best that we could.
But coming home his lovely wife cried,
and she plugged her schnoz up for good.
The lesson, my friends, has been made clear:
Drink up so you don't come unmoored;
your sea legs get better with each beer;
we won't let you drown, rest assured!

"Chug, chug, gulp 'em down glug,
drink like a fish out at sea!
Chug, chug, gulp 'em down glug,
throw one more back, you sardine!
Storms own the offing and waves the wharves swash;
pull up your oars and get sloshed.
Oh, storms own the offing and waves the wharves swash;
so pull up your oars and get sloshed!"

A sailor from Phlamoudhi, not to be
outdone, then took the rudder, leading them,

"A giant boatswain of our crew
once did a lovely girl pursue;
she set the hook and reeled him in
so he ditched us, his kith and kin.
Years later we passed by his home
from which she wouldn't let him roam,
a shadow of his former days,
his muscles sagged, his beard had grayed.

"Hunker down and plow away;
your flimsy oar will find the quay;
Fore and aft, abeam, astern,
rock till you start to feel the burn!
And when at last your load's discharged,
it's time you'd made yourself at large;
we're putting off from this old town—
pull out before you're anchored down!

"Played out by our rambunctious corps,
our dogwatchman sought peaceful shores,
whereat a filly jumped his bones
in pastureland, while all alone.
He cooed her on that grassy bed
then wooed her till she did him wed;
he crossed the threshold with his lass
where thirteen children romped en masse.

"Hunker down and plow away;
your flimsy oar will find the quay;
Fore and aft, abeam, astern,
rock till you start to feel the burn!
And when at last your load's discharged,
it's time you'd made yourself at large;

we're putting off from this old town—
pull out before you're anchored down!

"Disgusted by things maritime,
our helmsman scrubbed his grungy grime
and cast about for ball and chain
to live in cleanliness again.
He spoused the fairest that he saw,
spite protests from his mum-in-law,
who'd have no truck with that seadog,
and lo! she turned him to a frog.

"Hunker down and plow away;
your flimsy oar will find the quay;
Fore and aft, abeam, astern,
rock till you start to feel the burn!
And when at last your load's discharged,
it's time you'd made yourself at large;
we're putting off from this old town—
pull out before you're anchored down!

The tavern shook with drunk bigheartedness
as loutish longshoremen demanded more
such song, their arms slung round their newfound mates.
Thenceforward the carousal magnified,
the brutish bruit worked into choruses
until a hefty swab (whose years of beers
amassed around his waist and whom a stone
outwitted once, or so they say) slipped on
a tabletop and stove it, giving rise
to laughter that increased the more when he
bounced up as if in victory only
to be dragged out of doors by the alewife.
That woman feared for fistic forthrightness

reined in the multitude by threatening
to plug the aleflow, and although these men
would brave the deadly, storm-barraged abyss,
still their risk-taking had its upper bounds.

Some crewmen sat at table just across
from Aqhat, Gabbar, and Ameni—who
saluted them with frothy, upraised cups.
One of their kind, a shipman who'd sustained
a nasty scar across his eye and cheek,
observed the three mates' poorly guarded stares.
He drained his cup of ale, had it refilled,
then introduced himself to those at hand,
"You wonder where I got this scratch, do you?
They call me Awrikku. We've just returned
from Kaphtor, having been at sea for moons
on end—a struggle in its own right, as
you know—but amplified in our own case
by terrors that will haunt me till I die.
One night a sea dragon laid waste our fleet,
a horrid creature sporting seven heads
that wracked a number of our largest ships.
I manned one vessel, reaching in the waves
amidst the splintered flotsam and loud cries
to grab a fellow shipmate, but the beast
tore him away from me with one of his
wide heads before a second set of jaws,
impatient for his cut, ripped him in two.
I see our rowers brandishing their oars
like woodenheaded spears in self-defense.
Of our fleet four attained Siduna's shores,
including ours, and so we drink from ache
for those we lost, but also from relief.
Uphold your drafts; a toast to solid ground!"

A throng had ringed Awrikku round to catch sight
of the grotesque depiction he portrayed,
and when he had concluded, he inquired
what brought his table-mates to such a hall.
Distrustful yet intrigued by his fish tales,
and after having introduced himself,
Aqhat began to tell the sailors that
they'd traveled to the city seeking work,
but Gabbar intervened to vent the truth.
He'd relished seven beers; he threw back eight,
and knew that swabs who'd forborne Litan's wrath
would surely understand their chosen path.
They too had coped with gods and lived.
Among all men, before them rested those
who'd comprehend the hardships they'd endured
and sympathize, perhaps, with their just cause,
"We've also been assailed by hungry gods
along our northward march—by witches too.
In truth, the gods have not been kind to us,
forsaking or harassing us since our
belovèd home was pillaged and destroyed.
But we've not only fled—and now we do
much more than grit and bear our sufferings.
After descending deep into a cave,
a being called the 'Necromancer' spoke
to Aqhat of an ancient oracle
ordaining him to kill three gods this year
and so become a god in his own right.
We've journeyed here to find adept recruits.
Have you not seen enough to join with us?
Show them the Tablet fragment, take it out."

Aqhat recoiled from Gabbar's unconcern
and kept the fragment in his sack.

Though Awrikku and his companions checked
their laughter, many nearby sots guffawed
at what they'd heard and in their cockeyed state
ignited brushfires of mockery,
exclaiming, "All hail Aqhat, God Slayer!"
In jest they yanked him up, enwreathing him
with coils of oakum like a victor's sash.
Even those who'd not heard what Gabbar said
took part in the impromptu ritual.
Tiptoeing back inside, the fat oarsman
took cone-shaped cups and poured them on his head,
disporting them like horns of Baal Hadad
while spitting brewage torrents on the crowd
and belching thunder, pawing the wet floor.
An oldster's cane in hand, a wiry swab
then challenged him, evading his assaults
until he piked the lubber underneath
the arm, the large dope reeling to the floor
with one more table as a casualty.

Ameni, Aqhat, and Gabbar now strove
to flee the farce they led unwittingly,
receiving unsolicited support
from the alewife who strongarmed everyone
into the darksome night and slammed the door.
The general obstreperousness grew,
some moaning at their fate while others laughed
and parodied the Southerners' conceits.
The tavern's roistery now moved outside,
a woman leaned from her high window sill
and yelled at them, demanding they shut up,
but they extenuated their uproar
with slurred speech that she countered with clay bowls.
By now the hectoring woke all nearby,

so Aqhat, Gabbar, and Ameni gave
their tormentors the slip down moonlit streets.
A silent patron outraged at the insolence
of Gabbar's speech kept his distance, following
the foreigners with waxing malintent.
He lost them round an ordinary turn,
however, and their evanescence peeved
him, justifying his mistrustfulness.

A housemaid who'd awoken from the noise
looked from her window down into the street
and with maternal intuition sensed
some mothers' children's urgent needfulness.
She pulled Ameni through her door and waved
for Aqhat and Gabbar to follow too,
conducting them up to the topmost floor.
Another lady lit their lamps of oil,
inquiring as to why her housekeeper
had opened up their doors so late at night.
Adorning her trim frame as best she could,
a lamp in hand, its light unveiling part
of her allure, the woman turned to find
apparent transients within her home.
A snappy indraft whistled through the room.
When Aqhat's eyes encountered hers, he thanked
the women and insisted that they leave,
not wanting to disturb the two of them
and since their horses called for their regard.
But since she had already been aroused,
the lady bade them sit upon her couch,
requesting they make known their origins
and dispatching her maid to tend their steeds.

Gabbar began to speak, explaining that
they'd traveled north with hopes of finding work,
but well-versed in deception's artifice
and veridiction's subtleties herself,
she interrupted Gabbar's stock response,
"At ease—you're safe beneath my roof so long
as you speak truthfully. Depend on it.
They call me Laeya. If you've nowhere else
to go, you're welcome to retire here
until the morning. Eat, drink, stay awhile."

Considering her words, Aqhat replied,
"We thank you for your generosity,
but I fear honesty has been for us
more of a fiend than a devoted friend.
Can one speak plainly of uncanny things?
We'd rather not provoke unfaith from you.
But as we've wakened you, Laeya, and since
we're men of little means, perhaps a laugh
might reimburse your openhandedness.
My name is Aqhat. He is called Gabbar,
and he Ameni. This is why we've come:
Great war-ships from the sea destroyed our home,
the remnant of our village put to rout
across the desert where we made our home
with Shasu of the Seir Mountain Range.
But many felt attainted by some curse,
endeavoring to bring its cause to light.
Colluding with the dunbeards from our land,
the Shasu strongman came to understand
that Danel, my father—who long before
had promised Baal that he would sacrifice
that which he loved most to gain an heir—

had not appeased the god sufficiently.
To break the curse he spilt my sister's blood,
an act that ushered in prosperity.
Gabbar and I then quit that halfway house
to seek a psychagogue of whom we'd heard
to guide below the women we adored,
to aid and satisfy their roaming shades.
Along the way we just escaped the wiles
of Shegr, Ithm, and a foulsome witch.
But when we reached the Necromancer's cave,
he'd known of our arrival and much more
besides, presenting me with what was writ
upon this fragment hailing from the East."

Their host, who'd not yet laughed, received the shard
of clay from Aqhat, poring over it.
Her green eyes studied either of its sides;
her fingers ran along its graven glyphs.
She then inhaled, and with a weighty tone
asked Aqhat which alternative he chose.
Surprised that she could comprehend such runes,
he feared to answer her, his diffidence
response enough as Eliawa burst
into the room and interposed herself,
"You're all still up! I'm glad you get on well,
but in this house we've rules—we're no beer hall.
You mustn't worry for your horses now.
If Laeya so desires, the three of you
can quarter on the second floor below.
Yes? Good. Now go and take your rest at once.
Just make yourselves at home—but not too much."

The men bade them goodnight and walked downstairs
to their well-furnished room containing all

for which they could have hoped, including three
reposeful beds befitting royalty.
Ameni whispered to his boarding mates,
"Should we have told this stranger quite so much?
Don't you remember what occurred when we
entrusted ourselves to a woman who—
suspiciously—proved all-too-welcoming,
providing us a place to lay our heads?
She knows too much. Where did she learn to read?
Her good looks wangled everything from you."

Aqhat then remonstrated with his friend,
"Weren't you a stranger to us once as well,
and even more than this—an enemy?
I merely trusted to my breast's advice
when sparing you without reflective thought,
and had I acted by the rules, induced
by Shasu reason, we'd not be alive,
all thanks to your instinctive bravery.
The mainstay of my heart's supporting me
again, and who can tell if Laeya knows
men willing to avail our chosen course."

In this debate Sleep had the final say.
Above them, wide awake, their hostess gazed
upon the sea, apostrophizing thus,
"Oh Fate, sister who goes unseen in plain
sight like myself, if choice is fantasy,
why must we heft its yoke both night and day?
Have you brought me these godless men to seize,
transporting them to Lel to save its Lord,
my girls, and seventy and seven sons
from Aqhat's faithlessness, and in this way
be reconciled to those from whom I've fled?

To whom's allegiance owed if not one's kin?
No doubt my family would forgive my brief
retreat and welcome me with open arms.
And could I not share El with Shataqat,
to have, at least, one arm of his embrace?

"What am I saying! Who sees me as more
than just a vehicle for progeny?
El snubs my love, Baal contravenes my tact,
Mot disobeys my orders, and Anat,
my vilest daughter, sins without relent.
If absolution need be spoken of,
it's they whose shortfalls needs accounting for!
Our land deteriorates by the day,
its commonfolk dispatched for needless wars
while those at home endure Egyptian rule
and fear of retribution from abroad.
Nor have Resheph's cruel plagues come to an end,
despite my ex's ingenuity . . .

"No longer can I idly sit this out,
nor place hope in amends by way of words—
a recourse that I've tried eight thousand times.
What kind of godhead would I be if I
placed family ties above my people's care,
above my oathbound duties to this land?
If I revered the arbitrariness
of blood more than the ways of probity
I'd be no better than ground grubs and snakes.
But if a new arrangement could be forged
between the gods and men—a change profound
in goal and scope, in need of precedent—
then we might right this lurching, sinking ship."

In this way did such words barrage her heart,
preventing her from getting any sleep.
The morrow came and Eliawa left
with baskets for the local marketplace.
When Laeya found the men reclined within
the common area, belongings packed,
she asked to see the Tablet piece once more.
Unslinging his brown satchel made from hide,
Aqhat removed it, handing it to her.
As one about to overleap a gap
of chasmic depth, she took a breath and said,
"Upon this shard of destiny I pledge
myself to your incumbent sacrilege,
to help you slay those gods whom you so choose
within the year, to set aright what they
have blighted with besotted carelessness
and martial games. Where you go so shall I.
I'll share your failures and your victories,
expending and deploying what few skills
and ken I have that you might one day rule."
Her promise petrified the three of them.
When Aqhat looked his two companions' way
each nodded, ceding the alternative
to him, at which he welcomed her as one
of them and bade them sit so as to start
preparing, insomuch as possible,
for the momentous obstacles to come.

Not far away, Siduna's governor
Zimredda sat upon the courtroom throne
within his palace, flanked on either side
by troops outfitted in reburnished bronze,
no hand without a rounded shield or pike.
One guard accompanied a vizier

arriving from Hattusa to request
extended time to bring the barley, wheat,
and emmer promised him in good faith years
ago, but which the dearth of rain and Baal's
attack had all but made impossible.
The opportunity to hold that state
in debt to his assuaged Zimredda's rage,
so he proclaimed his clement leniency,
permitting Hatti's haulage one more year.
He had heard tell of that land's god-ordained
demise, not knowing its extent, but now
his storehouses and seaport felt the blow.
The Hittite wazir louted low and left.
Next came a courier that Uthi sent
when his defeat at young Tushratta's hands
seemed ineluctable; the man expressed
due obeisance to his superior
before depicting Washukanni's fate,
whose overmastery now disannulled
the prior treaties on which they'd agreed.
Zimredda grew still more annoyed with each
ensuing mouthpiece for ill-starred reports,
repining that he'd hear of nothing more.

A courtier now entered, asking if
Zimredda would admit a commoner
before they finished for the day, since his
importunacy pestered them and since
he swore his words concerned security.
In spite of his perturbed reluctancy,
the ruler deigned to let the man approach.
Forth stepped a dingy fisherman who said,
"My Lord, thank you for lending me an ear.
My name is Abibaal. I am a man

of simple means, a fisherman who's not
rebelled against your seat like other fools.
I've come to warn you of insurgency
that's brewing near the wharves, but not against
your person—no!—but even worse than this.
With my own ears I've heard such blasphemy
as I would rather not repeat aloud.
A Southerner who goes by 'Aqhat,' just
arrived with coconspirators, seeks out
recruits to slay our forefathers' divinities.
I followed them at first but lost their trail.
Such profanations cannot be excused.
The young are godless here and need to learn
respect for the old ways, which you uphold.
Siduna's sinfulness is on the rise.
I do not tell you this for any gain
but only as my upbringing commands."

Despite his name, Siduna's lord was not
considerably pious in his heart,
yet here he glimpsed an opportunity.
He stroked his beard in thought and made reply,
"You're right to bring such news to me, good man,
for coastal dwellings like our own cannot
forego their duties to the Conqueror
and Dread Anat, nor yet to Yam-Nahar,
to Litan, and to all the holy ones.
You say you know this 'Aqhat's' countenance?
Good. Work with my clandestine regiment
to hunt him down, accosting any who
would be so foolish as to follow him.
His capture shall ensure Hadad of our
devotion, standing us in his good stead.
Do this and you'll be handsomely repaid."

Now Abibaal conveyed his humble thanks,
retiring to direct Siduna's troops
and safeguard his belovèd, native shore
from reprobates who didn't know their place.
From fisherman to huntsman in a trice,
he swelled from his responsibilities,
determined to fulfill his chosen task
whatever hardships might present themselves.

Book XI

Ameni, Gabbar, and Aqhat sat down
with Laeya to discuss the way ahead.
His hands enclasped in thought, Aqhat led off,
"Our journey from the giant-ruined sea
has furnished me sufficient time to think
upon what recourses we might rely.
My brothers have suggested that we raise
an army to descend upon Mount Lel
or enter Mot's domain, since El and Mot—
Fathers of Life and Death who oversee
and fail to set aright the earth's despair—
comprise two deities we must lay low.
While we've already found an ally on
Siduna's shores, the Necromancer did
not say how many we might win while here.
I thus propose that we begin to cull
together anyone who vows to fight
with us, who swears to face the gods head on
and even die for what we shall achieve.
Of course, we must proceed in secrecy.
Our point of first attack will show itself
in time, although my odium for Baal
inclines my inner eye toward Zaphon's heights."

Encouraged by his sharpness, Laeya said,
"I know this city well. We'll find success,
I think, recruiting from the dispossessed
who've garnered little from their endless prayers
and toil and so have little left to lose.

We should split up in pairs to work apace
as Time, though silent, has unknowingly
pledged loyalty to our opponents' side.
But we will need far more support in terms
of strength and numbers than we'll have on hand.
As has become well-known, Hadad enfeoffed
Mitanni, setting up the puppet king
Tushratta who's forever in his debt.
Anat and Baal have sacked Hattusa too,
the news of which has found Amenhotep,
no doubt, who up until more recent days
has prospered from these lesser empires' gifts.
The pharaoh will consider Zaphon's moves
as a direct affront on his puissance,
thus we might ally with him down the road."

These words inspirited Ameni who
imagined heading convoys of his kin
with Aqhat, scattering divinities
abroad to win unprecedented fame,
his deeds recounted down through Nubia.
Gabbar leaned forward, speaking to his friends,
"It's true that Time, a god, supports his like.
Yet we must not become impetuous
but work neither too slowly nor too fast.
Ameni and I will explore the docks
and neighborhoods of fishers for recruits.
You two seek men among the urban poor.
Do you recall the backland fastness where
we camped between Siduna and Qrayé?
Let's use it as a barracks readying
and disciplining regiments until
our final stratagem solidifies.
If we discover individuals

who pledge their loyalty as Laeya did,
then we should mobilize them to enlist
like-minded fighters, every one of whom
should meet at the abandoned hideaway
in one month both with food and weaponry."

Concurring with his counsel, Gabbar's three
companions made to exit at his side
as Eliawa lolloped back inside
with drink and eatables, prohibiting
their egress till they'd breakfasted in full.
Throughout the course of her long life, few had
dared challenge her peremptory largesse,
and those who stood before her kept the norm.
Once having eaten they split up as planned.
Laeya and Aqhat walked Siduna's streets,
bypassing boys who chased each other, men
too old for work who argued with their friends
from habit and for fun, and blooming girls
who, practicing for motherhood, assumed
authoritative tones while teaching their
young sisters how to dance in synchrony.
Loud intermittent squawks cut through the air,
and whether these arose from the seagulls
who preened themselves atop high sunbaked quoins,
from infants kept indoors while mother worked,
or from some undeciphered colloquy
between the two—no expert ear could tell.

Around a corner, Laeya and Aqhat
heard shouts of men outside an ancient fane
which housed, traditionally, Athirat's
attendant cup-bearers and votaries.
They overlooked a crowd and heard a man

who stood upon the temple steps cry out,
"I am alive! I'm healed! Hey there, Mada'e,
have we not known each other all our lives?
When plague beset me, eating through my flesh,
my body blistered by apparent sin,
you acted like you'd never seen my likes.
Nor did you come, I'm told, to pay homage
to me upon my inhumation day.
But I don't care and I forgive you, friend,
for maybe I'd have done the same to you!
Just look, I'm well, back from the Netherworld
with hearty breath and not a boil to show!
Just like the sun I've peeped below the earth,
arising once again to tell of it.
Lord Horon took my hand when I gave up
my shade to him in prayer, escorting me
into his master's realm when on a whim
a goddess—she you see enthroned right there,
a gorgeous lady—took my hand away from his
and gently led me to the world above,
reciting spells that washed away my sores.
And I am not the only one, for there
are others who've beheld her haling eyes,
who knew infirmity and even death
but now live out their days with newfound thanks
to Shataqat, Redemptress of the Sick!"

Out of the temple seven priestesses
emerged, their hands beneath a golden plinth
atop which skyred a siltstone monument,
a carven replica of Shataqat.
Midst prayers the stolists primped the deity,
outpouring sweet libations in her name.
Laeya leered at the statue with disgust—

that thing whose wideset hips and hulking breasts
dissimulated infecundity—
as if that minx had borne a thousand gods,
creating and instructing them with love.
And when the huddled herd raised blats of praise,
Laeya took Aqhat's arm, conducting him
away from those who had disgraced her shrine.
The tightness of her grip bespoke her wrath
against the gods and reassured him that
in Laeya he had found a faithful friend.
As they departed down an alleyway,
Zimredda's troops appeared with Abibaal
along that temple's bright façade and scanned
the throng for Aqhat and his coterie.

While rummaging the city for recruits,
Aqhat and Laeya neared the palace steps
as guards dragged in resistant boys and slammed
the doors in front of which tall warders stood.
A group in tattered tunics who pursued
them with their farming implements now cursed
the doorwardens, one widow taunting them,
"You're all so brave! No doubt Siduna would
collapse if men in gilded chariots
relaxed their seizures of the destitute.
You think those boys know where your slaves have fled,
or that they'd squeal if they had any clue?
You say Zimredda's grain houses lie bare?
Then here, come take this mattock from my hands—
I know the perfect furrow for the thing!
You idiots imagine that surplus
arises out of barrenness, that those
of us with nothing have the most to give.
What lunacy! With your intelligence—

that's right, think hard—I guess that you'd infer
that fewer hands make farms more bountiful.
A very difficult idea, yes.
Why don't you take some time and give it thought,
releasing my three boys so we can work.
And isn't that what this is all about?"

Fed up with raving hicks, two sentinels
clanked down the steps to silence them for good,
and though the farmers' feet stood firm as roots,
Aqhat and Laeya intervened and stepped
between both sides while beckoning the men
and women to retreat and reassess.
Uneagerly, the peasantry stood down,
withdrawing toward the homes of relatives
to rest and reconvene on the next day.
The dowager who'd shamed the sentry men
asked who they were and why they'd interposed
themselves in matters not of their concern.
The two assured her that they'd common cause,
and while she doubted them, her careworn heart
endured them, habit welcoming the two
to company her to her relatives.

Inside, alone, the widow gave them drink.
When Laeya asked what angered her, she said,
"Inuya is my name. I farm the east
side of Siduna's outer no-man's-land.
My sons and I plow fields my husband leased
from wealthy landowners; since his demise,
however, and since Baal's withheld the rains
this year, we've been unable to produce
even the scrawniest of vegetables.
Unable to pay back our loans, much less

the tributes higher-ups demand—one half
of what the earth ekes out—we've racked up debt.
The large and well-off homesteads send no men
for military service or to work
for the temple, their fathers having paid
a onetime sum exempting their estate
from labor—even after they're long gone.
The temple takes this out on us just like
a testy older sister on her kin.

"And so, to debt slaves we have been reduced,
hacking another's land as bent-backed thralls.
The temple duns us for taxes that we
don't have then reprimands us with corvées.
We all owe things that we will never own.
The other day a group of fellow slaves
took off for unknown lands, deciding that
the danger of their flight proved better than
enduring endless servitude at home.
The high authorities suspect my boys
know where they've gone and that they had a hand
in aiding their escape, and so the guards
have captured them to winepress truth from them."

Laeya responded to Inuya thus,
"It's true then: Justice abnegates his role
on farmlets just as much as mountaintops.
My friend and I believe that you deserve
a better lot, a flourishing new start.
Zimredda doesn't care a bit for you
(on this we're both agreed), and Baal has not
made good on promises of winter rains.
But there is more at work than most detect.
Your problems' origins have distant roots.

Hadad has depredated city-states
beside his sister, breaking trade accords
that will incite Egyptian vengefulness.
Who do you think will bear the brunt of this?
A distant, noncommittal overlord,
Lel's bearded dotard, still refuses aid—
a drink in hand, a harlot on his lap.
And Mot debars your land from any yield.
Thus you'll not find your greatest enemies
within Siduna or its outliers.
You see, one must go after bigger game—"

Inuya fleered and interrupted her,
"Were I to need a lecture on the gods,
on whom two priests' words never coincide,
then I would be slumped over at some shrine.
That there are deeper reasons for the way
things are strikes me as true, but knowing them,
unriddling their beknotted mess won't free
my sons or yank up barley from the ground.
This widow has enough to fret about
without attending to concerns abroad.
Shall I go buy a boat and sail to Thebes
to knock upon the pharaoh's silvered door?
Or should I journey all the way to Lel,
reminding El of little folk like me?"

Aqhat removed the Tablet piece; to her
he handed it, responding to her cares,
"Where I'm from, little folk don't stare down armed
authorities without the faintest fear.
We've come to you because you've lion's eyes,
a dauntlessness of which we're much in need.
Some years ago my village was destroyed,

either by Baal's omission or command.
Since then, a Necromancer has bestowed
on me the power to kill deities
within the year, which we intend to do.
This Tablet shard contains the magic words
that augur my accession to divine
enthronement—which I'll use to help those like
yourself and others who are downtrodden.
You needn't give your answer on the spot.
If after more reflection you decide
to join us, we would gladly have your sword.
We hope you'll join us with likeminded kin
at the deserted garrison between
Siduna and Qrayé in one moon's time.
Whatever you so choose, we ask you keep
these plans within the circle whom you trust."
Inuya looked at him and wrung her hands,
declining them yet wishing them success
ere they turned elsewhere to solicit friends.

Ameni and Gabbar walked near the wharf,
along the side of which a train of men
upheld a sandstone god caparisoned
in dark-blue byssus robes behind whom danced
and sung a loud array of worshippers.
The content of the revelers descant
apprised them that the celebration day
revolved around the sea god Yam-Nahar.
They turned away from the parade just as
Zimredda's guards and Abibaal shot looks
in their direction, hoping to espy
the Southerners' cabal at the event.
The undetected roamed where Laeya said
there lodged communities of fishermen,

though few were found, most having left to keep
their tutelary's holiest of days.
Coming across two men in shabby rags,
Gabbar inquired as to why they stayed
behind, to which the older one replied,
"I've sailed and seined for long enough to know
that no libations, no amount of praise
can sate Nahar. Few are the men I've known
who've not been taken as an offering
to him and swallowed up before my eyes.
And I suppose he'll take me down one day,
but I am neither fearful nor dismayed.
When one has lost so many friends
one starts to care much less about most things."

His interlocutor replied in turn,
"What do you call yourself? My name's Gabbar.
I'm sure you know the songs of old in which
Hadad and Yam squared off, destroying ships
and drowning men without the least regret.
The songs recount that Mot availed Nahar,
omitting that El turned his eyes away
from the calamity, as did his sons.
I ask: What good comes from such governance?
I too have witnessed loved ones donated
to deities through slaughter's portalways.
Their lifelorn looks are branded on my heart.
But things don't have to be this way, for one
shall put the gods to sword, replacing them,
correcting the injustice that prevails.
We seek your help. Should you elect to join
with us, we welcome you and those you trust
to come to an abandoned garrison

between Siduna and Qrayé just west
of the main pathway when the next moon glows."

The younger fisherman horselaughed and said,
"You're madmen, truly. Abdu is his name,
and Abdu won't go slashing at the waves
like sand-castellans sallying the surf.
If you are telling jokes for shekels, I'm
afraid you've found a beggared audience;
and work on your delivery, for one
could almost think that you were serious.
Get out of here, you're standing in our sun."

Disheartened, Gabbar and Ameni left
to contract those of lesser scorn, yet most
replied to Gabbar's challenge much the same,
at which the man lamented that he had
no luck with fishermen or boatman types.
Ameni too began to question if
adopting the advice of a recluse
on where to locate friends made any sense.
The four met back at Laeya's tenement
that evening, breaking Eliawa's bread
and sharing details of their nonsuccess
while reconsidering their stratagem.
Each dawn they ventured out again, and while
a few inhabitants almost appeared
receptive, none committed to their cause.
How many people outright laughed them off!
With each recurrent letdown, Aqhat felt
duration's tightened grip around his throat.
The second candle meting Aqhat's window dripped.
Laeya's tenacity alone gave hope.

One afternoon, Ameni left his friends,
for he'd heard that Egyptian ships approached
and hoped to barter for a homemade gift
to repay Eliawa's selflessness.
He waited, watching Atum's evening-barque,
his feet hung from the peer's outjutting arm.
The god blazed bright against the skyline's calm,
the white and slate clouds being well-defined
until his distant downgoing atop
the cobalt water's coruscating scales
recalled his heat, the orange peripheries
beginning to cool down to lotus pink.
Soon only the perimeters of dimmed
blue clouds could be discerned, and all was still
except the keel preparing to tie up.

Ameni caught the painter that a swab
heaved underhand and helped secure the ship.
The tavern-beckoned seamen hopped off board
and ditched their pilot who began to thank
the shoresman for his help. In common tongue
Ameni welcomed the Egyptian skip,
"Prosperity and health, Son of Wadj-wer.
It seems that Renenut has smiled upon
your voyage even as the spring draws near.
Do you have scarab amulets for trade?
I've brought a skin of choicest wine with me
if you're inclined to pleasures of the sort.
How fare things on the Nile's Two Riverbanks?"

The merchant joined him on the bulwark's edge,
"Prosperity and health to you as well.
I've brought no amulets to trade, but here,
take mine, as I am parched and haven't had

a drop of wine since last time I was here.
Good man! You may want to hold onto that
awhile—its value's bound to grow if things
progress the way they are, for I surmise
that folks will harken back to olden times
before too long and miss Amenhotep,
regretting their ingratitude toward him.
You haven't heard? You've been away that long?
Amenhotep the Third died quite some time
ago and Akhenaten took his seat.
Admittedly he did some good at first,
completing Amen's house's entryway
in Karnak, fashioning another shrine
for him in Nubia—but now all's changed.
He's turned his early work and that of his
precursor on its head, commissioning
his yes-men to efface the Hidden's name
wherever it occurs and, even more,
to desecrate his father's hieroglyphs.
Word is he's siphoned Amen's offerings
and tribute Aten's way, forbidding praise
to Khonsu, Amen, Mut, and Osiris.
There's also rumor that the pharaoh hopes
to build a city for his patron god
from which he shall decide who merits life
beyond this one—and who'll be left to rot.
It's almost like this ruler thinks that there's
one god alone. I thought I'd seen it all."

The man's news left Ameni taciturn,
and so the merchant made an overture,
"Do you have family members back at home?
I lost a crewman on our voyage here—
a fine man, Wadj-wer bless his sunken soul—

and so I've got an oar in need of hands.
The pay's not bad, and I'd prefer to sail
back home to hoofing it if I were you.
A man can only stay abroad so long."

Disquieted by possibilities
he'd long since given up, Ameni brooked
these tidings and proposal best he could,
imagining his homeland's differences.
Beyond a certain period of time,
life changing as it will, do homes remain
much as and where they were, though altered or
expunged, or can they not depart from clay
and water, taking to the wind like ghosts?
And if they've gone, what can 'returning' mean?
A yen to feel the floodplains underneath
his toes collided with his present goals.
But in this murky maelstrom into which
the young man had been cast, one trusty chunk
of waveson propped him up with certainty,
to wit, that Akhenaten's likenesses
to Aqhat obviated any pacts
or common cause that might unite the two.
The merchant took another pull of wine
and told his countryman that they would leave
midmonth and that he'd save a foremost spot
for him amidships if he chose to come.
Ameni thanked him, turned around, and left.

He rubbed the scarab amulet between
his fingers, heading back for Laeya's house
where his companions spoke in privacy
about the options that remained to them.
Before he joined their likes, Ameni gave

the beetle to the steward of the home
and Eliawa, caught off guard, blessed him
before the erstwhile miner found his friends.
They welcomed him and Laeya spoke to them,
"We've little more than half a month till we
set out for the deserted cantonment,
which I'm afraid is likely to remain
as empty hence as we would find it now.
The failure of our present strategy
demands that we revise our action's course.
We must recruit if we're to know success;
yet no one rallies to our purpose here.
Thus here's what I propose: Let's venture south,
encamping in the vacant stead, and should
a handful come, we'll journey on with them
to Surri, Ashkelon, and other towns,
conscripting men-at-arms until we reach
Amenhotep the Third, petitioning
alliances against our common foes."

While Aqhat and Inumi's son reviewed
her notion in their breasts, Ameni told
them what the merchant had revealed to him.
Depicting Akhenaten's temperament,
intuiting what laws rang from his lips,
Ameni bore the crushing news that they'd
not find a single ally in the new regime.
His countenance alone snuffed out their hope.
Invisible, the goddess Silence slipped
among the foursome's presence for a time.
A moment passed, then yet another one.
Anticipating Aqhat's words, she flew
out of the window for new company.
Like ploughmen of surrounding farms he tried

to hardscrabble some hope from barren soil,
encouraging his friends to lift their chins.
His words feigned patience that he didn't feel,
advising them to seek likeminded friends
for three days, whereupon they'd travel south
ahorse and improvise their coming moves.

Yarikh descended and arose three times,
the intervals of which brought nothing new.
The four prepared provisions for their trek
and Laeya told the keeper of her home
that she knew not when she'd return to her.
Aliyan snatched his forenoon's worth of dates
from Aqhat's hands, excited by the sense
of change communicated by the weight
of stock and stores now laden cross his flanks.
They bid farewell to Eliawa's cheek,
bestrode their mounts, and southward made their way,
egressing through the gates without a hitch—
Ameni glancing backwards at the port.
Expending verve built up in idleness
by cantering through dawn's incipience,
the horses' geste contrasted with the mien
of those who rode them, each immured within
the downbeat premonitions of their hearts.

The hoofborne stopped to eat and rest beside
the dusty road. They'd yet to pass a soul.
A viscid wordlessness united them.
Restraddling their equid wayfellows,
the company moved on until they reached
the turn-off, following it slowly west.
Shalim the God of Gloaming scanned the land
beneath his ashen hood to take it in

as Aqhat and his tendance reined their mounts
down toward their hideaway which slank to view.
A downflooding of pleasant pain whelmed them—
dull aches originating from the stead's
drab vacancy, a tinge of pleasure roused
by the precision of their foreknowledge
admixed with tensive waiting's leavetaking.
They looked to one another, climbing down
in order to prepare for their next meal
when from behind a ramshackle doorpost
a chary face appeared; another peeked
above a further building's broken ledge.
These two came forward. Gabbar recognized
Abdu and Laeya knew Inuya's face
no sooner than they welcomed them, relieved
to find their month of work had yielded fruit.

They wondered if Inuya brought her sons
whereat she told of their untimely deaths
by lickspittles belonging to the court,
and all at once knew why she'd journeyed there.
The other claimed he had no better plans
at his age in a voice as gruff as shy.
Aqhat embraced the pair, acquainting each
to each before he tried to animate
those there by arguing that two more swords
were better than none, at which Abdu laughed.
A smile stretched out across Inuya's face
and met her whistle-loosing fingertips.
Like springtime vegetation, budding heads
approached the light and peeped through ruptured brick
while others curled their fingers over sills
to hoist themselves and gain a better view
till men and women showed themselves in full.

Now Laeya turned to Aqhat, questioning
his eyes till hers respirited the man.
In but a moment, upwards of ten score
recruits of peasant origin stood tall.

If heretofore Aqhat had half-believed
in his own cause, essaying to convince
himself and others at the selfsame time,
those present needful eyes that trained upon
his face, awaiting his decisive word,
now foisted on him full-scale leadership.
Intoning his newfound authority,
he called the people forth, and from his bag
he took the Tablet piece and held it high,
"My friends! Today shall be remembered hence
as where it all began, that twilit eve
which, like the spring's inchoate victory
surrounding us, presages better times
of harvesting and fruitfulness to come.
For it is prophesied upon this stone
that we shall undermine the ones who've shirked
their easy lot, who've long-forgotten us.
But don't deceive yourselves: The way ahead
will prove more difficult than you could guess,
for we shall do what none have done before,
that is, bring death to the immortals, those
who do not care for you—Baal, El, and Mot.
No undertaking is more perilous,
yet no rewards compare with those at hand.
And so I only call the dauntless forth—
those who shall pledge their sword and bow and spear
to me right now and when war's at its worst.
The rest can leave in peace and with no shame.
Of those who choose to stay, approach and kiss

this Tablet's sacred runes and swear an oath
unbreakable, whose breach shall summon death.
Take heart! A novel order has begun.
The gods' own twilight shows itself at last!"

Assenting roars responded to his words.
The people came to him, and one by one
with great respect they kissed the prophecy.
With each repeated oath, Aqhat began
to feel much as a father does when he
first holds his newborn child, in awe of what
such simple deeds effect, disquieted
by the severe responsibility
of untold time and weight that falls to him.
When all the enlistees had pressed their lips
upon the Tablet, Gabbar, Ameni,
and Laeya stood before him to renew
their troth (a sign he deemed superfluous),
yet they insisted, vowing faith in him.
Again the people's leader spoke to them,
advising them to rest since in the days
ahead they'd train with stark intensity.
Discussing how to organize their lot,
the foursome stoked a fire and roasted game
that Abdu'd hunted on his southward ride.
Considering the strengths possessed by each,
Aqhat asked Laeya to direct her thoughts
toward long-term stratagems, assisting him
and Gabbar with the military drills
when feasible, and to Ameni he
allotted the important oversight
of camp morale and peaceability.
They each agreed, still shocked by their success.

Within five days, the rhythmic discipline
of combat exercises had set in.
Northwest of camp, Ameni dug a well
with four strong women, dripping from their toil.
Having instructed his own regiment
in spearmanship all morning, Gabbar sat
with them, their middling weapons lain aground.
They watched as Aqhat practiced with his men
while Laeya fugled a recruit nearby.
She gripped a layered shield and he a lance
of pinewood, thrusting it with robust strength,
yet she deflected it each time with ease
so as to throw the piercer off his weight.
She laughed at his attacks and he smiled too,
suggesting that she train him one-on-one
from here on out and come break bread with him
that night to help the charge improve his thrust.
Averting this advance as well, she told
him that she promised not to lie with one
of whom her father'd not approved, and since
his death three years ago, she'd vowed to go
without a man's embrace for seven years.
She ran her left hand through her sideswept hair.

Their conversation addled Aqhat's poise,
in part because a fight should not be blithe.
Attending to the nervous novice whom
he'd trained with stolid patience up till now,
he set upon him with a burst of strength,
hacking the cringing tyro's upraised shield
with repetitious bluntness till this last
defense caved in and splintered, the recruit
pleading with him to cease. And so he did,
apprising him of warfare's gravity,

a lesson meant not only for the boy.
He helped him up and gave him a new shield,
commanding him to practice with the rest
while Aqhat walked away to wash his face.

A man recumbent on his elbow next
to Gabbar, seeing Aqhat's brandishment
of force, inquired how long he'd known the man,
whence came his might, his skills with bow and sword,
and what nobility had sired him.
Reflecting on their past, Gabbar explained,
"The origins of Aqhat prove arcane.
He comes from nowhere in particular
and has no kinfolk save those present here.
It would be false to say that he was born
like other mortals, for the gods had marked
him out before his time, electing him,
predestinating him for matchless feats.
The Tablet of Destinies bore his name
whole centuries before our land was formed.
His bow and quiver Kothar-wa-Hasis
constructed for him ere the boy could walk.
I've known him my entire life, and though
as his best friend I hold him in esteem,
still he surprises me at every turn.
We always trained for war as boys will do,
but it was on the Seir Mountaintops
and its encompassing, desertic waste
that he became a warrior in full."

Completing his account, he ordered them
to stand and to resume their martial drills.
The ragtag army practiced through the day,
acquiring skills and sound advice piecemeal,

locked swords sliding and griding edge to edge.
The makeshift host was growing, taking shape,
and had one cared to listen properly,
the subtly changing din alone would have
convinced them of their headway, for anon
the clumsy clangor grew still more precise,
a mutualness spreading through the camp.
At night small cookfires snapped and cracked, about
which men and women learned each other's names,
consuming game hauled back by hunting groups
Ameni orchestrated with due care.
A beardless man named Burianu cooked
a partridge, roasting it for Aqhat's meal.
Already sated, Aqhat thanked the man,
enjoining him to eat the food himself
before he wished those in his care goodnight.

Some evenings, when the Seir Mountaineer
retired to bed down in the garrison,
remaining fire-pokers shared their thoughts,
"I've learned some more about the one in charge.
It's said he didn't come into this world
as mortals do, not having a mother
or father but created by the gods.
His birth had been foretold—his whole life writ
upon the fragment that he carries round
before our earliest of cities rose.
He sensed his kismet and began to train
for war while young before adventuring
amidst the Seir Range to test himself.
Moreover, he's outwitted and repelled
a few divinities already, so
our future battles have real precedent."

One morning Gabbar sought his closest friend,
informing him that food supplies ran low
despite their best attempts at rationing.
Among his inner circle Aqhat stood,
considering the issue in his heart
before deciding that Siduna proved
the best place to replenish their supplies.
He turned to Burianu, asking him
if he'd accompany him on the trip—
an offer he accepted right away.
Yet Laeya questioned Aqhat's reasoning,
"Could you not send another group to go?
The longer we develop here the more
our weighty risks compound with equal step.
Last night I had a dream: A starving snake
pursued a shoal of fishlings from the shore,
but seeing him, the school escaped his jaws.
In deeper waters, slinking after them,
the serpent swam with silent twists and bends,
for he believed the shoal was one large fish—
with such a uniformity they moved.
His fangs snapped at the glinting caudal fin
which whacked him, so he turned and slipped away.
Continuing its flight, the shoal swam on.
Thinking the danger gone, a minnow left
his post to pinch a mote of floating food,
a few more following his freethinking
when from the depths the snake returned and picked
them off with ease, disbanding the array
until his gut reunified the rest.
The meaning of my dream requires no
complex interpretation. Stay with us.
Look after your community and send
another man for such a simple task."

In order to allay her needless fears,
Aqhat glozed over her ophidian
nightmare, explaining that sometimes our dreams
were only that and nothing more besides.
The two men gave their swords to Gabbar so
they might appear less menacing to those
in town as Aqhat gave his quiverful
and bow to Laeya, trusting them to her.
Her hands accepted them although her eyes
dissented from the choice that he had made.
The two men mounted up and Aqhat left
the Tablet fragment for his closest friends.
As Laeya clutched his bow she watched them leave.

Chagrined to be held up by hackneys like
the one atop which Burianu rode,
Aliyan loped ahead then circled back
round him on their Sidunan getaway.
His hoofbeats tallied twice the other's tromps
while Aqhat used this time to train his horse
to halt and run and wheel round on command
with dates from Mararat as his reward.
But even more impressively, he taught
Aliyan to rear up on his hind legs,
his chest held high, when Aqhat whistled twice.
The city gates attained, Aqhat advised
that he and Burianu split their tasks,
encharging him to gather victuals
while Aqhat bartered for new armaments,
accomplishing which they'd retrace their steps
to ride back south before the day was done.
They started their allotted work at once.

Although his facile tasks were menial,
they flooded Burianu with import.
He steered his packhorse for the marketplace
which murmured with its pullulating throngs.
From stall to stall he strode to purchase grapes,
green olives, cakes of fig, and salted fish,
and tested them as though he were a cook
before encumbering his jaded mount.
As Burianu pushed through crowds, a street
with vittles far exceeding those he'd bought
came into view; their size and hue alone
betrayed the blunders of his afternoon,
so Burianu whirled around and went
to those from whom he had secured his goods,
imploring them to take back what they'd sold.
As his requests flew in tradition's face,
at first they each refused, but whiny tones
and unbecoming importunacy
can whittle down a forest's stoutest pines
who've withstood centuries of williwaws.
The evening waned and Burianu raced
to purchase edibles befitting his
companions and bellwethers back at camp.

His sumpter laden, Burianu strolled
back toward the city gates, and when they rose
to view, he spied a mustering of guards
inspecting Aqhat's wares with diligence,
molesting him with queries and demands.
In panic, Burianu ducked behind
a wall and watched the troops bind Aqhat's wrists
and sling a noose around Aliyan's neck.
The head guard wore a self-indulgent smirk,

commanding those within his charge to take
the man away; he followed close at heel.
Maintaining mindful distance from the wards
who strongarmed Aqhat to Zimredda's court,
his counterpart pursued them, tarrying
until the stillness (though it be a lack
of movement) goaded him from wasting time.

He tied his horse, assuming a veneer
of nonchalance and laborer's fatigue
before he neared the Royal Court's perron
to sit upon a step, allowing time
to fritter by until he asked a guard
about the recent prisoner they'd detained.
The hulking courtwarden informed the boy
that such affairs were none of his concern,
yet Burianu justified himself,
explaining that his mother couldn't leave
their home, now bedbound in her final days.
Her last connection to the world came through
the tattle that he brought to her each night—
the juicier the livelier she'd be,
as if dread scandals slapped her back to life.
The porter stared through him, unentertained,
Aqhat's companion countering with gold.
The guard harrumphed, ensured the coast was clear,
then told him that they'd caught a heretic
whose insurrectionary blasphemies
would no doubt land him in Baal's island jail.
He thanked the guard, lamenting piety's
decline in these most decadent of times
before he casually stood up and left,
returning to Siduna's city gates

astride his horse and riding for the camp
as thunderheads unleashed their punishment.

When Burianu reached the camp, he roused
Ameni, Gabbar, and Laeya from sleep,
describing what had happened to their friend.
Ameni reprimanded him for his
unpunctuality, not having met
Aqhat in time to be of any use,
but Laeya intervened on his behalf,
remitting the mistakes of which she'd dreamt,
dismissing Burianu from their room
as images of Aqhat bound in chains
beset her heart, unbalancing her words.
Bestraught, the men expressed their wish to find
and slay the fools who'd riven him from them,
employing those they'd trained to test their swords
before Zimredda had a chance to send
him to some putrid cell on foreign soil.

Attaining some composure, Laeya said,
"Since Aqhat made me head of strategy,
I've given thought to how we should proceed.
Now that he's been abducted fewer paths
lie open to us, forcing us to make
the most of Fortune's forecast knucklebones.
To Alashiya Aqhat shall be shipped
and locked away in Baal's internment spire.
It's true we could waylay Siduna's troops
before they leave, but in so doing we
would forfeit many unprepared recruits
and sacrifice the one advantage left
to us, that is, our army's secrecy.

"My friends, take heed of what I purpose now:
I know a shipwright named Zelophehad,
my father's only living brother who
adores me with avuncular regard.
Tomorrow I'll ride home to sell my house
and everything within its well-built walls
in hopes that such a sum—to which I shall
adjoin fond memories of bygone days—
will furnish us with ships with which to sail
to Alashiya once the seas relax.
We'll pull up anchor, rescuing our friend
ere sailing up Puruna's waterway.
As neither Thebes nor Washukanni would
align themselves with us, we've only one
potential ally whom we might entreat.
Hattusa's lord will want revenge on Baal.
King Suppiluliuma, it is said,
grows more ambitious since his homeland's sack,
and if his army joins us we might march
back south to Zaphon, making war on Baal.
But meanwhile let us train and fan morale."

A deep uneasiness possessed the room.
If at the tidings of their friend's arrest
Ameni and Gabbar had sensed an end
to their endeavor, when their partner spoke
they knew that everything had just begun.
They were amazed that she would give her whole
inheritance to aid the cause, and since
they'd not her foresight or decisiveness
(much less her vista of the broader whole),
the two acceded to the plan set forth.
Without success the three then tried to sleep,
for each one pictured, in distinctive ways,

their friend's detainment, torture, and transport
to rot in Baal's impenetrable keep.

Not having merited a formal trial,
beyond the law by nature of the crimes
committed, Aqhat slouched and trod beside
like lawbreakers, the kind that worrisome
imaginations fear when walking home
alone while cities sleep—and rightly so.
He watched as nondescripts evaded him.
The sunlight's garish rays derided him
by forcing him to reexperience
the painful blows dealt out to him with more
reality than any memory
alone might do, albeit freshly carved.
Zimredda's guards encouraged those enthralled
with kicks and shoves toward their departure point.

Attuned to the direction of their march,
he knew they headed for the port from which
his captors likely planned to ship him off.
So also Aqhat understood that his
companions lurked nearby, prepared to free
him as they'd helped each other in all things
no matter what the cost or pitfalls be.
He knew that Burianu had escaped
and would have ridden full-stretch back to camp
to tell the others what had come to pass.
Should Burianu not have made it there,
his friends would have deployed a band of scouts.
Besides, they had an army at their whim.
A standing army that just stands around
will only stir up trouble for itself—
a truth his comrades surely grasped by now.

The prisoners reached a pier and clomped across
its wooden planks, spears prodding them along
and filing them into a slaver's hull.
When one man sought to flee, a soldier knocked
him down and kicked him in the wharfside surf
which, though not very deep, could not be tread
with metal shackles manacling one's feet.
A glance cast backward, Aqhat tried to spot
his friends' position when a spinal-blow
precipitated him abaft full-force.
The keel put off as fettered oarsmen rowed
by orders of a ferryman's whiplash.
About-faced, Aqhat met the tiller's eyes
though his weren't met in turn, for the old man
who steered their vessel was as blind as those
famed harpists who regale Egyptian kings.

Book XII

Between Siduna's barbicans she rode
alone, her busy heart examining
what she'd rehearsed since leaving camp behind.
Without directing rein-tugs, Laeya's horse
loped toward the portside home for which it longed.
Upon arrival Laeya climbed her stairs.
As soon as Eliawa sighted her,
she called her name, embracing her with force,
"Oh Laeya! How I've missed you! Where've you been?
The road's besmirched you, Shapshu burning you.
I'll draw a bath, whip up your favorite meal.
Drink this, a draft of wine will do you good—
now don't be rude, dear, take it for your health.
It's wonderful to have you home at last!"
Laeya had not envisioned such a squall
of kindliness and had to improvise,
surrendering to Eliawa's care
and finding that she'd spoken truthfully,
for having scrubbed the dirt and scurf from her
whole frame, and after tossing back two cups
of wine, redressing in washed vestiture,
she felt invigorated and refreshed.

Yet after unexpectant thunderstorms
one must get on with life, so Laeya said,
"I've missed you too. We all have, you should know.
I wish that I could cue you in on where
I've been, but I'm afraid you'd be ashamed
of me since I could never vindicate

the paths I've trod in frank and open terms.
I'm sad to say that I must go away
for quite some time, and I must sell this house
and all within it to afford the trip.
In doing so, you shall be freed of all
indebtedness to me, and I will set
aside a sum such that you'll never work
again, but rather have the means to do
whatever you desire most in life."

Taken aback, her caretaker replied,
"Laeya, you'd really sell your father's house?
What shall become of me? Have I not been
a worthy nursemaid since your early days?
Oh, lifelong help takes on a mother's role
in every way—except one can dispose
of us at will without the faintest guilt!
I want to care for you, my child, that's all,
yet if you go, a treasure hoard won't do.
I wish I'd never grabbed those derelicts.
Because of my impulsiveness you fell
for one, I'm sure of it. Is it Aqhat?
That handsome fool demands a dowry—yes.
It's unacceptable! No bride-price could
do justice to your smile or perfect hair.
That boy is trouble—of this I've no doubt.
But could I not come to the wedding feast
at least, to see you off and dance a bit?"

Denying her surmisals, Laeya kissed
her servant, almost starting to believe
that she'd looked after her since she was young.
She wished that she could tell her everything,
but she dared not appear mad for she feared

the thorough remedies to be prescribed.
Laeya assured her they would meet again
as soon as her affairs were set aright.
Ere Laeya left, her caregiver replied,
"Ever since thick hair sprouted from your head
you've run your left hand through it when you lie.
I'm wise enough to know the foolishness
of standing in love's way. Go if you must,
and may the gods look ever after you."
Laeya embraced her one last time then left
to find Zelophehad the Boatbuilder,
a widower who with his daughters lived
along the coast three leagues north of the wall.

The hard dirt road along the waterfront
passed steadily beneath her brown-maned's hooves.
Yet unbeknownst to her, a figure rode
behind her, following her from afar,
concealed within an hooded riding cloak.
Arriving at the shipwright's residence
and having tied its courser out of sight,
the shadow that pursued her ducked inside
the inlet's boatshed in which hung a keel
upheld by trusty hawsers fore and aft.
The boatbuilder heard whinnying and came
outside, a smile enlivening his face,
"It can't be. Laeya, is it really you?
My how you've grown! Girls, your cousin's here!
I haven't seen you since the funeral.
How are you getting on? You must be parched.
What brings you to our backwater shipways?"

Affectionately greeting him and his
four daughters, Laeya spoke to him, saying,

"Indeed, it's been too long. I've missed you all.
Look how you've blossomed, cousins! Suitors ride
up oftener than city-girls, I'm sure!
Uncle Zelophehad: Do you still build
seagoing ships as you did in my youth?
May I come see your latest craftsmanship?"
He threw his arm round her and led her toward
the dockyard lying to his homestead's west.
Her hidden hunter saw the two draw near
and, seeking cover, climbed into the bilge
above, the ropes supporting it strained taut.
Beside his homemade workbench Laeya said,
"In truth I've come to strike a deal, uncle.
I want to offer you my father's home,
including every item it contains.
You saw him fare well in commercial life
and know the quality of our estate.
But in return I'd ask for ten large ships.
I know—I'm quite aware that in this change
of hands I profit most, but I can't give
you more than everything your brother left.
Please, uncle, I will never ask a thing
of you again, and when my plans (of which
I cannot yet inform you) meet success,
you'll be repaid a hundred-thousand-fold.
But no soul must find out about your work."

Zelophehad explained why her request
proved most impossible with practical,
logistical, and fiscal rationales,
when the last strand of hemp that held the bow
aloft gave way and with a violent splash
fell forward, coughing up a hulking mass.
They smarted from the crash as Laeya grabbed

an adze in self-defense. But soon she saw
who floundered there and used the tool to pull
her startled caretaker onto dry ground.
His mouth agog, the shipwright gawked at her—
a small steamed dumpling of embarrassment
who, trusting her senescent eyes more than
the ones belonging to the age-old gods,
decided that attractive boys were not
the only ones who could adventure round
in secret to look after her encharged.

Laeya apologized and introduced
the sopping Eliawa to the man,
at pains to mend the bumbling mess she'd made.
However, he heard nothing that she said.
Observing that his first befuddlement
had given way to stifled prurience,
she joked that Eliawa's patina
came with her house's other goods.
And though the vast majority of jests
elude their mark, this one had better luck.
Before inviting his new guest to dry
herself beside their hearth and sup with them,
the love-mad man agreed to Laeya's terms,
ensuring her ten ships in three months' time,
the which he'd store within a secret cove
a little over one league to the north.

At daybreak, Laeya sat astride her horse,
all having come outside to see her off.
She asked if Eliawa wouldn't ride
with her for home, to which her friend replied
that she must stay to lend Zelophehad
a woman's hand since he'd much work to do.

Exchanging knowing glimmers, Laeya voiced
her gratitude then turned and southward rode,
her legs fixed firmly to her horse's flanks,
her hips in charge, harmonious in sway.
Like the adherents of an avalanche,
the ships she saw sped her and weighed her down,
each one reminding her of Aqhat's fate.
Upon arrival, Gabbar greeted her
and she informed him of the fleet to be.
Encouraged, he inquired when they'd ship out,
and when he learned that it would take three months
his thoughts grew cumbrous with resurgent doubts.
Congratulating her, he mustered hope
and with a warhorn called the camp to him.

Atop a rust-red rock he then announced,
"Come, listen! Unofficial rumors waft
about, so let me set the record straight:
In recent days field marshal Aqhat fell
into the hands of Baal-backed enemies
who'll ship him to the Alashiyan coast
where he will be imprisoned soon enough.
Please, calm yourselves! Though it's still in the works,
we have secured a fleet to rescue him.
Do not lose heart now that an obstacle—
the first of many, friends—has shown itself.
Remember once again the oaths you've sworn!
Your training shall continue as before
unless you have experience at sea.
Those with such knowledge should report to me.
Of those I deem most fit I shall appoint
ten captains, each of whom will spend their days
instructing us in arts of seafaring.

We'll sail for seagirt Alashiya soon
to free our leader—of this rest assured!"

Thus Gabbar. Soon a surfeit of requests
to pilot ships impressed upon his ears.
He listened to their claims and arguments
(which led to endless, petty infighting),
and chose at random from among the best.
Without delay the new ranks set about
preparing others, etching diagrams
of boats in dirt, explaining every part,
and helping all to memorize the swab's
impenetrable onomasticon.
As if this weren't enough, the pilots had
them sit athwart felled logs in ghost vessels
to plow imaginary waves with spears
until their bones ached, hoisting sails unseen
and bailing water from their earthen hulls.
For every exercise that he dreamt up,
the peasants pestered Gabbar with complaints—
the guaranteed reward of leadership.
And when clear images of Aqhat came
to him, he'd drill the nascent naval fleet
with more intensity, presuming that
he just might outmaneuver Fate with work.

Although the cedarn ship of prison-bound
was firmly masted, sailing with a wind
most favorable, still Zimredda's crew
would not allow the sails to be unfurled.
And while the steersman's savvy grip could find
a following sea on which they could coast,
he knew that such indulgences were not

allowed their pullers who must row the whole
day long beneath the heat's lash to forestall
potential mutinies once night set in.
A sun-seared man with flagging neck and back
asked why a strong and healthy captive lounged
astern—why he could not switch off with him.
The top dog sliced a hunk of apricot
with his knife, leaning on the figurehead,
and donning solemn airs explained that he
was no mere captive but a godly guest,
a valiant man who'd slay immortal ones
to usher in utopic days ahead.
The crewmen laughed; the scullers shot their scorn.
Aqhat drew inward, glowering abeam
into the endless uniformity
of slate mounds separating them from land.

Because the South Wind gusted with new force
come evening, swains untied the halyard knots
and lowered sail before their watch began
(being a mere formality, in truth,
for those who'd worked their oars of sandalwood
lay strewn about the hull as if deceased).
The helmsman didn't sleep. His hand held firm
the rudder while the sea breeze lost its way
in the thick rootage hanging from his jaw,
above which sat two waxen, glenting moons.
The night was calm, and stars alit the vault.
Addressing Aqhat—last to lie awake—
the graybeard introduced himself like this,
"This is my favorite time, when all have closed
their eyes, our bright ancestral kings above
protecting us on their nocturnal rounds.
I've never seen them but I know they're there.

Can those with vision hear the stars, or does
sight's favoritism cancel out their song?
My name's Sinaranu. What do you call
yourself, young man? I know that you're awake.
Alright, don't answer me if you prefer.
Perhaps you wrongly fear my mockery,
as if I were like those with swords and knives
aboard this ship. I'm nothing of the sort!
I merely make the voyages that kings
demand of me—possessive of my skill.
Nor would I snicker at the so-called crimes
of which you've been accused, as others do.
In fashioning our flesh and bone, the gods
accustomed that of which we're made to hands
with everlasting strength and safeguarding.
But our completion by those artisans
entailed a great diremption: Freeing us
in turn enchained us to our very lack.
Who doesn't long for immortality?
At least you have the valor to pursue
impossibilities like Gilgamesh."

That Eastern hero's name made Aqhat start
as shepherd gods galumphed into his heart.
He then revised Sinaranu's account,
reminding him that Lugalbanda's son
had lost Enkidu after they outfought
the Bull of Heaven, noting that the man
who would become the Sheepfold's king sought fame
and glory, not a life that knew no end.
The rudder-master chuckled at these words,
his eyes embrightening before he said,
"Young lad, who told you only half the tale?
And doesn't one seek out renown and might

as blemished stand-ins for eternity?
Lean back and I shall catch you up to speed
on what your truant eldermen left out.
If you don't learn a thing or two, perhaps
the deeds that I recount will help you sleep.

"It's true—Enkidu, Leopard of the Hills,
the Wild Man who helped Gilgamesh subdue
the welkin's longhorn, died as punishment
for their off-kiltering of things divine.
To Gilgamesh, the foundling was his kin.
For six days and for seven nights the man
lamented his friend's early passing-on.
He poured oil on his corse, perfuming it
and bathing it each day with hallowed rites
until a grub fell from Enkidu's nose.
In time the peers of Gilgamesh helped him
inter his friend, and yet his own fears were
not laid to rest but multiplied amain.
Although two-thirds divine and one-third man,
the shepherd had begun to fear that one
day he'd succumb as well and breathe no more.
He donned a lionskin whose canines clasped
his forehead (remnant of a fight the Wild
Man finished on a distant highland pass).
Embarking on a journey spirited
by spiritlessness, Gilgamesh roamed round
the earth; he trod through vacant lands and rowed
across the loneliest of icy tarns.
He bypassed scorpioid-men, caring not
for what they'd do to him, and hardly cast
an eye toward bushes on which gemstones grew—
unmoved by lapis berry clusters or
carnelian seeds in pomegranate rinds.

"While wayfaring down near the sea, the waif
caught wind of Ut-napishtim—he who lived
across the ocean, guardian of spells
the gods incant to grant eternal life.
The mourner longed to learn of him, but all
avoided him, for he wore grief upon
his dirty face and wildness brimmed his breast.
An alewife, old Siduri, fled from him,
but Gilgamesh implored her kindly aid.
She pitied him. Ensuring that the two
of them could not be overheard, she told
him of my ancestor Ur-shanabi,
the ferryman of Ut-napishtim's land.
Then with a word-wrought map she filled his ears.
He kissed her cheek and sped away to find
the tiller who took Gilgamesh aboard.
The pair set sail, and countless nights they passed
together—not unlike the two of us
beneath this sky—adrift, away from home.

"At long last they reached Ut-napishtim's lair.
That ageless one asked Gilgamesh why he
adorned himself with sullenness and fear,
and Gilgamesh recalled Enkidu's death,
explaining that he sought eternal life.
But Ut-napishtim warned him that all men
must die, and that he should give thanks to live
in postdiluvian times such as these,
for Ut-napishtim outlasted the flood
which Shuruppak's divinities unleashed:
He'd built a boat with six—no, seven decks,
outfitting them with plants, wild animals,
and any laborers of diligence,
and when a tempest purified the earth

of mortals, only those aboard drew breath.
The gods who hadn't been consulted raged—
the people of their cities floating by,
their quondam hymnic lungs now filled and stilled.
But Ea intervened, advising them
to let less ruthless means diminish towns
forevermore since accidents and long
droughts were as nothing in comparison
with the deluge that wiped away their work.
His words prevailed, and Ut-napishtim held
this dire history within his breast,
revealing it in full to Gilgamesh.

"Yet Ut-napishtim the Faraway's words
fell short of sating him, for he'd not sailed
across the sea in order to discuss
and contrast all the ways that men expire,
thus he continued flagitating him
until the arkwright couldn't but relent.
The ancient one gave Gilgamesh a quest,
completing which he would divulge the spells
which grant one full-fledged immortality.
Ut-napishtim instructed him to stay
awake for six days and for seven nights
with Ur-shanabi, ferrying unto
the Mouth of the Rivers to find a plant
with thorns and blossoms like a rose, yet which
grew only in that sacred, hidden dell.
The pair pushed off, and Ur-shanabi kept
awake to share his passenger's ordeal.
He prodded Gilgamesh with his wet oar
so that the man would not nod off to sleep,
and Gilgamesh recounted emprises
of former days to entertain his guide.

Once they had reached the trackless dale, they found
the plant and Gilgamesh uprooted it.
Sitting within the bosk, he tightly clenched
the plant's barbed stem to ward off drowse and dream.
Yet his grip loosened, Sleep outmatching him.
A serpent slithered to his side and snatched
the sapling, molting ere it bellied off.
Awaking, Gilgamesh repined his loss,
dejected at remaining one-third man,
then sailed away at Ur-shanabi's side."

With tilted ear Sinaranu confirmed
that Aqhat, unlike Gilgamesh, slept not,
and then explained why he had told the tale,
"All paths are bound and cyclical, young lad.
It's only fitting that one like yourself,
a man who's not afraid to turn his face
godward and raise his fists, a man who longs
for endless life like Lugalbanda's son,
should sail with Ur-shanabi's ancestor.
Of those I've met and freighted overseas,
as outwardly brave as they might appear,
most lack the candid courage to admit
that everything they do springs from the same
unsated wellspring from which you imbibe.
Men laugh at the inscrutable challenge
you've undertaken to unthinkingly
submerge the truth that they want just the same.
And even if you don't attain the fame
or name of vagabonding Gilgamesh,
at least you lived with his intrepid heart.
You have my deep respect. Now close your eyes
before the light of morning reappears."

His head between his knees, discovering
no solace, Aqhat spoke unto his heart,
"Who rules this life but Pain and Suffering?
The more I've tried to flee those enemies,
the more I've fought to rid myself of them,
the more incisive and resilient they've
become, gaining the upper hand with ease.
The falsity of everything's its truth,
our life a ruse worse than any drummed up
by Folly's oblates, those bucolic gods.
No—even life itself cannot contain
the farce that is the whole; do not Rephaim
reach out for blood and sustenance in death,
desiring tasteless, unfulfilling food?
Does such absurdity have no beyond?
Perhaps I've only gotten what a man
like me deserves, my pain a recompense
for my habitual unmindfulness.
I couldn't save my mother or sister,
and when I had the chance to mollify
their suffering, I put myself above
them both with shameless, wayward selfishness.
And now my friends and many more besides
await destruction by Zimredda's hounds.
For all this I'm entirely to blame."

The days wore on. The long oars plowed along.
The criminal who'd questioned Aqhat's place
within the keel had died of thirst, his corpse
unceremoniously heaved astern.
Aqhat assumed his place and rowed toward his
imprisonment by day while numbering
the sins and errors of his life at night.
Conceiving of his toil as punitive,

he leaned into the pain, and it was good.
One dawn, Sinaranu unwrapped a cage
of wood within which rustled a black bird.
Removing it, he kissed its silky scalp,
releasing it into the forenoon mist.
It flapped aloft and then incised the bleak
where none could see it; soon a distant caw
uprose, the boatsteerer adjusting course
toward his assistant's practiced signaling.
A moment lapsed before another call
arose, the prow now scything through the fog.
The steersman ordered those who rowed to cease.
The criminals complied without complaint,
although the turbid cloak unsettled all
aboard, as none could see beyond the bow.

Reentering diaphanous pale light,
the crew looked up, astonished to behold
a tower six and thirty stories high
beneath whose upper awning roared a fire.
Processing wavelets prostrated themselves
before the promontory's unshod feet
to wash them, laying down their seagrass alms
ere humbly backing up, their heads bent low,
their substance given to their next of kin
who'd carry on the timeless ritual.
Sinaranu's black bird sat perched upon
a solitary dock of rotting pine
extending from the headland's lowest point.
The tiller crowed and it replied before
the bird flew back, alighting on his arm,
delighting in its well-earned crusts of bread.
Both captives and their captors marveled as
their bearded helmsman guided their large ship

up to the dock, averting fallen rocks
such that no portion of the boat once grazed
a single object till its larboard kissed
the pier just like a bashful gentleman.
With swords unsheathed, the guards demanded that
those bound now bind the boat, and so they did
before they climbed the groin of stone-hewn steps
that led to cells which were to be their homes.

Arriving at the jail's surrounding walls
where Baal's armed wardens stood their ceaseless watch,
the crew conveyed the lawbreakers inside.
A guard shoved Aqhat in his penthouse cage,
a stone room with a thin embrasure that
looked south across the sea, a cedar door
restricting access to the corridor.
He met with callous silence when he spoke.
A guard tossed Aqhat's share of moldering
old bread upon the floor; he snatched it like
a starved cur, dying to revive himself,
and when he'd finished, all alone, he looked
out of his seaside slat through which the sun
alit his face. The vast sea lay empty.

For one moon Aqhat dwelt upon his sins,
routinely looking for his friends at sea,
his jaws bewhiskering, his hair unkempt.
But nothing happened. Days were much the same.
Oblivion's morose effluvia
slank up the tower walls and found his cell,
infusing it with unseen, noxious warmth.
He wept and beat himself for his mistakes
amidst the drudgery of his new life
until the self-inflicted suffering

by which he strove to expiate his faults
became an ordinary part of him.
Occasionally he would try to speak
with guards who thought him a malingerer,
so they ignored him as was protocol.
His muscles atrophied. His eyes grew dim.
At long last he accepted that his friends
would not at any point deliver him.

Undifferentiated from the last,
another month crept past as Boredom, sole
attendant of the inmates, made his rounds.
One evening Aqhat whispered to himself,
"Perhaps I'm seeing things with unclear eyes.
Complete annihilation waits for me—
what other being can lay claim to this?
Will not the Void, in which there's neither source
nor outfall, dissipate my toil and strife
and ache and loss as if they'd never been?
Just as a thankless and intractable
itch comes to fear its own dependency
upon the willing hand that scratches it,
demanding more relief with each reprieve—
unsatisfied in its satisfaction—
so too in every placated desire
exists the threat that, one day, our joy's source
will be no more, and so our wanting turns
to more imperious and desperate
resorts with failure as the foregone prize.
Or as we clench a stone so hard it seems
to throb with its own pulse, though lacking one,
so too have I clung tightly to this world,
ascribing meaningfulness where there's none.

"That's it! The Tablet fragment never vowed
to curse me with impending nothingness,
but rather blesses me in subtle ways.
I'll neither roam the world like Gilgamesh
nor suffer life nor rot in Mot's domain,
but disappear entirely, for good.
In being naught, there's nothing to be feared.
How strange that such a fate brings happiness
now that my ravenous desires have failed,
and doubly strange that I should find real calm
and wisdom now that I'm with no one else,
without the wisemen who pretend to know.
No more! I hereby swear off everything.
I shall allow the Void's great mystery,
its gifts that seem to come through emptiness,
to grant the peace that I have always sought.
To do so I'll deny myself those wants
that bear no fruit but only undermine
themselves in striving to endure and grow.
I'll neither work to keep my candle lit
nor blow it out, indifferent to that which
must be until at last I am no more."

He tore old fabric from his tunic's sleeve
and neared the sliver through which sunlight shone
to blot it out, returning to the wet
stone floor, eyes closed, his arms around his shins.
In nine days' time, the top floor's guardian
brought Aqhat's evening rations, knocking on
the door with hollow raps that echoed back.
He opened Aqhat's cell, a torch in hand,
preparing for an ambush, yet, surprised,
he only found an internee who slouched
against the wall, his bread and waterskin

of former days left on the floor, untouched.
The inmate raised his chin and bared a skull's
quiescent and emaciated grin.
At seeing him, the prison guard advised
a daytime jaunt along the open coast,
but Aqhat offered nothing in reply.
That night the watchmen held a festival—
so few and far between—and Aqhat's ward,
stirred both by pity and by drink, brought him
a roasted shank of lamb and cup of wine.
Come morning, back to work, the turnkey found
a swarm of horseflies buzzing all about
the gamey meat, the draft of wine undrunk.
Disturbed, the guard removed these things and left.

Eastward across the sea, on Zaphon's heights,
Baal laid recumbent on a balcony
from which he could behold the endless wood
that sprawled beyond his vineyard to the north.
Unwontedly attired in temptress lace,
seductively reclining at his side,
his sister doted on him with these words,
"Have you recovered from our recent wars?
My dear, I hope that you've enjoyed this time
of much-deserved unwinding here on high.
As one who loves you, I know what you love,
withholding my ambitions for your sake,
biting my tongue because I sense your needs.
Regardless of the doldrums I've endured
these many months, I've tried to play housewife
as best I can, but now I must speak up:
Our international endeavors have
met with success on every battlefront.
Great Washukanni caved beneath your club.

We've brought to heel the Hittite capital.
One foreign foe, one enemy remains:
the mighty pharaoh's red and black domain.

"Three moons ago, I secretly dispatched
my trustworthy Sutean Warrior,
Yatpan, to reconnoiter down the Nile.
Today my scout's returned, informing me
of changes that shall benefit our work.
With grand delusions like we've never seen,
progressing as if there weren't other gods,
imagining himself to be the son
of god (Aten's embodiment on earth),
the pharaoh scrimps on national defense.
Some people worry for his sanity
while others, on whom he has slammed the door
to life beyond the grave, revile his name.
His sandal-licking kin alone love him.
You see? I'd kiss Fate were she here with us!
Our final foe's already rent in two!"

Now sitting up, Hadad made answer thus,
"I do feel rested, ready for more war.
And you are right that only Egypt stands
between us and our dreams-made-manifest.
But we cannot just march an army down
the King's Highway to Horus' Way or sail
our fleet haphazardly into the Nile.
Despite the pharaoh's late moonstrickenness,
he still inherited his father's realm,
the footmen in its sphere of influence,
its far-flung bureaucratic tentacles
from Nubia to the Orontes' banks.
It's reasonable to assume their gods

already seethe at their rebated roles,
receiving lesser offerings these days.
They wouldn't hesitate to rally new
reactionaries to their promises
and so recoup their former eminence.
If we went head-to-head with them right now,
we might not win, and I will only fight
when victory and certainty align.
Additionally, you and I can't leave
Mount Zaphon as we used to do, for our
achievements on the battlefield incite
revenge and jealousy from every side."

Predicting his legitimate concerns,
Anat unveiled to him her master plan,
"Again you're right, my love, on all accounts.
You know that since their transplantation here
I've borne but ill-will toward Egyptian louts
who make themselves at home on stolen soil.
But evil things of every ilk turned toward
good ends become far less detestable.
Egypt's colonial yes-men along
our shores mislike this pharaoh's policies.
With perfumed promises we can transmute
their disapproval into bitter spite
and win them over to our point of view,
inspiring them to take their homeland back.
Once we have seized their hearts, they shall ship off
upon our naval keels with droves of our
own men aboard as slaves until they reach
the outfall of the Nile, continuing
to Memphis where our men shall be detained.
That city will rejoice in its new spoils,
relaxing since fresh labor has arrived.

"By then, our kinsman Kothar-wa-Hasis—
whom Memphis has forgotten owes his troth
to us—will have constructed and prepared
a cache of long spears, corselets, scimitars,
and shields, stockpiling them in armories
known only to our fleet, who on the night
that they arrive shall sack and burn and loot
the city with the men who brought them there,
rapining those who won't capitulate
(and maybe for some fun the ones who do).
If they succeed, the city shall be ours—
a beachhead from which we can operate,
constricting Egypt's central artery,
amassing allies, disallowing trade,
waylaying Akhetaten and Waset
with mercenaries from our vassal states.
But should that expedition fail, it will
appear as nothing but a slave revolt—
one more domestic hiccup to suppress.
Since we'll stand guard on Zaphon as events
unfold, should our clandestine strike fall through,
none will suspect our orchestrating role—
in which case we'll rethink the way ahead."

Astounded at the soundness of her plan,
Baal started to reply when Tallay came
outside, apologizing to each god
for interrupting them, explaining that
Ilisha's wife had broughten word from El.
Hadad invited her to join them, but
Ilisha's wife had little to report—
only that El now summoned him at once.
She didn't know the motive for his call,
but did express its seeming urgency.

Anat begged Baal to stay. He almost did.
But duty to the Superannuate,
Hadad's progenitor, outranked her wish.
For all his faults, El was the Patriarch,
the leader of their noble pantheon.
To humor her, however, Baal allowed
Anat to lay the groundwork for her plan.
They kissed, and he prepared to leave for Lel.

Ducking behind its wuthering cascade,
Baal ventured through Lel's portalway of stone.
A guard escorted him into a room
whose window overlooked the clouds and whose
opposing wall depicted El's defeat
of Anzu with exquisite strokes of paint.
Amidmost in the room a table sat,
upon which bowls of olives, nuts, and figs
surrounded jugs of wine to which Baal helped
himself, inhaling Mount Lel's pristine air.
Of Baal's ingression Elsh informed the Lord,
who walked with Shataqat to meet their guest,
an oliphant of wine in El's right hand.
At seeing Baal, El welcomed him and said,
"My son! Come and embrace the two of us!
We're happy that you're here. Do sit; drink up.
How do things fare upon your mountaintop?
Yes, eat. All that I have is yours as well.
Excuse the questions hurled at you and all
at once—I'm always eager to learn more:
How many of our towns are fortified
with mudbrick crenellations for defense,
and are their secret posterns tunneled out?
Have you been able to track down Resheph
or Athirat, or do you have new clues

as to their whereabouts? It seems so long
ago that all my sons and daughters supped
and sang here—when we laid the cornerstones
pertaining to our people's safeguarding."

More distant from his father than before,
Baal fiddled with his cup of wine, his eyes
transfixed upon the cloudbanks floating by.
Intuiting that something was amiss,
El motioned for his paramour to leave.
Once she'd cleared earshot, El engaged his son,
"I see. Then everything they say is true.
To Hatti and Mitanni you laid siege,
tantruming your way over capitals,
creating new alliances on which
our Council'd not agreed. Tell me I'm wrong.
You don't deny it, then? And let me guess:
You haven't laid a single rampart brick
or dug escape routes for one lousy town.
Have you lifted a finger to espy
Resheph's new hiding place or to track down
your mother, the Creatress of the Gods?
No! You deliberately undermined
the strategies your elders ratified,
inverting the decisions we laid out
to seek Ambition's tantalizing charms.

"My special love for you has blinded me!
I never should have delegated storms
and lightning to you or allowed our Smith
to build your separate palace on the sea.
The power you've inherited's a waste.
When your relations with Anat emerged,
I never came between you, letting your

perverted fun and games go uncondemned.
But now as an accomplice to her crime
she wields and uses you to mastermind
her many-fronted wars beyond our realm.
No longer can I look the other way!
I may have given purpose to the sea
whom giants poisoned with their tears and sweat;
I may have saved that Tablet on which Fate
inscribes her messages; I may have helped
ten thousand lives by forming Shataqat;
but what of my corrupted son, who's put
the aspirations of his sister-bride
above the safety of his fatherland,
above the counsel of the gathered gods?
How could I salvage the great mess you've made
now that our land's a target for revenge?
Among my countless children, you by far
are faithfulest in disobedience."

Steam bruming from Baal's nostrils, he rejoined,
"Spare me paternalist I-told-you-so's.
It's no surprise you don't know what to do:
Decision-making's not your specialty.
You lost the lives of Gerra and Adad
in battle, fleeing eastern lands for Lel
while dragging sloth and carelessness in tow.
In no time Egypt overran our ports.
Our people lost their pride. Megiddo fell.
'More walls,' you said. And how has that panned out?
Have pharaohs more or fewer fortresses
and governors along our coast today?
Which of our kingdoms knows autonomy?
You say you want our home's security,
but first it must become our own again

since one cannot protect something beyond
one's grip! Or can you safeguard Athirat?

"And Shataqat—you speak of her as if
she did much more than cater to your rod.
Until that harlot goes her separate way,
no one will find the Lady of the Sea.
At least I'm faithful to my love Anat,
who doesn't run and hide at my mere sight.
We speak to one another with frank speech,
and when her words are sound, I lend an ear,
as you once wisely did with Athirat.
For the first time, I've won great victories
for us, empowering our land in ways
surpassing that for which we might have hoped.
The empires of Mitanni and Hatti
no longer pose the slightest threat to us.
And who among our gods congratulates
or thanks me? Certainly no one from Lel.
Fine. Just don't stand before this juggernaut.
And so you know: The Council of the Gods
that harvesttime agreed with my advice
and not Lel's pussyfooted strategy.
Absent and drunk, you ratified nothing."

Irate and flabbergasted, El cried out,
"Usurper! Of one thing I can be sure:
You are no son of mine. Be gone at once!"
Baal stormed out of the room and down the hall,
rebuffing aid from would-be chaperones.
Possessed by rage, El stood alone and downed
his draft before he hurled the oliphant
against the mural lining the far wall.
He blankly gazed upon the sky, distressed,

till Shataqat returned, massaging him.
She asked what had occurred and he replied,
"If Zaphon's ingrates only grasp brute force,
if they need help remembering their place,
then I shall speak in terms they understand.
Dispatch one of Ilisha's wives to Yam.
Inform him that should Baal's warships debark
for Egypt's shores he is to sink them all.
My late permissiveness has reached its end—
as will Anat and Baal's destructiveness."

Without delay, one of Ilisha's wives
assumed a nighthawk's guise and winged her way
beyond the rocky shoreline out to sea.
With high-pitched shrieks she called out to the god
until gargantuan Nahar uprose,
a surly scowl inscribed upon his face—
whitewater running down his burly chest.
She lighted on his shoulder, altering
her outward form once more, her comeliness
subduing Yam's innate proclivities.
With honied phrases she imparted El's
commands, at which the deity harrumphed,
for on the one hand he'd disdained Hadad
since Baal had tricked and smote him centuries
ago, recovering from which roused shame,
while on the other hand surrendering
to Mount Lel's Goat annoyed him just as much.
He groused that he would do as he well-pleased.
The messenger departed with a kiss
and Yam plunged back into the salty depths.

Reclined within her home for one last time,
Laeya looked seaward, Aqhat on her mind,

absorbed with how their lives had intertwined.
One floor below, Ameni and Gabbar
paced round their room, awash with jumpiness.
Tonight, the members of the training camp
would sleep in their respective homes and bid
farewell to intimates, for come the dawn
they'd journey to the secret northern cove
in separated, unassuming groups.
Unless her uncle had backed out on them,
the company'd haul anchor by midday.
Prepared or not—the time for action neared.
The unknown future looming over her,
Laeya dispelled its dim uncertainties,
the past intruding on her unannounced.
A reminiscence barged into her heart:

During her second year on Lel, one day
ensuant on an argument with El
whose passion shook the walls, her husband came
to her and tied a blindfold round her eyes,
demanding that she put her faith in him.
His queen obliged him, though with reticence.
Up steep steps El directed her, and though
she couldn't see, she knew that soon they'd reach
the terraced roof where El gave vent to rage.
She feared his unresponsive secrecy
and started to protest, but much too late,
for now she felt his tightened grip and heard
the lonesome swash of heaven's highmost winds.
El then untied the cloth, permitting her
to gape at the botanical display
that trellised, sprung, and smiled before her view.
Bright chamomiles kibitzed amongst themselves
and crocuses empurpled in the sun.

Herbs hinted at the ways they might be used
(although they hoped to not be picked at all)
while yellow bee trumpets hit all their notes.
El took her hand, explaining that he'd stayed
awake all night, alone, to build this place
for her, a peristyle to call her own,
a garden for her cubs to play and rest.
She shed a tear and pulled him close, his black
and musky whiskers titillating her.

Book XIII

Departing from Siduna ere the dawn,
delaying briefly at her uncle's home,
Laeya embraced Zelophehad and his
wife Eliawa for a final time
before she gathered her supplies and rode
northward between Ameni and Gabbar.
Encumbered by the stores and wares with which
the new ships would be laden in due course,
the horses tromped along the esplanade,
the early summer sun a molten pink.
Inception of the arid season calmed
those waves that beat the shores in winter months,
a sight uplifting Aqhat's rescuers
who headed for the hidden northern cove.
Still, the momentousness of what might come,
of the sea's undecidability,
of what befell their friend on foreign shores,
impressed itself upon their cliffhung hearts.

Yet once their eyesight cleared the bluff that walled
the bight's near side, the riders froze in awe
before Zelophehad's woodworkmanship.
Below them beached upon the inlet's bank
sat brand new ships whose size and symmetry
won arguments for their seaworthiness:
Tall carven prows with arching backs embraced
their roles as vanguards to the cedarn walls
of strakes and garboards fitted to the keels;
long screens of wicker ran the planksheers' lengths

between which had been stepped boom-fitted rigs
capped off with crow's nests for an ampler view;
like giant bowstrings, lifts secured the masts
to stem and sternpost notches, pulling up
the hulls' ends like an archer's full-drawn bow;
twin quarter rudders rested on stanchions,
impatient to direct their oarsmen ranks;
and pierced weight-anchors waited for a dive.
Aqhat's companions smiled with wonderment
at one another, racing to the ships
to let their hands confirm their eyes' account.

While they unloaded what they'd brought—like swords,
longbows, fresh barley bread, plump waterskins,
and jugs of wine—the numbers whom they'd trained
began to trickle in, astounded by
the naval fleet that sprawled before their view
just as their leaders promised that it would.
Ameni helped ensure that the supplies
were evenly distributed among
the ships so all could eat and drink and fish
no more nor less than those on other decks
while Laeya greeted those who had arrived
to fan morale and reinforce their hope.
To each ship captain Gabbar made his rounds
to guarantee their readiness to sail,
pretending to a higher confidence
than he in fact possessed, his muscles tense
with knowledge that he couldn't tread or swim.
Observant of his worries, Laeya took
her comrade by the arm, deflecting his
concerns to images of Aqhat's joy
should they extract him from internment's grip.

Midday unveiled her face, yet one small group
went unaccounted for; their absence forced
the leaders to decide whether to sail
without them or to leave no one behind.
Although they disagreed on what to do,
the length of their discussion made the choice
for them, delaying them from setting forth.
But soon a distant figure came to view,
sprinting full speed and wildly gesturing
before all recognized the flailing man
as Burianu the Belated—dubbed
as such in jest (and so, in partial truth)
by Gabbar after his Sidunan trip.
Much slower runners tried to keep apace
with Burianu, losing stamina.
Interpreting his movements, Laeya gave
the order to push off at once, and all
obeyed except the vessel farthest east,
awaiting those who would complete their crew.
When Burianu reached his destined ship
(his breathlessness precluding lucent speech),
the reason for their panic showed itself.
Along the southern ridge strode Abibaal
atop Aliyan, Aqhat's mighty friend,
the frantic horse's muzzle bound with rope.
Behind this man rode sixty guards who on
his signal scudded full stretch for the cove.

Now Gabbar's caprine horn alarmed the fleet
to ply their oars while those who didn't row
began to flank their ships' larboards with shields.
Zimredda's dogs loosed litten arrows at
the ships while those in flight nocked flanes as well,
their aims' proficiency put to the test

far sooner than imagined or desired.
Diurnal shooting stars assailed the keels
as men pitched pales of water on the flames.
Dismounting, some of Abibaal's recruits
attacked the laggard boat on foot but met
swift sharpened bronze with other ideas,
the oars continuing to churn red froth.
By now the tenth and last ship had embarked,
although it strained to catch the other nine
as Burianu's arrows flew behind
his moving targets, ever swift of foot.
Blood christened the new decks as bodies fell
from topmost wales, relinquishing their breath
while Abibaal, who sensed his foes' defeat,
began to spur Aliyan with cruel kicks,
delivering a hiding with his lash.
He clutched a sling-bolt in his hand, a shield
emblazoned with his lord's insignia
across his other forearm, parrying
attacks, inciting soldiers to engage.

The coast's embayment now appeared before
the ships as though it were a finish line
whose prize was life itself, so scullers plowed
their oars with a decisive unity.
Now Laeya—who had lanced her share of men
with bract-tipped spears to send them flying back
the opposite direction of their mares—
unslung the bow that Kothar-wa-Hasis
had carefully designed for Aqhat's day of birth
and nocked an arrow, calling for the shields
in front of her to part, her target fixed.
Before a woman of her crew could douse
the planks afire nearby, their leader lit

her arrow's black, bitumen-covered tip.
Her shoulders drew the bow, her chest distent
as when an eagle opens wide her wings,
but Laeya—who had taught Anat to hunt
and wield a bow so many centuries
gone-by—had no need to invoke her now,
no need to beg the War Goddess for aid.
Some forty fathoms from her mark, she loosed.
The arrow pierced through Abibaal's rear skull—
the leader having turned around to rouse
his horsemen—looking on them now with one
eye skewered by an arrowhead aflame,
ignited and unsocketed just like
a piece of roasting flesh upon a spit.
He raised a shriek of pain, fell from his mount,
and struggled for his life upon the ground
for longer than those in his charge could bear.
They ceased to fight and let their quarry flee,
attempting to control Aliyan's rage.

The ocean gained, the hindmost crew jumped ship,
abandoning it, swimming for the ones
that weren't engulfed by all-consuming tongues.
Uphoisted by the painters tossed their way,
the crew and Burianu watched as Fire
and Water—diametrically at odds
with one another the majority
of days—consumed and wracked the trailing ship
as foes united in a common cause.
Dejected at their loss—dealt out, in truth,
before their seabound journey had begun—
the sailors of the nine remaining boats
attended to their injured kith and kin,
broke off long arrows dug into the strakes,

and scrubbed blood from the battle-tested decks.
As one, the rowers swept the open blue,
the helmsmen orienting them northwest.
With bleak remembrances of what had chanced
to pass and with forebodings of what lay
ahead the company imbued the sea.
In intermittent waves the bowsprit throats
choked on and snorted sprays of bone-white spume
till Fortune pitied them, endowing them
with following seas and converted winds.

Once night set in, the tillers held the course
as the exhausted remnant rocked to sleep.
While lost adream, a tall and muscular
galoot named Ash stood up and strolled about
while mumbling words his steersman found inane,
and so the latter ordered him to lie
back down before he stepped on anyone.
Continuing to sleepwalk, Ash replied,
"No, Mama! I don't want to lie back down.
What do you mean? How could you say such things?
I haven't had an accident in days!
Come see, I'll show you that my tunic's dry."
No sooner had he yammered on this way
than he flopped overboard, the cold salt sea
bewildering and wakening the man.
Ash cried for help and splashed amidst the wake,
arousing those on Laeya's trailing ship.
They tossed a rope his way and haled the man,
demanding reasons for his late-night dip
as Ash confessed to sleepwalking at night,
not wanting to have mentioned it before
so that he'd be ensured a place on board.
Some laughed at him while others, still unnerved

at having been awoken, griped aloud.
Hoping to fix the problem on the spot,
Laeya informed the charge that he would need
to be secured each night for his own good.
Embarrassed yet relieved that he could stay
to sail and fight, Ash gave assent before
men fastened rope around his waist and reeved
and looped the free ends through a sturdy thole.
The crew returned to their much-needed sleep.

One night, the fleet adrift at sea, a small,
horizonal glim glowered on the northern rim—
the flame atop Hadad's confinement spire
which Laeya recognized, instructing all
to veer windward toward Alashiya's cliffs
that fortify the island's southern ridge.
Her ship tacked westward as the other eight
adjusted course, and soon they found themselves
approaching seagirt Alashiya's bluffs.
Now that they'd taken in the oblong sails,
the argosy described the coast until
the lead ship chanced upon a grotto's mouth.
Laeya directed them to venture in,
and soon the nine ships entered through the cave's
black mouth and into its long gypsum throat,
their torchlight scanning ceiling crevices.

The keels collected in the windless delve,
Ameni, Gabbar, and Laeya convened
atop a limestone ledge to contemplate
the way ahead. Gabbar was first to speak,
"Can you believe we really made it here?
Our skirmish at the outset cost us men,
but our militia held their own against

Siduna's regiments—no meager feat.
If Baal's jail lies due east, we should attack
it straight away and not waste needless time.
The night shall keep our army out of sight,
assisting our besiegement of the fort."

Ameni disagreed, opining thus,
"Did you not see how many of our men's
strikes missed their marks when they assailed our fleet?
Our bowmen won't fare better in the dark,
and this terrain is unfamiliar yet.
Aside from these external sticking points,
our soldiers' inner lives demand our care.
We must avoid accustoming our troops
to skirmishing like brigands from the hills:
If we attack and flee like recreants
when it's convenient, none will learn to draw
true courage from within, but lean instead
on circumstance to found their bravery."

The former started to defend his case
when Laeya interposed herself, saying,
"Your words are very manly, but won't men
expect the plans of men? Consider this:
What hamstrings soldiers more efficiently
and with more ease than whettened spears and swords?
No thoughts? Come on, my friends, just take a guess.
Bad women and good wine! I recommend
the following: Let's hit them day and night,
but less with fistic arts than artifice.
Attend this scheme and tell me what you think."
Before them Laeya laid the plan on which
she'd dwelt throughout her ponderous past eves.
Receptive to her arguments, her two

companions charged a few men to protect
the grotto's entryway and with the rest
retired to sleep before the new day dawned.

Ameni and Gabbar awoke to find
that Laeya and her nineteen chosen girls
had bathed and cleaned their skin, massaging salves
and attar on their shoulders, arms, and legs,
their ears and necks embossed with simple yet
attractive jewelry filigreed by hand.
Their perfume ousted from the cave its frowst
and left behind a floral sweetness one
can still enjoy today (or so they say).
Upon a fire these women set a jug
of wine and brought it to a boil before
removing it, allowing it to cool.
Such sights ensorcelled many of the men
who gawped at them until a woman's brow
put loitering oeillades back in their place.
Laeya then ordered men to haul the jug
with five identical oinochoe
that brimmed with wine up to the land above
to place them on a wagon, whereupon
the leaders nodded one another's way,
relaying their unshakeable resolve
and equal comprehension of their roles.

Just following midday, the women left
the grot and scaled the foreland's knaggy face.
They pulled the laden cart onto a path
not far inland and wheeled it toward the east.
The Sun looked on with unsuspecting eyes
as Laeya led her cohort, readying
her heart and body for the deeds to come.

Before long, Baal's confinement tower rose
on the horizon, louring as they neared.
Their trodden seaside path passed close enough
to its foregate to guarantee that they'd
be seen, remaining far enough away,
however, not to raise undue alarm.
The women clenched a handful of their hems—
ostensibly in order to cool down
and stroll with greater ease—displaying bare
and svelte legs, chattering amongst themselves
as if oblivious to the erect,
important edifice due south of them.
They didn't look its way but talked and laughed,
bypassing it like ducklings on the move.

A bolt unlatched and six men exited
the keep, detaining the infringing girls,
interrogating them with swords in hand
as was their role (though some were now disarmed).
Laeya explained that they had traveled here
to relish Alashiya's coast with their
old fathers—merchants of varietals—
but in exchange they had to lug their wine
to eastern villages they'd yet to see.
Bidawa, one of the most gorgeous wights
accompanying Laeya, offered them
a cup of wine in gratitude for their
shieldbearance in so wonderful a land.
Whether their accents beautified their words
or word choice accented their beauty, none
could tell, the guards obliging them the gifts
that gave their knees redoubled firmity.
Auxiliary gaolers left their posts
as if these women and their wares required

the scrutiny of higher ranking men,
but Laeya now lamented that more wine
could not be offered at so low a price.
She thanked them for their doughtiness and charm
then turned to go, the other girls behind
her whispering with subtle, coy delight,
their furtive eyes now fancying a man,
now scampering away, like children who
love hiding just as much as being found.

Their leaving roused self-pity in the men.
By now the head guard had egressed, annoyed
to find his men distracted from their work.
Yet they were quick to justify themselves
by pointing to the bronze-hued foreigners,
relaying what had happened, offering
advice to him, which, had the circumstance
been different, would have been beneath contempt.
The warden stopped the women yet again,
suggesting that they stay with them that eve
because the nearest town was yet far off
and since the seaboard roads proved danger-fraught
once Shapshu snuffed her torch at daytime's close.
He then proposed that—though they had no coin—
perhaps their safekeeping might merit trade
for tastings of the vintage that they hauled.
The girls examined them and spoke amongst
themselves till Laeya thanked them but explained
that she and her companions found the terms
of such a bargain disproportionate.
Their hearts were crushed till, having second thoughts,
Laeya negotiated for a kiss
from each so that their deal might be made fair.
As when a well-placed arrow finds its mark

and makes a heretofore-calm fowl erupt,
a squab of lowest ranking squawked accord,
all others of like mind, a giddiness
before such luck ensembling each of them
as all their drudgery had never done.

The bolder of the men escorted those
they'd eyed inside as others, thinking back
as best they could to what their mothers told
them long ago, wheeled in the cart for those
they wanted to impress with courtesy.
Inside, ad-libbed decorum overtook the guards
who fetched the women cushions, charged the cook
to ready supper earlier tonight,
and lit what lamps and candles they could find.
The women laughed and calmed them, pouring wine
from every vessel save the one which they
had disempowered and dispirited,
declaring it of lesser quality
and thereby deemed unfit for noblemen.
Observant of the warden's general
unease—for he'd not planned for such a night—
Laeya approached the man and sanded his
sharp edges with cool wine and gentle words.

A voluble carousal filled the air.
Some twenty games of coquetry began,
and those unfortunate enough to be
sidelined were either satisfied to smooch
their cups or tried to vie for warmer lips.
When tensions flared between headbutting rams,
their prize would intervene, assuring them
that she was quite enough to handle men
in droves if need be—thus no fights broke out.

The wafts of roasting meat and randy squeals
ascended through the prison floors and filled
the jail cells, torturing the ones left out.
Enjoying being served, no guard refused
a welcome draft; instead, they struck up games
to prove their tolerance and buoyancy,
the women joining them with their flat wine
while feigning drunkenness with expertise.

Now that the night had grown late, Laeya took
the warden's hand and led him to the stairs,
proclaiming to the room that they required
their privacy and might be gone till dawn.
The men's yawls roused the warden who now grinned
with happy stupefaction at his fate.
Festivities continued as the two
climbed up the steps, the guardsman leading her
to the sequestered chamber where he dwelt.
Once they had entered, Laeya closed the door
with delicate, deliberate intent.
Excited, he began to grope for her,
his breath exuding smells of rotten fish,
but she delayed his touch with demure steps,
requesting that he turn away while she
undressed, and though lubricious, he complied.
She warned him not to peek then pulled a loose
brick from the wall and struck him on the skull,
ransacked his person for the keys, removed
a cloak bestrewn across his bed, and lashed
his arms and legs together, stuffing rags
inside his mouth and tying them with cord
so that, if he should wake, he couldn't yell.

With catlike steps she left the room and climbed
the guard-free tower's stairwell till she reached
a cedar hatch that opened to the roof.
A seaborne wind unnerved the lighthouse flame.
Along the rooftop's southwest side she held
the warden's cloak up high before the fire,
occluding and unveiling it three times.
Just south of her behind a headland's crest
awaited Gabbar—energized and nerved
by the alarum on which they'd agreed.
Checking their readiness a final time,
he drew his blade and then advanced upon
the southern gate with his armed regiment.

The ground floor's revelry had livened up
and some men dared a new recruit to go
see if their leader needed any help.
Abashed, the tyro finally gave in
to his uncomfortable reconnaissance,
tiptoeing up the steps and down the hall.
He put his ear up to the warden's door
and, hearing nothing, made to knock and check
that everything was fine and well inside.
But sudden noises soon deterred his hand.
A groan and muffled sigh escaped the room
accompanied by creaking table legs
and bellows bouncing off the bedroom walls.
The prudish boy flushed red and ran downstairs,
his betters horselaughing at his expense.
One man then called out for his favorite jugs,
deciding that he'd rather help himself
to refills than await Bidawa's aid.
He stood up, stumbling toward the remnant wine

to find that every ewer save the one
from which the women drank had been drained dry.
He pushed a girl aside to top his cup
then gulped a swig that dribbled down his chin
before expelling it upon the floor.
The toper looked into his cup, confused,
then sniffed the vapid drink and scanned the room.
He saw three women speaking soberly
amongst themselves and, growing paranoid,
alarmed the men that they had all been conned.

Unlocking the south gate, Bidawa met
Gabbar and his accoutered soldiery.
He thanked her and she hastened him inside
where guards had taken up their swords with hate
against the women whom they'd come to love.
Aqhat's salvation burst into the hall,
engaging topsy-turvy warriors,
the feast's rambunctious clamor now replaced
by the cacophony of clanging bronze.
Dispatching archers to the balcony,
Gabbar mowed down the men who came for him.
But as one clears good tilling land of weeds
to sow new crops, unable to avoid
an oaken giant of five hundred years,
a tree that's never bowed to anyone,
not even to the gales of breaking storms,
just so did Gabbar meet an axman, one
whose fenestrated crescent dripped with gore.

The giant swung for Gabbar's neck but missed
as Gabbar ducked and rolled off to the side.
Three bowmen shot the axman from above,
their arrows' fletching sprouting from his arms

and back and shoulders, but to no avail.
Gabbar's riposte collided with the man's
long helve and sent a shimmer through his bones
as one more arrow struck the man's left arm,
its penetration's depth enraging him,
inciting him to growl and whirl around
and hack with a berserk monstrosity.
Swift Gabbar dodged his fury. Countering
when possible, he sliced the man's right thigh,
a risk-fraught strike that almost cost his life.
The axman charged and chopped again but smashed
a pillar that upheld the colonnade—
exploding rubble blasting through the air.
The balcony beginning to give way
beneath her feet, an archeress slid down
the new declivity and leapt onto
the axman's shoulders, capturing his head
between her bow and bowstring from behind
before she yanked and turned it widdershins
so that the hulking brute could draw no breath.
Expelling chalky detritus upon
the stone floor, Gabbar gained his wits once more,
took to his feet, and then propelled himself
off of a riven stone to drive his blade
clear through the angry axman's tender throat.
The latter fell with a colossal thud
just as the archeress leapt safely off,
her bow bemangled, useless evermore.

Attempting to retrieve his sword dug deep
into the spinal column, Gabbar felt
an arm snake round his neck and pull him back,
a knife blade pressing on his jugular.
The drunken guard who'd sounded the alarm

before took Gabbar hostage, such that all
within the erstwhile sporting house could see.
Gabbar's surviving men-at-arms looked on,
unsure of what to do, and while their head
commanded them to fight, their loyalty
to him advised them to give up the fray,
for though few guards remained, still Gabbar's life
proved too important to abandon now.
Retreating, using Gabbar as a shield,
the injured and besotted hireling
began to dodder backwards from his foes
before he ceased to limp entirely,
a well-timed arrow puncturing his brow.
Stunned, Gabbar stepped away and looked aloft
to see Bidawa, empty bow in hand,
smiling with a robustious elegance.

A sanguine rush inspirited Laeya
as she began to search for Aqhat's cell.
A torch clenched in her hand, she called his name
and tried distinguishing his voice from those
who shouted from their cells for help, for all
by now had grasped that trouble was afoot.
Yet from behind one door no succorance
rang out, a silence full of meaning that
eluded her and beckoned for her keys.
She tried a host of them before one clicked.
Having flung wide the door, she stepped inside,
the flimmer of her torchlight going first.
Again she called to him without response.
A bundle in the corner turned her way,
a heap of rags with an anemic sight
within—an etiolated young man
of sallow countenance and sharpened bones.

Verklempt, she cried his name and ran to him,
her blood aswirl with gratitude that he'd
been found, with sorrow at his present state,
and with a boiling wroth for those who'd trapped
him here and treated him with such contempt.
He did not see her though, transpiercing her
as if she were a freshet or a breeze.
For all of her foresightfulness, Laeya
had not once thought that she would reunite
with Aqhat in such dark vacuity.
A scratchy pain constricted her airways
until the sound of her name startled her.

Bidawa and Gabbar had searched for her
and found her on the topmost floor with him,
yet Gabbar scarcely recognized the man
and, swallowing his sadness, spoke to him,
encouraging his friend to rise and leave
since they had cleared the tower of all threat.
But like a cavefish, Aqhat couldn't hear
or see him—coughing, mumbling shadowy
and incoherent words about the Void.
Laeya tore down the garment covering
his window, turned around, and spoke to them,
"His spirit rots as long as he stays here.
Bidawa, make ready the cart so we
can wheel him to our ships, and find what food
and drink remain so he can have his fill.
Once you have done this, free the internees
from these decrepit cellblocks, offering
the heartiest two scores a place upon
our keels—a new start and perhaps revenge—
if they swear fealty on the sacred Shard
of Destinies that unifies our cause.

The rest shall be allowed to go in peace
if they too swear to seal within their breasts
the costly means of their deliverance.
Gabbar, help me to carry Aqhat down
the stairs and transfer him onto the cart.
Let's get him to the ships without delay."

They did just as she bade, for shock before
some grave event ofttimes deters debate.
Bidawa cushioned Aqhat's vehicle,
informing her detachment of their luck
while tamping their excitement with the facts,
advising them to gather up their spoils
then make way for the cave—prepared to sail.
The warriors collected corselets, spears,
bronze swords, and helms of greater quality
than those they owned, their winnings tempering
the bitter news of Aqhat's feebleness
and of their need to brave the seas so soon,
for they were battleworn and sleep-bereft.
They also took what amphorae and cups
of Alashiyan-make that they could find,
and to this added copper braziers, oil,
and crates replete with salted bream.
Laeya and Gabbar hefted Aqhat down
the steps, positioning him on the cart
and giving him what food and drink they had,
though he refused them to their great dismay.

Benighted words slipped from their leader's lips,
"Who tries to lure me to my former ways?
Who tempts me with life's fickle niceties?
Oblivion is all I am and know.

I keep its nothingness and it keeps me."
This strange delirium aggrieved his friends.
These weren't the words of joyousness, nor this
the liberated leader whom they'd sought.
Some hex or madness overtook him now:
His muscles and his spirit atrophied,
the goal uniting them turned upside down.
While wheeling Aqhat westward down the path,
his friends began to wonder if the words
he'd spoken weren't in some sense accurate,
for how could such a leader—down and out,
determined, moreover, to stay that way—
how could a leader such as that revive,
much less conduct a theomachic war?
These thoughts transmogrified their victory
(so recently achieved) into defeat,
as though the words of Aqhat spellbound them,
as though the vanity of everything
had come about with Aqhat's saying-so.

By now apprised of Aqhat's bittersweet
salvation and affliction, Ameni
departed from his guardpost in the grot
to meet his friend's conveyors to the ships.
He found them on the road. They each stood back
to let him gaze upon the man who'd saved
him in the desert, now almost a corpse.
Clear images of their comradery,
the trying distances that they'd traversed,
and their close calls with once-pastoral gods
and sorceresses overcame his heart—
his eyes upwelling, vitric tidal pools.
Inumi's orphan told his counterpart

of what had fallen out in their attack,
repeating Aqhat's mutterings about
Oblivion to round off his account.

Ameni wiped his nose and said to them,
"Gabbar, you're sure those were the words he used?
Bidawa, Laeya—you both attest to this?
Perhaps there may be something we can do.
When I was still quite young, employed within
the Walls of the Ruler, I overheard
a merchant tell my father of some girls
who spoke of life and the Oblivion
as Aqhat does—verbatim, truth be told.
That merchant said a curse befell the lot
of them, such that life's pleasures turned to gloom,
its gloominess turned cause for pleasantries.
They manacled and gave themselves away,
interpreting the disenfranchisement
of their desires as hard-won liberty,
now deferent to blank indifference.

"The last one to possess these willing slaves—
a widower and landowner advanced
in years—decided that he'd find a way
to break the wretched chain that bound these girls,
for while he'd been a decent man, he thought
an act of selfless piety would set
things right between him and his household gods.
He sold his vast demesne and bought a boat
kit out with every furnishing desired,
his servants rowing cross the seas to find
whatever purgative or magic drink
would cure them of resentment toward the world.
He lived aboard that ship with them for ten

relentless years, pursuing mystagogues'
cold trails, petitioning seercraftsmen
and far-flung mavens, every time for naught.
At last in Keftiu he found success,
his former bondswomen revivified
and blossoming with magnified resolve
to see to their forgotten destinies.
Just how this came to pass remains obscure,
but legends and accounts agree in one
respect, to wit, that seagirt Keftiu—
the largest isle amidst the Western Seas,
the land that some call 'Kaphtor'—held their cure."

No words escaped their throats, the four of them
somewhat uplifted by Ameni's tale
yet rattled by the distance and the time
required to reach that western island's sands—
leagues opposite the Hittite watercourse
Puruna, up which they had hoped to sail.
Soliciting the helmsmen of their fleet,
Laeya inquired if they could find their way
to Kaphtor, and while all had heard of it,
Kalbu alone had voyaged to that land
when just a boy. She took the reins and said,
"We've saved our leader's body, but his soul
remains ensnared—without restoring which
we cannot help him overtake the gods.
In four days' time we sail for Kaphtor's shores
with Kalbu's knowledge of the wind and waves.
The yearlong window granted Aqhat shrinks
with ever-growing haste, so we must move.
Prepare to hunt and gather what we'll need,
for we won't cruise the reaver-riddled coasts
but sail the open water, come what may.

Bidawa, see to it that all the ships
refill their empty skins with freshwater
for one moon's journey at the very least.
And Gabbar, tend to Aqhat's needs—but pay
no mind to decadent words he lets fall
lest they prevail upon your spirit too."
Each set about their tasks, and in four days
the nine ships exited the grotto's mouth,
their bows bent westward toward their threadbare hope.

Five days thereon, three vultures flew across
the Alashiyan lowland, making swift
descent and then relinquishing their shape
for demigodlike form before Baal's gaol.
Unlike his kin, though, Gapn yet retained
a sable wing where symmetry required
an arm—a leftover he flapped and flailed
frustratedly while Ugar laughed at him
(not noticing he stood on claws himself).
Now Hirgab spun around—worn out from months
of scouting Hittite lands with birdbrained cocks—
withdrew his sword, and lopped off Gapn's wing
in one fell swoop, an arm now shooting forth.
As Hirgab's eyes met Ugar's, Ugar ran
and fell, their pecking order's highest rank
excising Ugar's bony, taloned claws
from which there sprouted proper, sandaled feet.
Baal's wayworn messengers had one last stop
ere they returned to Zaphon's majesty
to bring him knowledge of his realm's affairs.
The Father of the Vultures rapped upon
the tower's portal, eager for a bed
preceded by a meal for noble guests—
for though the tower lacked the finer things,

the memory of dozing on tree limbs
and beaking carcasses repulsed him now.
He knocked again, more forcefully this time,
but no one came to welcome them inside.
Perturbed, the courier stepped back, condensed
his strength, and kicked the gate to knock it down.
The three walked through the generated plume
of dust to find the hall in disarray
with signs of ransacking writ large across
the scene, not least of which were fallen guards.
In vain they searched each floor for any show
of life, disgusted by the grave affront
upon the holdings of their Lord Hadad.
Once they had reached the rooftop they resumed
their volucrine morphologies and soared
toward Zaphon's heights where Baal awaited them.

When they touched down before the silvered gate,
two stolid palace guards conducted them
through Zaphon's labyrinthine yet spacious halls
to weighty doors through which a taurine voice
bade entry, welcoming the couriers
into a vaulted bathhouse filled with steam.
Along its pool's perimeter relaxed
the handsomest attendants of Baal's manse,
the Lord himself chest-deep beside Anat.
Commemorating victories afield,
five artists painted the surrounding walls
with intricate and marvelous tableaux,
the torchlight adding motion to their work.
Sensing the business-talk to soon unfold,
Baal put a hold to their divertissements,
excusing his attendants and artistes.
Once all except Anat and Baal had left,

Hirgab began relaying Hittite news,
depicting Suppiluliuma's work
in reconstructing Hatti's armature.
Yet Gapn couldn't tolerate his dull
recountings, interrupting him like this,
"My Lord, forgive my haste, but you must know:
Someone's made inroads on your property—
your Alashiyan tower's been despoiled.
Its guards lie caked in blood, unburied yet,
the cells of every floor without a soul.
We searched the premises for any clue
that might betray the perpetrators' goal.
We had no luck. No witnesses remained.
What reason could one have to liberate
the world's worst criminals, the ones who spit
upon your name and desecrate your will?
What fool would walk up to a steer and poke
him in the eye, not caring if he's gored?
Don't mortals know the rains depend on you?
Do thundercracks not awe them anymore?"

Baal raised his dripping hand to quiet him.
He thanked his scouts and urged them to retire,
enjoying food and drink as was their due.
When they had gone, Anat made known her thoughts,
"Mere mortals wouldn't dare maraud your spire—
even that fool came close to grasping this.
We both know who would benefit the most
from disenthralling those opposed to you
in such a passive, underhanded way.
Our father has no time or energy
for full-scale war with you, so he attempts
to win his vengeance surreptitiously
in hopes you'll bow as vassal and as son.

To not respond to his affront in kind
would but condone his petty backstabbing.
The king Tushratta's subject to your will.
Command him to attack one of the towns
that El holds dear lest he grow bolder still."

Baal weighed her counsel, making answer thus,
"If we're to send our warships to the south
to capture Memphis, let's not whip up strife
or open infighting on the home front.
Dependence is obedience's soil.
Thus while in word El won't subject
himself to me so long as he shall live,
if he relies on me in deed, then I'll
blockade retaliatory attacks,
effecting real control throughout the realm.
Listen to what I now propose we do:
I'll fill enormous jars of azurite
with lightning, giving one to Pidray, one
to Tallay, and another to Yatpan
to place within the pinewood round Mount Lel.
When night sets in, the vessels shall explode
with deflagrating rage, alighting trees
who'll pass their torch one neighbor to the next.
As I'll prevent my clouds from circling Lel,
El won't suspect my thunderbolts as cause,
but he will need my rains to douse the flames,
requesting that I send his palace aid.
So humbled, I will summon thunderstorms—
a sign of my largesse and needfulness."
Anat adored the plan and mounted him.

The next day Yatpan, Tallay, and Pidray
departed for the wooded base of Lel.

With care they lugged their levigated jars,
avoiding eyes and ears of sentinels.
Yatpan tucked one within a chaparral
while Tallay and Pidray dug shallow holes
in separate valleys to inter their gifts.
They exited as swiftly as they'd come.
Shapshu delved underground as usual
before Yarikh assumed his nightwatch post.
The Wise One lounged within a portico
accompanied by Elsh who'd just returned
from unsuccessful recons for the queen.
While pondering where they might search, or what
they might now do to locate Athirat,
a blinding light midway between their view
and the horizon burst into the sky.
Two equal flashes followed it as three
explosions rocked the stone-walled citadel,
loud shouts of "Fire!" from the woodland's depths
antiphonal to screams from El's abode.
As if he hadn't aged a day, El sprung
up from his couch, ran to the banister,
and gaped upon the catastrophic blaze.

A god of action from his first of days,
Elsh scanned the conflagration down below,
advising El to call upon his son,
the Rider on the Clouds, whose rains could save
the pines before they were reduced to ash.
Such counsel fanned the Lord's contrarian
ire till it reached an apical degree.
He shot down his advice, which failed to take
into account intradynastic feuds,
directing him to muster everyone
of able strength beneath Lel's waterfall

whereat long lines should form to pass full jugs
of water to the sources of the fires.
Elsh found his Lord's command unwise, yet he
possessed enough good sense to know his place,
hying to spread the word to all he could,
including his own troops who grabbed what bowls
and amphorae they could to quell the tongues.
El's faithful (who'd slept soundly through the night
till now) self-organized in teams between
two roaring enemies—Lel's cataract
of freshwater and groves of fir ablaze.
They struggled through the night, and when the dawn
shone, trees predating El's arrival smoked
amidst annihilation's afterglim.
The Lord's plan worked, but at the great expense
of wooded neighborhoods who'd still stand tall
had he sought aid from Baal's abundant clouds.
El looked upon his realm and wondered how
the blaze began, regretting giving Baal
dominion over rain and thunderstorms.

When word reached Baal, confirming what he'd feared,
to wit, that his ploy to entrap Lord El
had failed, he glared across the Vasty Verd,
the anger swelling in his abdomen
just like a wicked fetus, hammering
inside as stormclouds clustered overhead.
The bolts within them veined like bloodshot eyes,
amassing ever greater might to match
his mood until the Thunderer let loose
the war-cry lodged within his breast—a squall
to quail even Anzu, if he had lived—
distending westward, whipping up the waves.

Kalbu directed Laeya's fleet with ease.
By night he starward gazed, their kingly light
reflecting on the spangled calm below
like speckled stretches of obsidian.
Only the mid-dream murmurings of Ash
would rise into the night until his mates
could brook no more and stuffed a sop between
his teeth to quieten the giant bairn.
The days were clear. Etesian winds kicked up,
upfilling sails and granting oarsmen rest.
Aqhat lay bundled inside Gabbar's bilge.
The latter tended to his body's needs,
providing sips of wine and chewing food
for him because of Aqhat's will-lessness.
Gabbar recounted what they'd done since he'd
been captured but his friend heard none of it,
the bane possessing him too strong for words.

One eve, the storm that Baal unwittingly
unleashed enveloped the far-eastern skies.
Bright flashes heralded ensuant roars—
the rockless rockslides of the firmament.
The crews began to panic out-and-out
and drove their ships away from the wind's eye,
the pilots bracing for their imminent
demise, commanding all to break their backs,
for none save Gabbar while in Shasu land
the night that Pugat died had seen such clouds.
The tempest salvoed on them in a trice,
fomenting groundswells as the nine ships heeled
like desiccated leaves acrawl with ants
careening downriver through whitewater.
Against the hulls and riggings spindrifts slashed
while stormwinds gusted, shearing through the sails

and casting rain-drenched mariners to Yam's
subaqueous empire beneath the waves.
And in this glooming, Aqhat grabbed the spar,
hoisting himself with nothing in the world
to fear, disciple of Void's nothingness.
He wondered if his final hour had come,
his vacant visage fixed upon the vault.
Gales fulminated at his arrogance,
but still he gripped the mast, indifferent now
to anything that might occur to him.
He stood so-poised, as if immutable,
until the white-rimmed grizzled clouds dispersed,
the savage storm relinquishing its raid
with one and twenty sailors as its price.

The morrow saw repatching of the sails
and jerry-rigging of the booms and yards
while pilots struggled to reorient
the spersed and sheveled vessels to their course
with Kalbu at the flagship's helm once more.
Soon word began to circulate about
the bravery of Aqhat in the storm:
Without the faintest flinching he'd stared down
the lightning till it disappeared for good.
Was it not obvious that he drove it
away from them? When had the man attained
such godly confidence, and how might they
begin to emulate and draw from it?
Undoubtedly, not everyone survived—
but most were Alashiyan internees
of suspect fealty whereas Aqhat's men
and women, by and large, had made it through.
In this way many spoke of him with awe.
Laeya and Gabbar, on the other hand,

were furious with Aqhat's wantonness.
Yet soon their swirling blood subsided just
as had the squall, relief replacing wrath,
allowing each to focus once again
on reaching Kaphtor's coast without more loss.

Book XIV

As if in mimicry of those aboard,
the vessels listed listlessly at sea,
the constant trials of sailing having drained
provisions just as quickly as esprit.
In private, Kalbu told the ones in charge
that they (by all accounts) should have arrived
in Kaphtor days ago. His worries sapped
from them what little strength that they'd retained
when from the lead boat's crow's nest rose the cry
of "Land!" whose joy transshipped, uplifting all
(save Aqhat) with new thoughts of dirt between
their toes, roast meats, and stationary beds.
Since they would play the part of traders here,
Laeya commanded every ship to cache
their arsenal below and bring the spoils
most fit for barter where they could be seen.
The ninesome veered southwest and traced the coast
in search of ports that might prove open-armed.
Anon a fleet far vaster than their own
appeared, approaching them head-on, the head
boat drawing close to Laeya's forerunner.
Down from the nearing flagship's afterdeck
there stepped a boy beside a brawny man
sporting a knee-length kilt, a belt to hold
his scabbard, and a leathern helm whose dome
and cheekguards were composed of tusks of boar.
This head of Knossos' warships, Madi, said,
"Good day to you, my seaspent voyagers.
With what designs do you cruise Kaphtor's coast?

Do you seek entry to our island towns
to trade or does some peril drive you here?"

Running her left hand through her walnut hair,
with one leg on the sheer, Laeya replied,
"My lord, we are but merchants from abroad.
We hail from many different climes: the Land
between Two Riverbanks, Siduna, Dor,
and metal-wealthy Alashiyan hills.
We braved the open seas so as to trade
unequaled goods with Kaphtor's fabled hosts
and wish to be your guests for one moon's time."

Now Madi turned to Talos, the first-beard
whom Outward-Looking Minos—Knossos' king—
selected to be groomed for leadership
of his revered and powerful navy someday.
Since whether they allowed the fleet to land
was not of consequence for an isle rich
as theirs, Madi deferred to Talos so
that he might feel command's peculiar weight.
The boy spied copper ingots, tripods, jugs—
perhaps of wine or olive oil—white tusks
of elephants, and many things besides,
remembering the way the market swelled,
the way the town lit up each time a fleet
of merchants similar to this put in.
With confidence he gestured Madi's way,
the latter welcoming them to his home.

Like children told of coming relatives
whose visit seems eternally deferred
expend their jumpiness once they've arrived,
embracing them and looking out for gifts,

so too delphinic chaperones propelled
themselves into the predawn air to catch
a glimpse of what these strangers hauled on board
while entertaining and escorting them
with Madi toward the docks of Amnisos.
Sleek boats cast nets beyond their yellow sides
embellished with ceil-blue clouds, tourbillions,
and dolphins, each stem raising floral gifts
as if the trawlers, though their function be
banal, could double as a house of prayer.
The vessels drew abreast to spacious piers.
Debarking from the flagship, Laeya found
the moorings' fixity unbalancing—
by now accustomed to the sea's sway, not
to say its inborn volatility.
She gained her land-legs and embraced her hosts.
Rehearsing his appointed role-to-come,
Talos addressed the emerald-eyed like this,
"Welcome to Amnisos, my friend, a town
that serves King Minos, Knossos' diadem.
They call me Talos. Madi is his name.
You're free to move about this coastal town.
The central market lies not far from here:
There you'll find artisans who'll haggle you
by day for all you're worth, inviting you
back to their homes come night where, over cups of wine,
they'll lavish you with gifts and drawn-out yarns.
Should you not need to hasten on from here,
I would invite you and three other guests
to Knossos' yearly Games twelve days from now
as it would not be fitting if you left
not having lain eyes on the Labyrinth's halls.
To be so bold: How do you know our tongue?"

As gracious guests are wont, she made answer,
"Our thanks, young Lord, for Knossos' openness.
You won't regret your hospitality,
and may our merchants profit equally.
It is with utmost gratitude that I
accept your invitation to the Games.
As to your final query, my old man
(who now rests peacefully beneath the earth)
was of Siduna's most respected skips
to fare the Great Green Sea, and he proved wise
enough not only to bequest his fleet to me,
but also to ensure that I could speak
the languages of those on distant shores;
thus he employed three tutors in my youth
who taught me everything I know today."

They spoke at some length, strolling down the dock
and toward a town where poros limestone homes
had huddled close to one another right
behind two towers topped with corbelled domes.
Her company secured their weathered ships,
unloading wares to swap for drinks and beds.
Ameni charged a random lot to guard
the boats by turns and told the rest to keep
low profiles while in town, to stir no frays,
insulting no one, keeping ready at
an eyeblink's notice to reboard the ships
if at some point he sounded the alarm.
Half-listening, the sailors made their way
landward where palm trees shot up where they willed.
Though few were expert hawkers, most waxed bold
at thoughts of what they might procure for their
hard-earned spoils from the isle's exotic folk.

Now Gabbar and Ameni hauled Aqhat
onto a cart that sat upon the pier.
Though Aqhat had regained a little weight
thanks to his friends' resolve, a darkness palled
him still, depleting him of hardihood.
Behind the rest they lugged their deadweight friend
toward Amnisos in which they sought an inn
where he could rest until the cure for which
they hoped (should it exist) appeared to them.
A smiling, crookback woman sighted them
and flagged them down, inviting them inside
her inn with words they couldn't comprehend,
and while they didn't know whom they could trust,
the dwelling of this boniface adjoined
a peristylic yard whose summer blooms,
fruit trees, and sun-bound ivy signaled that,
if like her garden she could tend an inn,
then she would make an expert caretaker.
In their own tongue they spoke to her and she
replied in hers, and while their words fell flat,
their gifts and gestures interceded on
behalf of both the strangers and their host.
She showed them to a cozy room upon
the terraced roof swept by a steady breeze.

Unpacking their supplies, the occupants
discussed how they would tend to Aqhat's needs,
one watching him the while the other worked
alongside Laeya to descry the spell
or magic antidote that he required.
The mass for whom they'd crossed the Great Green Sea
sat slowly upward on the bed where he'd
been lain, a caul stretched over both his eyes,
ere letting fall these words into their laps,

"All plans, all voyages are rendered null
in time—they come to naught no matter what.
Who are these idiots surrounding me?
Why do fools fret and fight and carry on
with their inane delusions? Pardon them.
They do not grasp the meaning of the Void—
that all unfolds and ends in emptiness."

Aqhat's companions flushed with crimson rage,
turning and storming from the upper room,
slamming the door behind them as they went.
Ameni ventured off to find a meal
in town while Gabbar headed for the coast
to walk alone and dry his misted eyes.
Returning from the pier, Bidawa saw
the man and greeted him no sooner than
she read his forlorn face and felt for him.
Attempting to conceal his cares from her,
he told her that he wanted to explore
the coast; she risked accompanying him.
Beside her Gabbar strolled the oceanfront
where, to the north, the turquoise offing rose
to meet the sky's cerulean expanse.
The hustle-bustle of the town died down
as they retreated silently, its din
surrendering to rustling fronds of palm.
She grabbed his arm to halt him, gesturing
toward constellated daffodil wherefrom
there sprung a cat that snared a waterfowl.
They spoke with one another naturally
while walking on—with silent interims
that neither burst with meaning at the seams
nor like a glutton beckoned to be stuffed,
instead entwining and renewing them.

Ascending a remote escarpment, they
looked southward where mowers scythed golden spelt.

Possessed of anima and waywornness
at once (in harmony comingled spite
their disaccord), Gabbar and Bidawa
sat underneath a quince tree, taking rest.
They plucked its yellow fruit and ate of it,
indulging in their isolated view
of sun-kissed workboats on the placid sea
and sipping wine Bidawa'd brought along.
Now summoning her courage, she inquired
what troubled him and he replied in time,
"I don't know why I love the ones I love,
or why I go to such great lengths for them
when everyone to whom I give myself
transforms with irrevocability.
Where death has not yet wrested them from me,
for such divisions living paves the way,
each minor change prefiguring the last.
How many times I've sat upon a bluff
with Aqhat, drinking wine, conversing as
we are right now, recounting tales of old.
Yet now I fear his spirit's gone for good.
I no more know him than one from a crowd,
nor does he recognize his longtime friend.
Why sacrifice for him? Or is it that
I only love those memories his face
reconjures, though devoid of life themselves?
I'm sorry. I should not be bothering
you with these extra burdens. Let us go."

Bidawa took his forearm and replied,
"You place no burden on me that I don't

desire to share, or I would not have come.
A childhood friendship's roots are strong and deep,
so much so that we oftentimes forget
that they can grow and die and be reborn.
Knowing how long they took to plumb the earth,
we balk before a sapling, fearing that
it too might fail to thrive—a waste of time.
Of course, we cannot know before the fact.
But I have seen you risk your life against
whole droves of warriors for those you love
and have loved—so I've faith that when you're faced
with fears for those you do or might or shall
love, you'll proceed with equal steadfastness."
Her words pulled them together till they both
enjoyed the fruit of one another's lips
with tenderness—then self-abandonment.

In Amnisos that night, Laeya brought peas
with roasted hoopoe to Aqhat's quarters,
but he refused the meal impassively.
She sat beside him as he laid upon
his sickbed, speaking though he couldn't hear,
"We'll find your remedy, Aqhat, I swear,
whether upon this isle or someplace else,
even if we must sail where none have gone.
Some days I blame myself for all of this.
Why did I stand aside and let you ride
off to Siduna after what I'd dreamt,
and with the likes of Burianu as
your only aid and means of armed support?
I'll never err in such a way again,
doubting the visions granted while I sleep . . .

"Remember when we met? So much has passed
since Eliawa dragged the three of you
upstairs into our hearth that welcome night.
Who would have thought what those lushes, their hair
disheveled from a recent scrap, confused
and bumbling (though decent-looking nonetheless)—
who would have thought what they would come to mean
to me before a half-year's time elapsed?
Unknowingly, you've saved me from so much:
a gnawing boredom, aimless restlessness,
imbedded feelings of futility,
and from things in my past that I . . . that I
long to explain to you—not here or now,
but someday, when the time is ripe. Goodnight."

With no discovery of purgatives
or spells or charms in twelve days' time, Laeya
and Gabbar hired horse-drawn chariots
to visit Knossos for its yearly Games.
Laeya rode with Ameni, holding firm
the reins as Aqhat slouched between their legs.
Abreast Bidawa, holding up the rear,
Gabbar controlled his two-wheeled wooden ride,
excited for the coming festival.
They took an unpaved road southwest through groves
of cypress, almond, and pistachio,
bypassing locals who saluted them.
Approaching Knossos' outskirts, they pulled up
beside a dwelling where they planned to sleep
that night and left their four-hoofed friends behind
with Aqhat, walking up the Royal Road
where metalworkers damascened bronze blades,
deft potters spun their wheels, and women worked

warp-weighted looms with callused fingertips.
Amidst the crowded street Talos emerged,
discovering his honored invitees,
his face exuberant, his garb pristine.
He proudly led them as his special guests
toward Minos' rivalless, fantastic fane,
its monumental walls of schist and vast,
carnelian propylaea looming large.

The five continued past the open air
theatral area and entered through
the sacred Labyrinth's northwest portico,
past the induction vestibule, and down
adjacent hallways lit by lamps of oil
and lightwells where each mazing turn revealed
frenetic tendants hurrying about
their tasks before exquisite, frescoed walls.
The jostling commoners and priestesses
alike forced Talos to conduct his guests
down narrow, zigging-zagging corridors
until they spilt into a sun-soaked Court
where some six hundred Knossians had thronged.
The fairer sex wore robes engirdled at
the hip with bodices whose slits allowed
their bronze-complected womanhood to breathe.
They styled their hair like turrets bound with cloth
whereas the men wore boots of oxen hide
with well-washed kilts or tunics gleaming white.
Those present toasted to each other's health,
downed cups of wine, compared their summer yields,
and shared what gossip they'd acquired of late.

Talos escorted his astonished guests
between the multitude toward a table

along the far wall, raised for all to see.
When they drew near, a royal entourage
of tattooed Libyans stood in their way,
that is, until the sovereign, having glimpsed
the future leader of his naval fleet,
commanded that his swords make way for him.
Forth from his lofted seat King Minos came,
a laurel chaplet set atop his head,
embracing Talos with paternal pride.
Queen Pasiphaë, noble yet reserved,
descended too, a tethered lioness
in hand, its collar lined with blushing pearls.

At seeing it, Aqhat's companions backed
away in fear—save Laeya—who approached
the wildcat with a gentle confidence.
It licked her fingers, nuzzling its soft head
against her hips so she might rub its neck.
Laeya complied, her nails remembering
just where and how to scratch without a thought.
Admiring her for this, Pasiphaë—
whose curls of long black hair were cinched with twists
of copper wire, her white dress fastened by
a bronzen fibula of tangled snakes—
observed her husband play the role of host,
a eunuch translating his overture,
"Good people from the East, we're glad you've come!
Talos has told me of your anchorage
in Amnisos and of your origins.
Please sit with us—it's best to watch from here."

Talos excused himself respectfully.
Attendants escorted the men behind
the king and to their elevated seats

beside him at table while Knossos' queen
took Laeya and Bidawa's hands in hers,
accompanying them to chairs reserved
for highborn socialites and priestesses.
Now throwing both his arms around Gabbar
and Ameni, the outward-looking king
addressed his visitants from overseas,
"I'm happy that you've come in summertime
to see our Games and celebrate with us.
I wouldn't have you sail back home to speak
of Amnisos alone as if that town—
although it has its simple charms—were all
our land and people have to offer you.
Though on a giant rock amidst the waves,
we're far from insular or hidebound folk;
just the reverse! Our ports embrace the world,
a world abounding with new contacts, lands
unsettled, and adventures to be had.
From one another we have much to learn,
of this I do not have the slightest doubt.
Tell me: The temples of the East—are they
just as preeminent as I've heard tell,
uniting everyone in common cause
and seeing to the proper ordering
of rulers with their ruled, of gods and men?
And are the lawgivers—from Babylon
to Ugarit and Egypt—just and fair,
controlling their domains with piety?"

Gabbar made to respond but was curtailed
by bellowing outsent from triton mouths
which organized the gathered crowds behind
a fence along the Court's perimeter.
Beside the queen a manservant delayed

and whispered something in her ear that made
her giggle as her husband leered at them.
Now twenty girls approaching womanhood
departed from the Labyrinth's sacristy,
their shining tresses falling at their waists,
their flounced white skirts revealing nimble feet.
They linked arms in a crescent near the Court's
north wall as on the south end doors flung wide
to outburstings of snorts and hostile lows.
Twin bulls emerged, the vastest on the isle,
each sporting horrid horns of sharpened bone
as all who stood along the three-railed fence
began to holler, cheer, and flout the beasts.
A train of Klawiphoroi now commenced
to beat large kettledrums, pluck silver lyres,
pipe boxwood woodwinds with increasing speed,
and clitter-clatter ivory castanets—
the semicircled girls becoming tranced
in rhythms that unnerved the pawing brutes.
Their swaying metamorphosed into dance,
their gorers taunted by its synchrony.

With no less rage than Heaven's Bull unleashed
upon Enkidu in the days of yore,
the aurochs blitzed the girls to do them in,
to finish their display of ridicule.
The first one charged, its horns about to strike
as Aqhat's friends (and many more) cried out.
The smallest girl had rushed to meet the bull,
flipped from the ground with sure-footed aplomb
onto its head before her hands propelled
her from its withers high into the air,
one leg behind the other such that her
white skirt assumed a scallop shell's fanned form

before the sprite resumed her earthbound step.
Six hundred cheers ensued as many sighs.
The second bull beset the other girls
as one distracted it and dove from right
to left between its muscled, rapid legs,
another springing left to right atop
its back ere flipping, twirling—neither scathed.
The multitude raised paeans for their feats
as the longhorns grew angrier and tried
to learn from their near misses, but without
success, for each attack was parried by
the children's lightsome, lissome somersaults.

From their assailants no girl fled but danced
the more intensely, leaping with more grace
the more their rushers fumed with vitriol.
Using their hands to form a sling, two girls
let fly a third who landed on a haunch,
and when it bucked to throw her off, she launched
from it, backflipping two times while midair,
her long black hair forming a perfect arc,
and landed on a kettledrum's downbeat.
In time, the jumping-whirling of the girls
wore down their dancing partners, sapped their vim.
The rhythms of the Klawiphoroi slowed
as from the bulls' horns girls hung for as long
as possible, depleting them of strength
until at last both animals collapsed
with praise redounding from the Central Court.

A white robe falling to his sandaled feet,
his face refigured by insignia,
the ministrant of ceremonies strode
outside, a labrys with quadruple blades

in hand, the Klawiphorois' tune changing.
Adulthood close at hand, the girls formed rows
behind both beeves on whom the ministrant—
his hands placed on their muzzles—whispered prayers.
The Klawiphoroi now began to sing
and the surrounding throng joined in with them
as the priest raised his visage heavenward,
hoisting the sun-flecked ax above his pate
and bringing it down full-force upon the first
bull's neck, its blood bestrewn upon the earth.
His axstroke fallen on the second bull,
the girls walked in between the severed parts
before the priest picked up each sundered head
and to a nascent woman handed them.
The leaders held their dripping gifts aloft,
processing to the northmost adyton
as mothers shed the happiest of tears.

Stewards emerged and brimmed the conical
winecups of men gladdened to see their girls
reach marriageable age, yet tristful that
some man would pluck their peonies so soon.
While slaves removed the carcasses and cleansed
the courtyard, maidservants brought trays of food
for everyone: rock partridge stuffed with thyme,
wild garlic, walnuts, and ripe pear—well-browned
and set atop a bed of lentil stew;
large porringers of olives and dark figs;
roe deer rubbed down with coriander, sage,
wild fennel, and oregano, slow-cooked
with care above a pit of oaken coals;
heaped plates of luscious strawberries and quince;
and fruit from the sea: fired flying fish,
tunny, and multicolored skaros fish.

Tall stirrup jars effused their garnet gifts
without concern for station or status
(even leashed monkeys supped like royalty).
Queen Pasiphaë dined upon the best
of offerings, however: octopus
first blanched in water steeped with onion, thyme,
and saffron, doused in olive oil and charred
till soft, its involuted tentacles
sea-salted—paired with citrusy white wine.

Enjoying Kaphtor's cornucopia
between games, Knossos' queen addressed Laeya,
"Please help yourself to anything you like—
the Games are not a time to look so glum.
Have you tried this before? Taste some of mine.
My dear, may I speak openly with you?
I've hosted people from unnumbered lands,
and you don't gladhand or prattle enough
to be a merchant's heiress—as you say.
So tell me why you've really come, my child,
and know your secret's safe with me, or I
am not the head of Knossos' Key-bearers."

Laeya beheld the nymph-born queen and told
her, just above a whisper, of Aqhat's
demise and of the rumors of this isle—
that it might hide historiolae, prayers,
or potions to restore him to himself.
Bidawa listened to her, stealing looks
at Gabbar when the times proved opportune.
The care in Laeya's eyes and forthrightness
in her concerns reminded Minos' wife
(though vaguely) of herself when she was young.

The queen stared pensively into the crowd.
Though eyeing nothing in particular,
the king's gaze trained on her and he knew that
she stared delightedly at one from his
retainer, his most muscular of guards.

A triton's call disturbed King Minos' thoughts
as all made way for two and thirty boys
adorned in codpieces, their longish shocks
of hair done up in prepubescent style.
They formed a row before their king, the priest
shearing a lock from each of them to give
in sacrifice to mighty Velchanos.
The men-to-be paid Minos obeisance,
now pairing off to test their fighting skill.
Though Minos couldn't hear the men across
the Court, he knew they offered bets amongst
themselves, despoiling temple rites with greed
and making playthings of the sacred Games.
Another conchblast spurred the boys to box,
the king's gaze fixed on Talos' every move.

Boys raised their fists and shuffled on their feet,
a deadly seriousness in their eyes
until one risked the first of many strikes.
Wide-browed Qadaro blocked Akato's swing
and slugged his kidney with a knuckled fist.
Akato tucked his elbows in and bluffed
left, boxing his opponent in the mouth,
the latter spitting out a loosened tooth.
Inflamed, Qadaro lost his poise and charged
with fury, pounding on his rival till
the latter could withstand no more, and fell.

The head priest sent Qadaro to the right
to stand and wait then walked Akato left
to sit where he'd be joined by others soon.

Young Duni chose to prove himself against
Talos, exchanging punches with his foe,
drubbing the former's ashlar abdomen
and drawing blood from Talos' lips and ears.
But for this contest Talos had prepared,
more skilled at doling out and taking blows
than most despite his middling weight and size.
A hunting lizard's patience and reserve
distinguished Talos' mien while he wore his
opponent down before he cloured his head
with a brain-scrambling clout—but rather than
debase his rival with a knockout blow,
he simply pushed him to the ground and walked
to join the first round's winners lounging on
the right, congratulating those who'd won.
From there he studied other pugilists
such as Alekrtruon, a boy by age
although a full-grown warrior in size,
who squared away against puny Puri.
The former danced round Puri, frightening
the boy with jokes and jeers until he took
a heap of marl and gravel-blinded him,
delivering a cheap and shameful blow
to Puri's boyhood, ending his short stint.

The victors partnered off to brawl for three
more rounds until two boys alone remained:
a tattered Talos and Alektruon.
The enemies rehydrated and staunched
their draining cuts as all looked on with great

expectancy (not least of whom were those
who stood to benefit financially).
As servants tended to Talos' right eye,
he saw Alektruon rub dirt upon
his hands, preserving some in his left palm.
Within the Court's interior the two
competitors met, Talos overmatched.

When both were set, the ministrant's command
ignited them, Alektruon the first
to swing but missing the spry Talos who
returned a counterpunch to no effect.
The latter landed two more body blows
before Alektruon upended him
by dealing a hardhanded uppercut,
yet Talos caught himself before he hit
the ground and dodged a fearsome finisher,
delivering two stomach jabs that irked
the one who thought he should have won by now
against this pest who couldn't reach his face.
Annoyed, Alektruon swung for Talos'
left temple, flinging dirt upon his face
as Talos staggered backward with his hands
pressed on his eyes as if he couldn't see.
The spectators encompassing the Court's
periphery delighted and cast scorn
as Talos backed away, Alektruon
now rushing him to land the knockout blow,
and just before succeeding, Talos spun
transversally, grabbing Alektruon's
long shocks of hair in his left fist, whirling
around his back to his front, twining
his braided locks like plaited rope, yanking
him downward toward him with momentous force,

and with an elbow shattering his nose.
The cracked bone echoed through the Central Court,
Alektruon collapsing to the earth
as cheers upsurged for this year's champion.

King Minos beamed with fatherly esteem,
inviting Talos to receive his gift:
an agate-pommeled dagger wrought of bronze,
its hilt plate riveted to the shoulders,
the blade well-flanged and direfully sharp,
its either midrib stylishly designed
with boxing scenes nielloed ebony.
Accepting it with gratitude, Talos
bowed low then raised it to resurgent lauds.
The acrobatic women now returned
from sacrificing as the newborn men
sought strong drink to abate their injuries.
The celebration amplified until
the ministrant of rites emerged to read
the summer's customary prophecy,
ofttimes auspicious after such a day.
All harkened as the priest proclaimed aloud,
"For too long have divine ways been ignored.
If Knossos should achieve prosperity,
and should our temple strengthen day by day,
then cast away outlandish rituals,
returning to the Horned God of Two Forms,
the Roarer, the Deliverer whose Home
Lies in the Sea—or else, so it is writ—
the Labyrinth shall be made to fall again."

The Klawiphoroi snuck enlightened looks
at one another, saying not a word

while Minos' heart recovered from the blow,
interpreting the oracle aloud,
"The gods speak through their representative,
not to foredoom us but to offer us
a second chance, an opportunity
to jettison outmoded practices.
We all know of the winds and seaquakes that
destroyed our first impeccable temple,
and now the reasons for it come to light!
Who rules the sea, comprising doubled form,
the one to whom we offered hecatombs
before impious women cast aside
the temple's rites to chant in clammy caves
and dance in sheep-shit covered leys, as if
this somehow pleased the Trident Brandisher?
No more shall we neglect Poseidon's needs
or act as if Enesidaon were gone,
abandoning observances to folk
who cannot even read, much less keep track
of whether, what, and how to sacrifice.

"Look to the empires of the Easterners!
Do they forget their gods in drunkenness,
in avarice, in lecherous forays?
No! Temple functionaries guarantee
adherence to the law and order life,
thereby appeasing openhanded gods.
If we're to reign the open seas, must we
not first learn to rein in our appetites?
Must we not master our own souls and free
pelagic deities from petty work
in order to hoist sail to seek new lands,
spreading our influence throughout the world?

"But do not think that I exempt myself
as tyrants do—the gods judge me as well.
From this day hence, the whorehouses shall be
shut down; but neither shall your king and queen
seek out another's nuptial bedchamber.
You may not reach intoxication's dregs,
but neither shall my house overindulge.
Lastly, let us abandon casting lots;
as you obey this law, so too shall I.
The priesthood of this Labyrinth will arrange
the means by which these laws will be enforced
and tabulate the offerings brought here—
here, mind you, not to primitive locales.
In such wise, in the fanes of our own breasts,
we will be unified and dignified,
averting the Earth Shaker's punishments."

When he concluded, Pasiphaë turned
to Laeya, having weighed her words, and said,
"I know the curse of which you speak, and you
were right to seek our help for your friend's sake.
With such a dareful purpose no one's come
for many years, yet some of us have not
forgotten the cathartic rites of old.
Though your friend Aqhat never shall become
exactly as he was, there yet exist
salvific mysteries we might enact,
although their secrecy must not be breached.
Cloak Aqhat in an elderwoman's shawl,
yourself in farmhand-garb, and meet me at
Mount Juktas' base when night falls on this day."

The Games now ended, all went home to pass
the afternoon with friends and relatives,

the western blood-orange light now shaded blue.
Shalim enshadowed Shapshu. Laeya dressed
her worldworn friend in elderwomen's clothes,
his sex and visage shielded by a shawl
before she steered their horse-drawn chariot
along a wooded path to Juktas' foot.
They lingered in the swarthy soundlessness
as nightmarish impossibilities
encircled Laeya; though invisible,
she felt their icy rasps upon her nape.
She wheeled back round to see an incubus
materialize—an agrimi skull
atop a woman's frame, a steer-goad clenched
in one hand, mallets in the other one.
No sooner did the driver make to flee
than Pasiphaë's calming hand arose,
the queen's look reassuring her within
white sockets once containing other eyes.
The leader of the Klawiphoroi dressed
her in an open bodice and a skirt,
tying her hair in one long sacral knot
and handing her the steer-goad as her own.
Climbing onto the chariot, the queen
conducted them beyond Mount Juktas' base
up rock-ribbed switchbacks and past long-armed oaks.

They summited to find dedicatees
behelmed with antlered skulls or elegant
headpieces cast in gold and repoussé,
their necklines garlanded with bryony,
their dresses hiding less than they divulged.
Some Klawiphoroi held tall staves wherefrom
there tintinnabulated copper bells
while others tended to the bonfires.

The queen brought Aqhat to the crest's east side
to sit abreast the toothless matriarchs
who, though they'd handed down these rites themselves,
now disremembered what they were about.
And yet they smiled to see the women there,
assisting one another with prep work.
Greeting the priestess Kesadara as
a sister, Pasiphaë introduced
her to her guest, the priestess' eyes enflamed
with pining to possess and be possessed—
a self-sufficient carnivore in heat—
her raiment like a spider's gossamer
showing her carinated torso's sheen,
her limbs replete with henna from her wrists
to shoulders with florestral patterning—
moringa oil combed through her rakish hair.
How can mere flesh and bone be mystical?
As berries beckon to be gormandized
by one who's gone for days without a bite,
their vibrant colors drawing lips to them
who're poisoned spite the satisfying taste—
just as one comes to crave their toxic juice
the more one must avoid them at all costs,
so too did Kesadara's onyx eyes
and godlike build repellently attract.

In cold sweat Minos woke within his room,
the details of his nightmare scurrying
for cover though he caught a glimpse
of two shapeshifters as they disappeared:
his strongest guard and Pasiphaë—nude.
He felt for her in bed, but she was gone.
In haste he clothed himself ere summoning

his villa's guard, demanding he apprise
him of his consort's whereabouts at once.
The guard read his distress, replying thus,
"My Lord, is she not in your room with you?
I saw her enter with my own two eyes,
and no one's come or gone throughout the night.
If you would like, I'll send my best-trained men
to seek her out and bring her back to you."

The king rebuked his plan, replying that
he'd go himself and bang on every door
until he tracked the woman down himself.
The man of the nightwatch implored him not
to venture out alone just then, as such
unpleasant and precarious employs
were best left for retainers of armed men.
Suspicion flashing from his eyes, the king
dispatched him to find Talos and to bring
him for a demonstration of just rule.
Reluctantly complying, he excused
himself, the sovereign hying up the stairs
to find a fragrant garment of his wife's.
At length, his new gift sheathed along his waist,
young Talos came and vowed the king his aid.
Taking his protégé's arm, Minos said,
"Today you proved your strength before the gods;
tonight, bronze-hearted man, I'll teach you how
one should direct such power through the law."
Together with the king's guard they uncaged
the royal hunting dogs, domestic wolves,
and Minos gave them Pasiphaë's scent
before the twelve men left to scour town
for traces of the queen's late vanishing.

Atop Mount Juktas' northern side,
Queen Pasiphaë stood between two pines
as kettledrums, cymbals, and auloi played
their midnight songs for dancing priestesses—
those sticky lily stigmas in the flesh.
Their leader raised her arms and prayed aloud,
"Come Lord of Souls, Oh Roaring One whose Home
Lies in the Sea; aroused by ancient song,
come fill our karanthoi with vintagefulls!"
Far north, beyond the sleep-rocked Amnisos,
a luminescent rondure breached the waves
like a diminutive sun, soaring south
on high as frenzied ululations rose
into the night to greet the summoned god.
Astonished, Laeya asked a celebrant
whether Poseidon were that golden light—
her guess rebuffed with grave intensity.
The orb drew closer till it reached the pines
and inward bent them one another's way,
the branches rearranged until a face
with a coniferous full beard appeared.
Green ivy retrograded down the trunks
and plunged into the earth ere tunneling
two rows from which their sprouted full-grown vines
with grapes that ripened right before their eyes.
The blazing, bearded deity exhaled;
his spirit blew the clusters to the ground.
Ecstatic from the recent miracles,
the Klawiphoroi danced on them, their juice
descending down a slight declivity
in runnels till they reached a limestone trough,
the elevated end of which sluiced drink
fermented outside time into their jars.

The mountain seethed with dithyrambic song
as in unceasing streams the red wine flowed,
enlivening the women's choral chants.
Like cranes the sylphs outstretched and whirled around,
unloosing pleasured cries into the night.
The febrous revelry also possessed
the matriarchs and brought them to their feet,
infusing them with such vitality
as they'd not known even throughout their youth.
When Laeya paused to glance their way she saw
that Aqhat's hands looked healthful once again,
yet Kesadara pulled her back and gave
her wine to drink as they began to dance.
The two drew close and kissed with unconstraint.
Regaining vision, Laeya looked and found
not women but the essences of fawns,
her wine turned blood. She wanted—needed it.
For and against the one the cosmos reeled.

In Knossos, Minos' wolves were on the scent,
the twelve men following their lead to doors
the guards kicked down for Pasiphaë's sake.
Yet each invasion only left a house
of half-clothed and befuddled commoners,
each failure hackling Minos all the more.
Cursing, the king invoked Poseidon, god
of the abyss, to aid him in his search
just as a lucent force rose from the sea,
ascending through the night toward Juktas' peak.
As if that sphere had rallied them, the dogs
began to howl and broke free, chasing it.
Enraptured, Minos sped his retinue
to mount their geldings, following the sign
with nothing but flambeaux in hand to light

the way of their predestinated path,
each horse switchbacking up the western slope.
Concerned (if not entirely affrayed),
the king dismounted well-below the peak,
desiring to approach Poseidon's sign
respectfully, that is, with mindfulness.

The peak awhirl with raucous jubilance,
its revelers rapt in infinite release
such that their brimful senses overflowed,
a dyad—apparitional and bright—
took shape and drifted Aqhat's way, unseen
by any present, floating at his sides.
They placed their hands on him as memories
inundated his muscles and his breast:
his mother's stories, songs, and tenderness
as well as her decease by cutthroat brutes;
Pugat's delighted laughs when pegged by grapes,
her blood drained by their father's ownmost hands;
skylarking in the groves at Gabbar's side;
this same friend nearly eaten by two gods;
his own stayed hand before Ameni's fear—
the second chance that boy returned to him;
the way his village elders cared for those
who had survived the raid; Shatanu's scowl;
the journey to the Necromancer's cave
where he had made a life-altering choice
before that cavern caved upon itself;
large drafts of ale enjoyed with fishermen
and Abibaal's indulgent cruelty;
and someone else (but who?) that he had met
who spurred and bolstered his resolve to put
gods to the sword before the year elapsed.
The figures at his side, who in that light

resembled Danataya and Pugat,
then slowly raised his chin, unhooding him
before oneiric scenes—unbounded girls
who raised euphoric chants, now gyrating
with manic speed, now giving suck to wolves.

Behind a temenos wall on the peak's
west side, the king took in the sacrilege
unfolding where Poseidon's sign had come:
Inebriated orgiasts defiled
their husbands' rights to them, yawping with strains
offensive to the ears of gods and men
and blurring lines between the wild and tame.
Without the temple's authorized consent,
libations drenched the mountain's rocky soil.
But lo! As if such anomie were not
enough, Queen Pasiphaë danced and drank
among those harlots, leading them in song!
His brand unsheathed, King Minos called his men
to arms and charged them to attack the sluts.
The first out caught a priestess unawares
and scored a spurting line across her throat,
its searing pain condoled by the entranced
whose screaks transfixed the vault, crescendoing
till they became their opposite—silence.

King Minos, Talos, and the royal guard
attacked, the fiery countenance amidst
the trees unleashing roars that shook the peak.
The image of his former self, Aqhat
stood up, cast off his cloak, and looked around,
discrediting his senses' exposé.
Ignited by their sister's death and by
the Roarer's battle-cry, the women raged.

Among their number Aqhat caught a glimpse
of her and cried aloud, "Laeya! Laeya!"
The power clutching Laeya lost its grip,
an ill-defined confusion stepping in.
Now recognizing who had called her name,
she ran to Aqhat with both joy and fear,
for while most celebrants counterassailed
King Minos and his meddlers, some caught wind
of more intruders on the mount's east side.
As Aqhat sprinted Laeya overran
him, pointing for her horse-drawn chariot
as seven priestesses raced after them.

Raising his blood-stained blade to fell the lot
of them, the next of Minos' guards set-to,
no sooner lunging for a libertine
than four agrimi-helmed devourers
beset him, biting through his jugular,
dislocating his limbs and flaying flesh
upon which they engorged their appetites.
Backup arrived for him (though far too late),
the rearguard cutting down three cannibals
just as two pine staffs whettened at the tips
whizzed through the air, one piercing a guard's thigh,
the other lancing through his partner's shin.
Beyond his toleration's bounds, the god
made manifest within the concave trees
took flight, the conifers in which he'd dwelt
recoiling as he flew back for the depths,
a tail of flaming light in hot pursuit,
its embers falling on the Labyrinth's heights.
His exodus benighted Juktas' crest
as those just recently transpierced by staves
retreated, stumbling through the black expanse

for cover as the gore-starved animals
gave chase, needing no light to flush them out
since clinking copper bells gave them away.

The bloodbath now on full display, the king
grabbed Talos' arm, commanding all fall back.
They hasted westward from pursuant eyes
and teeth and nails that sought to do them in,
vaulting the wall, precipitating down
the slope as swarming shrills gave chase en masse.
The swiftest priestess closed in on the king,
diving for him and grabbing his ankle,
pulling him down till Talos intervened,
stabbing her forearm as they fled once more,
the sovereign lord of Knossos out ahead.
At full speed Talos stumbled on a root,
collapsing on a gritty limestone slab,
the king delaying for a moment's thought
(now fathoms from the boy), then running on.
Descending on him with hyenic joy,
the pack of women ripped the young boy's spine
out, noshing on his numbles and his bones,
his future glory torn from him with ease.
Frenetic whinnies mourned for Talos' fate
before the revelers saw to their distress,
the royal geldings hitched to trees like bait.
While skirring, Minos tripped and hit the ground,
trundling down a steep declension off
a rock ledge, halted by a baetylus.
Befogged and wounded, Minos groped about
the jut from which he'd fallen, finding that
it opened, so he clambered through its mouth,
crawling and fumbling through the fusty cave
as far back as he could just as a mouse

is prone to scurry when besieged by fear,
just having scaped the taloned clutch of death.
Now prostrate, Minos closed his eyes and prayed.

Their twin-wheeled getaway attained, Laeya
and Aqhat stoked their destriers' alarm
with whips and curses, charging them to fly
down Juktas' shoulder as the priestesses
pursued them, anteloping through the brush.
As if to put their wheelwright's work to test
the four-spoked rims careered from side to side
while Aqhat and Laeya strived to forestall
a crash that at such speeds would mean their end.
Though running on bare feet, the huntresses
gained on their quarry's dust cloud, raising cries
of wrath and grief like demons boiled alive.
Unable to keep stride with Laeya's team,
the shrills of the possessed died down, replaced
by panting and the rotating of wheels.
Those fleeing reached the timberline's dirt path
where only shards of moonbeam lit the way.

Laeya decreased her horses' speed so they
could catch their breath and eyed her friend-made-whole
only to see a moon shadow disrupt
the stock-still boscage opposite his back.
She lashed the stallions to a run but not
in time as a wild priestess ambushed her,
the wilding's canines cutting to her collarbone.
The other six appeared as Aqhat pushed
the priestess from their car and took the reins,
escaping from their sight around a bend.
They crossed a lonely farmstead where a goat
who'd seen and felt the candent orb's retreat

awoke to browse, assuming dawn had come.
Her steer-goad ready-to-hand, Laeya hurled
it, sinking it into the caprid's flank.
It sprung for cover through a field of spelt
as priestesses gave chase, distracted by
the whiffs of blood that stained its matted coat.
From swishing stalks pathetic bleats arose.

Arriving at the local lodgings where
Bidawa, Gabbar, and Ameni slept,
the riders barged into their varied dreams
and wrenched them from their twitch-eyed peacefulness.
Though taken aback when aroused from sleep,
such startlement paled in comparison
to their bewilderment at Aqhat's state—
their leader's health returned to him in full.
Aqhat and Laeya raced for Amnisos,
the second chariot not far behind.
The port in sight beside the moonlit sea,
Ameni blew his horn for all to hear,
the followers of Aqhat wakening,
arising unforewarned from comfy beds
to gather what they could ere hurrying
for their respective ships, petitioning
for reasons for their flight at such a time.
Yet soon the grumbling company saw him.
A torch in hand, requickened as they all
remembered, Aqhat urged his faithful on.
Heaving aboard the goods which they'd acquired
and taking ship as briskly as they might,
they plowed their oarage northward from the pier,
a glim arising in the southern sky,
for Knossos' Labyrinth had succumbed to flame.

Book XV

Oh stay, Ilisha! Don't take wing just yet.
Late has your song saved Danataya's son,
rejuvenated by Mount Juktas' rites,
having escaped that night's calamities;
yet further from his purpose does he seem
than when we last invoked your hallowed name.
The time allotted him has dwindled, waned,
the space he must traverse to slay three gods
expanding with each rising of the day.
Surely you haven't towed us overseas
to leave us here, adrift in our suspense,
the echoes of Kinnaru's dissonance
permitted as our hero's final say.
Do sit! I'll fluff your cushion, fill your cup
with wine to liven up your tongue so you
can harmonize what's passed with what's to-come.

Alone on one of Lel's broad balconies,
hunched over deep in thought, El stroked his beard
to sharpen the perpensions in his heart.
Of late the Wise One had begun to doubt
the value of oneiromantic signs
and, even more than this, the truth of dreams
as such, for why, he wondered, had he not
been able to discover Athirat's
hideout, or harbinger the fires on Lel?
His last night's dream ate at him nonetheless.
In it, Tiratu had seduced his wife,
inviting her to cross the Great Green Sea

to Kaphtor where he owned a domicile
tucked high upon a claustral mountainside.
Agreeing to the god's proposal ere
he'd finished it, the Lady of the Sea
soon found herself stretched out supine on his
ship's forecastle, enjoying Shapshu's rays
and swashing waves bisected by the bow.
Reaching his private villa, Athirat
relaxed during the days but drank and danced
with him come sundown, making love till dawn.
The images of her ecstatic states
barraged El with a fly's bedevilment.

Lel's ruler contemplated what to do.
The search-and-seizure contrivance of Elsh
and his contingent had produced no leads
for months; a solipsistic Baal made war
with Dread Anat no matter what the cost;
Shegr and Ithm absented themselves;
and El already summoned Yam's support,
whether or not the sea-god would comply.
The other deities who had not heard
of Athirat's escape need not, as they
would either be of little use, judge him
for driving her away from home, or both.
In time an insight came unto the Lord,
a recourse whose audacity scared him
yet whose necessity proved obvious.
He would disparage Litan's habitat,
inciting the polycephalic dragon's
irascibility so that he would
destruct unnumbered ships on the high seas.
Though many innocents might meet their end—
which oft comes unannounced in any case—

he might well wreck his consort's ship as she
set sail for other lands, dispatching her
to Mot's domain deep down beneath the earth.
With that belovèd friend he'd then propose
a trade for his awaited runaway,
returning her to Lel where she belonged.

El looked beyond the lofted balustrade
below which rushed his blue cascade, the source
of water filling freshets and cold rills.
He hesitated—knowing that his act
would spurn a god not easily consoled,
thereby imperiling unnumbered lives—
no sooner than Tiratu's mug (grotesque
as pain) appeared to him, emboldening
the Father of the Gods to follow through.
Clearing his throat, he hocked a ball of phlegm
and spit into the giant fountainhead,
an accident innocuous enough
when done by sailors, yet when El demeans
in such a way, a god offends a god,
unhallowing his sense of due respect.
The spittle disappeared and left no trace
for any eyes to see or ears to hear.
Although beyond two hundred leagues away,
roaming abyssal depths for decomposed
cadavers southwest of the Cyclades,
the seven-headed Litan caught a whiff
of Father's slaver ere it reached the sea.
And from those trenches which no light can pierce
reverberated soughs of malcontent.

Mounting the Upperworld's terraqueous
rim, Shapshu honed her daybreak beacon on

each midship beam until her broadened light
expanded to encompass everything—
a shortened reenactment of the way
that each one in life's dawn misconstrues
his own importance, racing here and there
beneath the sunlight's singular regard
to find with eld, alas, that the concerns
of other beings overstretch his own.
A seabird's carp woke Aqhat from his drowse.
Pulling a blanket from his face, he scanned
the dawn-gilt waves surrounding them before
beholding Laeya, up to whom he rushed,
embracing her with reborn happiness.
She smiled as he looked sternward for his friends
on trailing ships, and seeing Ameni
and Gabbar, called their names and waved to them—
but they persisted in their work, heads down.
Perplexed, he turned to Laeya, asking her,
"Can they not hear me from so far away?
Why don't they greet me? Whose nine ships are these?
Was I not captured in Siduna, rowed
to Baal's damp gaol, and left there to decay?
If so, how did I flee? Where are we now?"

Insisting that he sit, Laeya began,
"It's true then—you remember not a thing?
I can't believe that you've returned to us
after so many long and trying months!
Zimredda's warriors accosted you,
transferring you to Alashiya's coast
where they retained you in their custody.
While you were locked away, your friends took charge,
deciding the way forward best we could.
Knowing your prior wishes and our need

for motivated allies, I had ships
assembled to release you ere we sailed
up the Puruna seeking Hittite aid.
We made our way toward Alashiya's bluffs,
an ancient grotto sheltering our fleet.
A group of women infiltrated Baal's
lighthouse and duped his guards, and when I climbed
onto the roof, I covered and revealed
its fire three times to signal the attack,
which Gabbar led and ended expertly.

"Yet when we found and liberated you,
we mourned the state into which you'd devolved,
for some fey spirit had possessed your heart
and limbs and senses, hemlocking your health.
We put our meager hopes in Ameni,
who thought that Kaphtor might possess the cure
that you required, whatever it might be.
Through calm and storm Ameni and Gabbar
saw to your safekeeping and nourishment
until we reached the docks of Amnisos,
where denizens of note invited us
to Knossos on whose nearby mount a rite
returned you to yourself and to your crew.
The way's not been an easy one for us,
and that which clutched your being ridiculed
the ones who'd given up their lives for you.
The stingers of your words remain beneath
their skin, so give them time to ease them out."

He glanced abaft upon his stalwart friends
then on the seascape, searching for right words,
"Never could I repay you—all of you—
for your unyielding faithfulness and love.

While I succumbed to who-knows-what-dark-spell
so easily, you three accomplished more
than had I been there to abet your work!
And where I waffled in my plans, unsure
of which resort to choose, of whom I should
lay waste in one year's time, the three of you
refused to hesitate, acting as one
in common cause for this unworthy man.
You're right, Laeya, as you have always been:
Let's seek support from Hatti's men-at-arms
and ride along the Puruna's waterway
before returning south to Zaphon's fields
where Baal shall be the first to meet his end."

Catching a steady southerly, the ships
unfurled their sails; the backsore shipped their oars.
They bent their prows northeast from Kaphtor's shores,
hoping to hop along the Lukkan coast
until they lighted on Puruna's firth.
The men and women reclining aboard
Aqhat and Laeya's vessel bided time
by showing everyone what they'd obtained
while trading in the stalls of Amnisos.
For his spoils Abdu claimed a lightweight helm,
a breastplate, and a pair of sheet-bronze greaves,
each riveted by bronzesmiths next-to-none.
Inuya, on the other hand, acquired
a dagger damascened by practiced hands;
she sliced through cable twined with fibrous palm
to demonstrate its edge before their eyes.
For his sought-after gold and copper bars
Belated Burianu swapped an ax—
the mighty labrys for which Kaphtor's famed—
the which he proudly wore across his back.

When time it came for Ash to tell what he
had gained, Attanu heckled him in jest,
as he seemed to have lost more than he'd won.

With unfazed confidence, Ash told the crew
that he'd made out the best, in fact, although
no richer by material account.
He stood and playacted what had transpired:
"Hoping that Kaphtor was indeed an isle
of magic cures, I sought one for myself.
I pestered potion peddlers with no luck
until a woman, Sami, overheard
me, by the hand escorting me to fair
Tuweta, Lady of the Lonesome Wood.
Arriving at her isolated cave,
I told her of my strange predicament.
She turned from me and in her cauldron poured
strong extract from Egyptian lotus, clumps
of ground hemp, Alashiyan poppy seeds,
galaktar from green Kizzuwatnan leys,
and fourteen drops of viper's bugloss oil.
Atop a flame she brought them to a boil
and muddled the concoction into paste
ere straining it, extending it my way.
The Lonesome Wood's enchantress then took hold
of me and led me to an open plot
of dirt within which she commanded me
to sit while she began to moisten it
with buckets filled with water from a stream.
With an old oar she smoothed the ring of mud
surrounding me, ignoring my misdoubts.

"Tuweta then commanded me to look
upon the sun and down her remedy.

I deeply drank (though with unease) before
my heavy eyelids tempted me to sleep,
whereat the women loosed strange whooping cries
and thus prevented me from nodding off.
Put out, I stood and cursed their fraudulence.
Tuweta smiled and asked me where the sun
had been and how the earth had looked when I'd
drunk her decoction two eyeblinks before.
Her pointless questions angered me the more
until I realized that Shapshu shone
not on my face but on my neck and that
the muddy plot surrounding me had dried—
with not a single footprint formed in it.
Now comprehending that I'd need not be
tied down, my sleepwalking nights at an end,
I hugged the women, promising to give
them everything I could, but they refused
my stuff, requesting two nights all alone
with me instead—as if I would refuse!—
and afterward they bade me flushed farewells.
A lesser remedy than yours, Aqhat,
but still, how wonderful it is to sleep the night
away and wake refreshed in the same place!"
All present cheered for Ash's turnaround
before they laid their heads, entrusting their
well-being to the helmsman's steady hand.

A scarlet-shrouded Shahar leered above
the sealine in the morn, and as if his
attire had not sufficiently unnerved
the sailors, by midafternoon the sighs
of northern gusts portended heavy rains
and forced the crews to take in sail and row.
The captains ordered all to brace themselves,

commanding them to plow in unison
against the headwinds, violent as they were.
Just as one can't ignore a broken leg
though one desire to flee the future pain
of setting it—this second snap far worse,
not least for its foreseeability—
or as one can't avert the scalding blade
to sear shut open, gushing battle-wounds,
so too could Aqhat's fleet find no escape
from the array of charging thunderheads,
for had they sought to set a different course
instead of meeting them head on, as one,
they'd only give them time to gather strength,
postponing ineludible affronts.

As madcap whitecaps hammered at the hulls,
the bowsprits breasting saw-toothed waves
now high and mighty, now abject, the Sun
looked down and watched the boats—so bantam, meek,
and of no consequence—become engulfed
by stormclouds smothering the sallow sea.
A norther hurled its curses at the fleet
as in return garboards and sheerstrakes groaned
amidst the helter-skelter of loud shouts.
With drenched and veiny arms the tillers clenched
the quarter rudders, trying to prevent
the roaring ocean, frothing at the mouth,
from swallowing the ships they'd sworn to guide
while thinking: Who, in the last instance, can
withstand its infinite, digestive force?
Anon this beast became a lesser cause
for fear, supplanted by the high-pitched shrieks
of something neither man nor animal
that lurked beyond them in the ebon drear,

its contour barely visible by turns
when intermittent bolts transpierced the sky.

With Kothar's bow in hand once more, Aqhat
barked orders to his company, and while
few heard what he had said, they swapped their oars
for lance and spear, preparing for the worst
as some large mass shrithed underneath their keels,
its presence sensed although it moved unseen.
A moment passed, then yet another one.
Upsurging from the deep amain, Litan
shot through the fourthmost vessel, splintering
its planks and through-beams as the rigging snapped
and flew into the billows with the crew
who had been underhandedly dispersed,
the breaching monster crashing on the waves.
From the ensuing groundswells every ship
yawed violently, most slipping on the decks
and fumbling to regain their footing as
he reemerged, his fourteen serpent eyes
and seven fang-filled jaws in search of prey.
Terrified, those on crafts intact loosed spears
and arrows at the god—those hitting home
molesting him as if mosquito pricks.
While weltering midst evil-minded waves,
those drowning grabbed ahold of jetsam, cried
for help, soliciting Nahar with prayers.
And yet those selfsame pleas gave them away,
occasioning their sordid opposite
as Litan's gullets overstuffed themselves
with blood and cracking bone, his ghastly eyes
like those of whole fish roasted over coals,
scanning for leftovers who'd not gone down.

Fuming, Aqhat shot one of Litan's jowls
above the teeth and just below his lips,
piercing the god's black gums and forcing him
to drop the torso he was feeding on.
Like lightning Aqhat hove bronze pikes, the third
of which impaled one of the beast's bright eyes
at which he shrieked, unsnarling his next meal
who plashed into the seafoam from above.
Climbing into the crow's nest's basketry,
Laeya let fly a bronze harpoon that plunged
into one of the monster's necks before
with tentacles he circumvolved a ship,
ensnarling it, exerting concave force
that stove it in and clove it bow from stern.
Another creeper twined around the boat
near Gabbar's as the latter whirled and whipped
a grapnel, sinking it in Litan's arm.
He tried to manage the appendage but
fell down, so Burianu held his waist,
attempting to forestall catastrophe.
Aqhat looked on with terror in his eyes
as Litan yanked the two men overboard
into the sinister imbroglio.
Yet both held to the rope as Gabbar dragged
himself with Burianu on his back
until they gained their footing on the beast.

The shipmen fought and watched as the two men
drew swords and, winding rope around their wrists,
began to hack and saw the tentacle
while Litan wrawled and reeled in agony.
As both men carved into the god's own flesh
which retched its oozing gore onto their chests,
the steersman of Aqhat and Laeya's ship

informed his leader that the South Wind blew
and that they had a moment, maybe two,
to seize its breath before it changed its course
and thereby flee the unsubduable.
Aqhat turned round and watched his lifelong friend
dispart the tentacle that they assailed,
another knocking Burianu square
into his crewmate, both companions cast
into the aleatoric abyss.
Bidawa and Ameni screamed, restrained
by Ash and Abdu from a reckless act.
A new arm sprouted from the monster's gash.
Repeating Gabbar's name amidst the rain,
a total grief sluiced over Aqhat's heart,
his hand reacting in the only way
it knew, without postponement raising up
his horn and sounding it for all to hear.
Brave women piloting the ships not yet
destroyed unfastened cords from yards as men
unbound the aft-tied halyards, opening
gray sails that with the gale winds bellied out.
Just as a heron stabs and gulps down fish
corralled into a shallow shoal, so too
did Litan gnash and nosh on everyone
unfortunate enough to flail or float
atop that ossuary deep and cold.
The rhombic sails of flaxen weft drew taut,
the remnant vessels hasting with the wind
which for a time hauled anguished cries in tow
as if such souls, remaining audible,
might scape their bodies' final perishment.

Thrown far off course, the broad sea's cloud cover
preventing orientation by stars,

the battered ships continued north, or so
they hoped, assuming shorelines would appear
eventually, though when no one could say;
nor would they if they could, perhaps, for deep
despair befogged and jaded everyone
save Aqhat—swelling with a silent rage
at Litan's unprovoked maleficence.
He clenched his teeth and teemed with enmity.
The images of Gabbar's end now joined
the scenes of Pugat and his mother's deaths,
as freshly graven on his unstaunched heart
as if the gods had taken them that morn.
Laeya interpreted his eyes, which said:
"To what depravity will gods not stoop
to propagate their pointless tyranny?"
She felt the fullness of his rising wrath
within her feet and thighs up to her chest
and neck, reminded of their common plight
as one more travesty united them.
Without a word the crews repaired the booms
and masts and gangways damaged in the storm.
An atmosphere of doubt enshrouded them.
Even when sighted shores broke up the sea's
monotony to ground them, none exclaimed
at seeing it. It promised no relief,
and no one cared what such a land might hold.
The seven vessels beached upon the sands
as men and women pitched their tents, began
to search for freshwater, and started fires.

Aqhat unslung his quiver, entering
a tent where Laeya sat alone, and limned,
"When we had no more than eleven years,
Gabbar asked me, abashed, if I might teach

him how to swim, since he had yet to learn.
I promised that I would another time
if he would play at swords with me that day;
what exploits and adventures did we risk
that afternoon while traipsing through the fields!
I failed to keep my end of the deal, though,
for no real reason other than the fact
that I desired to choose what we would play.
Did I enjoy possessing one more skill
than him, delighting at my upper hand
against a boy I loved with all my heart,
though at that time I didn't use those words?
I even kidded him about his lack!
And now that friend who crossed the seas for me,
who conquered fears I never remedied,
restoring me to life, and health, and you—
that irreplaceable friend breathes no more."

Without control he trembled and bewept
Inumi's orphan, Laeya catching him,
embracing him as he collapsed aground
and kissed his forehead, gently rocking him
as she too mourned for those they'd lost of late.
Allowing their emotions room to run
till they began to taper, Laeya held
him in the silence and consoled him thus,
"All children and—unfortunately—all
adults do selfish things to suit their needs,
but any such occurrences between
the two of you were overshadowed by
the far-from-childish bond connecting you.
Ask any of those here—they'll say the same.
Above all others Gabbar understood
the risks of roving over desert wastes,

through cities, into necromantic caves,
and—most of all—upon the storm-churned seas.
He acted freely, motivated by
his love for you and by our common cause.
Were our friend still alive, he would demand
that you dispel the Void that tugs at you,
remembering your chosen destiny.
And are we not set on destroying Mot?
If so, we'll have to enter his domain,
the House of Death where Gabbar might be found."

Like one who's drowning Aqhat fought for air,
returning Laeya's reassuring hold
to thank her for her stouthearted support,
affrighted, suddenly, at losing her.
To find Ameni he now exited
as Laeya sat, recalling times remote
when she and El had fashioned handmade gods:
El had been young, and so had she—no signs
of aging scrawled themselves upon their skin.
How muscular and handsome was her Lord!
How many centuries had passed since then?
No matter. Both had kept the evening lamps
alight in order to produce a son.
Materials and tools for creaturecraft
lay strewn about their private, warded room
as El and Athirat recited spells
and chiseled banded agate (so it seemed)
comprised of swishing black and yellow whorls
ere furbishing its bright exterior.
El warmed the final product with green fire,
allowing it to braze as Athirat
and he stood back, beholding what they'd formed—
an egg ten times the size, one hundred times

more beauteous than those in ostrich nests.
They smiled and kissed their handiwork before
Qodesh and Elsh transported it to where
Lel's waterfall became a watercourse.
There Yam-Nahar arose, acknowledged El
and Athirat who watched him from above,
assumed their handicraft and, diving down,
swam seaward whence he came to bury it
within the Great Green's muddy floor where it
would incubate and ages later crack
as Litan forced his way beyond its shell.
What trace retained he from his mother's side?
No more than had Anat, Laeya inveighed.

Emerging from the isolated pool
where he had bathed and mourned his comrade's loss,
Ameni wrung his hair and donned his robe
of particolored patterns, sandalling
his feet and taking in the forenoon sun.
He felt the stubble on his jaw and gazed
at his reflection in the water's calm,
conversing with it (that is, with himself),
for though he found himself on far-flung shores,
he found it strange to find a stranger there,
"When did you swap that tunic for your kilt
and shirt, and why wear footgear now when you,
in emulation of the gods, required
no shoes before the Shasu captured you?
My wardrobe's but the least of my concerns
when storms and gods and storm-gods strongarm me.
In truth, I'm hounded by what would befall
my spirit should I perish like my friend.
Have you forgotten that Duat awaits?
If you have not, adventure without fear

until the Jackal-headed welcomes you!
Assuredly, Duat's not slipped my mind.
Let's say I fall in battle. Even if
my friends should seek to honor and embalm
me with that science of the sciences,
my vitals treated, were I to appear
before Anubis, would he—knowing that
I'd left my home, meandering in ships
jam-packed with Asiatic mutineers,
intent on helping them lay waste to gods
who, after all, might be his distant kin—
would he adjudge my lifetime one well-spent?"

Footfall broke up this two-way monologue.
Ameni turned around as Aqhat came
his way, a hint of love within his eyes.
Before Ameni spoke, Aqhat led off,
"I'd almost started turning over rocks
or climbing trees to find you, my good friend.
Ameni, please forgive me for the ways
that I've offended you in recent days.
While witched, it was as though another spoke
and acted in my stead—does that make sense?
I'm told that you suggested voyaging
to Kaphtor, so I owe my life to you.
I can't repay dear Gabbar now, but you,
comrade, should speak whatever you desire,
and if I can I'll give you what you wish
since your fidelity deserves reward."

Enheartened by his friend's recovery,
Ameni clasped his shoulder and replied,
"One can't forgive another where no wrong
has been committed, as you no doubt know.

With Fortune's aid I've kept the oath I'd sworn
upon the Tablet fragment—true enough—
but I am not alone in this regard.
When we encountered Litan's virulence,
I felt so powerless. What could I do?
A bystander amidst grotesquery,
I feared for all your lives as I did mine.
While I am not a warrior like you,
remaining a mere onlooker who throws
occasional harpoons will not suffice
to be protected—much less to protect.
I'm tired of serving as a menial.
Aqhat, install me as your head of scouts,
a subgroup answering to me and I
to you so we can obviate attacks
before the fact, preventing needless deaths."

Touched by his words, he happily obliged
as both made for the shoreside tentage where
Aqhat announced Ameni's newest role
as head of scouts, entrusting him with those
he chose to form a special battery.
Ameni wasted little time that eve,
selecting topnotch charges to account
his own, like Yaduaddu and Shaya,
Shubammu and Abiya, Abishar
and Ummihibi, all of whom took pride
in being singled out for furtherance.
At first light the Egyptian sallied forth
with his detachment to descry if folk
inhabited the place they'd chanced upon,
exploring the interior afoot.
In time they found a homestead in a vale
behind which rose a massive limestone bluff

appearing to uphold a residence
of wooden make quite like an eagle's nest.
A rustic stepped uneasily outside
and introduced herself as 'Huwarlu,'
gesticulating willingness to help
the men and, in her local dialect
resembling Luwian, petitioning
the men surrounding her for clemency.
With syntax jumbled and words mispronounced
Ameni calmed her nerves and promised that
they meant no harm, their fleet sojourning on
the nearby beaches to restock their hulls.
He asked Huwarlu if their overlord
lodged on that summit, to which she replied
that while a queen indeed inhabited
the clifftop, she was not of local stock,
transplanted from her distant fatherland,
Hattusa, where her erstwhile husband reigned.
Astonished by her words, Ameni asked
her to repeat them to ensure that he'd
not simply heard that which he wished to hear.
She did so and he laughed at their windfall.

Returning to the camp with lightened step,
Ameni shared their tidings with Aqhat
and Laeya who could scarce believe his words,
congratulating him on his success
and hoping his report would turn out true.
Enjoying just-speared seabream and wheat bread
from Amnisos, the leaders tossed around
ideas as to how they might proceed,
deciding that a smallish group would leave
once morning came to introduce themselves

to Suppiluliuma's divorcée.
And so they did. Ameni took a band
of seven to the northern mountainside,
Aqhat and Laeya hiking side by side
while hashing out how she'd address the queen.
The mountain's foot attained, Ameni led
his friends round its colluvial hemline
to switchbacks wending toward the aerie's heights.
They summited before the eventide,
Laeya assuring the queen's hierodules
of the unwarlike nature of their needs,
requesting but a moment's time with her.
Seeing they'd traveled without arms, the guards
conveyed the visitors to a jardin
behind her circular abode of wood,
presenting them to her with deference.
She pruned orange orchid stems and fed a swift
who'd lighted on her, not the least afraid.
She raised her eyes to Laeya and Aqhat
and asked her servants why this couple came
to her and why she'd not been notified.

Advancing toward their uninviting host,
Laeya presented her with linen robes
dyed violet with the aid of murices
from Kaphtor's coves, addressing her like this,
"My lady, please forgive our unannounced
arrival—we don't wish to bother you.
My name is Laeya. These men are my friends.
To cut to it: It's rumored that you know
King Suppiluliuma of Hatti,
a man with whom we hope to join ourselves
as allies, seeking vengeance on our foes.

If you would deign to offer but some small
advice or means to such an end, we'd be
most gracious and forever in your debt."

Annoyed no small amount, she made reply,
"So am I even now—a thousand leagues
away from he who banished me to this
remotest outlook, torn from my dear sons
and royal habitudes, cast out without
a say in whether, how, or where I'd go—
am I still nothing but a cold stone step
ascending to my ex's lofted throne
or an appendage surgically excised
yet living, diagnosed as incomplete
without the life-source of my amputee?
Why does his name pursue me round the world
unintermittedly, nipping my heels?
In this case, Rumor whispers verities,
and to that loudmouth's truths I offer mine:
My name is Henti, Hatti's exiled queen.
I'm not inclined for or against you, dear,
for I know nothing—don't desire to know
a thing about the king who bedded me.
Yet as one loath to help an enemy
or harm a friend from ignorance, I'll cede
the purpose of our meeting to the gods
since no decisions keep them up at night."

Queen Henti charged one of the hierodules
who had accompanied her from the East
to seek out the Ornithomanceress,
the land's trustworthiest practitioner
of augury's interpretative arts.
The former Tawananna led her guests

out of the garden to a broad stone floor
around which hovered crowding pine trees who
like spectators within a theater
shushed one another, making their own stir.
As evening fell, a rangy woman nighed
the furthest tree line, clinging to a leash
extending to an ostrich on whose back
bestrode an eyeless boy of seven years.
Her visage curtained by long, matted hair
from which excresced a beak-bone brim,
the wrinkly talons hanging from her sleeves
outmeasuring their human counterparts,
ill-shapen Paskuwatti cleared the wood.
Glissading wraith-like on the smoothened schist,
the seer neared the ones who'd serried there
and silenced Henti who'd begun to state
the reasons for her summoned expertise.

At length the auguress took centerstage,
gazed welkinward, and raised her voice in prayer,
"Oh Thousand Gods inhabiting our realm,
both simpletons and royalty alike
beseech your all-pervasive points of view.
Annarumenzi, show yourselves to us!
Delineate your vault with omina,
Marwainzi, that your succorers might know
your will for them throughout the days to come."
The shadowy Ornithomanceress
then towed her giant, flightless bird to her
as the unseeing boy presented her
an ivory flute, outholding smudging herbs
whose redolence the newborn winds inhaled.
Playing erratic sounds that even one
who's never heard a bird long for a mate

would understand through music's tensities,
the sibyl piped her song—stopping to hear
its chorus from the mountain's farmost side.

Responding to the echoed harmony
with august variations on the same,
she placed the flute down, proning out aground,
each bony arm outstretched, her palms face up,
a lidless eyeball bezeled in each wrist.
By these she stared into the sky as swarms
of common kingfishers rushed into view,
consorting in an undulating dance
of azure eddies, summersets, and dives.
Assembled in an improvised array,
each one and none moved of their own accord
until a flock of bearded vultures soared
onto the scene, one larger than the rest.
Red-annulated eyes locked on their prey
as widespread wingspans gathered growing speed,
the scavengers divebombing through the waves
of swooping commoners, attempting their
disbandment into fractured congeries.
The vultures' strategy met with success
as each one beautified its claws with blood
while Paskuwatti's pupils darted to
and fro, ingathering arcanic signs.
All of a sudden, collared doves arose
and beat their wings about the warmongers,
their lightsome songs infuriating them
till they left off their meals and flew away.

The gods' own living words departed now,
their peroration having reached its close.
The moved Ornithomanceress arose,

wheeled round, and nighed those looking up at her.
With surety and gravity she said,
"The gods have spoken unequivocally:
The strangers seeking armies in the East
shall neither venture cross the Great Green Sea
where Litan and lightning are wont to strike,
nor roam across the steppes and crooked spines
that separate us from that distant land.
Instead, their host shall offer them her best
of dragomen and pilots as their guide.
Yet in return they'll cautiously transport
the doves that Henti has equipped and trained
to carry embassages to her nest
and give them to her hatchlings so that they
might govern with a mother's acumen."

To clarify the sky-writ of the gods,
Hattusa's exile made to question her,
but Paskuwatti slowly raised a hand
to silence her, the sleepless eye within
her wrist adfixedly inspecting her
before the seer turned around and left,
towing the ostrich-mounted boy behind.
Now Henti looked to Laeya and began,
"The gods have spoken, making known their will
which, even though auspicious in its tone,
extorts a share of pain as recompense.
Mere mention of my sons reopens wounds
that Time—impassible in passing—scabbed.
Do you have children of your own, my dear?
But even so, how different do things stand
for queens like me, who've sworn to guide their sons
and daughters in the way of rulership
only to have their high vocation stripped,

deprived of witnessing their lives unfold.
At least some hope now blunts my fears, for if
you bring my sons my white-winged messengers,
I might still carry out my role abroad.
Oh sweet Telipinu, to one day know
that you still think of me from time to time!

"Yet as regards the gods' intent for you,
you'll have Nuhati, my most capable
of guards and guides from Hatti to direct
you through the northern Sea of Maramar
to the River Marassantiya's mouth.
Along that artery Nuhati shall
deliver you to Hatti's heart, where you'll
present my sons with doves to call their own
without their father's knowledge of my gifts.
Please tell them that I love them just as much
as when I sang to them in my belly,
to send me messages when possible,
and to remember my advice to them."

Nuhati walked beside his escortees
the next day, five of whom held doves encaged.
With now Ameni and now Laeya's help,
Nuhati spoke with Aqhat of the course
that lay before them: Ahhiyawan isles
detached from the Karkishan littoral
at first, proceeded by constricted straits
aligned with oyster bars and pirate fleets
that lead to the Inhospitable Sea.
On reaching the encampment, Aqhat told
his followers of what had come to pass
and introduced Nuhati, charging them
to care for him as he would do in turn.

When some embraced him he helped stockpile drink
and wares that they would need in coming days.
With pride Ameni watched Nuhati work,
the outgrowth of the former's scouting trip
developing before his very eyes.

Ere long the ships pushed from the sandy shore
and made sail northward, Aqhat and Laeya's
boat in the lead, Nuhati perched arear
with Kalbu the boatsteerer, guiding him
past Milawanda's cape and Lazpa's reefs.
To Henti's cooing exports Laeya fed
handfuls of seed in hopes thereby to make
their waterborne imprisonment less glum.
One eve, as Aqhat held onto the stem
while standing on the bulwarks—Kothar's gift
at rest between his montane shoulder blades,
Etesians playing with his locks of hair—
Laeya beheld him and, for the first time,
succumbed to seasickness, her head grown light.
She doused her face with ocean spray and trained
her focus on Wilusa's distant shores
where, had she keener ears, she would have heard
a teenage goatherd, Alaksandu, sing,

"I dreamt of a girl whom I've never seen,
she must frequent faraway shores
where she awaits me, her gold tresses pristine,
Oh, for her I'd fight lifetimes of wars.

"Yet how shall I meet her confined to this place,
of which poets shall never write songs?
Just let me away and I'll find her one day,
lying next to her where I belong.

"Let none come between what the Fates have well-spun,
lest they wish to rouse a good fight.
We'll take them head-on, or set off on the run,
for true love transcends wrong and right.

"I dreamt of a girl whom I've never seen,
she must frequent faraway shores
where she awaits me, her gold tresses pristine,
Oh, for her I'd fight lifetimes of wars."

With unimpeded course on waves unstirred
by beast or gale, the crews reclaimed a sense
of meaningful directedness once more,
although none, to be sure, would dare give voice
to their decided turnaround of luck,
lest in so doing they should forfeit it.
Suspicions of their guide's ulterior
intents soon dissipated, falsified
in part by piecemeal guesswork's stillborn claims,
in part by sea-time's just-so steadiness.
Yet groups of like mind need not feel alike.
In truth, it must be said, not all enjoyed
this relatively breezy northward push:
Her feet bedangled from a larboard side
at the armada's rear, her once-long locks
shorn just below her ears, with eyes that blazed
from love and battle now reduced to slag,
Bidawa watched her vessel's riven wake
continually diverge and enervate
and disappear, never to touch again.

Book XVI

An isle's retreating, green-cerulean
ebb tide revealed its daily offerings—
in large part average droppers-by like rocks
and kelp that frequent such low watermarks—
although impeccant, unsoiled sands like these
expect the sea's profounder gifts as well.
A gang of seafowl hovered overhead
to estimate and tabulate the haul,
unable to refrain from gossiping
about the noteworthiest sacrifice.
Six fathoms of a bulky, sable vine
with thorns along its side had washed ashore.
One thinner, scandent tendril of light brown
coiled round the vine, beneath whose far side lay
a corpse bedraggled with sea spume and blood.
From caution rather than respect the birds
perused the pungent waifs in intervals
before the corpse eructed seawater
and swatted them away confusedly.
His eyelids batting open, pained, Gabbar
began examining himself and his
environs, wondering just when and why
he'd come to such a place, and by what means.
A grapnel rope was tethered to his wrist,
constricting blood flow to his weakened hand,
its bronze barbs still impaled in Litan's arm.
At seeing this, the castaway relived
the night that monster ambushed all of them

and how with bravery or foolery
he'd climbed his tentacle to sever it.

With difficulty Gabbar gained his knees,
uncoiled the grapnel's cord from round his wrist,
and scanned the shoreline for some sign of life.
A fighting-flapping swarm called out to him
as he stood up, now realizing that
warm blood dripped from a deep gash in his thigh.
He ripped a soggy strip of tunic cloth
to cinch it, wincing, hobbling toward the fray.
He shooed and scattered them then vomited
once more at his discovery—a corse
almost past recognition, shriveled up
from face to feet and stippled with gooseflesh,
its limbs abrased and belly bloated, eyes
unclosed and gawking at the callous sun.
With welling teardrops Gabbar bade farewell,
"Though late for everything in life, your death
comes far too soon, brother Burianu.
So young, you were most faithful to our cause,
and maybe to a fault, for look where plight
has landed both of us. You shall be missed.
Perhaps one day those riding in the boats
from which you leapt so dauntlessly will find
and rescue you from Mot's decrepit lair."

Closing his comrade's eyes, he then began
to dig a grave with Burianu's helm,
collapsing afterward until he found
a jot of strength to drag him into it,
while doing which, he heard the grate of shell
on metal, finding Burianu's ax
from Amnisos still fastened to his back.

He took the shining labrys in his hands,
a gift which couldn't have been timelier,
expressing gratitude to the deceased,
interring him as he would have his kin
(had he been able to that night so long
ago when his own shore had met with death).
Resurging violently, a stabbing thirst
and famishment impelled him toward the trees
where Gabbar lapped the morning dew and chewed
fistfuls of bitter dandelion leaves,
his makeshift tourniquet soaked through with blood,
betokening the awful act to come.

Collecting desiccated fronds of palm,
brown nests of life-stripped milkweed, unclung bark,
and hunks of flintstone, Gabbar sought refuge,
assembling tinder of the lightest stuff
beneath the serrate spears, and struck the flint.
Ten times the spark extinguished in the wind
until a flamelet nestled in the brush,
its fragile life embowered by his hands
until a crackling fire took hold and grew
just like a child, avowing readiness
for bigger bites, so Gabbar added logs.
Unbandaging the unhealed wound from which
his life outflowed sans promise of a scab,
he clenched a branch within his teeth and held
his ax above the flames until it glowed
like aught from Kothar's fabled forgemanship.
He inhaled, exhaled, pressing it against
his open wound which hissed and cauterized
while Gabbar groaned and champed his bit just like
a courser who, enraged at being speared,
bites through his mouthpiece, stumbling to the earth,

his mounted warrior forethrown with force.
The singeing whelmed him as he fell facefirst
onto the sand, the fire keeping watch
and warming him throughout the livelong night.

Salt-scurfed and grungy, Gabbar woke at dawn
to find his gruesome cut had ceased to bleed.
His metal heirloom ready-to-hand, he
limped shoreward, dropped his labrys on the beach,
disrobed, and in the surf he scrubbed the grooves
of grime that caked his sculptured nakedness.
Now Pugat, now Bidawa on his mind,
no sooner did the thought of rescue by
his friends present itself to him than its
extreme implausibility razed it:
For even if a single ship survived,
and even if it strived to search for him,
electing long digressions for one soul,
still fleets one hundred times the skill of theirs
could not outpace, much less outmatch Litan.
Who—having seen that beast, even should one
do so from shore, not having fought against
his cataclysmic might while witnessing
one's fellows rent asunder with incensed
disportiveness—who'd dare say otherwise?
This brutal fact triaged the work that fell
to him, in which a stable garnering
of food and water held the foremost place.

Gulls flocked around the washed-up tentacle
some ways up shore, commotion that enticed
the sea-bathed to investigate the arm.
His tunic donned, he grabbed his ax and walked
toward Litan's limp appendage, scattering

the opportunists ere he prodded it.
The waterfowl had torn their way through its
external layering of pliant skin
to dine on pearly, oily flesh within.
He carved a portion of the topmost meat,
returning to his cookfire's living coals
and placing it skin-down atop their heat.
Ambrosial scents upwafted from the flesh
as fat-drippings unnerved the hissing ash.
As if a sacrifice turned on its head,
Gabbar crosscut the godhead, offering
the first piece to himself, enjoying its
delicious taste (resembling melted ghee,
both mild and buttery), improved the more
for granting strength from his late enemy.
He tossed aside the hardened, useless skin,
relieved to know that he would not soon starve.

While searching for a water source, Gabbar
discovered nettles, amaranth, wild thyme,
black nightshade, and dark juniper berries
(the likes of which he'd seen for trade on carts
in Kaphtor), hoping they were edible.
Within a half-day's time he'd circled round
the folkless islet where he'd been marooned,
redoubling the effects of lonesomeness.
In time he found a spring of freshwater.
He guzzled from its flow until he ached
(as he and Pugat and the rest had done
ere entering the desert years before)
and scooped a helmetful for later use.
Returning to the seaside firepit
where he would make his camp—so that should ships
sail by or come ashore, he might be saved—

Gabbar relit the flames and rinsed the greens
he'd gathered in the sea ere steaming them
on Litan's rind which doubled as a plate,
consuming them with roasted tentacle.
He then reflected to himself aloud
while leaning with his back against a tree
about what sort of lean-to and which type
of wood would suit his circumstantial needs.

Expecting answer from himself, he looked
about in fear when rumbled forth a voice,
"Before you fell my trees and pilfer fruits
that you've not helped to grow with your own sweat,
what do you bring your landlord in return?"
The challenge seemed to come from everywhere
and nowhere such that Gabbar only thought
to answer to the island as a whole,
"A stranded man abandoned by his friends,
I fear I've nothing much to offer you.
I've lost my kin to savage plunderers
from foreign lands, my friends to vengeant gods
or to revenge against those selfsame gods
no matter what the cost—like childhood's bonds.
I've not a single laborer to plow
the inland soil—no milk-producing cow
to weed and prune and fertilize your greenery.
Bereft of women whom I loved too late,
unable to lay generational
foundations on this solitary rock,
I've all but lost the will to carry on.
I render you my dwindling gratitude,
however insubstantial it might be."

A silence followed his rejoinder as
the Sun made her quotidian descent.
Anon the broad deep voice responded thus,
"Time out of mind, a people came to me,
and I was soft and foolhardy enough
to grant them residence upon my back
just like a man adopts his orphaned niece
and nephew when their sickly father dies,
though he's not seen them since they crawled on fours.
This influx of exilic immigrants
brought cattle, seeds, and tools by which they fed
themselves and offered thanks for my support.
In time, however, they invited friends
and kin to join them here, uprooting trees,
exhausting soils, and bickering for space
and resources that never were their own.
My body wearied from their infighting
no less than from their rampant burgeoning.
Now: Sleepless anger often drives a soul to do
odd things from which he'd normally refrain,
and so it was with me who, making not
a sound, invoked the goddess Silence here
and wordlessly implored her to dispense
with every ingrate who with hand and tongue
attenuated my forsaken needs.
The goddess granted my request that night,
upstirring warningless and hastening
floodtides wherewith to drown the parasites.
A few escaped by boat while most behaved
unselfishly for once and gave themselves
to creatures of the sea for sustenance.

"Like you, I've lived through enervating times,
self-consciously unpeopling myself.
Since you inhumed your friend within my flesh,
affording me with more than you've acquired,
I have permitted you another day.
Should you continue to give back more than
you glean, then you may stay and dwell with me.
The lacks you listed are prerequisites,
in point of fact, for calling me your home.
So do now what you will. I've said my peace."
He ventured a response but stopped, unsure
of whether he had heard another's voice
or whether paltry aliment and days
adrift at sea now took their toll on him,
and so he stoked the fire and laid his head
to sleep—the labrys as his bedfellow.

When roseate Dawn shone, Gabbar filled the helm
that Burianu had consigned to him
with seawater, set it atop the flames
until the water bubbled and reduced,
allowing what remained to dry before
he gathered up the remnant shards of salt.
Forethinking that the gods themselves decay,
he ground the juniper berries and salt
with wild thyme, dredging strips of tentacle
in order to preserve the most he could.
Each day he cut and cured more, hollowing
the tendril, leaving Litan's skin intact.
Before he finished, the tentaculum
had straightened and rigidified beneath the sun
as if it were a giant's javelin point.
Gabbar hiked inland, made a second fire,

and burnt a little more than half the flesh
(the isle's admeasurement) just to be safe,
retiring to the humble lee he'd built
to put to rest his stomach's loud complaints.

A month elapsed ere Gabbar'd settled in,
his new home's cornucopia of rest,
tranquility, and rhythm changing him.
From yews he fashioned twin-barbed fishing spears,
impaling unsuspecting mackerel
along whose silver-chrysolitic sides
ran wavy streaks of black paint not-yet-dried.
He neither gave nor followed stern commands,
beclothed himself however he saw fit,
and satisfied his needs when they arose,
bethinking to himself the odd advice
that Shegr and Ithm had forwarded.
While Gabbar missed yet hated those who left
him on his own, the island's vibrancy
effectively forbid submission to
the prickly pleasures of despairfulness.
Receding and upwelling like the tide—
which though ostensibly identical
to that of yesterday, exchanges drop
by imperceptible drop its entire
makeup—the images of former friends
would populate his heart from time to time
only to lose their contours and the strong
affections tied to them with each reprise.
Creation's beautiful untrammeledness
distracted him from past and future cares,
and the divide that separated work
from rest—which life inculcated in him

while growing up—dissolved, the islander
beginning to partake of something like
Enkidu's early years of happiness.

Meanwhile, Nuhati'd led the seven ships
comprising Aqhat's followers northward
just as the Auguress had bidden him,
stealing into the Sea of Marmara's
first strait at night past tight-lipped oyster shoals
and nid-nodding hulls raising no alarm.
Disporting ensigns of Tumanan ships,
the vessels gained the Inhospitable
Sea, scudding coastwise, stopping for supplies
at outposts where Nuhati's confidants
held sway and happily restocked his ships
as small remittance for past services.
As if clairvoyant, Aqhat's dragoman
would tack their steerage seaward when the coves
from which Palaian sea raiders were known
to sally forth appeared, then back toward land
when their provisions needed topping-off—
as when they beached upon an untrod shore
leagues west of the Marassantiya's mouth.

While most made camp per usual, Laeya
solicited Bidawa's company
while fowling just beyond a nearby ridge.
Together they sought out the green-winged teal
Bidawa'd shot as Laeya asked (although
intuiting the thoughts she held entombed)
why airs of mourning hung about her face.
Finding the duck and taking it in hand,
Bidawa drew the arrow stained with blood
out of its heart, replying in due time,

"We've all lost shipmates journeying thus far,
and insomuch as they've been nothing but,
the lot of us knowing beforehand that
such pains were possible, our wounds will heal.
But there was one among us who surpassed
the ranks of those I held as intimates.
Although unscathed in Alashiya's fight,
an arrow from Astarte or Athirat's
bow pierced me as I fought at Gabbar's side,
and though I sailed from there without a scratch,
account me of the fallen nonetheless.
Upon a shaded bluff near Amnisos
(perhaps before) a goddess lanced him too,
our tender openings enfastening
the two of us together through a pain
as satisfying as incomparable.
How overreaching and uncountable
are love's imagined probabilities,
even—that is, especially when fresh!
He's gone, and yet the world's still rife with them,
their unreality oppressing me.
If only we had run away right then.
Or better yet, if only we had lain
upon that rock until the end of days.
If nothing that I say rings true, ignore
me, Laeya, till my wits return to me."

Laeya embraced her, saying not a word
for quite some time before she made reply,
"The agony you feel's unique to you.
Nor you nor I can leaven it with words.
But be that as it may, know that I've lost
a lover, though in ways dissimilar.
I also fell for him beside the sea.

Exuding youthfulness, of noble birth,
creative, wise, empowering: He was
the god for whom I'd dreamt since I was young.
In time, however, my fine cavalier's
edge blunted from an overindulgence
in privilege's inane amenities.
A myriad of voices weakened his,
disheveling his will, cajoling him
until his onetime wisdom was no more.
Such faults and many more besides a wife
finds ways to pardon, yet when he employed
his creativity to be untrue
I left him, never again to return.
But in that time I had been someone else,
and now it's like I've never loved before."

Continuing the hunt, Bidawa asked
if Laeya'd felt love's longings since those days.
Laeya alluded to the warden she'd
seduced to win a laugh and smile from her
before responding in the negative
and with her left hand brushing to the side
the tress a zephyr'd wisped across her eye.

Attending to the haulage and stowage
of expeditionary articles,
Ameni and Aqhat coworked in camp
until Yasiranu, now overwrought
with worry for his wife whom he'd not seen
since yesterday, entreated them for help.
Ameni calmed the man, advising him
to strike out with three scouts to the southeast
while he and Aqhat looked southwest for her.
Should they have no success by nightfall, all

were to return, abandoning the search.
Without delay Yasiranu set off,
enlisting those he thought most capable
of aiding him, Ameni and Aqhat
departing for their unknown stretch of wood.
The latter plodded underneath old firs
and spruce and alders, listening for sounds
betraying Milka's hidden whereabouts,
yet both men only heard the distant Wind
who strolled along the valley's other side
and ran his fingers through the foliage
in order to communicate in tongues
well-known to isolated brooks and streams.

Ameni turned to Aqhat, asking him,
"May I disturb the silence with some things
that I've been pondering, although I've kept
them to myself to not be bothersome?
The gods have never slept alone, you know.
If you indeed slay three gods in the year,
will you, like many of the holiest
of gods, not take your sister as your wife
if you can free her specter from below?
Or shall your consort be divine from birth?
For while a god can lay with anyone
he chooses, as all know, yet he cannot
espouse a mortal made of different stuff."

Taken aback, Aqhat replied to him,
"How strange these speculations you unearth!
And yet it's true that I've been fixated
upon the Tablet's central mystery
concerning godly death by human hands,
leaving all matters of the heart aside.

If I'm victorious, will my old loves
and tastes be out-and-out transformed, perhaps
in other instances reversed, destroyed?
I cannot know these things before their time,
my friend, so maybe they're best left alone.
At all events, your questions counsel me:
I will not give myself to anyone
lest in so doing I should give the Void
the upper hand or lead another on;
no good could come from acting otherwise."
He spoke this resolution just before
its truth occurred to him, a truth that he
resented for escaping from his lips,
for now his promise could invoke its rights
to rein his passions in and master him,
vows striving to exert their potencies
and will to live like aught that's animate
no matter who decides to challenge them.

They halted—boar grunts frightening the trees.
Ameni clutched his spear and Aqhat nocked
an arrow, slinking toward the stertorous,
repeated lows that rose as they sped on.
Rounding a bend, Ameni gestured toward
a ragged man who thrust himself upon
a half-dressed Milka, shackled and knocked out.
Aqhat let fly a bronze-barbed arrow shaft
that spit the man's right lung, at which he howled.
The two men rushed his way as Aqhat kicked
him on his back to find Rashapabu
(whose moaning changed its tune) as the culprit.
Aqhat renocked a flane and drew it taut,
the bowstring raring to release its stress
while concentrated on the rapist's face.

Ameni unbound Milka, finding that
she breathed, relaying his discovery
to Aqhat who'd grown deaf with vitriol.
The latter asked of Rashapabu if
his crime had been worthwhile, a bloody grin
the man's retort ere Aqhat ended him.

Aqhat retrieved his arrows, bending down
to Milka, lifting her to carry her
back when Ameni asked what they should do
with Rashapabu's corpse, to which his friend
replied that blowflies and pale maggots would
administer to him the rites he'd earned.
Dumbstruck, Ameni didn't question him
but followed Aqhat northward toward the sea.
By dusk they neared the camp's perimeter,
the cries of seagulls pointing out the way.
The ravaged beauty cradled in his arms,
the Seir Mountain Man returned to camp
as startled countenances gazed on him.
Examining his every move, Laeya
deplumed her fresh kill absentmindedly
and pressed a plucked quill's tip into her thumb.

Ere long Yasiranu caught sight of them
and ran with joyous incredulity
to take his battered wife into his arms
while asking Aqhat where they'd chanced on her.
He started to reply when Milka stirred,
"Yasiranu, my love! Are those our ships?
What happened to me? Last thing that I recall
is Rashapabu telling me about
a local goddess who revealed herself
atop a nearby stream, informing him

that only women could approach the site
or gather water from the riverbanks.
Imploring me to come and lend a hand,
I followed him for many leagues it seemed.
Assuring me the stream was not far off,
he kindly shared his waterpouch with me.
Why am I covered with this dirt and blood?"

She fainted and Yasiranu whisked her
away to tend to her afflicted state.
By now the scandal's attar had aroused
the whole encampment's interest, so Aqhat,
exhausted and infuriated, climbed
a boulder, summoning his followers.
When all had gathered round he raised his voice,
"If we consider wrong the bearing off
of one's belongings, all the more if he
be family, then just how anathema
should we regard the stealing of a spouse?
And if to desecrate a neighbor's house
is impermissible and frowned upon,
then how much worse is it to violate
the bond because of which one makes a home?
Not least of all: If Fate has destined us,
united us to undermine three gods
for their injustice, treachery, and lies,
while doing which we are attacked by sea
and land by other deities, then why
reach out to them for aid amidst a storm
or heed their whisperings as anything
but rank, self-seeking underhandedness?
Friends, we have traveled much too far, have fought
too many beasts and warriors, have lost

too many kinsmen to grow lazy, weak.
Our greatest challenges still lie ahead,
so look within yourselves, right here, right now,
and either recommit yourselves or leave,
breaking your oath as Rashapabu did.
First thing tomorrow morning we make sail
for the Marassantiya, the last leg
to Suppiluliuma's citadel.
Prepare yourselves and ready every ship,
but only if you're truly one of us."

Thus Aqhat, who inspired discipline
within his followers, respect among
his friends, and love in his admirers.
They put to sea at dawn, arriving at
the outfall of Hattusa's waterway,
ascending its discrepant tendencies
with oarage when the wind ran short of breath,
carving between acclivities of green
sporadically bedecked with gray fieldstones
behind which crested snow-blotched mountainsides.
At local docks they harbored for the night
(if any were available) and snatched
what news and know-how locals offered up.
Some men of one town in particular
provided for the fleet's requirements:
Zaipuwa's circumspective magistrates
supplied Nuhati's friends with victuals.
While coasting up the quiet riverbends,
the ships braved onslaughts unannounced by tribes
of Kaskan rogues, each marginal escape
emboldening and centering the fleet,
ensuring them that Fate was on their side.

At last the products of Zelophehad's
precise and weathered hands came to a quay
on the Marassantiya's riverside
where they'd retire, their holiday well-earned.
They berthed along a bustling mooring-point
where soldiers, mongers, fugitives, and thieves
fled from or headed to the capital
along the highways of the emperor.
Prepared Nuhati had associates
assist unshipping keels then traded them
for chariots and horses for their trek
while Aqhat, Laeya, and the seafarers
transitioned to their roles as foot soldiers
and, after little more than two nights' rest,
set forth along the empire's thoroughfares
that cut between the mountains like dried flumes.

They rode till saddlesore then rode still more.
The outskirts of Hattusa now in sight,
Nuhati counseled them to bivouac
as groups of armed and foreign legionnaires
would not be welcomed in the capital.
They heeded his word, Aqhat and Laeya
bedizening themselves as diplomats
from faraway and wealthy metropoles
ere naming the Egyptian aide-de-camp
to see that peace and order were maintained.
With Henti's doves, Nuhati, and four guards,
the leaders cantered for Hattusa as
the city's western walls rose into view,
wide sections towering symmetrically
at intervals with mammoth battlements,
each one adorned with crenelated crowns.
The dragoman conducted his encharged

up to the gateway flanked with leonine
defenders of the city, each maned beast
on guard with eyes of hematite wherein
one found oneself the object of their scrutiny.
Tremendous watchtowers held up the rear.
Before the portalway Nuhati spoke
among and reasoned with the gatewardens,
identifying dignitaries whose
regalia signaled their significance.
Three days' admittance being granted them,
the seven passed between the lions' jaws
and sought the upper town to take their meal.

Some city quarters lay in disrepair
from Zaphon's leaguerment not long before,
though Suppiluliuma had dispatched
a host of architects and brickmasons
to reconstruct and fortify what walls,
canals, and shrines Baal's troops had pulverized.
While Aqhat, Laeya, and their ward explored
the upper city's spicy marketplace,
Nuhati, man of many contacts, left
to locate Prince Telipinu, the son
most prized by banished Henti and, among
his father's sons, the most persuadable.
Sneaking into the Shaushkan Garden where
Telipinu would stroll to clear his head,
Nuhati startled and delighted him
when he removed his hood, enclasping him.
Barraging him with inquiries, the prince
asked how his mother fared. Nuhati said,
"It's by the queen's command that I've returned
across the Inhospitable Sea's swells,
up the Marassantiya's snaking course,

and over highwaymen-infested roads.
Your mother lives, although her vast remove
from you and from your brothers tortures her.
She has entrusted me with precious goods
for each of her belovèd kings-to-be.
A small flotilla of stout seafarers
has fended Henti's presents from the start,
its leaders hoping to deliver them
to you in person, here, at dawn, thereby
attaining closure to their pilgrimage.
Thus if you're so inclined, corral your kin
in secret—Mursili and Zannanza,
Piyassili and Arnuwanda too—
insisting that they join us privately.
Oh, how she'd smile with tears to see you now!"

The prince accepted his enticing plan,
delivering the news to his own blood
who, though far less excited than he was
(held back by duty and suspicion's tugs),
caved to his earnest importunacy
and to the universal love of gifts
that binds both stately lords and grunts alike.
The next day, Aqhat, Laeya, and their guide
rode through the Shaushkan Garden's entryway,
clip-clopping under arbors and down paths
embosked with fruiting pomegranate trees
until they reached the heirs of Hatti's throne,
alighting from their stallions, kneeling down.
King Suppiluliuma's sons bade them
arise as all exchanged formalities.
Aqhat presented them with olive oil,
red wine, and arms of Knossian design
and provenance, their rarity well-known.

In nearly-fluent Nesite—beautiful
despite, or rather, due to her slipups—
Laeya told how they'd met the erstwhile queen
as Aqhat handed each of them a cage,
"Receive these alabaster doves, with whose
safe transport your dear mother trusted us.
Though in the flesh she cannot be with you,
yet with you she desires to share advice,
encouragement, and even everyday
occurrences—a mother's right, no doubt.
Nuhati brought these birds aboard his keel
when he accompanied her to the coast;
there they were reared and trained as messengers.
Now that they've reached their birthplace once again
they'll know the journey west, allowing you
to speak with Henti as if she were here.
Although you cannot barter with or sense
her final present to you, nonetheless
esteem it higher than the rest: She sends
you more affection than our fleet could ship."

A fragrance reminiscent of childhood—
a coriander perfume Henti wore—
bespoke the white doves' authenticity
as love, despond, regret, and gratitude
rolled down the princes' outcropping cheekbones.
They heaped thanks on their visitors and poured
them drafts of wine as Arnuwanda asked
how they might reimburse their porterage,
assuming (rightly) that the one who'd sent
them on their voyage hadn't financed it.
Laeya replied to Arnuwanda thus,
"It's true—our journey cost us quite a lot.
And while we do not bring you things for trade

but only what your mother and the gods
ordained, if we could be so bold to ask
for an event instead of worldly things,
you'd honor us and leave us in your debt.
Word of your father's greatness travels far—
even the foreign peasant knows his name
and by his deeds compares his higher-ups.
Could we but for a moment meet with him?"

The princes' sidelong looks of reticence
and idle beard-strokes gave the lie to just
how difficult her favor was to grant.
Mursili spoke up first, explaining that
the emperor had trying days ahead,
the stress of which would leave him indisposed
to entertaining any visitors.
Zannanza added that the constancy
of ill tidings depressed their genitor
and made his recent tasks unbearable—
suggesting that Aqhat and Laeya name
what gleaming riches they preferred instead.
But young Telipinu, who fed his dove,
considered all such counteroffers rude,
their mother's embassy deserving just
what they had asked for and, in truth, much more.
He noted that the promised couriers
from Nubia with whom the emperor
had planned to meet that day had never come
and freed a space for them to congregate.
Though wary of the soundness of his words,
the siblings of wide-eyed Telipinu
agreed to usher Aqhat and Laeya
to Hatti's Royal Citadel that eve
on the condition that they not bring up

their mother under any circumstance
nor mention that they'd helped them see the king.
The two agreed, both sides contented now
as Hatti's lords invited them to eat
and quaff strong drink with them till dinnertime.

Telipinu led Aqhat and Laeya
up to Hattusa's Royal Citadel
engirdled by embravened, looming walls.
They entered through a turreted portail
as guards bowed to their escort solemnly.
Vast forecourts opened up before the three
as priests and scribes concluded their day's work,
the scent of incense clinging to their cloaks.
On reaching Suppiluliuma's Court,
the prince explained to the doorwarden that
he'd brought important, foreign viziers
to greet Hattusa's sovereign majesty.
The guard bade them await as Temetti,
the emissary of the emperor
to eastern lands, related what he'd heard,
"Your Eminence, Ishuwa's king has sent
us word ensuring that he'll do his part
to quell rebellions in Hayasha's towns
and pledge his fealty to Hattusa's crown
if you would send Muwatti as the king's
betrothed before the full moon takes the sky.
Such is the good news. Yet the Upper Land
remains entirely impassable,
precluding her conveyance to the king.
The monster Ullikummi savages
the hills and pinelands senselessly, tromping
and smashing everyone who interlopes.
Of a battalion sent to take him out

one man alone's returned, relaying that
the mountain crushed his men into the earth—"

"That's quite enough!" the emperor broke in.
Temetti genuflected docilely,
recusing himself from all argument.
Attendants signaled for Aqhat and his
companion to approach, Telipinu
becloaked, remaining in the vestibule.
Advancing toward the dais of the king
and bowing when they neared, Laeya began,
"Your Eminence, Hattusa's Saving Sword,
they call me Laeya; Aqhat is his name.
We've traveled here with seven ships of troops
to meet with you and hoping that our bone-deep
affinities and hatreds might align.
Just as Anat and Baal wreaked havoc on
your city, so have they devasted us.
On Zaphon we propose declaring war.
Should you seek vengeance too, we welcome you
to join us on our military march."

King Suppiluliuma studied them.
A moment passed, then yet another one
before the king exploded with guffaws,
his belly heaving up and down just like
a bellows, teardrops streaming down his cheeks.
The High Court's magistrates erupted too
as Suppiluliuma caught his breath,
"My side is split as from a mortal wound!
Who kindly sent these entertainers here
to close our day with such hilarity?
Exceeding the palatial satirists

and jugglers that I've witnessed heretofore,
these two have played their parts with flawless charm!"

A sycophant along the wall chimed in,
"My Lord, perhaps these heroines had hoped
to vanquish Abihumbaba as well,
for how else could they reach Mount Zaphon while
the Snake Commander still protects his turf?"

Confounded, Aqhat and Laeya turned round
to exit but the emperor desired
to keep the game alive, resummoning
his guests and following the last man's cue,
"Don't go! My councilman speaks well for once:
If I'm not wrong, then errant warriors
in search of high reward—alliances
with emperors, for instance—must subdue
dread beasts to prove themselves. Is this not so?
In that case, I propose the following:
Immobilize the gritty demigod
called Ullikummi—he whose biceps swell
as hillcrests with a headland for his head—
and render me a portion of his heart.
Along the way, take out Humbaba's son,
the guardian of Kizzuwatna's woods
who bears six serpent heads atop his frame,
returning with a scale of his as proof.
Do this and by the Thousand Gods I swear
that Hatti's horses, battle-tested men,
and chariots are yours to commandeer!"

To the High Court's uproarious delight,
Laeya accepted his mock overture
and thanked him, turning round to take her leave,

those gathered wishing them heartfelt success.
Not knowing what they'd said, Aqhat asked her
as they rejoined with Prince Telipinu,
who blushed vicarious discomfiture.
He led them from the Royal Citadel
and to an empty, nearby alleyway
where Laeya translated what had occurred
to Aqhat who grew mad and ill at ease.
Telipinu apologized for what
had fallen out, assuring them that had
he known the content of their suppliance,
he would have striven to dissuade their aims.
With fingers pressed against his sweating brow,
eyes closed, Aqhat expressed that he could not
believe that they had failed—that they had placed
their every hope upon the charity
of Hatti's crown without a backup plan,
and that they'd sailed so far and wide for naught.
The prince asked what they'd do when Laeya said,
"The king did not deny us out of hand,
his overt ridicule allowing us
a way, however periled, to lay claim
to what we traveled here to bring about.
In irony lies opportunity.
Although the challenges he set to us
might well exceed our strength, we can't lay waste
to gods successfully without his arms."

Incredulous at such temerity,
they looked at her then one another's way.
And when the prince had come to understand
that no expostulation, no good sense
could bridle her insistent suicide,
he led them to a torchlit tunnelway

beneath a temple's adytum and through
a door to which no priest possessed the keys
until they reached a mural set apart
with Ullikummi painted on one side
and Abihumbaba on the other,
divided by columnar hieroglyphs.
Reluctantly, Telipinu began,
"If I cannot prevent your obdurate
and reckless ventures, then at least I might
reveal to you those words passed down to us
regarding those against whom you're dead set.
I've brought innumerable generals
before this diptych, counseling each one
to contemplate its hidden mystery
so that, when leading their battalions through
Hayasha's hills or Kizzuwatna's woods
to carry out Zababa's bloody chores,
they might at long last incapacitate
the monsters staving off our empire's growth.
But of those few who haven't scoffed at it,
even they've not deciphered its purport.
So I implore you: Take these words to heart."

Running his fingers underneath the glyphs,
Telipinu intoned them like a prayer,
"Among the outlands two brutes dwell,
entirely incongruous.
By opposites one does them quell,
all other ways prove ruinous.

"Of everything the first conceives—
the realm of wisdom's his domain.
There's nothing he cannot perceive,
nor anything he won't explain.

"No force the other mollifies,
insensate and belligerent.
Impressed by none he liquefies,
his lapis heart's indifferent.

"Unto the senseless one bring sense,
whereof he shall be grounded.
And to the first's intelligence
propound something unfounded.
In such wise—not with lance or bow—
can one these demigods lay low."

The prince permitted them to ponder what
he'd just divulged before he led them out,
rethanking them for Henti's downy gift,
imploring them to maintain vigilance.
Aqhat and Laeya then retired to camp,
apprising their Egyptian adjutant
of what transpired, deciding that it would
be best for him to run the camp so they
might undertake their challenge undeterred.
With well-disguised begrudgingness,
Ameni vowed to oversee the camp
and wished the pair a quick and safe return.
They thanked him and outfit themselves with gear
and vittles for their trek of unguessed length,
delaying not a quarter-moment's time
before they galloped south beneath the moon
and toward the Anti-Taurus Mountains' heights
with little but the prince's promise that
they need not spoor for Abihumbaba
for long, as he'd discover them with ease
and make himself apparent all too soon.

Book XVII

A string of scintillating gilt-head bream
in hand, Gabbar strode through the surf up toward
familiar wooden homes with wattled roofs
as Shapshu bronzed the bare skin of his back.
He bypassed Danel, judge and Harnemite,
saluting him and asking whether he,
Aqhat, and Danataya wouldn't like
to take their meal with them once evening fell.
The pious man accepted his invite
with graciousness, returning to his tasks.
Gabbar then entered through his mother's door.
She soaked her purpled feet in a washtub,
the harvest's squidgy labor having stained
her soles—but noticing her son she rose
and stumbled headlong, kicking the bucket
and spilling dirty water everywhere
as Gabbar caught her midfall, laughing at
her unilateral, impromptu hug.
He gifted her the choicest fish he'd speared.

In the attempt to catch him up to speed
on backlogged news, Inumi spoke full tilt
and handed him a brand-new skin of wine.
He took in all the content of her words
to humor her, anticipating brief
caesuras so that he could hurry home,
but after six mistimed escape attempts,
he kissed her, thanking her and ducking out
as she concluded what she had to say

between the jambs, her voice raised to a shout.
Along the town's periphery his own
home now came into view, and when he neared
its door, Bidawa stepped outside,
her fingers laced around her budding waist.
As he approached his wife a fly alit
upon him and he shooed it till he roused—
that dung-eater alone having been real.

Reveries like these—some stranger than the rest—
had frequented his lonely nights of late,
and though he grasped their unreality,
such knowledge hampered none of their allure.
The island's goods, though better than the gifts
for which most mortals hope, turned drab before
familiarity's ingratitude
and from comparison's corrosive bite.
The taste of unblent wine—of olives, dates;
the drowsing hum of townspeople at work;
and most of all, the taken-for-granted
companionships that render life worthwhile—
these now-departed phantoms beckoned him,
discoloring the haven he had found
until his haunted homesickness won out.
Once Gabbar had determined to sail home—
to start a new life in his fatherland
whatever hurdles might oppugn his rough
return—the phantoms rallied to his cause.
They floated new ideas as to how
he might, at long last, get where he belonged.

Although unknowledgeable in the ways
of shipbuilding (except for what he'd learned
in recent months), Gabbar turned over types

of deep-sea craft within his breast and put
to work the fantasies that pestered him,
enchaining, redirecting their reserves.
The seven-headed monster's tentacle,
now straight and stiff, its remnant flyblown flesh
once-thought deprived of usefulness, appeared
potentially salvific once again.
He knew its buoyancy, and from the plates
he'd fired, hoped to make it watertight.
With Burianu's labrys Gabbar flensed
the rancid meat and tossed it to the gulls,
inlaying the tentaculum with fronds
before he planed the hardened, lateral
topsides into symmetrical gunwales.
A sturdy crosswise thwart endowed the hull
with proper curvature and doubled as
a trusty transom seat from which to row.
To seal the rearmost end that once received
its nutrients from Litan's many mouths,
he clinched the opening and fired it,
occasionally singeing his own hands,
shaving and fashioning a nearby barb
beneath the keel's stern side into a skeg.
Lastly, he raised a makeshift baldachin
cut from his tunic's upper half so as
to weather Shapshu's sweltering regard.

The island's single, kilted habitant
equipped his dugout with eleven spears,
the butts of which he tied to coils of rope.
Provisioning the craft with salted fish,
plump waterskins, a sundry aggregate
of fresh comestibles, two paddles carved
from carob trees, and the Belated's ax,

he put its seaworthiness to the test.
The bowsprit he reheated and reworked
(uplifting it like those he'd seen before)
while flattening the belly of his craft.
One placid morn he gorged himself like one
whose broken their first drawn-out fast and brimmed
himself with water till he heard it slosh,
embarking northward as he leapt aboard
to row for any peopled continent.

Beyond Hattusa's sphere of influence
by now, Aqhat and Laeya rode southeast
with little time to pause and catch their breath.
A swale embosomed in a mountain pass
called out to Aqhat as the best way through,
and so he clenched his thighs and spurred his mount
in that direction, Laeya at his rear.
Like obelisks erected by the Skilled's
strong hands, the pines in that part of the world
outstripped the ones on Lel in girth and height
(though these were capped with cream-hued, melting snow),
and Laeya wished she could examine them—
could stop to run her fingers down their bark.
Without so much as saying so, the two
knew that the wood's pulsating quietude
betrayed its underlying savagery,
the ever-present possibility
of ambush marshaling deterrent force,
a martial law unspoken, untransgressed.
This stifling aura of forbiddenness
exacerbated the austere restraint
wherewith they disciplined their bodies' needs.

"And to the first's intelligence
propound something unfounded . . ."
Aqhat reflected on the mysteries
Telipinu had read to them and wished
his childhood friend were right there by his side.
He thought about the games they once had played,
about Shegr's nonsensical charades,
about how Gabbar beat back Litan's wrath.
"Of everything the first conceives—
the realm of wisdom's his domain.
There's nothing he cannot perceive,
nor anything he won't explain."
His scattered flashbacks interposed themselves
between attempted riddle-work and doubts.
At one point, when it seemed that they had gone
in circles, Aqhat vented his dismay,
"How many detours can we undertake
provided that I have so little time
to kill three gods? My candle's fuel runs low.
How can you be so sure that we must take
the present path—that there's no other way?
Should we not reconsider our approach?"

Pinpricked by his misgivings, she rejoined,
"Our Alashiyan search and rescue, then,
and voyages to Kaphtor and across
the Inhospitable Sea were nothing more
than pleasure cruises, roundabout delays?
I've no more certitude than you have got.
Whatever angle we decide to take,
we only have a finite set of moves
when Fortune casts our chancy knucklebones.
Or wouldn't you have saved Gabbar and sped

from Litan had that choice availed itself?
So go ahead. Rework our strategy.
And when you light on tactics better than
the present ones we'll tack the other way."
Approaching Kizzuwatna's timbered steeps,
they rode in silence at a hand gallop
until prodigious footfall halted them.

Reminded of a scent of old which yet
escaped precise location in his thoughts,
Abihumbaba—grisly guardian
of Kizzuwatna's woods, columnar-legged
and from whose frame there sprouted serpent heads—
employed his forked tongues to investigate
the air until his dozen eyes descried the source
of that delectable perfume, to wit,
defiant mortals clothed in scrumptious flesh.
Excited for his supper yet incensed
by these two dimwits' insolence, the snakes
addressed the pair and lisped amongst themselves,
"Does gall or sheer stupidity propel
you into realms where you do not belong?
Which one of you has duped the other one,
convincing him that my existence proves
akin to characters in old wives' tales?
Why do you ask—who cares? Their blood's so fresh,
and when you stress them out their meat turns sour.
Not true—it's fish you're thinking of, you schlub!
With bread-eaters one must filet and strike
them over and over until they're soft.
Do so if you so please; I've waited far
too long for sustenance, and so I'll shear
my own slice off and swallow it uncooked.

A suitable method for a big mouth.
Ah, quiet! Let them say their sad so-longs."

A frisson shocked the onlookers, the hair
upon their guardless necks like hoarfrost spikes.
But feigning some composure, Aqhat said,
"We are no trespassers and mean no harm.
You might be right to guess stupidity's
the reason for our trip, though whether it
be ours or has its source in someone else
is largely why we've come: You see, it's said
that you're unreasonable to a great
degree, that you're a thoughtless oaf who does
his father's bidding, ready to give up
all freedom just to gorge on forest fowl
and traipse about, conversing with yourself.
Wait! You've a right to be annoyed, so just
another moment, if you'd be so kind.
You see, I too was angered by such lies.
I argued, contrary to popular
belief, that any demigod with time
to contemplate the world and its beyond
within the woodland depths could not but be
the wisest one who ever walked the earth.
Moreover, I said, one with many heads
must be still wiser than the gods, since they
are of a mind to deal with practical
affairs (and for our benefit, praised be)
and thus must set aside the mind's ordeals,
attending to ethereal concerns.

"While in a tavern late one night, I set
forth arguments like these and, thinking that
they'd shut me up for good, a rowdy lot

rebuked me, saying, 'If that monster be
the paragon of wisdom, as you claim,
then there exists no riddle such that he
could fail to grasp its essence from the start.
No normal puzzle'd really do the trick.
For one with such unmatched intelligence,
the only fitting obstacle would be
to act unreasonably. So, head off
into the forest (bring a witness, too)
and set this simple trial before his feet:
to do just one unreasonable thing
and nothing reasonable ere the moon
ascends above the treeline on that night.'
Inspired by brazenness and too much drink,
I seized their proposition, and so here
I stand, a sober man who's proud, at least,
to see your glistering eyes at long last.
Were you successful in this no-brainer,
we'd straightaway ride back into those towns
to tell the tale, repairing your repute,
and all would know we'd spoken truthfully
since no one's ever entered this dark wood
to come back in one piece—or so they say.
But if aspersion doesn't bother you,
no matter how inane or libelous,
however far and wide they smear your name,
then act on instinct—do as you see fit,
thereby confirming common sentiment
and my apology's great foolishness."

Now, most who find themselves with surplus time
become adept at piddling it away,
but Abihumbaba preferred to plumb
life's paradoxes, sharpening his mind.

He'd scratch the gulars of his sixfold heads
while lost in thought until an insight flashed.
Without permission to abandon his
legated realm, however, and without
new adversaries to antagonize,
his inner lives had dipped into a lull
of late, and so the six consented to
take up the facile challenge, wondering
what it would be like to be hindered by
the unrefined and thickish thoughts of men.

At once they put their sibilance to work,
"Alright, let's get this over with, as my
stomach's grown sickly from its emptiness.
Of course, although your stomach's not just yours.
There's but one spot to start, brothers: Let's ask
this boy to first set straight exactly what
'unreasonable' means, and do something
that falls inside this sphere. Perhaps . . . No, stop,
you fool! Investigating something's sense
is not the least nonsensical, and to
act sensibly would be to do something
most reasonable—don't you understand?
That's sound. Let's not consult trespassers
whose single goal is to deceive us all.
But wouldn't such a recourse—to rely
upon one's foes—be unreasonable?
In this case, it's in our best interest, no?
Ask nothing from those two unsubtle souls!
The challenge, anyways, was set for us.
Let's separate unreasonable things
from everything opposed to these in kind.
Who'll mark the first division? Must I be
affixed to you slow-witted imbeciles?

To make distinctions, even if they be
unsuitable or silly, implicates
oneself in reasoning at least somewhat.

"He speaks well, does he not? We've overthought
a contest meant for thoughtless doofuses.
Let no one say another worthless smidge.
Do whatsoever springs to mind, since to
act unpremeditatedly's the lot
of idiots—a purposeless purport.
At this point, anything we'd do would be
directed toward restoring our renown
in order to consume the halflings here.
But surely any soul who has some end
in mind (albeit stashed within his gut)
and acts accordingly to benefit
himself and blood relations must be deemed
at least a slightly reasonable sap.
It's like you've secret potencies to find
exceptions in abysses lacking them.
I'd rather see too much than have a mind
that's so exceptionally abyssal!
Perhaps I've solved it, then: I'll slash your throat
with these envenomed fangs, concluding this
absurdly wordy whirlwind since we're stuck
together and since injuring oneself
could not be sensical. You wouldn't dare!"

At this the disputatious adder nest
began to snap and furl upon itself,
a central snake assaulted from both sides
until, in self-defense, it scragged the maw
of its aggressor, kinsman though he was.
As often mortal hands will comprehend

some challenge that the mind cannot prehend,
so too that brute's claws tried to reinstate
the peace among the pestilential swarm.
A spluttered insight gave the serpents pause,
"Hold on, that's it—the puzzle has been solved!
Though shedding blood is proof of neither truth
nor falsehood, here such rules need not apply:
Instead of inference, violence has won out
in the attempt to truly strike our mark.
And since persuasion through malignant fangs
involves a full-blown lack of reasoning,
we have succeeded spite our differences.
What nonsense! Reasoning has never swayed
one's kin, much less a raucous multitude.
Where mindless chaos threatens to expunge
the public good, it's only sensible
and reasonable to resort to force.
In other words, we've not advanced at all.
That's it! You both are right and wrong at once.
Consider our debacle heretofore
a singular event: Endeavoring
to turn our reason into unreason,
or unreason ourselves out of reason,
we've conjured cross-purposes from thin air.
But what could be less reasonable than
self-contradictions never meant-to-be?
Ridiculous! How so? What do you mean,
'How so?' Exactly what we all would mean.
Speak for yourself. This is preposterous!"

The beast's ophidic heads lashed out at one
another yet again, but this go-round
with more resolve, their hissing echoing
down through the corridors of conifers.

A second time he reached up, yanking them
apart as one in grief pulls out their hair.
Their sneers intensified—his necks afoul.
Abihumbaba clutched an asp in hand
and squeezed its throat (although he felt the pain
as well, that neck belonging to himself).
Defending one beside whom he'd grown up,
an adder fanged Abihumbaba's wrist
whereat the sixfold shrieked in agony.
As if a mauvish marsh the site distent.
In fits and starts the forked-tongues settled down
yet realized that their challengers had fled.

Just as Anat lifts her flagitious scourge
of scorpion tips which cluster in the air
behind her ere they strike in unison,
so too did Abihumbaba's long necks
whip forward toward the earth with unified
decisiveness, enraged at being fooled.
Upon all fours the dread brute flung himself
in order to hunt down the charlatans.
His tongues immediately caught their scent.
Licking the air, Abihumbaba loped
between the cedars over underscrub—
familiar with the twists of his domain.
He ran full-stride and slowed down only once
to verify their spoor, at which he slewed
their way with reinvigorated hate.
Like rising-falling gunnels of a boat
that broaches-to between competing swells,
the monster's shoulder blades rocked back and forth
atop the churning of his legs and arms,
some newfound virulence investing him

with such prodigious potency it brought
a spate of violent vertigo in tow.

Despite their head start, Aqhat and Laeya
could feel the earth convulsing underhoof.
Humbaba's son loosed shrieking wyverns' roars
that bristled all the brushland's follicles,
the forestland itself on high alert.
While fleeing, Aqhat signaled for Laeya
to ride away from him as he unsheathed
his sword and cut his arm, drawing black blood.
She fumed at him until he bade her go
again, his partner yielding to his plan
ere both raced through the dusking bosk, alone.

The mongrel gained on Aqhat, unseen wreathes
of blood provoking and attracting him
as wounded schools do sharks from leagues away.
With confidence the monster slowed and skulked
into a dell with sportive grimaces
as if to have enjoyed the game in full
yet eager to lay claim to his reward.
There Aqhat sat atop his frighted horse,
alone, outnumbered, pinned against a bluff,
and in that moment thought how stupid he
had been to challenge Kizzuwatna's beast
who'd all-too-soon devour his unwept corpse.
Encroaching on them, slavering for meat
of horse and man alike, the serpent heads
began to think of one accord once more,
no longer muddled by mock challenges
of human speech—so feckless, so absurd.

The demigod resumed bipedal form
and cracked his knuckles, striding toward his meal
till two mere fathoms separated them.
One snake head opened wide its mouth to taunt
his kill but hitched for air, an action that
confused his brothers as they sought the cause,
deducing its alarm-inducing source.
Forgetting Aqhat, every serpent head
descended toward their suppurating wrist
to suck the self-inflicted toxins out
(as eels contending for a hippo's leg
in dark lagoons will spin and lash and bite),
disgorging their extractions on the earth.
All hands on deck did not suffice withal.
The manhunt's fury'd pumped his veins with bane,
resulting in extremities that froze
then scalded in successive, random bursts.
In unison the vipers vomited
black purulent goo upon the earth and shrilled,
writhing and kinking in a knarry mess
without the least control of their intents.
The serpentine heads thrashed spasmodically
in jolts at first but then began to squirm
with rash convulsions and paroxysms,
his poisoned throats encoiled and paralyzed.
His weakened heart continuing to throb,
the tutelar of the timber lost his minds
and like a humbled cedar struck the earth.

That thud reverberated through the woods,
alerting Laeya who now feared the worst.
She found her partner standing petrified
in disbelief and gazing on the heap
before she rent her sleeve to stanch his cut.

Just having stared death in the face, worn out
from riding, jubilant at their success,
Aqhat recounted all that had occurred
in detail as she bandaged up his arm,
and when he told her how the poison coursed
through Abihumbaba's entire mass,
he took her wrist to demonstrate what had
transpired and pressed his lips upon her pulse
as if to leech hot venom from her veins.
His energy transfused her and she flushed
like one about to fall from high aloft,
now recommending that they carry on.
Sliding his blade beneath the squamous mail
of one of Abihumbaba's six necks,
he pried two scutes as proof of victory
and with these spoils sought Ullikummi's realm
deep in Hayasha's long-abandoned tors.

Over the Anti-Taurus' snow-fleeced spine
the rovers rode while alternating leads.
Aroused by their approach, an antlered stag
caught sight of them and coolheadedly led
his two red does, a mother and her fawn,
beyond the ridge to safer pasturage.
Aqhat and Laeya fought against short spells
of sleet which melted from their bodies' warmth
and Shapshu's sultry rays only to freeze
again when she departed from the world.
These battles back-and-forth between the moist
and hard as such exhausted them and brought
to fever pitch the need to mount their beds—
two unrolled throws of hide and fur on which
to take their rest once Aqhat pitched his tent.
At times, awakening to stoke the flames,

he glanced to see if she still slept and if
she'd rolled away or toward him while adream.
When Aqhat slept she kept watch much the same.

Reduced to edging under cornices,
shambling along cliff shelves, and sliding down
loose scree, the thoroughbreds endured their slog
with a forbearance only matched by dogs.
Their alpine crucible had nearly done
them in when, having gained the highest lee
south of Samuha and the headwaters
of the Marassantiya, anguished brools
and seismic temblors rocked the mountain ridge.
The travelers forthwith hitched their four-hoofed friends
and peered with caution just beyond the range
where rose a basalt mountain on two legs
one thousand times the size of barbicans;
whose fists brick temples envied for their size
and their propinquity to heaven's gods;
whose face, though stony, bore those humanlike
characteristics which allow for one
to show emotions like unease and wrath.
There Ullikummi towered, treading trees
like sedge and pummeling the nearby peaks,
large chunks of which Aqhat and Laeya dodged.
From provocations as of yet unguessed
the living mountain squalled, his timberlined
and rimy beard convulsing from the sound.

And then, as unannounced as he'd begun
his havocking, the megalith sat down,
his rugged chin set on his sighing chest.
The two looked on with just as much surprise
as grim duress—for Abihumbaba

now seemed a plaything in comparison.
Exchanging rough ideas and half-baked
proposals, each of which the other knew
to be foreclosed without experiment,
the pair felt their gigantomachic task
impinge upon and all but quash their hopes.
"No force the other mollifies,
insensate and belligerent.
Impressed by none he liquefies,
his lapis heart's indifferent."
They made camp for the night so as to give
due thought to better stratagems but were
aroused at daybreak by a tantrum much
the same as they had witnessed recently.

When Ullikummi stopped and took his rest,
Laeya continuously banged her head
against Telipinu's abstruse two lines,
their meaning barred behind a bolted door:
"Unto the senseless one bring sense,
whereof he shall be grounded."
A moment passed, then yet another one
before an insight breached the surface, its
circumfluous effects diffusing waves
around their origin until her neck
and spine and feet partook of logic's joys.
Smiling, she turned to Aqhat, questioning,
"What force could move the mountains from their sleep?"
He gawked at her, not knowing whether she
had wished to complicate the riddle more
or whether she had asked rhetorically.
Before he spoke, she cried out, "Delusions!"
extrapolating her outburst like this,
"Though he has gaping caves for mouth and eyes,

for ears and nostrils, Ullikummi yet
cannot perceive a thing by means of them.
His flesh is rock, and so he doesn't feel.
He smashes this and that, stomps here and there
before returning to a peaceful state.
So what alarms him if he's never sensed
the world around him—what could rile him up?
It must be that he suffers from the same
disturbances as Ash, our sleepwalker—
although what shape they take I couldn't say.
From what do senseless beings, though their heads
be ever vacuous, construct their thoughts?
But think! If recent memories have not
departed us, we can try the recipe
whose contents Ash recited on our ship!
That merchant who provisioned us two days
ago—might he not have the stuff we need?"

Astounded by her breakthrough, Aqhat said,
"Magnificent! That just might do the trick.
And yet—how does a living rockface eat?
Does Ullikummi have a gut, and if
he doesn't, how could he digest a thing?
If we cannot induce him toward his cure
by means of smell or sight, then I'm afraid
we'll have to enter into him somehow
in order to release Tuweta's cure."

They contemplated such logistics while
retracing their own hoofprints due southwest.
Eventually they found the crookback pass
that they had taken to restock their gear
and grub at a secluded trading post
set back behind a cavern's entryway

along the Anti-Taurus' jagged feet.
The shopkeep Zashapuna noticed them,
inviting them inside as he would friends,
making a grandiose display of things
that neither they nor anyone would want.
Aqhat broke in and itemized their needs,
"Good Zashapuna, man of wondrous wares,
we come to you with little time to spare,
although we'd love to pass whole months with you.
Our list is quite specific: Do you have
blue lotus extract, viper's bugloss seeds,
galaktar from green Kizzuwatnan leys,
dried clumps of hemp, and poppy seeds to trade?
If so, we'll take as much as you can give.
Such items aren't for our consumption but
required by a troubled friend of ours."

The small, eccentric merchant laughed at him,
"Ha-ha! Ah, yes, of course! No one I've met
ingests such things—though friends of friends indulge.
I say let judges judge and traders trade!
But in all seriousness: Do you know
the going rate of that for which you ask?
A tiny satchel (a beginner's bag)
exchanges for eleven chariots
or hefty treasure hoards of equal worth.
And since you seem deprived of either one—
no credit at this stall, I'm sad to say—
should I possess what you were looking for,
and loads of it, it might exceed your means.
But if you—I mean—if your friend enjoys
such pleasures, I would recommend this skin
of wine brought from Maliya's hills, preserved
with resin of the pine and terebinth,

maturing at the proper temperature.
Here—taste it. Better that I let it speak."

Aqhat uncovered one of their two spoils:
Abihumbaba's adamantine scale.
It shone like vitreous obsidian
as Zashapuna—failing to maintain
disinterestedness (since no one who'd seen
such scales had ever lived to tell of them)
and knowledgeable of the sad truth that,
if it can harm, there's profit in its trade—
beheld the plate as though it were a god.
Now Aqhat told him how he'd won the prize,
from whose neck it had come, and deigned to let
the awestruck man attempt to gauge its worth.
The merchant gave it back to Aqhat, turned
around, and hastened deep into his delve,
returning only after quite some time
with four herbaceous and substantial sacks.
He swore the bags contained their listed needs,
producing two more wineskins free of charge.
He bit the inside of his cheek until
his buyers clasped his hand to seal the deal.
They tasted supper with him, sleeping well,
and parted happier than when they'd met.

Laeya and Aqhat headed back northeast
to try their hands at the unthinkable,
discussing ways to infiltrate their foe.
A pair of days passed by before they heard
the montane monster's terrorizing tromps,
preparing to effect their ad hoc plan.
Atop a shelving shoulder they stood by
like racers on their mark, their muscles tense,

their mounts disburdened from excess supplies
but fraught with jumpiness before the groans
and earthen dunder rising through their hooves.
When Ullikummi yawned, reclining on
another mountainside to rest his bones,
the riders lashed and sped their stallions down
the slope at rockslide speed until they reached
his feet, dismounting to surmount the brute.
They scrambled up his calves and dug their nails
in crevices to keep from plummeting
so many leagues below to certain death.
Since Ullikummi's chest heaved up and down
the hikers lost their footing by and by
as liberated stones fell far from sight.

At length they reached the leveler's upturned,
volcanic mouth and dared to enter it.
Their meager torchlight threatened to blow out
each time that the somnambulist would snore,
but to his gullet Aqhat and Laeya
held fast, spelunking down stone vertebrae,
depending from his costal ladder rungs,
and dropping to a sternal prominence
from which they spied his lapis heart of hearts.
With Zashapuna's sacks secured to her,
a cord tied round her waist, Laeya abseiled
below with Aqhat as her sole lifeline.
Beyond his sight she touched down on the heart
which glistened like a frozen, sunstruck sea.
Unfastening the satchels, Laeya set
them blazing with her torch's fire and sent
each one careening into the abyss.
She next removed a bronzen adze, inhaled,
then struck the monster's core time and again

to gather proof for Hatti's emperor.
But on the sixth strike Ullikummi roused,
unleashing chaos on the outer world
as Laeya lost her balance and fell down
while like a godsent heraldess at night
the torch flew from her grip and disappeared.

As when alternatives will pull a choice
unmade from side to side within one's breast
in oscillating, dilemmatic turns,
arousing fear that weighs one down because
its outcomes threaten those whom one loves most,
so Laeya swung above that stone-cold heart
while Aqhat strained to hold the willow rope.
The mountain's rocky bones and chawdron quaked
with Ullikummi's steps and blows just like
the Necromancer's cave had done before,
imploding and collapsing overhead.
In dank and floral fumes the litten bags
rose from the deep as Laeya lighted on
the heart and struck where she'd been hammering.
She broke a portion off to carry out
as hand-over-hand Aqhat hoisted her,
his legs clenched round a wet stalagmite's base.
When she drew near he pulled her up and both
collapsed upon the stone and gasped for air.

They'd gathered stamina to go again
just as the herbal plumes took full effect—
as much on Ullikummi as on them.
The basaltic behemoth laid himself
procumbent on another crest, his mouth
and nose no longer options for egress.
With playful, overstated politesse

they helped each other over obstacles,
the giant's hiccups titillating them.
A soft flush flimmer from the evening sun
shone through a narrow, rising passageway,
appearing as the only route outside.
They climbed. The higher that they got the more
their gnawing worries faded from their hearts.
The magnitude of what they'd set about to do
evaporated—all things lost their edge.
Ascending through enflowered evergreens
from which small blackened berries drank the light,
they crawled upon all fours, some of the leaves
and blooms hitching a ride on Laeya's locks.
The cliffside overlook attained at last,
they peered down to see what they could make out
to find they'd scaled the monster's ear canal.
Both laughed until their weakened knees gave out,
hushing each other ere remembering
the brute was stone deaf, laughing still more,
the other as the other's lone support
till even strength enough for this gave way.
They soon began to catch a second wind,
exultant to have been victorious,
distracted by the other's perfect flaws . . .

She burned to be with her beloved,
repining over Aqhat's touch—
the one whom Death gripped in his clutch.
No less did he want her, that girl
with lips like dates from Mararat,
whose eyes were beautified with kohl.

Laeya braved Tharumagi's mouth
where Horon, God of Little Deaths,

vowed entry if that Conqueress
of Hearts both mortal and divine,
anomalous in that dark place,
obeyed the ancient rituals.

Oh, let us come together now,
enlocked in raptured unison!

His vision clouding from the smoke
of sacrificial offerings
within the realm possessing him,
Aqhat explored the unknown land
before him with regardful care,
aflutter with desire to see.

Without her constant vibrancy
collapse beset the living realm.
The earth dried up and cattle died.
All life refused to multiply
as sable scarabs rolled their orbs,
their sunbaked young entombed inside.

Oh, let us come together now,
enlocked in raptured unison!

For days and nights she traveled down
until she reached the Netherworld,
yet he was first to find her, glad
to pluck the laurel from her hair
as she her lapis trinket shed—
a lovely goddess, to be sure!

After their fingers intertwined,
however, a great asp aggressed

at Mot's behest until, enclosed
within a cave, it drew her blood—

Oh, let us come together now,
enlocked in raptured unison!

—but not before she'd bested it
and drained its pulse up to the hilt.

Emerging from that raucous fray,
they ferried over Mot's black stream,
ascending skybent from below.
Earth fructified where all things green
and golden tryst, and from within
the scarab's sphere there burst new life.

Illumed with love's fatigue, reclined beside
the man she'd pined for, Laeya said to him,
"I feel that for the first time I can rest.
Attempting to conceal itself from me,
my love for you has been a shapeshifter
becloaking itself in so many looks,
affections, options, and reluctances.
From time to time, just when I thought that I
had glimpsed that changeling's essence, it bilked me
and thereby frustrated me all the more.
But now I have it—have you—for my own.
Why have we frittered so much time away?
Your eyes, your lips, this stubbled chin have been
in front of me for almost one whole year!"

To which profession Aqhat made reply,
"In truth, your very being tongue-ties me.
My love for you has hounded me nonstop.

And while I sensed its growth, I half-ignored
it—rushed and self-engrossed as I have been.
And now I balk to give it voice, for who
can speak of love without embarrassment?
Aware of every thisness one's beloved
deserves to have extolled, one borrows this
or that cliché—and knowing just how far
each one falls short, by just so much lovers
sense the indignity of their remarks,
offending their beloved and love itself
(a downright unforgivable misdeed).
But I will say this much to you, Laeya:
If hatred for divine injustice bound
our thinking in Siduna when we met,
bestowing us with purpose hitherto,
then what will stop us now that we are one,
now that our very bodies coalesce?"
Anon Sleep pulled them from the waking world
but failed to pull them from each other's arms.

Sometimes a seam along a dam wall cracks—
a mishap irrigating the parched ground
till builders, learning from the accident,
divide the separated elements
again (and this time much more thoroughly).
But other times a dam downright displodes,
its water flooding to the riverbed
from which it had been cleaved and with which, since
that time, it felt the urge to reunite;
repairmen throw their hands up, daring not
to drive another wedge between the push
and pull of either pertinacious side.
The love that joined Aqhat and Laeya can
be likened to this second sort of break,

this second, rarer sort of unison.

He kissed her bare and briny shoulders as
she halfway roused with far more quiet grace
and luminance than any sunrise might,
for one's newly belovèd showers light
from one end of the earth to its beyond,
imparting and conditioning the sheer
allure that others borrow for a time—
yet she's deprived of naught, not once dislimned,
even in her predictable routine.
She is the very reason for the day.
A reason for tomorrow, too. What does
it matter if the one who loves her should
discover her—disheveled, dirty, dank—
inside the brambled earhole of some brute?

She woke and smiled to see her man reclined
beside her as she kissed him upside-down,
her whole world topsy-turvy for the best,
upturned by that disorienting joy
which makes babbler and orator swap roles;
the coy turn bold; the brave tuck and turn tail;
great kings become servants and servants kings;
the godless fall upon their knees to make
due sacrifice while holier-than-thous
neglect their former gods for chosen ones.
Although they wanted to lie next to one
another thereabout forever, both
had now foretasted what unending life
together would be like, the requisites
of which still lay before them, unachieved.
So Laeya and her lover dressed, hiked down
vast Ullikummi's somnolent rockface

that gently snored, crestfallen and content,
and rode west for Hattusa, this time slowed
by love's uncompromising give-and-take.

With part of Ullikummi's lapis heart
and one of Abihumbaba's black scales,
the victors galloped through Hattusa's Gate
of Kings, the proof of their accomplishments
vouchsafing them the right to pass its wards.
Conglomerates of densifying throngs
around the northern temple signaled that
one of the city's many festivals—
a blessed extravaganza which the plebs
looked forward to each year—was underway.
Rightly expecting Hatti's emperor
to hold its pride of place, Laeya and her
beloved cut through the crowds that let them pass
with double-takes and neighbor-nudging nods
as Rumor's forest fires sparked and spread.
Most commoners had heard tell of the pair
the last time that that goddess made her rounds.
Accounts and jokes about the foreign fools
who'd somehow stridden up the royal steps,
requesting Hatti's regiments to fight
the gods, dissuaded by quixotic quests
still more ridiculous than that first posed
(to the uproarious High Court's delight)—
such news had whipped across the capital,
the comedy's costumery and props
reworked with each production while its cast
of actors and effect remained unchanged.

Approaching to a temple's wide perron
atop which Suppiluliuma sat

enthroned, alighting from their destriers,
Aqhat and Laeya knelt and hoisted up
the fruits of their impossible emprise.
The king wished not to forge alliances
with the two Southerners before him now,
but he could not rescind his well-known vow
lest mobs accuse him of apostasy
and lies, his word denuded of its force.
Great Suppiluliuma, piloter
of the magnific ark whose deck of stone
stretched out before his view, his grip upon
its rudder's arm yet having felt the lurch
that called in question his authority,
his crew misdoubting his omnipotence—
this sovereign ruler had no choice but heed
his multitude without their knowing it.
With outstretched arms he welcomed them and said,
"Come, friends of Hatti, bring to me, upon
this holiest occasion, that which I
had charged you to go forth and win for us.
Behold! A scale from Abihumbaba
and souvenir from Ullikummi's breast.
The Snakeheaded One and the Monstrous Mount
have been dispatched by these fine warriors
who'll help us to exact our just revenge!
My people: Now begins our empire's rise,
its broad expansion to the South and East
for which I've purposed all of us since Baal
attacked our populated capital
alongside his rapacious sister-wife.
Up to Zababa raise your brimming cups!
Pour him potations. Guzzle down your fill.
For while we sing and dance and celebrate
right now, tomorrow we sketch battle-plans

and whet our swords, dust off our bronzen casques,
accoutering our eldest sons for war!
As you forget no sacrifice today,
the blood of oxen on your hands, prepare
yourselves to wade knee-deep in battle-gore,
the everlasting war-god at your side!"

Like storm-tossed surges pounded by dark rain,
the ocean's din becoming deafening,
the waves of serried people bayed assent
as Suppiluliuma bade the pair
ascend the steps and sit at his right hand.
And so they did, presenting him their gifts
while forth came Suppiluliuma's sons
to welcome them and introduce themselves.
If hitherto said princes had been fond
of Aqhat and Laeya, they now looked up
to them as toddlers do their older kin,
with hopes to emulate and follow them—
their admiration laced with hidden fears.
The king commanded that all talk of war
be tabled till festivities surceased,
requesting that his godsent allies tell
of how they'd undermined and neutralized
the demigods with whom Hattusa'd fought
and struggled since time immemorial.
With winecups which the servingmen refilled
before they'd emptied, Laeya and Aqhat
drank deeply and recounted their brave feats
while Suppiluliuma and his sons
beheld their validating evidence,
the more impressed with each ensuing word.

Along the moonshot shores of Zaphon's base
there stretched a fleet of slavers to embark.
Upon the top decks and within the holds
Egyptian mercenaries whom Anat
and Baal enlisted from the towns nearby
made final preparations for their trip
with help from warriors of local birth.
With his intrepid sister flanking him,
Hadad called to attention his devouts,
addressing them so all could feel his voice,
"Tonight begins King Akhenaten's end.
That would-be pharaoh thinks himself a god,
unbalancing interimperial
affairs with overweening recklessness.
He spits upon the deities of old
and threatens to undo, in one fell-swoop,
the trade uniting cities on the Nile,
Mitanni, Hatti, and our very home.
Who benefits from his self-centered gall?
Since his accession, have your lives improved?
His chaos havocs offshore colonists
and mainlanders alike, whatever be
their stock, their family's place of origin.
But not for long thanks to your sacrifice!

"When this armada nears the Delta Lands,
tie up the Asiatics' hands behind their backs,
enfastening long ropes to their lip rings
to simulate their subjugated state.
In Memphis Kothar-wa-Hasis—my kin
by birth, now an Egyptian resident—
impatiently awaits your anchorage.
Once you have gained its quaysides, look to him,

that Peerless Armorer, to fit your out—
both slave and slave-driver in unison—
with smithy-fired and mallet-sired gear
to ambush and reclaim that central nome.
Recruit the populace by any means
deemed fit and fortify the city's walls,
dispatching messengers to us at once
so that we'll know what backup to supply.
Enough! You've been informed of all of this
so many times by now—you know our plan!
I'll not delay your passage anymore.
Set sail—and may our blessings speed you on!"
Baal's navy cheered, beginning to shove off.
Not one to mope and bellyache and plead
her father for a bull from heaven's heights
as Ishtar had, Anat took what she pleased.
She neared her husband, grabbed his nose ring, pulled
him close, and passionately bit his ear.

Book XVIII

Embayed along the matchless Lukkan shores,
west of the River Kastaraya's mouth,
there curls a beach with pine-draped mountaintops
just to its rear, a godly harborage
where bright, untended watchfires feed on stone,
uprising from deep, chasmic pores to flag
down and seduce bypassing mariners.
Here it was that eleven masted ships
belonging to displaced Mitannians
had seen those fuelless flames and made for them.
The crews comprised some folk from whom Hadad
marauded—with Tushratta's helping hand—
the meaningfulness of life: the men
and women—mere civilians—whom they loved
and who had died in Washukanni's siege.
With neither kith nor kin, these orphans sold
their second-rate inheritances, joined
together, traded for a seedy fleet,
and pledged their common fealty to the sea.
Their latest venture (whether judged to be
highhearted or foolhardy, they cared not)
had filled their holds with rare and coveted
Pelasgian commodities and gear.

Said eastbound sailors dropped their anchors near
this stretch of Lukkan coast to hunt and rest.
A clan of passing nomads welcomed them ashore
by means of kindly gestures known around
the world and through the fleet's interpreter

whose Luwian locutions missed their mark
and pricked them—tickling them with malaprops.
The tribe's apparent spokesman, Shekelesh,
had four of their sheep gralloched, broken down
to roast atop the hill-begotten flames.
The flagship's pilot, Wullu, then dispatched
his built son Akawatil to unload
their olives, saltfish, wine, and bread to share
with Shekelesh and his attendant clan.
Before they ate the marbled cuts of lamb,
old Shekelesh looked vaultward, praying so,
"Oh Arma, Herald of your People's Prayers
come night when Father Tiwad journeys down
below—bright Wanderer who Waxes, Wanes:
Transport this char-encrusted offering
with our thanks to Hapantaliya's feet.
Without her we'd be lost—you know this well.
And look! This yearling's flank we gift to you.
Please smile upon our newfound friends tonight
and grant them a safe passage—you who see
all goings-on, even amidst the dark."

The land- and sea-rovers now huddled by
their beachside fires and passed around the skins
of wine to warm themselves, reciting tales
and news to one another as the ships'
sole translator worked hard to earn his keep.
As pulls of wine became more animate,
so did the entertaining epopees.
A daughter of old Shekelesh who had
attracted ogling eyes now won all ears
by borrowing a goddess' hymnic voice.
Once she concluded, having roused their hearts,
the sailors' translator attempted to

reiterate the meaning of her song
when, from the fire's far side, a wizened man
chimed in, explaining that Mitannians
had songs of coiled monstrosities as well.
Alike transhumant and seafarer begged,
implored the man to sing one, at which he
quaffed drink and cleared his throat, allowing time
for his mind's eye to visit olden days
before he solemnized them with this song,

"If you tilt your ear you can often still hear
all their names carried over the ocean.
Returning cold gales that once billowed taut sails
cross the Dark Water home of our bosuns.
In an age long ago when the white hawthorn shone,
a year's bounty marked us out as chosen.
The apricots gleamed and the honeycomb teemed,
with our dragnets and wains overflowin'.

"Upon such excess our proud leader couldn't rest,
taking thought as to how we might prosper.
On a warm summer's night he called every last wright—
for a fleet he would laden their coffers.
They felled evergreens for the pegged joinery,
working stout keels and planking of cedar.
Soon one hundred boats looked toward Egypt's coast,
and they set sail to brave the Dark Water.

"The Lord of the Sea gave Sertapsuruhi
to the Grain God for personal reasons,
who with due forethought a sea serpent begot:
Hedammu the bane of all seamen.
To slay the Storm God was the Sea Asp's lone job,
and the two fought like ravenous demons.

Their battle wrought human collateral
till Hedammu dove down through the deepness.

"Throughout the long days bright Allani lit the way
for the flock of one hundred wood seabirds.
But come the cold gales they took in their sails
as the prows cut through sea spume to leeward.
Beneath the packed troves the strained mortises groaned
as the Sun Goddess went down before them.
From deep in their breasts the young shipmen couldn't wrest
the thought that they'd not see her come mornin'.

"Amidst the Great Green sailors heard rumblings unseen—
sounds like the roll of fell thunder—
when in the wan light they beheld their last blight:
the argosy's fork-tongued affronter.
The men took to arms and then hove long bident barbs,
hoping therewith to drive him back under.
Soon all became calm and the beast carried on,
for he'd wracked our brave brothers asunder.

"What kind of deities do just as they please,
giving barley and fish when it suits them,
then looking back round turn our fates upside down,
slaying slews of good men in so doing?
On eaters of bread don't the Thousand Gods depend—
on the sweat of our sword and our sickle?
At our offerings' dearth will Kumarbi plow the earth?
What makes the gods all so damn fickle?

"All's started anew under puce hawthorn bloom,
where the fortunate young kiss their women,
while we who are old still sing songs of the bold
to remember our Hurrian shipmen.

Down near the pier you can still sometimes hear
all the names of our brothers and bosuns.
Returning cold gales that once billowed taut sails
carry their dirge across the Dark Ocean."

Although they comprehended not a word,
the nomads understood the elder's song
to such degree that not a cheek was dry.
Now two boys of the tribe who'd been at play
down shore burst in and interrupted them,
panting, explaining that something had beached.
The well-wined leaders followed them and drew
their knives, prepared for anything (they thought).
A crew of others followed in their stead
until they lit upon a wondrous sight—
a seaworn waif (beyond fatigued) who knelt
beside a dugout and addressed them:
'*a-na ia shi shul-mu a-na ka-a-sha lu-u shul-mu*,'
which translates, 'It is well with me; may it
be well with you'—Ameni's handy phrase.
Old Shekelesh and Wullu then dispatched
a man to fetch roast mutton and red wine.
They both assisted the young castaway
onto his feet and asked from where he hailed,
examining his tentacle-cum-boat
and recent scars with eyes incredulous.
The runner having just returned, he gave
the man a cup and Gabbar emptied it
before devouring fatty hunks of lamb
as all looked on like Uruk's shepherds when
Enkidu took his first meal at their side.

The translator interpreted his words,
"Would that all folk were generous like you!

I'm Gabbar. Left for dead by former friends
while facing Litan—hacking off this arm
amidst his grim assault upon our fleet—
I drifted to an isolated isle
where Chance the Lot-Caster abandoned me.
For days unnumbered I enjoyed that place
until my truthful fatherland called out
to me, insisting that I head back east.
Unable to withstand its forceful tug,
I fashioned Litan's arm into the craft
before you here, endangering my life
upon the seas once more where giant fish
and octopi rose from their seabed lairs.
Ill-luck for them! I gored them with harpoons,
the creatures pulling round my watercraft
all while their strength flagged and I hauled them in
unnerved and plashing till this labrys struck
its mark and chummed the sea—a warning sign
for all averse to going belly-up.
And now I've landed here. But where is 'here'?"

By nature, fishing tales lack evidence,
yet these onlookers faced excessive proof:
the tangible, tentacular canoe;
a blood-stained labrys; Gabbar's gruesome scars;
a massive fish tooth carved into a dirk;
and two beaks from gigantic octopi.
Beholding him, the captain Wullu said,
"If what you say is true—and I believe
you, speaking for myself—then you must be
some kind of god, for who has fought Litan
('Hedammu'—as we call him in our tongue),
awakening come dawn to speak of it?
Yet here you voyage in his sundered arm!

You've run aground on Lukka's pristine shores—
no better place to gather up your strength.
As pilot of our flagship, I invite
you to accompany us to the east
where lies your destination and our goal.
We've need of men like you aboard our ships.
Of course, we wouldn't charge you anything,
but I would recommend that you not leave
your craft behind as emperors would trade
whole kingdoms for an article like that
(although they'll take your hero's credit, too).
We'll tie it to a sternpost, if you like,
and tow the dingy east to Ugarit."

Accepting Wullu's offer, Gabbar joined
the others round the fires as two men pulled
his boat toward theirs, each individual
not satisfied until they'd run their hands
along the deity's enhardened arm.
With no need for antediluvian
exaggerations, Gabbar told his hosts
about what had befallen him that year
before the exiled Washukannians
shared sorrows of their birthdom's sack with him.
At first light Shekelesh and his tall son
showed Gabbar the unending flames nearby
and Gabbar gave his son the fish-tooth knife
in graciousness for everything they'd done.
Ten days thereon the tribespeople and crew
would part ways, sharing one another's tales
and news with those who chanced to cross their paths.

Inside Hattusa's Royal Citadel,
Telipinu led Aqhat and Laeya

up stone steps to the high-ceilinged war-room
where Suppiluliuma and his sons
awaited, sipping gobletfuls of wine.
In his right hand the king clutched his new rod,
a stately scepter measuring five forearms
from cap to base, ultramarine in hue.
He'd had his private lapidary cut
the staff from Ullikummi's splintered heart—
an heirloom to be known around the earth
and handed down from emperor to son.
When his new allies entered through the doors,
he poured them hearty cups and then began,
"Well-met, friends! Come this way and drink with us.
I hope my empire's celebrations filled
your hearts with joy, replenishing your might,
for now we plan another festival
where rougher masses swarm to sing their hymns
of invocation, try their hands at games
of strength, libate large drafts with far-flung prayers,
and slaughter untold offerings to see
which side the gods will favor on that day.
A first draft for Zababa, Quenchless God
of War; may he inspire our strategies!

"And you have not proposed a mundane war,
highhearted Southerners, some hit-and-run
assault on oath-forsaking mutineers
who breed like rabbits on our borders, but
protracted siege upon the gods themselves—
a mad war had you not immobilized
the Monstrous Mount and the Snakeheaded One
to win my confidence and clear two paths
for our expansion to the South and East.
A keeper of my word, I'll march with you

to Zaphon followed by ten thousand troops
and thirteen hundred blazing chariots.
Anat and Baal spilt Hittite blood in our
own streets, exterminating innocents
with savagery—I've not forgotten this.
So in a fortnight let's send forth our squads
to win due vengeance in our homeland's name."

Mursili took due thought and then replied,
"Well-spoken, Father. Justice shall be ours.
Yet we should take precaution not to be
outflanked, for once kings to the east catch wind
that Ullikummi blocks them off no more,
receiving tidings of your southward push,
our strong defenses having left the nest,
Hattusa will lie open to attack.
Because elite Ishuwans bend the knee
now to Mitanni, now to us, their high
court smolders with a drive to be unyoked.
Provided chance, they'd squander everything
on mercenaries to restore their pride
and take advantage of the opening
to liberate their appanage for good.
As our instructor Walwaziti says:
'Resentment rears Humiliation's heirs.'
Rears them for full-on blood sport, I would add.
Should some of us not convey Muwatti
east to Ishuwa's king as he had asked,
and thereby seal his vassalage in stone?"

Reflecting, Arnuwanda gave answer,
"Muwatti's far-too precious for a king
like him—even his sons aren't suitable.
Yet no one in their court's laid eyes on her,

so why don't I conduct an armored train
of brides-to-be to him—of varied age
but equal in immeasurable looks—
three gorgeous women he could not refuse,
quelling his sensed inferiorities
while putting him in greater debt to us?"

His brother Piyassili laughed and said,
"So while our vast platoons march south, the rest
deployed as ministers to monitor
affairs at home, you get to caravan
about—a brothel-master on the road?
The heavens will collapse before you could
be trusted with a eunuch's enterprise!
And if Mitanni's king Tushratta finds
himself another ally short, will he
not marshal loyal warriors to take
Ishuwa back by forthright force of arms?
Ishuwa needs our soldiers to defend
the kingdom's borderlands, yet we'll have few
to offer him according to your plan."

While Hatti's bloodline fell to bickering,
Laeya began to hatch new stratagems.
She polished off her wine and intervened,
"My friends—Protectors of Hattusa's Realm:
Each of your talking points have struck upon
something we'd be remiss to overlook.
The emperor speaks truly when he says
that we must send to Zaphon giant hosts
to maximize our chance of victory.
Mursili, Piyassili—you're correct
to note that, of necessity, the war
we plan to wage will not have just one front.

Let's not forget: Tushratta fought with Baal
in your home's savage onrush, shield-to-shield.
If we're to conquer Zaphon's Conqueror,
Mitanni can't go unaccounted-for.
And lastly, Arnuwanda's subterfuge
is not without its merits, since we should
seize on Ishuwa's claim to loyalty
and put their standing army to quick trial.
So, this is what I would suggest we do."

She voiced her battle-plan, outlining each
advancement with contingent fallback routes
and marshaling supporting evidence
from past campaigns—a few of which the king
himself survived, though many harkened back
to wars his father's father might recall.
When she left off her masterminding speech,
King Suppiluliuma said to them,
"As is, this Southern woman's ill-prepared
for war—no doubt you'd all agree with me."
Her eyes blazed spitfire-green at his affront,
the king now gesturing to Mursili
who exited through silver-paneled doors.
Before the spiteful words within her breast
burst forth—Aqhat unsure of what the king
had said—Mursili joined them once again,
presenting her with shield and thrusting-lance.
The gathered council beamed before the gifts
as Suppiluliuma said to her,
"Receive the fruitage of our allied cause.
While Aqhat slings between his shoulder blades
a godsent bow and quiver, and while my
five sons and I have weapons aplenty,
we thought a warrioress like yourself

deserved to gear up like the rest of us.
My own official armorer reworked
Abihumbaba's ebon scute into
an aegis, sharpening its sides like blades
ere riveting enarmes onto the back,
plied fourfold with bronze layering and hide.
He likewise smithed the tempered thrusting-lance
that you now hold, its lethal spearpoint shaped
from what remained of Ullikummi's heart.
May they enable you to long outlive
and drive beneath the earth your enemies."

She clutched and studied her new armaments,
thanking the king before the company
commenced the delegation of its roles.
Once finished, Aqhat and Laeya returned
to camp beyond Hattusa's khaki walls.
Espying a new lightness in their step,
congratulating them on the success
which Rumor'd circulated through the camp,
Bidawa and Ameni seized their friends.
Ameni's noncommittal eye-contact,
however, gave him up, and Aqhat asked
him to unpen whatever news he had.
Ameni told them of the robberies,
two murders, and desertion of six men
embrangling Aqhat's camp in disarray.
Chastising him for letting things devolve
to such a state, Aqhat apologized
and turned the blame onto himself instead.
He washed his face, departed from the tent
(his friends not far behind), and blew his horn,
assembling undirected layabouts
before the ridge of stone on which he stood.

When all had lumbered over, Aqhat said,
"Good friends, at last your patience has paid off!
We march for Zaphon in a fortnight's time!
Accomplishing the emperor's demands
of us, Laeya and I immobilized
the guardian of Kizzuwatna's woods,
Abihumbaba, who until that time
debarred our passage to Mount Zaphon's heights.
So too did we put Ullikummi down,
the Monstrous Mount whose terrorizing wrath
blockaded easy contact with the East.
Never before have such things been achieved!
Your faithfulness to me and to our cause
have not passed by unnoticed—from day one
in our well-weathered hideout till today,
I've watched you grow in wisdom and in strength.

"In due time myriad of you shall serve
as officers with squadrons at your back
and beck, large-scale battalions who will heed
your war-cries, following you through the thick,
dependent on you for their livelihood.
But how could you pretend to lead these troops
if you have minds for petty theft or kill
your very brothers out of jealousy?
If once you were a highwayman—no more.
If once you plowed the rain-forsaken earth,
you soon shall plow and hack our enemies.
If levy-looters in your former life
subjected you to legal discipline,
enough! You now shall discipline yourselves.
For one last time: Repeat your fealty oaths
and kiss the Tablet shard that Laeya shall

hold out to you, recalling to yourselves
the quintessence and purpose of our ways."

Their hearts renewed, his partisans espoused
their theomachic mission once again,
kissing the Tablet piece and readying
themselves to march on Zaphon's citadel.
War-preparations underway, Aqhat
deployed Ameni and his regiment
ahead of them to scout and spy on Baal's
defenses and emplacements, seeking out
the best spot to dig in and make camp.
They clasped arms and Ameni took his leave,
relieved to put his skills to better use.
Within a half-month's time, Telipinu,
Zannanza, and prince Arnuwanda had
become acquainted with the commoners
whom, spite their accents and their origins,
they found deserving of respect for all
they'd done and all they'd set about to do.
The camp became a capital outside
the capital as Hittite conscriptees—
preparing for the haul ahead of them—
pitched tents around those of their officers
in rippling, widening circumferences.
Sons whettened bronzen swords their fathers had
let slip while matrons, charged to vindicate
their brothers slaughtered in Hattusa's fall,
filled quivers with fletched arrows, practicing
their aim in duty to the Huntswoman.

On the appointed day, the field marshals
Laeya and Aqhat met at the Sphinx Gate
with Suppiluliuma and his sons.

Each bade farewell to one another, prince
Mursili and Piyassili to join
their father's eastbound convoy totaling
eight thousand foot soldiers and five hundred
war-cars with expert drivers at the reins,
whereas Zannanza, prince Telipinu,
and Arnuwanda would accompany
the others south, assisting as war-chiefs
to master their twelve thousand men-at-arms
and seven hundred hoofborne chariots.
The two colossal armies parted ways,
Hattusa's walls atremble from the force
of trundling wheels and marching sentry-lines.

That night, midway between Zaphonian
Hadad's environs and their trailing host,
encamped beneath snow-bearing sprays of fir,
Ameni kept watch, shivering with cold.
Even the Necromancer's cave seemed snug,
inviting, and secure compared to here,
where boulders pulled their moss-spreads to their chins.
Swift gales swooped down from perches high aloft
to claw Ameni's face, invisible
and graspless though they were, and so he sat
down, pulled his knees up to his chest, and tucked
his windbrent nose within them to keep warm,
recalling images of sun-drenched nomes.
A moment passed, then yet another one
as his newfound position thawed him out.

Macabre screaks awakened him as eight
gray wolves who'd stolen into camp attacked
without a warning, speeding those who slept
that night on to their final night of sleep.

Malnourished and cadaverous, one wolf
tore through Shubammu's neck as fitful streams
of bright blood spurted forth and singed the snow.
Not having heard a cautionary word
escape Ameni's lips nor any neigh
that might have readied her for a fair fight,
Abiya met Mot in much the same way.
Ameni smarted from the raid and grabbed
his sword, essaying to disband
the pack, his comrades in the direst need.
Her eyes and snout Anubian in make,
her thickset pelage prickled to the touch,
the hulking she-wolf holding foremost rank
impeded his advances, dodging his
aggressive swordstrokes, countering with snaps
as her affiliates wrapped up the job,
uniting for a disuniting end.
As Ummihibbi's final lifebreath fumed
into the frosty air, so did the ghosts
of Shaya, Yaduaddu, Abishar.
Ameni backed away and tried to calm
his horse, eventually mounting her
and racing full-stretch northward through the vale,
the chiefess of the pack content to glut
her jaws upon her butchers' choicest cuts.

The tear-streams trickling down Ameni's face
congealed as through the haunted hills he raced,
desisting rarely, momentarily
to feed and water his surviving horse
at snowbanked brooks, allowing her to rest
(although the weight she bore was less than his).
After a lengthy ride he came upon
the army Aqhat and Laeya helped ford

across the River Marassantiya
to Kizzuwatna's northern mountain pass.
He found his friends inside the marshals' tent
and stammered what befell him and his scouts.
Bidawa and Laeya helped him lie down,
attending to his hunger, wounds, and thirst
while Aqhat sucked upon the sour thought
of his first loss—to lanky dogs no less—
occasioned by Ameni's negligence.
He counseled that his commissary rest,
informing him that he'd redeem himself
as nightwatchman of the field marshals' tent.
Ameni gave an acquiescent nod.

Gapn, Hirgab, and Ugar burst into
the wide hall where Hadad and Dread Anat
were supping to relay the urgent news,
"Forgive us, Lords—you'll want to hear us out.
A massive Hittite host with chariots
has crossed the River Marassantiya,
descending our direction in full force.
While their intent remains unknown to us,
they pose a threat to peace within the realm.
In hopes to spare you from afflictive news,
we divvied up great northern tracts to scan
for the Snakeheaded One—who'd rout the lot
of them for the sheer pleasure of it—but
despite our wide surveillance of his wood
(and even having summoned him) we had
no luck; Abihumbaba's left his post!"

Anat held up her hand to give them leave,
and turning to her brother-husband said,
"Did I not argue that Hattusa'd need

to be subjected with more force and more
protracted scion hunts than you allowed?
Instead of storehouse spelt they send us spears!
We never humbled them sufficiently,
and now their sovereign's prideful seedlings snap
through winter's glass with dew-eyed confidence,
with no sense of their knotty origins,
without respect for their dependence on
the rains by which you sate their very roots.
Better to prune new branchlings that jut out
before their proper time than let them drain
a sturdy tree of its lifeforce, for come
the first frost they will die in any case.
Pull back your naval fleet at once, prepare
your ground forces for war, and call upon
Tushratta's rank and file to lend us aid.
I'll drench my scorpionic punisher
in plague-blood—anyone who flees alive
sent packing with Resheph's fell souvenirs!
Let's set upon Zababa's idiots
before they've left the Kizzuwatnan wood."

Thus Anat. Baal Hadad replied to her,
"I didn't further subjugate Hatti,
if you'll recall, because they didn't put
up much resistance and because one can't
lord over those whom one annihilates.
A shrill rebellion rises in the north.
So what? Such is the normal course of things.
It doesn't overhaul our broader plans.
Tushratta must remain at home so that
his folk habituate themselves to his
inchoate, sedimenting governance.

Nor should you cast aside our navy's ruse—
the offspring of your ingenuity.
Lastly—and here you've lost your wits, I fear—
forsake all use of pestilential arms.
The curses of Reseph cannot be tracked
and could recoil upon our garrisons.

"Through the Amanian Gates I'll deploy
a cavalcade of snowclouds to waylay
and snuff the flames of Hatti's firebrands.
Should Fortune save some squadrons that maintain
their lusting for some forlorn hope, then they
can give us practice, weeding out the weak.
You do not really fear these fools, do you?
What do they plan—to leaguer deathless gods?
Attritional war's central strategy's to hold
in place and starve one's circled enemies.
So will this horde put to a halt the bread
and meat and wine and varied offerings
that mortals all around our realm raise up
to us in sacrifice each month, each day?"

As ever, Baal laid claim to the last word,
retiring to the upper balcony
and glaring northward ere he closed his eyes,
controlled his breath, upraised his hairy arms,
and mustered massive, grizzled cumuli
which in conformity with his intents
rolled headlong toward his inexpectant foe.
When he had ceased, his chest heaved from fatigue
at the enormity of what he'd done,
thus he sought out his bedchamber to sleep
a few days' time, regathering his might.

All the while, Wullu's freighted fleet arrived
at Ura's harbor—Gabbar and the crew
now disembarking to restock their hulls.
The haven sheltered ships of every ilk,
some hauling grain to Ugarit and Dor,
some shipping slaves to Milawandan kings,
and others bound for Akhenaten's quays.
Now Akawatil, Wullu's only son,
led Gabbar to the nearby mudbrick House
of Flowing Ales where fishers drank like fish
and shipmen kept afloat on amber swells.
Some threw back bready cups of bubbly ale
while Akawatil and his newfound mate
tried beers with honey, grape, and saffron notes.
A coterie of trawlers friended them
in brief, amalgamated strings of words
from different tongues before exchanging rounds.
One fisher, Pikku, animatedly
described their recent struggle with a fish
unprecedented in its heft and length,
revealing scars from where it gouged his arm.
Not one to be outsung, Akawatil
recounted Gabbar's run-in with the god
disporting seven heads, encouraging
his mate to show his fire-soldered wound.

They smirked at the impious myth (although
they had enjoyed it to the full, no doubt).
An Adaniyan trader hunched nearby
could not but help to overhear and said,
"Last year I would have laughed him off as well,
yet spite the thought that I have seen it all,
these days I hardly know what to believe.

Some time ago I visited my kin
who call Hattusa home to celebrate
one of that city's famous festivals.
On the last day, two foreigners the king
had charged to undermine Humbaba's son
and Ullikummi stood before his grace,
presenting him their hard-won battle-spoils—
two relics from the beasts that they'd lain low.
I glimpsed their proof with both my trusty eyes,
neither of which have once missteered my barque.
And now with Suppiluliuma's boys
those two seek vengeance on the Conqueror.
While sailing down the Shamri waterway
I saw them camped in Abihumbaba's
forbidden territory—thousands strong—
and while I've sighted the Snakeheaded One,
I've never known a soul to beard his realm.

"One always knows less than they first supposed.
As with my laden ship, I try to steer
my thoughts between opposing riverbanks,
the land on one side named Mistrustfulness,
the other known as Gullibility.
There's profit in this outlook, after all.
The richest man among my clientele—
a godnapper and relic-purveyor
who works in secret—has assured me that
a great change in the world is underway,
instructing me to keep a watchful eye
for blessed and cursed materials alike
(and granting me the means for it upfront).
So maybe this young man sheared Litan's arm.
And if you have, with any proof besides

the bumps and bruises everyone has got,
then show us and I'll make it worth your while—
make you a man far richer than a king."

Though Gabbar didn't take the merchant's bait
(distracted by the thought of former friends),
with steady cup-poundings and eggings-on
Wullu's son pestered him to show them how
he'd fled the isle as other squabs joined in—
though knowing not the cause they seconded.
Relenting with a deep, defiant draft,
he exited as Akawatil sped
the merchant, trawlers, and inquisitors
outside to their flotilla brought to port
and towing the tentacular bateau
hand-over-hand until it reached the dock
where all might probe its actuality.
The dugout dumbfounded the regulars
and filled them with vicarious prestige.
Rebrimming Gabbar's cup with malty brew,
the Shamri-sailing salesman threw his arm
around him, leading him along the shore
to test the waters of the man's desire.

Beyond well-rested, Baal awoke and stretched.
He threw his gilded tunic on and nighed
the casement of his bedchamber to breathe
the morning air only to find a host
of Hittites camped on Zaphon's eastern foot
just where the treeline starts to thicken most.
Wheeling and bolting through his door he stormed
down involuting steps of stone to halls
where the god's soldiers—native-born devouts
and Blackland mercenaries side-by-side—

clankered about with orders from Anat.
Baal found his bronze-accoutered wife inside
the armory and she addressed her spouse
while sharpening an edgy khopesh sword,
"Well there you are, my love! Did you sleep well?
I hope you don't care that I've set my mind
to playing housewife—tidying a bit,
prevailing on our lazy servantry
to make due preparations for our guests,
and seeing that we've stocked up food and drink
to ready supper for your homecoming.
I worried that, just like our visitors,
you might have come down with some kind of chill.
But I'm relieved to see that I was wrong!"

Baal smarted at her sarcasms before
demanding that she bring him up to speed
on every unilateral decree
she'd made, to which the Bellicist replied,
"Our parapets house archers night and day,
each group relieved in alternating shifts.
Our mercenaries have begun to dig
long trenches fronted by outworks of pine
around our mountain's natural glacis,
constructing sally points for chariots.
Battalions of outfitted foot soldiers
stand at the ready, waiting our command,
the vanguard anxious to protect their Lords.
Although our armament should easily
outlast the coming siege, our victory
must prove decisive not only in deed,
but also in exemplary display—
by brutalizing every renegade.
Thus my Sutean Warrior, Yatpan,

has taken flight for King Tushratta's realm
for extra men, the Father of Vultures
Hirgab sent off to call our navy back.
What good are our expansionary plans
if we can't call upon our subject kings
when needed, harnessing their vassalhood,
or block our seaport from Hattusan ships?"
Her disobedient effrontery
vexed Baal almost as much as did his foes'.

Aqhat's battalions, having set up camp,
drank wine while roasting mountain stags and fowl.
The march had proven arduous, and all
knew that the biting blizzard they'd endured,
in which good souls and sumpters froze to death
or met their end by avalanche—all these
survivors knew that Baal Hadad deployed
that manless vanguard to destroy their hope.
And though the storm had thinned them out, one more
defeat before the battle's start, it had
not weakened but enkindled their resolve.
While Laeya and Aqhat surveyed the land,
appraising possible advantages
of which they might make use despite their need
to fight on upsloping terrain, war-priests
schooled in Hattusan battle-rites prepared
to please Zababa and to purify
his faithful servants, Hatti's men-at-arms.
The hundred priests had hawthorn arches built
along a rivulet of meltwater
with bonfires set ablaze on either bank.
To drubbing drums foot soldiers, shieldbearers,
charioteers, longbowmen, stone-slingers

and more came to the rill to lend their ears
and eyes and unclean souls to the war-god.

Appareled in brocade, great scimitars
in one hand, leashes in the other one,
a hundred acolytes led billy goats,
piglets, and puppies to the liturgists
to whom they handed over their encharged.
As one, the war-priests raised their hands and prayed,
"Internecine Zababa, Slakeless God
of Warfare, harken to the prayers we lift
to you in supplication on this day!
Make clean again the faithful instruments
through whom you actuate your artistry
and grant us strength to carry out your will!"

The acolytes held firm the animals
as celebrants their sickle-swords held high
to halve the caprids, swine, and newborn whelps.
With bloodied hands the priests' aids used each half
to form a grisly path behind the gates
which led down to the snowmelt watercourse.
Not knowing whether they should intervene,
having neither the wherewithal nor hope
of doing so successfully, Aqhat's
disciples watched or joined their counterparts.
To the presiders their assistants came;
elect, obedient, and pure of heart
they faced the priests of war on bended knee.
Zababa's mouthpieces dissevered them,
disparting them to consummate the paths.
Now one-by-one the soldiers walked beneath
the hawthorn gates, between the offerings'

partitions, and into the ice-cold brook
where they besprinkled water on themselves.
Once cleansed, the soldiers bedded down as well
as any can upon the eve of war.

Betimely Shahar rose and roused the troops,
his presence livening and menacing.
Platoons geared up and sharpened shiny swords
and lanceheads, not because they'd lost their edge,
but from their fingers' need to occupy
themselves and from desire to stroke the ones
on whom their very life-grip would depend.
Field marshal Aqhat's followers made rounds
to their encharged, intoxicating them
with gruff, apocalyptic rally-cries
as Aqhat, waking next to Laeya, kissed
her lips and then her midriff, setting out
with his retainer to confront Hadad
(Kothar-wa-Hasis' bow slung round his back),
riding for Zaphon's eastern, basal plains
where Baal, impatient to size up his foes,
alike departed from his lover's side
with Gapn, Ugar, and Hirgab on hand.

Eyes locked, the Conqueror and Aqhat met,
the latter challenging the god like this,
"Hereby do I, the Seir Mountain Man,
proclaim destruction on Mount Zaphon's gods.
Before my birth you swindled Danel, Man
of Rapiu, my father, offering
that pious judge an heir for a blood-price
exceeding value and to which he'd not
consent had he perceived your sanguine sense
of righteousness—in which the fallible

must kill the very ones for whom they live.
Whether by negligence or your own hand,
you shed one person's blood a hundredfold,
accursing and exiling us from home
until my father paid the dreadful debt.
In some sense I'm your son. To that extent,
suckled and reared on what you think condign,
I've come to give you what you're owed, that is,
to drench your mountain battlefield and home
with gore—that of your lackeys and your grace."

Baal marveled at the man's audacity,
turning to his attendants to inquire
as to the meaning of the sacrilege
expelled from one of whom he'd never heard.
The three took thought until Ugar recalled
to them their stopover along the coast—
now many years gone by—when they had heard
a man named Danel pray and toss them scraps.
Through a collective haze the memory
(inconsequential, and so lain aside),
came forth, still seeming neither here nor there.
Baal leered at Aqhat, hoping that he'd cow
the man into retreat, voicing his response,
"Young man, to you I benefacted life
itself, greathearted as I am, yet here
you stand, another ingrate child like all
the rest, condemning me for circumstance.
The Sortileger Fate acts on her own.
This Danel never taught you to judge well,
it seems, or you'd not make such grave mistakes.
You called your father 'pious.' Piety,
however—as you seem not to have learned—
means following the wishes of the gods,

incomprehensible as they might seem,
for some such wishes harbor tests of faith
to raise the simple from credulity
to better knowledge of their place on earth.
Behold your god, whom few have seen and lived,
who generously grants you once last chance
to judge correctly—to choose holiness:
Throw off your irreligious arrogance
and march my Hittite army home at once,
and I swear that no harm will come to you.
If you do not, Mot's Pit's spacious enough
to house the lot of you, with room to spare."

Meanwhile, field marshal Laeya sat atop
her horse, her lapis-headed pike in hand,
the Tablet fragment in the other one,
Abihumbaba's aegis on her back.
She marshaled the enormous host, each line
belèd by generals and Henti's sons,
addressing them with her commanding voice,
"Almost a twelvemonth gone, risking his life
in order to commune with his mother
and sister's souls, your leader visited
a Necromancer who possessed the writ
that foreannounced our coming victory.
Open your ears to what was said that night:
'To him shall come a Querent, One who seeks
Communion with the Shades of his Mother
and Sister when the Saffron Moon ascends,
and ere a Candle of a Shekel's Weight
expires, this Visitant, whose Given Name
is 'Aqhat,' shall decide between Two Roads.
Either he shall forsake his Arms and burn
his Bow and Arrows, offering their Smoke

in order to empower and appease
the Gods of Old, and with Apposite Rites
he shall, this Night alone, communicate
with the Deceased Ghosts whom he cherishes,
bestowing on them Sustenance and Rest.

"'Or he shall seek a Power yet unknown
to Mortals, infinitely greater than
any the Earth has seen before this Age:
the Mettle that belongs to Gods Themselves.
If he indeed desires such Potencies,
then let Duranki's Priest incant the Spell
befitting this Decision—Magic Words
that shall empower him to slaughter Three
and only Three Gods ere a Year's elapsed.
If down this Path he sets, then when the Third
One breathes no more, his Hands shall run with Blood,
and with the Squall of Warfare he shall roar
as Light surrounds and captures Sin Itself.
He'll never come to Death, and with his First
Words he shall name himself and thus become
Immortal, living to the End of Days,
his Reign inaugurated by Old Song.
If Aqhat should slay fewer than Three Gods
within this Time, henceforth he'll never know
a Mortal's Life, a God's Life, or the Life
of a Rephaim, but shall dissolve into
Oblivion for all Eternity,
that No-place without Form or Hope—the Void.'

"As each of us has done by marching here,
he chose to vindicate the ones he loved
by waging war upon those deities
who've broken us through life as well as death.

Unsheathe your blades, unsling your reflex bows,
brandish your spears, and raise your war-hammers!
The one who felled Humbaba's son, who put
to rest the Monstrous Mount, has summoned you
to force the fickle gods to beat retreat
and set aright the chaos they've unleashed.
I swear to you that such a day's at hand!"

With raucous roars the rows of soldiery
replied, saluting Aqhat's riding in
from parley with the enemy, their swords
upheld as he gave order for the van
to make for Zaphon's serried men-at-arms,
and so they did, twelve thousand regulars
processing west in unison with cars
of war that flanked those pulling up the rear.
Their treading quaked the earth as swordsmen plied
their metal hilts as mallets on their shields
to drum up blood-lust and intimidate
the warriors—some fourteen thousand heads—
who'd formed for battle at the mountain's base.
Atop an overhanging balcony
adjacent to their bedroom, Dread Anat
and Baal surveyed the field day by which they
would judge their army's future requisites,
whether in horsemanship or stamina,
communication or defensive stands,
perceiving those amassed to challenge them
as nothing more than sieves through which their weak,
unskilled, or partially committed chaff
would separate themselves from hearty seed.
Baal overlooked Anat's gargantuan array
and raised his hand at which the foremost lines
leveled their lances horizontally,

the rearward archers nocking bronze-tipped shafts.
He trained his eyes on Aqhat, ordering
his soldiers to attack, his enemy
commanding his recruits to do the same—
the war of gods and men having commenced.

Book XIX

Vast rows of soldiers fell in and fell to
stampeding head-on and breakneck
for adversaries cross the battlefield
in gross, stentorian cacophonies
until—like cymbal-clangs that finish off
the deep percussive movement of a song—
the clash of bronze-on-bronze erupted forth,
once-throaty voices now reduced to wails
amidst the leveled, nearly finished-off.
The vanguards hove or drove their javelin shafts
according to a fighter's combat-style,
innumerable hafts half-painted red
while saddled elephants with sharpened tusks
ran roughshod over Aqhat's foremost lines,
asphyxiating foes approximate
to them ere skewering late rescuers.
Beyond forefallen troops the next-up sped,
salvoes of barb-tipped arrows tracing arcs
in opposition over wintry skies,
impaling those in bowshot ere they'd swung
a bit and splintering thick oxhide shields.
Swifter than orderlies on chariots,
heraldic winds sped war's effluvia
of blood and greasy grime to rearguard lines
as high aloft Anat looked on and wrung
her hands with lusty eyes and malintent,
a flesh fly brooding on its future feast.

Deep in the thick, Kessi the Hattian
went on an unimpeded killing spree.
A bronzesmith from Hattusa's Lower Town
who fired sacred tablets for the priests
of Hannahanna's temple on the side
to make ends meet, Kessi heard Hatti's call
to arms, deliberating whether he
should go to war given his mother's state.
She lay upon her sickbed, withering
away, dependent on her son who heard
the evocation of the Thousand Gods.
While yet undrilled in warfare's rudiments,
who spent more time with weaponry than him?
And though illiterate, what hardheaded
man tended to the gods' words with more care?
Such knowledge would ensure his victory.
Decided, Kessi melted his housegods,
recasting their pure bronze into the tool
by which he'd shatter Zaphon's warriors:
a giant war-hammer to stave in ribs
and pike skulls with its opposing peen.

A young Egyptian readied to attack
this Northerner intruding on his lands.
The last-born son of simple colonists
who'd settled on Orontes' riverside
a century before, Harkhuf fought off
the Hattian aggressors threatening
to overtake his family's tillage plots.
Supposing that they'd either made their home
beyond the reach of Tefnut's aptitude
or that they'd angered her, Harkhuf's household
capitulated to the status quo,

enlisting him in Baal Hadad's brigades
to guarantee protection and good rain.
Having adapted to his given lot
and humoring Anat's insistence that
they undergo rote training every day,
he now fought through the furor, struggling hard
in hopes that, soon enough, he'd go back home.

Harkhuf struck first, his blade like horned Yarikh
when on the final days of humankind
he'll plummet to the earth to usher doom,
but Kessi's upheld shaft forestalled his death.
The bronzesmith made reply with counterstrokes,
the sixth of which knocked Harkhuf's crescent sword
out of his tingling double-handed grip.
A pounding thwack to Harkhuf's chest sent him
careening breathlessly backward into
the runway of eight heedless chariots
whose spokes and felloes were befouled with guts,
their chargers snorting foam, champing the bit.
Not a moment too soon, Harkhuf escaped
disaster to rearm himself with sword
and javelin, each one borrowed from a corpse.
The juggernaut of war-cars having passed,
his Hittite enemy engaging him,
the ambidextrous warrior Harkhuf
used his left arm to fling his newfound spear
which Kessi knocked aside as Harkhuf twirled
and with his other hand let fly the blade
that whirled far faster than a potter's wheel
to scythe both of the Hittite's greaveless shins.
He fell before his feet—a baseless lump.
Harkhuf rolled Kessi over with his heel
and wrenched from him his hammer, raising it

high, bringing it down with full force upon
his breastbone, claiming his new weapon as
the Hattian wheezed through deflated lungs.

Although the regiment Inuya led
had passed her up due to her agedness
and from its lust for battle, nonetheless
that erstwhile debt-slave gladly joined the fray
beside men who'd have been around her sons'
ages had not Zimredda murdered them.
For their sake, honoring their lives, she hacked
her way into the tumult unafraid—
for she'd lost everything a year ago,
had voyaged to the earth's far side and back,
and had outlived the Seasnake's wroth to boot.
A lanceress of local origin
named Nuriazu, having sensed Inuya's
preeminence as chiefess of these troops,
elected her and set on her at once.
Inuya read her purpose, clutched her sword
and layered shield, and readied for a fight
as Nuriazu dead-set on her foe
leapt through the air and downward thrust her lance—
a kill-shot thirsting for the old bag's heart.
With unflapped grace the debtor dove and rolled
away as for her shin she counterswung,
her sword blocked sightlessly and answered by
an upward lance turned quickly to the side
as Nuriazu kicked her in the chest
and backward through the air onto the earth.
Hadad's recruit expent no time and jumped
to plunge her spear into Inuya's chest
as the hardscrabbler from Siduna's fringe
deflected it, its force interring it

before Inuya grabbed her leathern shirt
ere burying her sword into her neck,
blood clogging Nuriazu's throat, her eyes
protuberant as Mot devoured her.

The strength of Aqhat's infidels-in-arms—
who stood their ground like dug-in palisades—
began to disconcert the Thunderer.
Because the opposition held their own,
offsetting Zaphon's onset, Dread Anat
determined to unveil her new surprise.
She turned to Baal and grinned mischievously
while near the balustrade she blew a horn.
A moment passed, then yet another one
when from above the palace's west side
there soared Baal's vulturine ambassadors
ahead of skyborne birds of a feather.
Some of the scavengers clutched tarpaulins
of river stones while Hirgab's echelon,
like Anzu at the Battle of Hehe,
flew overhead with boulders in their claws.
Neither diviner nor astrologer
were needed to decrypt these omina.
The first air-raiders loosed large carpetfuls
of hurtling rocks that strafed men on the ground,
dislocating their shoulders, shattering
large wooden shields, and pulverizing brows.
Into the piebald skies the archers loosed
sleek arrows—felling birds with well-placed strikes
just as the second surge bombarded men
and women with colossal limestone chunks.
The Seir Mountain Man held Kothar's bow
full-draw and shot an arrow, skewering
Hirgab's black pinion, forcing the godling

into a flighty doubling-back for home
while other buzzards risked their lives for spoils—
nosediving on the carnage, ravening
on hunks of carrion as their reward.

The execution of the airborne raid's
tide-turning run aroused the Conqueror
who tabled his large winecup to approach
Anat and pull her close, massaging her.
She had been stimulated by the screams
and mounting little deaths below, and now
his bestial muzzlings brought her to the edge.
The Bull unclasped the belt of human skulls
engirding her as she let fall her sash
of severed hands, impassioned by his strength.
As Zaphon's army reimposed its will,
obliterating those whose relatives
they'd killed in Hatti not so long before,
Baal's wife looked on before he carried her
to the adjoining master bedroom where
he barred the portal, making love to her
all afternoon and sleeping into night.

The bloodbath swelled in tandem with their lust.
A khopesh sword in hand, just having dodged
the worst of Zaphon's aerial assault,
Aqhat fought front and center, heading throngs
against a thickset row of brawny brutes.
In giving battle and in giving up
the ghost men belted out their cries of war
as blood and mud begrimed their visages.
Upon his taking out another two
Egyptian sell-swords, Aqhat wiped his eyes
and caught sight of a leading general,

Yashaddu, perched atop a gray-black horse
still just as wild and dappled gorgeously
as on the night Mutbalu's trusted men—
surveillants of the River Jordan's dale—
provided Aqhat with that willful mount.
Yashaddu'd stridden Abibaal's purebred
when Laeya's marksmanship unhorsed the man.
Promoted by Siduna's hierarchs,
Yashaddu rode Aliyan to the north
to spearhead the Destructress' latest ploys.
From head to toe expensive battle-gear
adorned the arriviste, a carapace
of metal armoring his mortal flesh.
An echt admirer of Abibaal
and sculpture come to life, he bayed commands
unquestioningly followed by his men,
his presence witness to their cause's right.

Aqhat fell back and flagged a chariot.
Leaping aboard he told his copilot
to gain speed, breaking through the thinnest row
of phalanxed infantrymen come what may.
Yashaddu watched a raving Aqhat point
his spear at him and welcomed his bravuric taunt
with open arms, unscabbarding his brand.
Unready for the brazen chariot's
breakthrough, the weak point in Yashaddu's line
gave way as Aqhat's charioteer sped
their war-car full-speed through them, the chargers'
chests knocking shieldsmen down and trompling them
as Hittites hurled their spears to clear a path
until a lance transfixed their leftmost horse
who cried out from unfathomable pangs,
careening and collapsing in the dust,

propelling Aqhat from the car of war
which rolled and craunched its reinsman underneath.
Regathering himself, Aqhat picked up
his lance, Yashaddu riding hard for him,
lashing Aliyan's head with a stiff switch
to bring the foaming-mouthed to full-gallop,
his flowing mane now plaited, tightly bound.

Anat's recruit sliced Aqhat's battle-shirt
and carved a reddle gash across his chest—
a scar-to-be, not fatal as of yet.
Yashaddu flayed Aliyan's upper thigh
and wheeled around to make another pass.
He charged, the hardly broken horse breaking
the solid ground with every hoofbeat's pound
as Aqhat dodged his strike and spun about
to heave his spear for his attacker's back—
Yashaddu having sensed the counterstrike,
positioning his shield to block the blow.
The spear impaled his shield but missed his arm.
Unscathed, the glinting statue of a man
let fall his newly fashioned spinning top,
irate at Aqhat's bold recalcitrance.
Aqhat unslung his god-wrought gift and nocked
it, drawing taut its string, the bow on edge.
He whipped a bronze-barbed flane Yashaddu's way
which struck his armored clavicle and clanged
aside, not having made the slightest dent.
Aqhat unloosed another arrow which
Yashaddu swiped aside with his épée,
encroaching on him with malevolence.

Conspiring nesciently to decimate
the man who in Litani's rapids risked

his life to drag him to the other bank,
his jetty equine eyes now swollen slits,
Aliyan couldn't meet his victim's gaze.
Aqhat drew back before he took a knee
then whistled twice, Aliyan rearing back,
his chest and forelegs rising heavenward
the way that Aqhat trained him moons before.
Caught by surprise, Yashaddu raised the reins
to keep his balance, opening a patch
of unprotected flesh above his hip
into which Aqhat sank a whizzing shaft
that traveled through his entrails to his spine.
Yashaddu fell and broke like an idol
cast down in some iconoclastic raid.
Aqhat raced to Aliyan who reared up
and neighed in agitated self-defense
till Aqhat's intonations hit their mark,
remembering the one to the other.
As Lugalbanda's son after the fight
with Heaven's Bull came to appreciate
and love Enkidu all the more—untoward
and never outright tamed deep down—so too
did Aqhat burst with love for his wild friend.
Becalming him as much as possible,
he mounted him, his soldiers looking on,
inspirited to just the same degree
as their foes blenched now that Yashaddu'd died.
The Seir Mountaineer undid the pleats
of the ungelded who shook out his main,
not head-shy to the East Wind's fingertips.

Come nightfall the contending sides pulled back,
war-weary and in need of bandages,
mixed wine, coal-fired meats, and Sleep's attent.

Within their tent, Laeya and Aqhat saw
to it that each received their proper care,
undressing to address each other's wounds
and downing drafts before they bedded down.
She wanted to unveil her godship, here
and now, unburdening herself of truths
kept from her heart and body's other half—
for whom she'd suffer seven thousand deaths.
But would he understand the reasoning
behind her mortal cloak, why she refused
to jeopardize the freedom that she'd found
(strange as it seems) among the race of men?
Should El's belovèd Mot catch wind of their
intent to vanquish him—his servile spies
reporting back to him—he'd barricade
both Tharumagi and Targuziza,
defending every entry to his world
to nullify their chances of success.
Or what if Aqhat should take umbrage at
her secret once disclosed, either because
she'd not divulged her essence earlier
or due to her relation with the gods
they'd come to hate, their bitter opposites?
No—it was still too soon. Once Aqhat had
apotheosized he'd be readier
to bear such revelations in their time.

In Zaphon's billets men took rest asprawl,
their field day having gone far worse than planned.
One of the Craftsman's arrows Aqhat shot
still fixed within his left arm, Hirgab knocked
upon the door behind which slept his lords.
Bade entry, he and an ambassador
dispatched in order to secure backup

from Washukanni passed the porters by.
Anat commended Hirgab for the raid
he led that afternoon and he thanked her
before depressing her with ill-starred news,
"Our aerial attack—the progeny
of your creativeness—marked our assault's
high watermark, I am afraid to say.
Yashaddu fell by Aqhat's bow, his horse
despoiled immediately afterward.
Without his generalship and firm hand,
the central units fell to disarray.
A few troops out-and-out surrendered, but
our enemies gave quarter to no one,
now leaving us with half as many men
as we possessed before the day began."

Irate, Anat strode toward him, both eyes locked
on Aqhat's arrow, studying its make.
She grabbed both sides and broke the shaft in two
inside the Father of the Vultures' arm,
dispersing spates of agony throughout.
She analyzed its make: the arrow shafts
plucked from the reedbeds of the Nile's black soil
and fletched with feathers from young avocets;
its head a fusion of Mitannian
copper and tin shipped from Assyria.
The War Goddess asked Hirgab whence it came
and he confessed that Aqhat pierced his wing.
She wondered how that boy had come upon
a weapon forged by Kothar, but her drive
to confiscate the bow far overmatched
her short-lived curiosity and awe.
Baal intervened and, hoping for good news,
requested that the other herald speak.

Though nervous to relay the rumors, he
boiled down Mitanni's new predicament.

Among their host of fifteen thousand strong—
excluding twin-wheeled chariots from home
and from Ishuwa's king—Piyassili,
Mursili, and Suppiluliuma
supped underneath the umbrage of a tarp,
just one of countless others compassing
the walls of King Tushratta's capital.
The faithful Khabur Tributary had
switched sides and helped the Hittites hem them in,
providing the besetters drinkwater
and barb-mustachioed, flat-headed fish.
Mursili quenched his thirst with wine and said,
"Although descending from the Upper Land
proved arduous, I'm ready to knock down
the city gates, to lead our squadrons on
to victory however you see fit.
While the Ishuwan sovereign sets to work
on making heirs of common blood with his
new wives, his hefty bride-price of platoons
will shed their blood for our empowerment.
Their relatives back home can lionize
their valor, but they fight for Hatti's sake,
exchanging one yoke for another one.
Why sit around? Which day shall we begin?"

King Suppiluliuma made reply,
"Now's not the time for onslaught. Now we wait.
We could besiege the capital today,
of course, but as you've noted, we would lose
whole scores of our Ishuwans doing so.
Though most are lowborn grunts, the troops we've bought

with ersatz brides would readily perceive
their use as bait and fodder for our war.
To sacrifice them, killing the morale
of those left standing—such a battle-plan
plows furrows for desertion and revolt.
No, my sons. We shall take this stronghold soon,
just as we'd planed, but we've not marched this host
down the Euphrates' snaking riverfronts
to squander such an opportunity.
Begin to think on grander scales, my boys!
Just as the very thought of losing her
only two boys in battle far away
can kill an anxious mother from within,
so too the stress produced by siege can fell
a citadel without a drop of blood—
for which our grubs and theirs will honor us.
Glory awaits you on the battlefield,
and well I know how it uplifts the soul.
But one day you'll be old like me and need
to seal your power in abiding ways.

"The leaguer of this city is to be
our first of many in the years to come,
for once our work is finished here, we'll west
beneath Arinna to appropriate
Nuhashe, Qatna, Qadesh, Ugarit,
and other regions, Rundas permitting.
Those swearing fealty to Mitanni will
submit to us while Akhenaten's sheep,
whom he lost long ago—that lunatic—
will cede their vassalage to sounder minds.
You see, Hadad and his bloodthirsty wife
are not the only ones to comprehend
that solely they who dominate the Great

Green's eastern rim at the expense of one's
imperial competitors can rule
without the constant threat of overthrow.
I may not live to see stability
of such a sort—but you, my princes—shall."

In Washukanni's council chamber, wise
advisors huddled round Tushratta's seat
to lend him decades of experience.
Agèd Kikkuli was the first to speak,
"My Lord, excessive time goes by without
a stratagem to guide our action's course.
Our resources diminish by the day
as commonfolk imagine what they'll eat
once water and provisions peter out.
I'd counsel you to send a messenger
pretending that you'll abdicate the throne
to Suppiluliuma come the dawn.
Midnight, when they are least expecting it,
you'll sally every sword-bearing recruit
beyond these walls besieged by Northerners,
surprising our aggressors in their sleep.
A swift and all-out strike's our only hope."

Before Tushratta could reply to this
advisement, Hallu-shenni took the floor,
"Your Worship, you can ill-afford to vex
the god to whom you owe your sovereignty,
and Zaphon calls on you to lend support
in this, its rare and trying time of need.
We won't survive a Hittite siege for long,
nor can we overtake them hand-to-hand.
Baal had you dig evacuation routes
for hapless circumstances just like this.

Let's muster everyone we can and flee
to Zaphon, lending Baal the aid he needs.
When you've fulfilled your promise to Hadad,
will he not help you to reclaim your throne?
The two of you—"

Tushratta raised a hand to silence him
before responding to his counselors,
"Lord Baal requested our platoons to give
them practice, not from weakness on his part.
You know Mount Zaphon's unassailable.
Yet when he welcomed us to join with him
for military exercises, he
may not have known the impasses we face.
Once he discovers why we have delayed,
and when he quells the uprising at home
(which won't be long in coming), he'll ride here
to squash this infestation from abroad.
When he assails the Hittites from the rear,
we'll join him, setting on our foes full-force
until their emperor exhales his last.
Though difficult in the extreme, control
of self must guide our judgment here on out.
I thank you for your guidance and your trust."
Each bowed before their emperor as he
excused himself to tend to other needs.
Kikkuli, Hallu-shenni, as well as
Artatama, the Second of His Name,
remained behind closed doors without their king,
discussing what alternatives remained
to them as Washukanni's advocates.

Alighting on a new plan to which each
advisor gave assent, Tushratta's aids

inaugurated its accomplishment.
Once night fell, Hallu-shenni, Kikkuli,
and Artatama ventured to the court
in order to make known their overture
to King Tushratta who prepared for sleep.
The royal doorwards rapped upon his door
before allowing his advisors in.
Surprised by their ingression, Mitanni's
enthroned asked why they'd come at such an hour,
at which Kikkuli gestured to his king
with a clay tablet, indicating that
its words would vouch for their late dropping-by.
Kikkuli set the sacred writ upon
a tabletop around which each man stood,
explaining that it documented past
beleaguerments of Hurrian demesnes,
affording lessons for the days ahead.
Somewhat perturbed, and quite reluctantly,
Tushratta brooked his aids' persistence in
their fervor for prudential governance
as Hallu-shenni limned historical
encirclements of Washukanni's walls
by foreign and unwelcome infantries.
Tushratta interjected as the night
grew late, acknowledging his gratitude
to them as he reiterated that
his previous decision hadn't changed
when he stuck out a long and bright red tongue—
the blade of Artatama's dirk thrust through
the king's nape, silencing his rationales
and speeding him on to the Hereafter.

Abreast of Zaphon's lowdown and without
consent or knowledge of his overlords,

Hirgab took flight for Lel on mended wing.
For all his loyal scions who had died
in recent battle following his lead,
he risked petitioning support from El.
The Father of the Vultures soared aloft,
transmorphing back into his wingless state
near Mount Lel's waterfall, behind which he
ascended, led by El's guards to the room
in which the Ageless One held audience.
On bended knee before the Lord of lords,
Hirgab addressed the Wise One, speaking thus,
"Oh Father of the Gods, revered for your
compassion and forgiving heart, I come
as one of your descendants, pleading you
to set aside the just hostility
you bear your reckless children—Zaphon's lords.
I will admit that they're headstronger than
a pair of worn-down, shiftless drayhorses,
but children are ungrateful by design.
As I'm sure that you've been informed by now,
a host of reprobates has set upon
the stronghold Kothar fashioned for your son,
and while we've staved them off at present, more
attacks will follow in the days ahead.
I humbly ask for backup: Send us Elsh
and his trained soldiery to do away
with the impious mortals threatening
to kill your children ere they turn upon
your southern populace and Lel itself."

El polished off his gold-rimmed oliphant,
his cupbearer refilling it, then said,
"Has Rumor the Gossipmonger not reached

Mount Zaphon's summit? Baal's no son of mine.
I've spoken it, thus it has taken hold.
And since his sister seems inseparable,
she likewise merits disinheritance.
My seed are thankless, to be sure, but gods
who've lived for eons—childish though they be—
cannot exempt themselves as children do.
It pains a parent to give good advice
to have it spat upon at every turn.
You are a father too, if I recall.
So how can you, in one and the same breath,
advise compassion and forgiveness as
if they were always easygoing friends?
If I forgive my former son (who has
not come to ask for it), permitting him
to carry on to his self-detriment,
is this compassion? Don't I do him wrong?
The wise know when to teach hard truths and when
to let them show themselves from in themselves.

"But all's not lost, for Baal aligned himself
with Washukanni's highborn majesties.
Surely they've not reneged their sacred pacts,
so why not fly to them and ask for aid?
Nor should the lords of Zaphon fret about
Carchemish, Qadesh, and the lands between.
I once suggested their defenses be
built up, improved, but Baal and his right hand
chose other, more offensive stratagems
apparently, of which this war's a part.
Since they know what they're doing, I'll refrain
from intermeddling, leaving you to it.
You are excused. My guards shall see you out."

Wing-clipped twice over, Hirgab hung his head,
escorted out by stolid sentinels.
The Lord dropped an impassive stare into
his winecup as a scowl possessed his face.
With might and main he cast the oliphant
across the hall, wine far-flung from its mouth
before it broke against the ashlar wall.

Disgustful flesh wounds and the memory
of friends-in-arms cut down amidst the last
onslaught some days before depressed the hearts
of all in Aqhat and Laeya's war-camp,
and spite their circumscribed successfulness.
Nor did it help that Baal called up the rains
to cleanse the sloping middle ground of gore,
a bloodened salt tide washing through the camp
like flooding rivers of the Underworld.
Laeya advised her love that they not wait
and dally in the rot, allowing those
who couldn't fight to rest, enheartening
the remnant to requite their fallen kin.
He heeded her, informing generals
to ready their brigades to war at dawn.

When Shahar reäppeared, the companies
sloughed off the painstricken state of their souls
and took their place upon the battleground,
confronted by the best of Zaphon's troops.
As when a tusker's hackles stand on end
before a wolf whose hundred thousand hairs
stand to as well, both feral beasts prepared
to draw first blood, their muscles tense, alert,
just so did Aqhat's squadrons hoist their swords
and raise their spears in uniformity.

Premeasuring the tempo of the fight
to come, six thousand heartbeats drummed apace.
Opposing waves of soldiers surged and stormed
against each other at their horns' command,
their anger cresting just before they crashed
together, spuming blood and sweat and spit.
The second waves collided, undeterred.
Bidawa raged with fearless elegance
and ran her blade through checkered bodices
of leather, smashing rounded, hide-bound shields
of pine to shatters, tending to her kills
with focus, giving meaning to each one.

Huraya's hatred lighted on her now.
A young assassin shaped by Yatpan's hands
to equalize unsettled debts and crimes,
she sensed the going rate of blood-prices
with more exactness than a city's head
of commerce tabulates imported goods.
Bestowing wives of less-than-holy men
free passage to the House of Death below
became that specialty for which the few
who knew of her employed her services.
She plied a massive mace—a femur bone
with crocodile teeth fastened to the head,
the whole club overlaid with coats of bronze
and graven with gigantomachic scenes.
She much preferred that head of teeth to speak
and to negotiate on her behalf—
quick to the point, conversant in a tongue
all knew, and always getting the last word.

Demanding that her reinsman alter course
to run Bidawa down, Huraya fixed

her right foot on the guardrail of her car
then jumped from it and clanged Bidawa's shield
which countervailed the weapon's vehemence
and spun her round, allowing her to knock
back her assailant with the baldric's edge.
The cutthroat's counterblows bit through her shield,
but Laeya's confidante stood up to each
with deft evasions and surprise ripostes
when suddenly a wayward arrow ripped
into Bidawa's shoulder, missing bone
but lodging underneath her olive skin.
Expending not a moment's time, the trained
assassin dashed upon her, battering
her aegis till it flew out of her hand—
disfurnished of her scimitar as well.
Huraya relished every blow she dealt
her unarmed enemy who coughed up blood
when cudgeled in the navel or her side.
Each clobber disempowered her the more;
her eyes glazed over, welcoming an end
in which to pride herself, for she'd known love,
had sailed across the Great Green Sea, had fought
alongside friends without betraying them,
and had achieved still more with excellence.
Athwart her battle-shirt she crossed her arms
and, tear-stained, looked up, emptying her lungs
in a great war-cry as Huraya swung
for one last time, the former tearing out
the arrow from her shoulder, sidestepping
Huraya's blow to ram the arrow through
her jowl beyond her skullcap, hoisting her
aloft beneath the sun (as kings pike heads
as warning signs) until Huraya died.
Rescabbarding her bloodied, blunted sword,

Bidawa stripped Huraya of her mace
and claimed it as her own as one of her
assistants ran to tourniquet her wound.

Rechristening Suppiluliuma's
engifted lance and shield with viscera,
Laeya deflected and impaled the men
so eager to deprive her of her gear.
They got the close look each of them desired
but not the end result for which they'd hoped.
She parried ax-swoops with her burnished scute
and gaffed men's vitals, whirling round her shield
to slice through armor simultaneously,
dispatching Ahnabbu and Merisu—
Khun-Anup, Sneferu, and Padiya.
In broad daylight her lapis lazuli
spearhead empurpled as she covered Ash
and Abdu's backs—a favor they returned
as Shapshu curbed her westering decline
in hopes of seeing who'd come out on top
while Zaphon's rulers fell to quarreling
about the surest path to victory.
They brandished arguments like armaments.
Though battle-weary, Laeya scanned the front
where Aqhat fought atop Aliyan's back.
At catching sight of him she swelled with strength,
their host gaining the edge with each advance,
outfighting and outnumbering Hadad.
Such was that effort's hard-won apogee.

Forth from the east the devastating blare
of war-horns rose as El—enarmored in
the furbished gear he'd not strapped on since named
'Ninurta' in the olden days—waylaid

the Seir Mountain Man's pitched garrisons
with dashing reinforcements from Mount Lel.
Elsh and his men set fire to the tents
and made quick work of convalescent lugs
as large infernal tongues engulfed the camp.
El ordered Elsh to run down and accost
a fleeing man who sported the clean garb
befitting some authoritative role.
The Lord's attendant gave Ameni chase
and gained on him, delivering a clour
that wholly incapacitated him.
Elsh slung the hostage on his brown-maned's back.
Upright and sober, El commanded that
his footmen headlong charge into the thick
to slay the infidels. None disobeyed.

Alarmed by ancillary footmen whom
their rearguard could detain awhile at best,
Aqhat gave order for his infantry
to disengage and pull back to the left.
Since onslaught from the east had never seemed
a possibility, they'd not prepared
for it, now surely paying with their lives.
His generals and horsemen echoed his
behest over the battle's riotous
bedlam as Laeya led the leftmost flank
southward to nowhere in particular.
But the divinity to whom she was
espoused veered left as well, his troops prepared
to herd the fold into the deep-set trough
of Zaphon's southern rim, corralling them
like droves of cossets led to sacrifice.

Chaos clopped roughshod over friends and foes
alike as Order's callused hands held tight
the charger's overtautened, fraying reins.
A codependency united them.
The reinsman knew he needed constant war
to spread his influence, but couldn't wage
campaigns without his untamed opposite.
War's indeterminacy and misrule
allured the destrier as well, and yet
without a modicum of mastery
Chaos felt labile, inadvertently
engendering a patterned peacefulness
that compromised its devious desires.
The terror instigated by this team
evacuated life of certainties—
such as assurance that one would awake
to greet the day; the unreflective sense
of why and for whom one exhausts one's bones;
the myriad 'at leasts' that motivate
a person to go on; and knowledge that,
if one feels pain in some particular
location, seeing that it's caked in gore,
that it does not belong to someone else.

Bursting into their private back-and-forth
with happy tidings, Gapn scused himself
before Hadad and the Goddess of War,
informing them that backup had arrived—
destroying Aqhat's camp, positioning
themselves to take their foemen from the rear.
Down halls the gods of Zaphon sped until
they gained the lofted parapet from which
they witnessed El, their Father, Wisdom's Source,

putting to flight their hated onsetters.
Gapn enticed them still more, declaring that
not even this exhausted his good news.
As if an overeager child he led
them round the rampart walkway till they reached
the citadel's opposing overlook,
now iridesced with Shapshu's blinding rays
completely uninhibited by clouds.
With shielded eyes Anat and Baal looked out
across the seascape over which the moist
and mighty zephyrs of the wet season
propelled a silhouetted naval fleet.

Short-lived affections of humility,
relief, and thankfulness emerged from deep
in Baal's tempestuous interior.
He took his queen's arms, looked her in the eye,
and then acknowledged that she had been right
to call upon their navy for support,
that he'd been wrong not to perpetuate
their first assault on Hatti, and that he'd
amend his future acts accordingly,
beginning by deferring to her now.
Returning eastward down the battlement
on lightened foot, Anat submitted that
they summon and relocate longbowmen
to where they stood so that, should El succeed
in hounding Aqhat's throngs into the pass,
they might rain fire on them until their fleet
arrived en masse to finish off the job.
Baal grinned then sought out ancillary troops
to set in motion Dread Anat's advice.

El's men-at-arms engaged the hindmost lines
who, in a last-ditch effort to delay
the inescapable, charged them head-on,
thereby allowing friends who'd risked their lives
while raging in the vanguard to escape.
Like spademen who have next-to-nothing scraped
from barrens, transporting their trifling yield
to market and demanding more for its
exchange than any costermonger would
accept, the cultivator's poverty
impelling him to get all that he can
(if not by theft then violence), so too did
the rearguard, knowing how much work they'd put
into their being, valuing it beyond
what those attempting to lay claim to it
would grant—so too did they demand far more
than any of their purchasers could stand
in their grim truck and trade of life for life.
Although some men got ripped off from the first,
most Hittite foot soldiers struck bargain deals
of three- and four-for-one in Mot's bazaar,
despoiling El's men of their better swords,
holding them off as long as feasible,
succeeding in the forlorn hope by means
of which Aqhat's foreguard took to the vale.

On fleet-hoofed mares men doubled-up and clung
to trundling war-cars, racing at top speed
into the dale at Zaphon's southern foot
until they came in range, at which Anat
commanded that her archers nock and loose,
their recurve bows unleashing bolts aflame.
Torrential fire rained down on Aqhat's troops,

transfixing them like spitted, crackling slabs
while other blazing barbs impaled the rails
and frames of war-cars, glutting on their wood.
More than a few of Hatti's bravest troops
incinerated with the Great Green Sea
in sight—their only hope gone up in smoke.
Zannanza won his shieldsmen's eyes and ears,
aligning them along the vale's north rim
to block whatever arrowshots they could
as Arnuwanda wheeled his troops around
to face and brace for their pursuants' charge.
Field marshals Aqhat and Laeya led scores
beyond the shooters' ambit, but by now
all knew they'd been entrapped, observing Baal's
black fleet make for the shore near which they stood.
Outfoughten footmen caught their breath as Ash
and Laeya mustered outfits of fatigued
last-ditchers to back Arnuwanda's force.
Now Laeya and her love cast parting looks
each other's way, the latter serrying
what troops remained to make their beachfront stand.
Bidawa joined him, rallying her men.

Impatient raptors hovered overhead
as Arnuwanda's front lines clashed with Lel's.
The sun's slight semicircle ducked behind
the skyline, parting for the Underworld
where in due course whole scores would find themselves.
The once-calm sea began to stir with swells
and spindrifts midst whose blackened blustering,
far off atop the offing's razor edge,
there cut foul figureheads of beastly form
as warships dug their sculls into the waves.
Just like the sightless heart knows when to pound

deep in the dark recesses of one's chest
when new external threats present themselves,
so too did that armada set about
tattooing drums of war amidst the gloom.
Loud plashing oarage timed itself against
the magnifying thumps as on they raced.
Anon the foremost galley beaked into
the sands, a shadow dropping from the bow.
It tromped toward Aqhat and Bidawa as
rear vessels plowed their furrows on the beach,
stout warriors debarking in the surf,
withdrawing blades and clobbering their shields.
Bidawa raised her hand to ready those
who on her mark would loose what arrows that
remained and storm the landing argosy.
She grit her teeth. The captain then unhelmed
his full-faced casque, approaching those ashore,
his eyes unhanding both of them at once.
With tears and stupefaction Aqhat ran
to him, embracing him and crying out,
"Gabbar, you've come back from the Netherworld!"
Bidawa shoved the man aside and kissed
her love, the one she'd given up for dead—
the cold world disappearing in a trice.
They saw the wounds that one another bore.
Turning to Aqhat, Gabbar made reply,
"I never perished. Mot's domain awaits
us yet—or wasn't this our destiny?"

Cries higher up the gradient made short
shrift of the friends' reunification.
Gabbar entrusted those who'd sailed with him
to Wullu and Akawatil as he,
Bidawa, and Aqhat attacked uphill,

bypassing Arnuwanda's shouting troops.
Gabbar's auxiliary seafarers—
whom he'd persuaded to accompany
him eastward on the well-provisioned fleet
for which he'd traded Litan's tentacle—
these merchants, trawlers, and adventurers
from Kizzuwatna and Washukanni
counter-waylaid the forces of the Lord
midst flames antagonized by seaborne winds.
The Wise One's gilded retinue had not
at all envisaged any such reprise,
and spite the vantage of their lofted ground,
their formal training, and their implements
of far superior make, nonetheless
they lacked the stamina to cope with them.
Aqhat took Laeya's side, her deadly spear
and his sword making short work of El's troops
while Gabbar's double-bitted labrys cleaved
through bone and muscle, hewing men like wood
that over time has rotten inside-out—
Bidawa flourishing Huraya's mace
as if it had been shapened for her hands.

Atop their fortress' battlement Anat
and Baal could hear the griding, ringing arms
whose labor echoed through the firmament.
Their jittery imaginations joined
these sounds to warm, anticipative thoughts
as well as to their known advantages,
concocting visions which, although unseen,
enveiled by night, denoted victory.
In time the clankorous cacophony
died down as cheers of triumph filled the air.
Baal hugged his consort from behind then told

a handmaiden to fix a sumptuous meal
for El and his salvific legionnaires,
their repast to be followed by warm baths.
She turned to leave as god and goddess strode
toward Zaphon's Eastern Gate, awaiting El
astride his ivory horse, his guards close by.
Indeed the Father of the Gods soon came,
yet with a sullen, irritated lour
and fewer men than he'd led into war—
a combination that dejected Baal
while angering his sister overmuch.
A servant hastened well-aged wine to El
which he imbibed before his taurine son
led him and his retainer to table,
no word arising in the interim.
Presenting Zaphon's hostess with a gift,
Elsh asked Anat where she'd prefer it stored,
whereat she gestured for the dungeon guards
to show Ameni to his holding cell.

After their meal (not dismal for its want
of gourmet offerings but on account
of the exhaustion and despondency
that gripped the festal hall) two chambermaids
showed El his room and drew a steamy bath.
Well-cared-for and reclothed, the Lord dismissed
his handmaidens with gratitude as Baal
rapped at the door and came inside to sit
beside his father, wearied from the fray.
In due time Baal began to speak his mind,
"Remember when you granted me control
of lightning when I begged you as a boy,
and how I nearly razed our library,
upset about my tutor's stringency?

In truth I only wanted to show off,
to bare my strength, exert my will, and use
your recent gift to garner your esteem,
entirely forgetting where I was.
I've come to understand that moment as
a seed, a starting point from which have shot
forth tangled roots and disparate offshoots.
I wanted to impress you, then as now.

"When I pursued Tushratta, allied him,
wanting Mitanni and the Hittite's realm,
deploying my fleet (whatever's become
of it) to Egypt's heartland down the Nile,
I sought to court your favor—strange as it
might sound—by disobeying your advice.
To win great wars and backers as Adad
my namesake did with you—such was my wish.
While growing up I understood my role:
to emulate your grandeur while at play.
But as I aged my games turned serious,
their consequences losing levity.
Still overshadowed by your umbrage, how
could I accomplish deeds as great as yours?
Having been raised beside her, loving her
as kin already, trusting her more than
some transshipped consort, and requiring her
propensities for war, I joined Anat
by choice and yet compelled by destiny
in order to effectuate our dreams.

"Today our troops would have been routed had
you not descended from your mountain home
to ambush them; we're in your debt, and I
am grateful for your unexpected aid . . .

Does wisdom help you grasp my foolishness,
as if perceiving it from my own heart,
conciliating us, or does it put
you at a greater distance, rendering
our disaccord irreconcilable?
Your children need you more than ever now
and hope this period's predicaments
might yet solidify our lineage.
Forgive us, Father. Help us prove ourselves."

The Lord took thought before he made reply,
"I well remember Athirat's dismay
at all the sacred writ that you rebaked
by happenstance, and how she scolded me
for giving you your powers far too soon.
Yet learning can't occur without mistakes—
at least not any worthy of the name.
I stand by my decision to entrust
you with control of fire-bolts and rain,
aware of the responsibilities
and the anxieties it brought in tow.
I gifted you dominion over clouds
because I loved you most of all my sons.
Perhaps I thought you knew I treasured you
and didn't make my favor or esteem
explicit as one must with growing hearts.
I longed to make you strong, self-disciplined,
reliant on yourself instead of me
or others, yet it seems I went too far,
withholding how I felt, in part to keep
your siblings' green-eyed rivalry in check.

"You've erred, as you have said, yet so have I.
Let us imbibe these acrid truths and turn

them toward the betterment of our domain,
which I'd have you lord over in due course.
Receive forgiveness as my son once more,
forgiving me in turn for my own sins.
This done, rest well, for come three days from now
Anat and you shall do what I could not
and march our host against the enemy
yourselves, exterminating them from Earth."
After he'd spoken, Shataqat, who'd been
escorted to Baal's palace by Lel's guards
when safe to do so, entered through the door,
embracing them and gladdened that her Lord
had followed her advice and made amends.

The sound of clacking footsteps echoed down
nine hundred involuted steps that plunged
deep into Zaphon's limestone viscera.
Flambeau in hand, the Dread Godhead of War
the nadir reached—a dungeon just as damp,
frigid, and tense as is a child clutched by
a nightmare, struggling to unbind herself
from herself though it be impossible.
Cross-legged, alone, like Ptah before he spoke
or Atum's hand before he loved himself,
Ameni waited in his cell and read
by candlelight the glyphs scratched in the walls
where prisoners commemorated their
decease with ravings and admonishments.
He faced Anat as she approached. She said,
"A literate Egyptian far from home,
forsaking countrymen to war beside
unfaithful, Asiatic turnabouts—
they must be treating you remarkably
well (better than an equal, I

would venture) to employ the services
whereby you risk your spirit's permanence.
This solitary place tries to impart
its wisdom, helping one reorder life
before their Judgment Day extends its hand.
Some former residents, you may have seen,
found ways to liberate their fettered souls
while others chose disintegration's out.
I'd wager that you're of the former sort.

"As a divinity who's spent her share
of time amidst the Field of Reeds, I've come to know
Osiris and his two and forty squires,
Anubis and Sokar, Isdes and Thoth,
befriending fertile Isis and Nephthys.
Throughout the centuries we've grown quite close,
although I must admit that their humor's
a little dark for me most of the time.
What do you plan to say to them when your
time comes, that is, if you are mummified
pursuant to the proper rituals?
I can assure you: Those compatriots
who will survive you on the battlefield
will not embalm your corpse or bury you,
protecting you from graveyard dogs with prayers.
What of your friends? Do they know what we do,
how life-forces and personalities
must be preserved and duly unified?

"Your army's ultimate defeat draws near.
As you saw, El's auxiliary troops
have vanquished most of yours; renewed support
will soon arrive from allies in the East.
However much I love these battles, though,

they're matters of inconstant transience,
whereas farsighted men like you prehend
that with eternity no time compares.
I'm going to set you free before the dawn.
Retrieve your master's bow and quiver, bring
them back to me, then voyage home by way
of Ugarit, and you shall spend your days
in Akhenaten's palace, after which
I'll disemburden your unrighteous heart
and put in a good word among my friends."
Ameni stood, beginning to refuse
her offer ere she silenced him and told
him to allow the thought to germinate
as did the spark in Nun's primeval egg,
turning around, ascending up the stairs.

Book XX

On Zaphon's crest the sun poured molten light
that disembogued into the rocky trough
down to the beach where soldiers lay in tents
provided by the fleet in Gabbar's charge.
Up from his hold the aforesaid emerged
to take the morning's beams before his love
arose as well and kissed him from behind.
They broke their fast with Aqhat and Laeya
onboard as Gabbar told them of the isle
on which he'd washed ashore, how he'd interred
their comrade Burianu, fed himself
on Litan's flesh and herbage found nearby,
escaping in a dugout that he'd made
out of the monster's indurated arm,
persuading those he'd met at Ura's port
to fight with him against the god whose storms
assault all life reliant on the seas.
Before recounting further stories though,
Gabbar insisted that his company
describe what had befallen them in turn.
Aqhat tossed spongy bread his way before
rehearsing their run-in with Henti who
entasked Nuhati, her famed wayfinder,
to guide them through the Inhospitable
Sea and along the Marassantiya
to Suppiluliuma's capital.
From there they felled two brutes with luck and wit,
thereby aligning with the emperor
who now blockaded Washukanni's walls.

Each knew that fleshing out the details they'd
passed over would require far more time
and turned to matters much more imminent.
Field marshal Laeya, having taken stock
of their affairs, propounded a return
uphill in three days' time to battle on
the leveler plain where they had fought before.
A few would stay behind to guard the ships,
preparing them for possible retreat.
Gabbar concurred with her. As she began
suggesting tasks for them, the camp's north side
upstirred, arousing their solicitude.
They rose and through the crowd they pushed their way
to marvel at another friend thought dead—
Ameni—smothered by his intimates
before those in authority pried them
away and mobbed him, shedding tears of deep
relief and asking what became of him.

Ameni outlined his close call with death:
Collecting water close to camp when El's
assault commenced, he hastened north and hid
until the morning when he stole away
and tracked his friends by traces from their clash.
Enthralled, Aqhat proposed they throw a feast
to celebrate their friend's improbable
return and sate their war-torn flesh and bones.
No plaints arose and troop esprit soared high
as Akawatil and Wulllu threw food
and wineskins to their men along the surf.
Two dozen Urans brought the fish they'd speared
at dusk and roasted them on driftwood fires
while those encharged to Abdu, whom he'd sent
to hunt, arrived to dress the local game.

Carousing in a motley mix of tongues,
Mitannians and Hittites, sons of kings
and former slaves forgot their dead, forgot
their Fate-allotted statuses, and shared
large drafts and slowly roasted venison,
united in the joy of having lived
to drink and fight at least for one more day.

By midday Arnuwanda had returned
with scads of loot contributed by El's
late troops, amassing it upon the beach.
Before he let his generals compart
the haul among the men in their command,
Aqhat gave precedence in choosing their
deserts to Gabbar and Ameni, they
who'd cheated Mot and lived to tell of it.
Surveying the agglomerate of spoils,
Ameni picked a scimitar whose haft
concluded with a hooded cobra's head.
Bidawa, Laeya, Aqhat, and Gabbar
drank to his fortune, seconded by all.
Gabbar the Castaway was next in line.
He lifted and examined corselets, helms,
and shields to torturously toy with those who had
selected their reward before their turn,
arousing disapproval and guffaws.
At last he chose a bronzen dagger cast
with one mold (following the cutting-edge),
its ivory haft well-suited to his grip.
He hoisted it and brought forth festive roars,
all present gladdened that the one who'd come
to help them beat back El had his reward.
Aqhat now had the princes parcel out
the pile among the generals, whereat

the latter gave them to their warriors
whose reasons to wassail remultiplied.

As unmixed wine admixed with fighters' blood
throughout the eventide, words that would pass
as jocular to sober ears now rang
as challenges to family name and pride.
A brawl between ten Kizzuwatnan louts
and thirteen Hattians broke out, and when
by different means their leaders intervened
to break them up, they came to blows themselves.
Departing from their mirthful fireside,
Laeya and Aqhat carved a flume through men
with their unhappy, transfixed line of sight.
The field marshals stood by the row until
the emerald-eyed had had more than enough,
her booming voice commanding them to cease.
She pressed all to remember to themselves
the reasons for their unity, the war
that bound them, and the work that lay ahead,
demanding that they clean the beachside camp
now that they'd ended the festivities.
The men complied. Their leaders then retired.
Inside their tent, Aqhat and Laeya spoke
about the dwindling discipline among
their troops and yet acknowledged that the day's
enjoyments far outweighed its grievances,
for if Tiratu's gift spurred men to fight,
so too it cleansed attainted memories.
Now Aqhat froze. He whipped around and asked
his love if she'd seen Kothar's armaments.
A panicked anger overtook his face.

Their days of preparation scurried by,
the coming combat and Ameni's flight
impinging on the leaders' careworn hearts.
They fronted regiments now standing-to
upon the battlefield, Zaphonian
Hadad's thick rows of infantry en face.
Yet now, as when they smote Hattusa's walls,
Anat and Baal prepared to head the charge,
the former riding Yatpan's war-car pulled
by lionesses stolen from Mount Lel.
Anat slung Aqhat's quiver round her back
and gripped the bow that once belonged to him.
With Driver the remorseless club in his
right hand, a rock-hard aegis in the left,
Baal hoofed it, eager for the blood sport's start.
Just as a master brings his hound to heel
before some scrap of food or chaseable
diversion to breed self-restraint, and though
upon its hindquarters it shakes and shifts
he counsels patience nonetheless—so too
did El look down from Zaphon's battlement
as chargers champed the bit and warriors
deadlocked their enemies with grinding teeth
and stares impregnated with violent thoughts
till El unleashed his war-dogs on their prey.

The battlelines collided head-to-head
as Baal clubbed troops in the opposing van,
projecting broken bodies through the air
and over openmouthed Hattusan troops.
He summoned thunderheads, discharging bolts
upon his foes with incandescent cracks.
A spear and shield in hand, Aqhat broke right,

his sights upon that god whose governance
or lack thereof destroyed his kith and kin.
Above the rest the horn-helmed deity
ascended, brazen barbs deflecting off
his breastplate, falling to earth like windblown
pine needles dying at their source's foot.
Four fighters ambushed Baal at once with cries
of war, but stooping to their level he
dove forthright and transpierced the first two men
while bucking those attacking from behind.
By now Gabbar the Castaway had helped
to clear a path for Aqhat and his horse,
the pair of whom beset the god amain.

Now with his long lance Aqhat thrust for Baal
whose aegis knocked aside its lethal tip.
Alighting from Aliyan, squaring off
to face him hand-to-hand, he stormed the god,
the twain attacking and evading strikes
such as King Minos' Labyrinth's never seen,
the Castaway's contingent fighting off
attempts at intermeddling in their bout.
The god delivered Aqhat brutal blows,
the least of which would decimate most men.
His spear raised on his shoulder, Aqhat made
as if to hurl it at the Taurine One
but let his palm slip down along the shaft
and like a stave he gripped it, whipping it
beneath Baal's buckler, fracturing his shin.
Sharp pain shrieked from the impact site as Baal
unloosed a low like Heaven's Bull had done
when fighting with Enkidu long ago.
Baal whirled his shield at Aqhat, knocking his
defense from him, now charging him full on,

his rancor overpowering his pain.
Hadad lunged horns-first for his enemy.
While Aqhat dodged his inborn weaponry,
the god yet pinned him to the bloody earth,
his forehead pressing downward on his chest.

The Seir Mountaineer could draw no breath
as Baal compressed his lungs, nor could the man
withdraw the sword still baldricked on his back
because Hadad held firmly to his wrists.
About to suffocate, with Nothingness
encroaching on his spirit, Aqhat pulled
his kneecap toward his chest and slipped his foot
inside Baal's golden nose ring, kicking down
and ripping it from his dissepiment.
The Bull reared back and roared as Aqhat gripped
the god's left tine and pivoted midair,
the mortal's legs secured around Baal's neck
till Aqhat, mustering the love and wrath
that drove him ever onward, pithed the god,
continuing to strangle-ride him as
dark ichor gouted from his riven neck.
Baal breathed his last and thudded to the ground—
a sprawling banquet for Oblivion.

His blade upheld with joyous rage, Aqhat
decapitated Baal in one fell swoop
and by the scalp he raised his trophy high.
With trichotillic groans El mourned his son,
besmearing dirt upon his tear-streaked face
as waves of blinding sorrow battered him,
now fever-pitched by grief and foundering,
supported by the arms of Shataqat.
Here Aqhat turned before his infantry,

most rallied by his victory, the rest
of whom took knees in awed humility—
for from their point of view it seemed as though
their leader had assumed the god's own head,
despoiling him of power and of form.
Their act of worship reinforced his strength.
Anat the Dreadful witnessed Aqhat's grave
defilement of the brother whom she loved.
She drenched her scourge's scorpion tips in blood
from victims of Resheph's ensorcellment,
demanding Yatpan run the killer down.

Field marshal Laeya, having seen Anat's
debasement of her golden pride, went on
the warpath, skirting armed impediments
intent on stopping her at any cost.
To Yatpan's speeding war-car she gave chase.
Its team of lionesses trampled throngs
of soldiers, biting, clawing their way through
until Anat reached Aqhat, whiplashing
the shield with which he held off her assault.
The goddess circled him. The Dread One's scourge
pulled back then whipcracked forward round his shield,
its stingers puncturing his mortal flesh.
Anat yanked back upon her captured prey
with such élan that Aqhat lost his brand.
The goddess hauled him toward her chariot
as if he were a giant fish, and once
she'd dragged his body sternside, she coldcocked
him neither once nor twice but seven times
till darkness overcame his faint world-grip.
His body heaved aboard, the Bellicist
commanded that her driver beat retreat.

The deft Sutean Warrior obeyed.
With Aqhat's godsent bow Anat cleared swathes
of soldiers from their new trajectory,
removing any in her way until
a whettened shard from Ullikummi's heart
impaled her shoulder blade, the force of which
sent her careening from her driver's side
onto a rocky mound that stole her breath.
Once she came to—her heart a hornet nest,
a slaughterous and apoplectic swarm
set off by someone's suicidal wish—
she ordered Yatpan to continue on
and pulled the spear out of its exit wound,
bewielding it against the reckless bitch
who'd heaved it at her, soon to pay the price.

A matchless sword of Knossian design
unsheathed, Abihumbaba's stone-honed scale
in her left hand, fleet-footed Laeya flew,
remaining even-keeled atop the gore,
her calves and sandals ruddled in the sludge
like Klawiphoroi when they press their grapes.
She leapt and with a plunging thrust attacked
Anat, her devastation held in store.
Anat responded with a clanging swipe
then butted Laeya's shield, twirling her spear
around and slicing her opponent's waist.
War's mayhem flared on every side yet they
remained engrossed in battle, each assault
deflected or absorbed with brusque ripostes,
counteroffensives, and propulsive blocks.
Though burning with volcanic vehemence,
each moved with cervinesque agility—
yet Laeya better understood the spear

Anat plied than that goddess did, attuned
to the exceptional requirements
for its cooperation in the field,
foreknowing its propensities and wants.
Anat drove Laeya's javelin overhand
and missed her jugular but grazed her ear
as Laeya gutwrenched her from underneath
with an incisive upthrust of her shield,
along whose foreside innards spattered down.
Befogged and moribund, Anat let fall
her armament, her wrathful gaze deprived
of sense till she beheld her mother's eyes,
succumbing to her filicidal strike.

Doorkeepers opened Zaphon's Eastern Gate
for Yatpan who drew rein before the Lord,
the lionesses' gilded coats stained red.
El glared at Aqhat who began to stir.
Observing that some life remained in him,
the Ancient One demanded that his men
now hang him by his wrists outside the wall
and high enough for everyone to see,
left there to strain and contemplate his sins
while El considered whether questioning
the man or using him to sue for peace
proved wiser given their predicament.
Baal's retinue—now his to lead—complied.
Ascending Zaphon's eastern parapet,
El overlooked the battlefield and blew
his horn to start the pullback of his troops.
The desperate army harkened to his call
and disengaged, now turning tail to flee.
Their foemen hunted them, pursuing them
till they drew near the Eastern Gate—and ceased.

Strung high aloft was Aqhat, he in whom
they'd stored their hopes, his arms unsocketing.

The pendent hero coughed himself awake,
expelling bile, each movement riling up
the aches both sharp and dull afflicting him.
The deep incisions that the Dread One cut
into his back and shoulders festered, itched,
but he could not alleviate their sting.
He watched as Zaphon's men-at-arms rushed through
the gate and sealed his troops from entry, but
neither the welfare of his allies nor
his victory against the Thunderer
recalled themselves before his inner eye.
Instead, his cobweb core caught gadfly-thoughts
of his Egyptian friend, Ameni, as
they flitted by—a swarm of memories
of how they'd saved each other, warded off
Shatanu's cunning, delved into a cave
from which a multitude had not escaped,
recruited forces to waylay the gods,
and voyaged over untold leagues of sea—
only to break asunder. And for what?
Had he collaborated with Anat?
What good can rival friendship's pride of place?
Surely not Kothar's handmade weaponry.
Bequest Ameni Kothar's very tools,
his skills, and every resource to construct
ten thousand quivers, longbows, and sharp flanes
to use and trade and marvel at—what good
are these without a friend for whom one lives?

Infuriated, Laeya glowered at
El's work: degrading Aqhat to a lure.

But lionesses are deliberate:
They wait and prowl and muse before they maul.
Bidawa, Gabbar, and some generals
who had survived looked on aghast as well,
Laeya's right hands discussing what to do.
To her companions Laeya spoke these words,
"See how the Lord thought wise, compassionate,
gives quarter to the people he provokes—
how he exalts the downtrodden on high!
He plays with us and tempts us to lay siege.
Let us exult in disappointing him.
Bidawa, send your men back to the ships
to have them transport tentage, victuals,
and wine to us, for we'll make camp just out
of arrowshot, remustering our might.
Gabbar, send horse-drawn teams to gather up
the corpses of the gods. Watch over them.
Inuya, Abdu, Ash: Devote your time
to tending to the injured, sending those
who cannot fight to rest near Gabbar's fleet.
Be quick! Our leader's life depends on it."

Two moons remained to come into their own
ere Aqhat's pre-appointed time ran out,
and now Yarikh—a portion of his face
concealed from sight—waxed overhead among
the transmigrating kings of Ugarit,
the only lights aside from Zaphon's torch
to mitigate the tenebrific night.
Only El's mercenaries slept that night.
Shahar was long in coming, followed by
the Sun, the two of whom had forecasted
the residues of such a war, although
a myriad of endings moonstruck them.

Arising from the side of Shataqat
and contemplating how his detainee
might serve his interests, El beclothed himself
as chambermaids began to sandal him.
He ventured to the citadel's war-room
where generals and gods of lesser note
demurred and counterargued finer points.
Those present stood to render obeisance
as Hirgab filled the stillness with his thoughts
no sooner than the Wise One silenced him.
El took the floor, addressing them at once,
"I've taken thought as to our way ahead.
Not much deters the predators outside
these walls from fomenting their war-bent path—
nor fear of death nor shame nor piety.
Our best resort's to strike a deal with them,
to offer them our hostage in exchange
for absolute retreat and the remains
of my own progeny, Anat and Baal.
I have not finished! First, and with respect,
they'll leave the bodies of my children at
our Eastern Entry, whereupon they shall
abandon Zaphon, whether on their ships
or for some distant city, I don't care.
Should they accomplish this, I will release
their irreligious prisoner of war.
If they refuse, I welcome them to starve
and watch this Aqhat do the very same."

Ensuring that the Lord had said his peace,
the Father of the Vultures gulped and said,
"My Lord, your hostage perished overnight."
El's baggy eyes spread wide and scanned the room.
Averted glances and bleak soundlessness

disquieted the room, confirming that
the message Hirgab had relayed held true.
El stroked his beard and reassessed their lot,
"Foredoomed are they who seek to fight the gods.
Perhaps Mot favors us and intervened,
preferring that we should display our strength
before those who'd defame our pantheon.
At times grim Warfare's cauldron overbrims,
unable to contain the blood upfilled
from either side, and when that moment comes,
armistices once-thought impossible
appear and augur respite from the gloom.
We leave the sinner as a sign of our
determination till our foes return
our fallen, whereupon they shall have theirs.
Gapn, relay our terms to those beyond
the walls and grant them three days to decide.
The rest of you, see to it that your troops
have taken drink and every kind of food,
outpouring red libations to the gods
who fought and gave their very lives for us."

Even the most experienced and brave
of heralds never grows accustomed to
conveying ill tidings which, like the wind,
seem immaterial until they strike
full-force, destructing everything in range
with wanton unpredictability.
Gapn was no exception, taking wing
with fear amassing in his hollow bones.
Near camp he morphed back into godly form,
invited to approach with ninety bows
flexed taut like runners' tendons on their marks.
Bidawa, Gabbar, and Laeya approached

the courier who broke the news to them,
"Good people, I bring terms of peace from El.
Why must we hack each other limb from limb?
Or is our soil so poor in nutrients
that, lacking inundations every year,
we must enrich the ground with brooks of blood?
Our Lord desires a truce and asks of you
to let him mourn his children properly,
as you no doubt should also like to do.
If to the Lord you give his unwept son
and daughter's bodies, marching home your troops
from Zaphon, then he'll give you Aqhat's corpse."

The earth itself yawed under Laeya's feet.
She grimaced, leapt onto her courser's back,
and galloped headlong through the predawn fog
till she could see the palace's east wall,
looked up, and saw her lover's lolling head,
his strung-up body rocking in the wind.
A keen more violent than the benu bird's
erupted from her throat as she wheeled round,
removed a knife, rode full-stretch back to camp,
and whipped it at El's royal errand boy.
Gapn resumed his vulturine physique,
upstirring dust clouds as he beat his wings,
the blade—lucky for him—crosscutting his
left leg instead of puncturing his heart.
He disappeared into the hazy mist
as Laeya's eyes confirmed her friends' worst fears.

Unhorsed by grief she dropped and clawed her cheeks,
her forehead pressed into the earth while like
a ruptured bellows soughs and hitching breaths
possessed and pumped her lungs spasmodically.

She felt her heart rip open as a fog
belonging to the Void enshrouded her,
depriving the totality of sense,
direction, and their brittle unity.
Abhorrent and unfathomable Whys
shapeshifted through her breast as pointless skirls
escaped her hollow being, for to whom
do gods turn to endure their suffering?
Bidawa and Gabbar sped to her side,
partaking in her thrashing threnody.
Inuya, Ash, and Abdu then declared
nine days of mourning for the one they'd lost.
The period would not suffice to grieve
but gave the generals a modicum
of breadth to contemplate expedients.
Bereaved, the friends of Aqhat dwelt inside
their tents, an emptiness consuming them.

As nighttime cast her cope, both warring sides
embraced whatever contributions Sleep
afforded them, and she proved generous.
When all except the nightwatch on patrol
lay still on Zaphon, Shataqat awoke,
departing from her dreaming lordship's side.
Donning invisibility, she left
their bedchamber and crept down palace halls,
bypassing unsuspecting sentinels.
She found a window Kothar had advised
that Baal not add (yet he'd done as he pleased).
El's mistress grasped its frame of stone and slipped
onto a gusty ledge that overlooked
the forest leading to Assyria.
With wary step she sidled down the ridge,
her fingernails dug in the masonry

till she arrived at Aqhat's drooping corpse.
Knowing he'd died from blood corrupted by
Resheph's disease, sworn from her first of days
to treat its victims, Shataqat laid hands
on Aqhat's ankle, susurrating spells
as wind whipped up the citadel's façade.
Her words bore no results and Shataqat
returned the way she'd come, reentering
her room and sliding into bed with El.

Entrapped in fog both blustery and cold,
Aqhat glimpsed Danataya and Pugat.
His spirit strained to reach them yet he woke,
his lungs expanding with inrushing air,
his gaping eyes adjusting to the night.
Reacclimating to the life he'd lost,
Aqhat remembered what had come to pass
and struggled to twist round to face the wall.
Eventually he lodged his toes into
a crevice, pushing down to give the rope
some slack and stretch his blood-strapped fingertips.
The possibility of breaking free
now dawned on him, and Aqhat grit his teeth,
prehent the bonds that tethered him, leaned back
until the rope drew taut, and brick by brick
began to scale Mount Zaphon's outer wall.
Two times his footing failed, two times he sent
loose rubble through the air and out of sight,
yet spite his chafing wrists and aching arms,
he never shrunk back from his escalade.

When he approached the window from which he'd
been thrown, Aqhat heard two Egyptian guards
discussing something in their common tongue.

When one of them drew near the limestone sill,
he throttled and defenestrated him,
replacing him within the lookout room.
The other guard unsheathed his blade and swung
for Aqhat, only managing to slice
his cord as Aqhat dodged two more assaults.
His wrists still bound, El's hostage grabbed the rope,
and when the moment came he spun around
the warder, deftly cutting off his breath.
The victor seized the fallen scimitar,
dissevering his bonds before he donned
the nightwatchman's equipment, dressing him
in his own garb and fastening his wrists
before he lowered him to take his stead
along the citadel's unfeeling face.
He then gave thought as to how he might flee.
Anon a dangerous yet pivotal
idea spoke to him, inciting him
to steal away toward Zaphon's topmost point.

Decked out as one of Baal's reserves, he slunk
through dimlit halls, preparing to defend
himself should any henchmen notice him.
With luck he lit upon Mount Zaphon's spire,
beginning to ascend its coiling stairs
when from afar a soldier halted him
with foreign words. Without thought he replied,
'*a-na ia shi shul-mu a-na ka-a-sha lu-u shul-mu*'
('It's well with me; may it be well with you').
The saying seemed to calm the nightwarden
who hailed him and continued with his rounds.
Up and up Aqhat climbed until he found
the Keeper of the Torch, whom he dispatched

before disrobing him and holding up
the Keeper's lengthy cloak before the flames,
removing it in intermittent threes
to send his friends their surreptitious sign
should it by chance find an interpreter.

In camp, a lookout came to Laeya's tent
(as was the man's routine) to update her.
Considering her present state of soul,
he offered to return another time,
but duty's habitude outmatched her tears.
She bade him fill her in as usual
and he obliged, reporting little new
save rumors that the flame on Zaphon's torch
now flickered in successive bursts of three.
In haste she thanked him, exiting her tent.
Astride her horse she rode hard to the west
where she observed the very sign they'd used
to liberate their leader from Baal's gaol.
And yet she also saw that Aqhat hung
where he had been. Was he not higher up?
What trick of light made him appear so large?
She spun her sleek-haired round and galloped back
where she informed Bidawa and her man
of what she had been told and what she'd seen.

Exasperated, Gabbar said to her,
"Laeya, he's dead! The Void has swallowed him.
I wish his fortune had been otherwise.
And yet we saw him hanging, spiritless.
Why do you seek out that which torments you?
The seaborne winds lash Zaphon's torch, no more.
Let's not play necromancer, listening

for words and reading signs from the deceased,
but really mourn our comrade's death until
we're able to admit its horrid truth."

Fresh tears of doubt and anger filled her eyes
as Laeya made reply to Gabbar thus,
"Not long ago and by a god's own hands
you too passed on before our very eyes.
What if we'd doubted our impressions then,
though stone-set and unshakeable they seemed?
And weren't the hopes of locating your love
correct spite their irrationality?
I swore upon the Tablet fragment that
I'd fight for Aqhat till I breathed my last.
I've reason to believe he's signaling
for us to meet him at the Southern Gate
to open it just as Bidawa did
for you on Alashiya's southern coast.
I'll lead a small reconnaissance brigade
tonight and would appreciate support."

Sheer silence and empathic earnestness
conveyed their final, negative response.
Laeya departed from their tent and set
to rounding up whomever she presumed
would fight for Aqhat even now—the troops
whose truth and troth was most unflappable.
Inuya, Ash, and Abdu pledged their aid
with fifty of their best-trained warriors.
Some seafarers who'd sailed in Gabbar's fleet
had hauled jars of bitumen to the camp
for flaming arrows; Laeya commandeered
the tar to camouflage her rescue corps,

each one bepainted black like priests of war.
Once they'd equipped for battle, Laeya led
the band by foot to Zaphon's southern ridge,
the which they summited unseen, unheard,
now sheltering behind a precipice.
Like Kaskans set to raid a mighty king
they waited—common sense lampooning them.

When time eterne had seemed to run its course,
a small gate opened, three guards walking out.
Each scoured the land before the trailing man
cut down the others and unhelmed himself.
Laeya ran out to Aqhat, kissing him
to verify her senses' messengers,
deluged with an impossible relief.
Forth crept her charges, dumbfounded to see
him standing taller than he had before
ere learning where patrolmen kept their watch.
With feline stealth they entered through the gate,
unmanning and annulling nightwatch posts
until three hirelings sounded the alarm,
intensifying combat on all sides.
Amidst the darkness, fearing for the worst,
some mercenary gangs abandoned El
by any exit-point available.
Those fleeing through the Eastern Gate ran hard
and straight into stampeding warriors
forefronted by Bidawa and Gabbar,
whose cries gainsaid their former disbelief.
Their pressing throngs mowed down the runaways
ere funneling into the citadel,
diffusing through its corridors and rooms,
surmounting crenelated battlements.

El smarted, waking from the caterwaul
of consummate defeat as Shataqat
hung on to him aquiver, shedding tears.
Hirgab and Elsh burst through the chamber door,
alerting El to what he had surmised.
The Wise One ordered Zaphon's viziers
to save whichever of the pantheon's
divinities they could and make for Lel.
Their dumbstruck hesitation vexed the Lord
who thundered his command a second time.
Embracing Shataqat the Fine, El kissed
her, promising her safety in their hands.
Ere long he watched as Hirgab flew his love
away, Yatpan bestriding Gapn's back,
Elsh clutching Ugar's plumage with both hands.
Alone within his stately bedchamber,
the Ancient One accepted his demise,
"What else, Oh Time, makes up this world and its
particulars but your ephemeral
events—those holdouts tug-of-warred between
That Which Has Passed and That Which Will Have Been
who're dead set on becoming That Which Is
though mostly non-existent they remain.
It's you, Oh Time, the greatest god of all,
who conquers everything and everyone.
I bow to your impartial equity,
which neither gods nor mortals can evade."

Begrimed with blood and sweat, Aqhat found El
at last—unguarded, ready to abjure
the pantheonic seat he'd meant for Baal.
El held his hands to either side and said,
"May you be wiser than your parentage"
as Aqhat sank his sword into his chest,

ensuring the pretender Lord of lords,
his second kill, departed for the Void,
El's ichor pooling on the cold stone floor.
Laeya had entered just in time to see
the deed done—never to be unperformed.

Enlivened, Aqhat sped his way unto
the center of the citadel to back
his infantry, but when he came upon
a lofty battlement, he recognized
that every coup de grâce had been dealt out.
His stout contingents spied him and he said,
"Tonight I pulled myself from death's black shore
to finish El, my second chosen god,
in line with the Tablet of Destinies.
Brothers and sisters: I have you to thank!
This palace—what a foothold to secure!
Still greater things await you nonetheless.
Your loyalty's engraven on my heart,
and there it shall remain throughout my reign.
But now: Attend your wounds and lie abed
wherever you desire; tomorrow we'll
enjoy those gifts the gods denied to us!"
Cheers rose into the night, as did the chant,
"Hail Aqhat, Slayer of the Deathless Gods!"
With great triumphant whoops and beaten shields
the victors rocked Mount Zaphon's very walls.
Aqhat's companions celebrated his
returnment from beyond the veil of life
before they bathed and fell upon their beds.

Come evenfall the next day, Aqhat strode
into the vaulted festal hall beside
the lady he intended as his queen,

the two bedecked in garments finely spun
by royal seamstresses as offerings
to honor Zaphon's prior overlords.
All those at table rose and welcomed them
with accolades, but Aqhat bade them sit.
Laeya looked fondly on her warrior
and took the dais at his righthand side.
In due time Zaphon's servant girls appeared
supporting earthen tuns of ruddy wine
that genuflected when to cups came near,
relinquishing strong drink, commoving guests
more heartily than any earnest prayer.
Lithe girls brought fig cakes set in porringers
with bowls of raisins, nuts, and apricots,
arranging them near tallow tapers who
foretold with fragrance courses yet to come.
The hall doors opened once again and men
brought trays of bread and safflower oil inside,
accompanied by twelve legs of lamb
confit'd and fatling cuts prepared by cooks
with cumin, sumac, onions, thyme, and salt.

Rejoicing overbrimmed the crowded hall:
With split sides Abdu and Inuya laughed;
Ash added to his spoils by emptying
his winecup faster than Hattusa's best;
Kalbu and Akawatil chronicled
their wildest voyages across the seas,
outdoing one another with each round
and, as a shipwright puts to test the wood
acquired for its strength and pliancy,
they shaped their stories, bending truth to fit;
along the other side the Castaway
and Wullu limned specific battle-scenes,

delighting in the details of each one,
Bidawa relishing her repast yet
by subtle, gravid pinches signaling
to Gabbar that she longed to mount their bed;
Zannanza, Arnuwanda, and the young
Telipinu raised toasts to fallen souls,
with anecdotes remembering their deeds;
the hostess' pride of lionesses lounged
beside her, swallowing large table scraps
and nuzzling Laeya's hand for a massage.

Anon the God Slayer addressed the room,
"My friends, it pleases me to see you here
enjoying food and drink and fellowship,
but as the night grows late, I think we'd be
remiss to squander convocations such
as these (since rarely do they come) without
discussing tidings that concern us all.
Perhaps as some of you already know,
King Suppiluliuma's leaguerment
of Washukanni met with swift success.
Tushratta—learning little from his past—
proved so unwise to think that enemies
beyond his boundaries posed the greatest threat.
The halfwit! Those he should've feared the most
hadn't a need to manufacture plans
to escalade his city's walls, for they'd
been machinating from the inside out,
awaiting their rebellion's proper time.
A junta of advisors ended him
and pledged their fealty to Hattusa's king
who indirectly governs them as planned,
now marching westward to attain more land
and troops to join his forces to our own.

With such an army—one the likes of which
the world has never seen, brigades comprised
of footmen from the four winds' origins—
we shall fulfill our work and conquer Mot."
With pounding cups and shouts each roared assent,
the chamber vibrating above their heads.
As songs and tales of war betrayed no sign
of letting up, the heads excused themselves.

Their faces halfway glimmed by candlelight,
entangled in each other's arms and legs,
Laeya and Aqhat laid their heads. She said,
"I can't believe you're here in flesh and blood.
To see you strung-up like some animal
for skinning, fading then devoid of life—
I'd rather die ten thousand times than see
them so humiliate and torture you.
What magic rescued you from breathlessness?
However you outmatched the Emperor
of Rot this once, he still remains a threat
so long as he has regency below.
Tomorrow marks the new moon, giving you
one month—no more—before our time runs out.
Let's make for Tharumagi, setting forth
as soon as possible; our downgoing
into the Netherworld will not be quick,
nor will it be without its hindrances."

He kissed her, trying to reduce her fears,
"I shall not perish, as the Tablet vows.
I now believe this in my very bones.
We made short shrift of El and Baal, and Mot
shall get what he hands out. There's time enough.
Our warriors need rest. They've earned the right

to sleep and drink and heal a bit before
we wage our war on Death and his command.
Remember that our average soldier's not
like you—designed to muster argosies,
recruiting swelling empires to her side
only to kill the War Goddess herself
and, most impressively, put up with me
without begrudging me at every turn.
Let Sleep revive us, bringing clarity."

As if inside a sewer barnacled
with breathing sores, she found herself amidst
a near-impenetrable shadowland,
myopic torchlight pointing out the way.
Cut off from her battalion, Laeya heard
the cataclysmic echoes of a war
reverberate through shafts like panicked bats.
She hurried, stumbled toward the shrieks and shrills
through limestone tunnels, under alcoves, past
deep meres of liquified obsidian,
and up an unforgiving passageway
until she reached a high-hung precipice
whose vista seethed with dismal butchery:
The ranks who'd followed Aqhat heretofore,
emboldened by their latest victories,
confronted fiends familiar and unknown.
The dogfaces they'd slaughtered not two days
before took up their arms once more, although
the gashes that they bore had not improved.
The dead invited them to join their ranks,
and when they'd tasted blood they caught a whiff
of life and fumed at having lost its touch.
Beside the fighters spanned a tarry sea
incised by ghastly figureheads of Baal's

armada—sunken by Nahar at El's
behest—vindictive landfall in their hearts.

Supporting these offended companies
were Malakuma deities, the kings
of Ugarit who'd handed down their crowns:
Ugaranu, Amqunu, and Maphu
led generations of departed while
Ammuharrasi and Ammutamar
inspirited their files of grim Rephaim
who fought for everlasting bragging rights.
Rapanu, Lim-Il-Sarri, Ditanu
Ibbiranu, and Yaduraddu held
the rear, impatient to engage head-on.
These fearsome generals were masked with casques
of hippo skulls, and those who raged with them
clenched ferrous instruments within their fists.

An inhospitable sea all its own,
the waves of multitudinous reserves
allied themselves to fell monstrosities:
Baboon-like creatures sporting ivory horns
bullwhipped cacodemonic flying goats
that swooped and strafed oncoming warriors
with fulgurations of pure lapis flames,
a hundred thousand urnfuls flitting round
till blackened snowdrifts formed along the roads.
Thick serpents slithered toward the frontmost lines
with commination flashing in their eyes.
Belowground Biters and Detachers grabbed
men unawares and pulled them out of sight—
at times with limbs left fending for themselves.
Employing armaments of iron make,

hyena-headed women squeezed the reins
of hirsute war-pigs with engraven tusks.
Each being had their hierarchic place
by virtue of tradition and their ilk.
The strongest answered to the war-cabal,
among whom could be found Usharaya,
Gataru, Milku, Horon, and the like.

Beyond this horde of beasts stood Mot's abode,
an ashen mountain piercing through the brume
and circled by abysmal waterways
infested with enormous octopi,
white crocodiles, and omophagic eels.
Beyond Mot's den a massive outcrop loomed—
an earthquake-fashioned balcony atop
which stood the giant Og who with one eye
alone directed every thanatoid
commander with uncompromising calls.
Yet Og was far from angry or upset.
Most fortunate for him, pure deicide
returned his long-lost partner to his side.
Anat beheld her visions actualized,
her eyes bedewed by warfare's culminance,
hugging the giant for his faithfulness.
Twin henchman—gibbous, hairy creaturelings—
presented her the contents of a sack.
They dumped a broken Aqhat at her feet.
Anat stepped back as Mot the God of Death
approached and raised his double-bitted ax
to speed the mortal to Oblivion.
Resorting to her magic, Laeya tried
to intervene, effectuating naught.
The Emperor looked up. Their gazes locked.

With curt finality he dropped the blade,
his armies trampling over the foredoomed
and upward, upward to unite their realms.

Awakening from her oneiric view
of what would come to pass, Laeya sat up
and screamed, alone, her blankets soaked in sweat.
A bodyguard came in with sword withdrawn
for her assailant, but he scabbarded
the blade, observing that she'd poorly dreamt.
She asked where Aqhat went and he replied
that he'd sought Zaphon's vineyard to the north
to stroll about and repossess his thoughts.
With hastened gratitude Laeya dismissed
the guardsman, dressed, then walked down corridors
and to the Northern Gate, her downbeat heart
attempting to interpret her nightmare.
Had he not sought *a Power yet Unknown*
to Mortals, infinitely greater than
any the Earth has seen before this Age:
the Mettle that belongs to Gods Themselves,
just as the Tablet presaged he would do?
If Aqhat were to *never come to Death*,
how could the Emperor of Rot win out?
Aqhat's grave run-ins with Oblivion
had tortured her, but should he *never know*
a Mortal's Life, a God's Life, or the Life
of a Rephaim, forever sentenced to
that No-place without Form or Hope—the Void,
how, why would her existence be worthwhile?

She fled the citadel, its vineyard now
in sight as Shapshu watched her from on high.
She noticed Aqhat standing midst gray rows

of grapevines, pruning branches one by one
as though he were a migrant laborer
content to undertake the season's work.
Laeya inhaled and tried to calm herself.
When she came near him he reminisced,
"So many years ago, when I was young,
I'd travel with my mother and sister
to trim the dormant vines—a tedious,
benumbing job—but when the harvest came,
when we cut drooping clusters to ferment,
enjoying one another's company
and making games of work and singing round
the fireside—then our winter's work paid off.
So too have you and I begun to prune
unbalanced gods whose excesses do far
more harm than good, and when our labor's done,
our struggles bearing fruit, we shall retire
as vintners and the land will fill with song."

Her secrets quavered in her breast, Aqhat's
professions deafened by the *Magic Words*
that had empowered him to slaughter Three
and only Three Gods ere a Year's elapsed.
As if to shield her from what would transpire,
Yarikh in all his fullness made his way
toward Shapshu, covering a part of her.
Laeya beheld the Moon-God's act of love
and came to understand why *when the Third*
One breathes no more, his Hands shall run with Blood,
and with the Squall of Warfare he shall roar
as Light surrounds and captures Sin Itself.
Observing woebegoneness underneath
her strong veneer and unsure what he'd said
to bring her sorrow, Aqhat reached for her

and kissed her as she took his hands in hers.
Grasping the hand in which he held the knife,
she cut her wrist, and by the time he saw
what she had done, he worked to stanch the flow
and gazed at her, dumbstricken, horrified.

He strove to put her deed to question but
she silenced him to justify herself,
"I am a god—the third through whom you're saved.
I'm Athirat, adorned in human form,
ensnared between eternal life without
you by my side and the Oblivion.
I've made my choice—grant me this selfishness.
My light, I love you, more than you could know.
Remember this when you assume your crown."
Yarikh now shielded Shapshu's burning eye,
a ring of brimstone light surrounding him,
enshadowing the earth as likenesses
of fallen kin appeared to Athirat,
"Gods against gods, men against men, each kind
against each other: Who is in the right?
Truly, which ones could ever conquer Death?
Who, who shall bring this madness to an end?"

Aqhat replied, "I am who, I am!" but
the very reason for the day went out.
The reason for tomorrow, too. What does
it matter if the world becomes one's own
if one's beloved's not there to brighten it?
Thus did he take the fitting name 'Yahweh,'
existing simply in and for himself,
Immortal, living to the End of Days.
Forth from his lips there burst a war-cry while
he held the lifeless Lady of the Sea

within the hands she'd stained with her own blood,
her vibrant life cut short.
He qualmed and soughed and crumbled to his knees,
considering how he might end his life,
his Reign inaugurated by Old Song
as Shapshu swept aside her lunar veil,

"Long labor has left my feet well-worn,
these hands strained and stained as if torn.
There's naught come next but seek out rest
alike the Sun on ruddied mornes—
who in the morn our faces tanned
and warmed the naked ochre sand,
afore high-hung but now far-flung
she sighs and plumbs the hinterland.
Her presence she as yet betrays
with softened alpenglow displays
that disappear as I hide here—
horizon's flame fading away.
My life she's still engendering
as I sprawl out remembering
day's good and ill now that all's still,
this solitude my rendering.
The twilight's secret's yours and mine,
reminding us there comes a time
when gone are cares for life's affairs,
and all that's left's to drown in wine."

Glossary

Abdiyarah: Kum-U's son who reveals the general location of the Necromancer to Aqhat.

Abdu: An elderly Sidunan fisherman whose support Gabbar and Ameni seek.

Abibaal: A fisherman from Siduna who learns of Aqhat's intentions, going to Zimredda to seek support for Aqhat's seizure.

Abihumbaba: A demigod and son of Humbaba. The snakeheaded guardian of the pine forest north of Mount Zaphon. Commander and summoner of the earth's snakes.

Adad: Mesopotamian storm god and son of Anu.

Ahiram: A Canaanite elder. Father of Bitea and Hayya.

Ahmose I: The leader who overthrew Khamudi in Avaris.

Akawatil: The young man who sails abroad with his father, Wullu, after Baal and Tushratta's seige of Washukanni.

Akhenaten: The son and successor of Amenhotep III as ruler of Egypt.

Alashiya: Modern-day Cyprus.

Alektruon: A large boy who boxes against Talos in the Central Court of Knossos' Labyrinth.

Aliyan: Aqhat's hot-blooded courser whose name means 'mightiest.'

Allani: A Hurrian goddess of the Underworld, known as the sun goddess in some Hittite texts.

Amen: A creator and southern warrior deity of Egypt whose name means 'the hidden one.'

Amenhotep III: Egyptian pharaoh and son of Amen. Married Giluhepa of Mitanni. Succeeded by Akhenaten.

Ameni: An Egyptian saved by Aqhat during a caravan raid.

Ammittamru I: King of Ugarit.

Amnisos: A harbor town in Kaphtor serving Knossos.

Anat: Canaanite goddess of war and the hunt. Sister-wife of Baal and daughter of El.

Annarumenzi: Luwian deities; 'the forceful ones.'

Anu: Mesopotamian god. Father of Ellil, Adad, Gerra, and Shara.

Anubis: Jackal-headed Egyptian god of mummification, embalmment, and the afterlife. Patron of lost souls.

Anzu: Mesopotamian god. A lion-headed eagle born out of Mount Hehe's side who guarded the doors of Duranki and stole the Tablet of Destinies.

Apis: A sacred bull of ancient Egypt.

Aqhat: Son of Danel and Danataya; brother of Pugat.

Arma: Luwian Moon-god.

Arnuwanda II: Son of Suppiluliuma and Henti.

Arinna: The Hittite sun goddess.

Arsh: An attendant monster of Yam-Nahar.

Artashumara: Son of King Shuttarna of Mitanni and brother of Giluhepa.

Artatama II: A member of King Tushratta's council.

Ash: A brawny member of Aqhat's company afflicted with constant sleepwalking.

Ashtabi: Hurrian god of war.

Astarte: A Canaanite goddess of war, hunting, and love.

Aten: The solar disk worshiped by Akhenaten.

Athirat: El's wife. Creatress of the Canaanite pantheon. See also 'Laeya.'

Athtar: Canaanite god of the morning star. Son of Athirat.

Attabi: The Western Hurrians' god of war.

Atum: Egyptian solar deity associated with the evening sun prior to Akhenaten's reforms.

Awrikku: A sailor who claims to have survived an attack by a sea dragon.

Baal (Hadad): Canaanite storm god. Brother and husband of Anat. Lives on Mount Zaphon.

Bidawa: An attractive woman who plays a role in the infiltration of Baal's prison on Alashiya.

Bitea: Daughter of Ahiram. Sister of Hayya.

Burianu: A young follower of Aqhat who accompanies him to Siduna. Gabbar dubs him 'the Belated.'

Danataya: Wife of Danel and mother of Aqhat and Pugat.

Danel: A local Canaanite judge. Husband of Danataya and father of Aqhat and Pugat.

Death: See 'Mot.'

Duat: An Egyptian term for the Underworld.

Duranki: Ellil's temple.

Ea: The Mesopotamian god of wisdom and fresh water.

Eanna: Anu's temple.

Eya: Hurrian manifestation of Ea.

El: Patriarchal head of the Semitic pantheon. Husband of Athirat. In this epic, formerly known as 'Ninurta.'

Eliawa: Laeya's maid in Siduna.

Ellil: The Mesopotamian god who decreed the fates. Son of Anu. Father of Ninurta. Brother of Adad, Gerra, and Shara.

Elsh: An attendant of El and Athirat.

Enesidaon: Poseidon's chthonic aspect; his name means 'earth-shaker.'

Enkidu: The wild man created by Mami. Servant/friend of Gilgamesh.

Ereshkigal: Sumerian goddess and sister of Ishtar.

Gabbar: Aqhat's close friend from childhood. Son of Inumi.

Gapn: One of Baal's messengers whose name means 'vineyard' or 'vine.'

Gataru: A chthonic deity of vegetation and warfare.

Gerra: Mesopotamian fire-god. Son of Anu and brother of Ellil, Adad, and Shara.

Gilgamesh: Mesopotamian epic hero. King of Uruk. Son of Lugalbanda and Ninsun.

Giluhepa: Daughter of King Shuttarna II of Mitanni, who married her to Amenhotep III. Sister of Artashumara and Tushratta.

Hadad: See Baal.

Habayu: A Canaanite figure with two horns and a tail.

Hallu-Shenni: One of King Tushratta's counselors.

Hannahanna: Hittite mother-goddess who gives advice to other deities.

Hapantaliya: Luwian pastoral goddess.

Hapiru: An ethnically heterogenous group of people throughout the Bronze Age Levant commonly referred to as robbers and troublemakers in Egyptian texts.

Hayya: Son of Ahiram. Brother of Bitea.

Hebat: A Hurrian goddess.

Hedammu: A large male sea monster from Hittite mythology. Likely the offspring of Kumarbi and Sertapsuruhi.

Hehe: The mountain from whose side Anzu sprung.

Henti: The Tawananna ('Great Princess') and former wife of Suppiluliuma, exiled from Hattusa to an island in the far West.

Hirgab: A messenger of Baal's. The Father of the Vultures.

Horanu: A deity of magic and exorcism.

Hudena: Hurrian goddess of conception and childbirth.

Humbaba: The fire-breathing guardian of the Pine Forest in *Gilgamesh* and predecessor of the Greek gorgon.

Horon: A god of the Underworld. Serves as an emissary for Mot. Father of Astarte.

Igigi: Sumerian group term for the sky-gods headed by Ellil.

Ilisha: The Canaanite herald god.

Inbubu: Anat's mountain home.

Inhospitable Sea: The Black Sea.

Inumi: A friend of Danataya; mother of Gabbar.

Inuya: A dowager and debt-slave whom Laeya and Aqhat try to recruit in Siduna.

Isdes: The Egyptian god of the plumb-bob, which ensured the accurateness of the Scales of Judgment.

Ishtar: The Mesopotamian goddess of love and war. Sister of Ereshkigal.

Isis: An Egyptian goddess and the sister-wife of Osiris.

Ithm: A rogue son of El. Brother of Shegr. God of cattle and sheep.

Juktas: An important mountain site located a few kilometers from Knossos.

Kalbu: A helmsman of Laeya's fleet who knows the way to Kaphtor.

Kaphtor: An ancient name for Crete.

Keftiu: The term Egyptians used to designate Crete/Kaphtor.

Keldi: A Hurrian deity.

Kesadara: A Klawiphoros whom Laeya meets on Mount Juktas.

Khamudi: A Hyksos king from the 16th century BCE, overthrown by Ahmose I.

Khonsu: A youthful Egyptian lunar deity. Son of Amen.

Kikkuli: One of King Tushratta's counselors.

Kilamuwa: A Canaanite priest.

Kinnaru: A divinized lyre.

Kirta: A Canaanite elder.

Klawiphoros: 'Key-bearer'; a term for a Minoan priestess.

Knossos: An important city on Crete/Kaphtor.

Kotharat: Canaanite goddesses of conception and childbirth.

Kothar-wa-Hasis: The Canaanite craftsman-god whose name means 'skillful and wise.'

Kumarbi: Hittite grain deity.

Kum-U: Abdiyarah's father who led the flight of his village to their current location.

Kurnugi: A Sumerian term for the Underworld.

Laeya: The name that Athirat takes for herself when she assumes human form.

Lel: The mountain upholding El's temple.

Litan: A sea monster with seven heads. The Canaanite precursor to Leviathan.

Lugalbanda: The father of Gilgamesh.

Madi: The leader of Minos' navy.

Makhadu: Ugarit's main port.

Malakuma: The deceased kings of Ugarit who inhabit the Underworld.

Mami: The great Mesopotamian mother-goddess.

Marwainzi: Luwian deities; 'the dark ones.'

Milka: A woman of Aqhat's company and the missing wife of Yasiranu.

Milku: An divinity of the Underworld.

Minos: King of Knossos; husband of Pasiphaë.

Mot: The Canaanite god of death and ruler of the Underworld.

Mursili II: Son of Suppiluliuma and Henti.

Mut: An Egyptian goddess; consort of Amen and adoptive mother of Khonsu.

Mutbalu: The ruler of Pella.

Muwatti: Suppiluliuma's daughter.

Necromancer: A former priest from Duranki who moves northwest to a cave after Anzu steals the Tablet of Destinies.

Nephthys: An Egyptian goddess and the sister of Osiris, Isis, and Seth.

Ninurta: Mesopotamian warrior-god. Son of Ellil. Receives the name 'El,' or 'the Lord,' after defeating Anzu.

Niqmaddu II: King of Ugarit and contemporary of Suppiluliuma I.

Nubadig: A Hurrian deity.

Nuhati: Henti's finest wayfinder and pilot from Hattusa.

Nun: An Egyptian deity who represents the boundlessness, darkness, and turbulence of the primordial waters out of whose chaos Atum-Ra created the world.

Og: A one-eyed giant. The last of his race and the head general of Mot's army.

Ornithomanceress: See 'Paskuwatti.'

Osiris: The Egyptian king of the dead.

Pasiphaë: Queen of Knossos and head priestess; wife of Minos.

Paskuwatti: The Ornithomanceress, or practitioner of augury whom Henti calls upon.

Phlamoudhi: A coastal town in northern Alashiya.

Pidadaphi: A Hurrian goddess.

Pidray: One of Baal's female attendants.

Piyassili: Son of Suppiluliuma and Henti.

Poseidon: The Minoan god of the sea, at times associated with bull's horns. Also transliterated as 'Poteidan.'

Ptah: The creator-god of Memphis who thinks of and speaks all the gods into being.

Pugat: Daughter of Danataya and Danel; sister of Aqhat; wife of Yarimmu.

Qodesh: Athirat's attendant.

Ra: Egyptian creator-god and sun deity.

Rabbim: An enemy of Baal and Anat.

Renenut: An Egyptian goddess; the deified concept of fortune.

Rephaim: The deified dead of the Canaanites.

Resheph: The Canaanite winged god of plague. His name means 'plague' or 'flame.'

Rundas: The Hittite god of good fortune and hunting.

Samal: The Canaanite mother of vultures.

Sertapsuruhi: Hittite goddess. Daughter of the sea-god; wife of Kumarbi.

Shahar: The Canaanite god of dawn whose name means 'the shining one.'

Shalim: The Canaanite god of dusk.

Shamash: Mesopotamian sun-god.

Shamhat: The prostitute from Uruk who seduces Enkidu.

Shapshu: The Canaanite sun-goddess.

Shara: Son of Anu and brother of Ellil, Adad, and Gerra.

Sharelli: Daughter of the Shasu leader.

Shatanu: A witch who lives in an abandoned town north of the Seir Mountains and south of the Dead Sea. She maintains relations with the Necromancer, although the nature of their relation remains unclear.

Shataqat: A goddess fashioned by El to do away with Resheph's plagues and who also becomes El's mistress. Her name means 'she expels (disease).'

Shaushka: A Hurrian/Hittite goddess of love and war.

Shay: The Egyptian deified concept of fate.

Shegr: A rogue son of El. Brother of Ithm. God of cattle and sheep.

Shekelesh: The spokesperson of a small clan of nomads traveling along the Lukkan coast.

Shunama: One of El's sons.

Shuttarna II: King of Mitanni. Father of Giluhepa, Artashumara, and Tushratta.

Siduri: The alewife who informs Gilgamesh of Ur-shanabi's whereabouts.

Sin: Mesopotamian moon deity.

Sinaranu: The blind tiller who transports Aqhat from Siduna to Alashiya. In this epic, he claims descendancy from Ur-shanabi.

Sirion: The mountain range today known as the Anti-Lebanon Mountains.

Sokar: An Egyptian deity of cemeteries, metalwork, and life after death.

Suppiluliuma I: Son of Tudhaliya II. Eventual king of Hatti. Ex-husband of Henti.

Taduhepa: Daughter of Tushratta, given to him by Astarte.

Tudhaliya II: Ruler of the Hittite Empire. Father of Suppiluliuma I.

Talan: A Hurrian deity.

Tallay: An attendant of Baal. Her name means 'dewy.'

Talos: A young boy whom Minos favors and hopes to one day lead his navy.

Targuziza: One of the mountain entrances to the Underworld, according to the Canaanites.

Tawananna: A term denoting the wife of a Hittite king.

Tefnut: An Egyptian goddess of rain and moisture.

Telipinu: Son of Suppiluliuma and Henti.

Tharumagi: One of the mountain entrances to the Underworld, according to the Canaanites.

Thoth: A wise advisor of the Egyptian gods.

Thukamuna: One of El's sons.

Timegi: Hurrian solar deity.

Tiratu: Canaanite god of wine.

Tiwad: Luwian sun-god.

Tushratta: Son of King Shuttarna II. Brother of Artashumara and Giluhepa. Father of Taduhepa.

Tuweta: Kaphtor's Lady of the Lonesome Wood who provides the remedy for Ash's sleepwalking.

Ugar: One of Baal's messengers whose name means 'field.'

Ullikummi: A senseless and mountain-sized monster made of basalt stone.

Ur-shanabi: The boatman who transports Gilgamesh to Ut-napishtim.

Usharaya: A chthonic deity whose sphere of influence includes divination, oaths, and justice.

Ut-napishtim: The man to whom Gilgamesh journeys while in search of immortality. Hebrew Noah.

Vast Verd: The Mediterranean Sea.

Velchanos: The original Minoan name of Zeus.

Wadj-wer: Egyptian fertility-god. Personification of the Mediterranean Sea.

Washukanni: Capital city of Mitanni.

Wullu: Father of Akawatil and leader of the fleet of merchants and adventurers who flee Washukanni after Baal and Tushratta lay siege to it.

Yadi-Yalhan: One of Athirat's sons.

Yam-Nahar: A Canaanite sea-god, referred to as a 'judge' or 'ruler.'

Yarikh: Canaanite moon-god.

Yarimmu: Pugat's husband.

Yashaddu: A hierarch from Siduna promoted to serve as a general in Baal's army.

Yasiranu: A man of Aqhat's company who cannot find his wife, Milka, when their fleet is beached on the southern shores of the Inhospitable Sea.

Yatpan: Anat's attendant and henchman. Also referred to as the 'Sutean Warrior.'

Yattanu: A potter of Aqhat's town of origin.

Zababa: Hittite god of war.

Zakir: A Canaanite elder.

Zannanza: Son of Suppiluliuma and Henti.

Zaphon: Baal's mountain dwelling north of Ugarit.

Zashapuna: A shopkeeper operating out of a secluded cavern on the northern side of the Anti-Taurus Mountains.

Zelophehad: Laeya's "uncle." A shipwright who lives with his daughters north of Siduna.

Zimredda: The ruler of Siduna.

References

The following sources proved most helpful in conducting some of the background research for this poem.

Bar, S., et al. *Egypt, Canaan and Israel: History, Imperialism, Ideology, and Literature.* Boston, MA: Brill Academic, 2011.

Benz, Brendon C. *The Land before the Kingdom of Israel: A History of the Southern Levant and the People Who Populated It.* University Park, PA: Eisenbrauns, 2016.

Castleden, Rodney. *Minoans: Life in Bronze Age Crete.* London: Routledge, 1992.

Ciraolo, Leda, and Jonathan Seidel, eds. *Magic and Divination in the Ancient World.* Leiden, The Netherlands: Brill, 2002.

Coogan, Michael D. and Mark S. Smith, eds. *Stories from Ancient Canaan.* 2nd ed. Louisville, KY: Westminster John Knox, 2012.

Cross, Frank Moore. *Canaanite Myth and Hebrew Epic: Essays in the History of the Religion of Israel.* Harvard: Harvard University Press, 1997.

Dalley, Stephanie, ed. *Myths from Mesopotamia: Creation, The Flood, Gilgamesh, and Others.* Oxford: Oxford University Press, 2008.

Dickinson, Oliver. *The Aegean Bronze Age.* Cambridge: Cambridge University Press, 1994.

Euripides. *The Bacchae and Other Plays.* Translated by John Davie. New York: Penguin Classics, 2006.

Gaster, Theodor H. "A Canaanite Ritual Drama: The Spring Festival at Ugarit." *Journal of the American Oriental Society* 66 (1946) 49–76.

Gibson, J. C. L. *Canaanite Myths and Legends.* Edinburgh: T. & T. Clark, 1977.

Hoffnery, Harry A., Jr. *Hittite Myths.* Atlanta, GA: Scholars, 1998.

Jeffers, Ann. *Magic and Divination in Ancient Palestine and Syria.* Leiden, The Netherlands: Brill, 1996.

Kahn, Dan'El. "One Step Forward, Two Steps Backward: The Relations between Amenhotep III, King of Egypt and Tushratta, King of Mitanni." In *Egypt, Canaan and Israel: History, Imperialism, Ideology and Literature*, edited by S. Bar et al., 136–54. Leiden, The Netherlands: Brill, 2011.

Liverani, Mario. *The Ancient Near East: History, Society and Economy.* Translated by Soraia Tabatabai. London: Routledge, 2014.

Melchert, Craig A. *The Luwians.* Leiden, The Netherlands: Brill, 2003.

Moran, William L., ed. *The Amarna Letters.* Baltimore, MD: Johns Hopkins University Press, 2002.

Mouton, Alice, et al. *Luwian Identities: Culture, Language, and Religion between Anatolia and the Aegean.* Leiden, the Netherlands: Brill, 2013.

Muhlestein, Kerry. "Levantine Thinking in Egypt." In *Egypt, Canaan and Israel: History, Imperialism, Ideology and Literature*, edited by S. Bar et al., 190–235. Leiden, The Netherlands: Brill, 2011.

Pardee, Dennis. *Ritual and Cult at Ugarit.* Atlanta, GA: Society of Biblical Literature, 2002.

Parker, Simon B. *Ugaritic Narrative Poetry*. Translated by Mark S. Smith et al. Society of Biblical Literature: Scholar's, 1997.

Reeves, John C. "The Feast of the First Fruits of Wine and the Ancient Canaanite Calendar." *Vetus Testamentum* 42 (1992) 350–61.

Richard, Suzanne, ed. *Near Eastern Archaeology: A Reader*. University Park, PA: Eisenbrauns, 2003.

Rochberg, Francesca. *The Heavenly Writing: Divination, Horoscopy, and Astronomy in Mesopotamian Culture*. Cambridge: Cambridge University Press, 2004.

Smith, Mark S. *The Early History of God: Yahweh and Other Deities in Ancient Israel*. Miller. Grand Rapids, MI: Eerdmans, 2002.

Steiner, Margaret L., and Ann E. Killebrew, eds. *The Oxford Handbook of the Archaeology of the Levant c. 8000-332 BCE*. Oxford: Oxford University Press, 2014.

Stiebing, William H., Jr., and Susan N. Helft. *Ancient Near Eastern History and Culture*. London: Routledge, 2018.

Trimm, Charlie. *Fighting for the King and the Gods: A Survey of Warfare in the Ancient Near East*. Society of Biblical Literature, 2017.

Tyldesley, Joyce. *The Penguin Book of Myths & Legends of Ancient Egypt*. London: Penguin, 2011.

Van de Mieroop, Marc. *Philosophy before the Greeks: The Pursuit of Truth in Ancient Babylonia*. Princeton: Princeton University Press, 2016.

Wachsmann, Shelley. *Seagoing Ships and Seamanship in the Bronze Age Levant*. College Station: Texas A&M University Press, 1998.

Walsh, Carey Ellen. *The Fruit of the Vine: Viticulture in Ancient Israel*. Boston, MA: Brill Academic, 2000.

Wilkinson, Toby. *Writings from Ancient Egypt*. New York: Penguin Classics, 2016.

Wilson, Eleanor Amico. *Women of Canaan: The Status of Women at Ugarit*. Whitewater, WI: Heartwell, 2013.

Wright, David P. *Ritual in Narrative: The Dynamics of Feasting, Mourning, and Retaliation Rites in the Ugaritic Tale of Aqhat*. University Park, PA: Eisenbrauns, 2000.

Yoder, Tyler R. *Fishers of Fish and Fishers of Men: Fishing Imagery in the Hebrew Bible and the Ancient Near East*. University Park, PA: Eisenbrauns, 2016.